Connecting

❧

also by Sandy Sheehy

TEXAS BIG RICH

Connecting

THE ENDURING POWER OF
FEMALE FRIENDSHIP

❧

Sandy Sheehy

*To Joanna —
In celebration of your
friendships and in
gratitude for the insights
and experiences you shared —
They made the book stronger
and more vibrant —*

〰 WILLIAM MORROW

An Imprint of HarperCollinsPublishers

*Sandy Sheehy
October 11, 2000*

HarperCollins books may be purchased for educational, business, or sales promotional use. For information please write: Special Markets Department, HarperCollins Publishers Inc., 10 East 53rd Street, New York, NY 10022.

FIRST EDITION

Designed by Fearn Cutler de Vicq

Printed on acid-free paper

Library of Congress Cataloging-in-Publication Data has been applied for.

ISBN 0-380-97430-4

00 01 02 03 04 QW 10 9 8 7 6 5 4 3 2 1

This book is for all my female friends.
You inspired this book and enrich my life.

Contents

✦

Acknowledgments

This book owes its heart to the girls and women who shared their friendship experiences with me. It owes its insights, in large part, to the social scientists and clinicians quoted in the pages that follow and especially to Joan Berzoff, Phyllis Gillman, Helen Gouldner, Christine Hejinian, Judy Jordan, Joan Lang, Jean Baker Miller, Stacey Oliker, Karen Roberto, Irene Stiver, and Sharon Vaughn. Their intellectual generosity touched as well as inspired me. Any errors in interpretation are mine alone. I am also indebted to the resourceful research staffs of the University of Houston Electronic Publications Center and of Galveston's Rosenberg Library.

My former agent Stuart Krichevsky and my friend Judythe Wilbur gave me crucial early encouragement and guidance. From finding the right publisher for the book to shepherding its development, Charlotte Raymond has been the wisest and most nurturing of agents. My acquiring editor Charlotte Abbott sustained me with her faith in the book, which Tia Maggini and my current editor, Krista Stroever, continued. In addition to making the book more readable and more focused, Tia's tireless attention to detail put lie to the complaint that editors no longer edit. Marcy Allen, Bonnie Bryant, Jo Ann Colon, Jill Folzman, Shari Hall, Heather Maynard, and Cynthia Nolan helped me bring women's stories to life by transcribing my interview tapes.

The hospitality of friends and family made my research both more affordable and more enjoyable. Bill Barrett and Nancy Uscher, Nan Birmingham, Gracie Hamilton Cavnar, Bob and Leslie Granville, Rob Granville, Dan and Nancy Heller, Martha Holstein, Betty Hoskins, Earl Kamsky and Shan Leonard, Laura Kramer, Kip Leonard and Jody Miller, Liz Maggio, Karl and Mildred McKenzie, and Mary Ann Wilson all gave me places to stay. My father, Bob Granville, also loaned the financial support that allowed me to take my interviews nationwide.

Ironically, writing this book about female friendships challenged my own. I was less available, more distracted, often so absorbed in my work that I made dull company. Yet my friends remained steadfast and supportive. I am especially grateful to Maida Asofsky, Kathryn Casey, Faith Einerson, Rhoda Ferris, Sharon Itaya, Faith Lagay, Lynn Randolph, Carol Safran and Bernice Torregrossa. My women's group (Marilyn Brodwick, Michele Carter, Sharon Goodwin, Evelyn Markides, Julie Penrod-Glenn, and Marilyn Schultz) helped me keep my balance, and my book club (Kathy Cunningham, Charity Gourley, Faith Lagay, Julie Reichert, Chula Sanchez, Luanne Stovall, and Bernice Torregrossa) helped me keep my goal in sight. Above all, I am grateful to my husband, Tom Curtis, whose support of all kinds made this book possible.

Author's Note

In conducting interviews for this book, I asked 204 girls and women to be candid about their friendships—the hurt as well as the joy. Despite the sensitive nature of what many revealed, most women gave me permission to use their real names. In a few cases, they asked me to use a pseudonym when describing a particular incident. Other women made concealing their identities a condition of being interviewed. Then there were the friends my interview subjects mentioned. Except in the few cases where I interviewed both parties in a friendship, these women had no opportunity to grant or withhold permission to use their names. I felt obliged to protect their privacy.

To accomplish this without having to interrupt the text to indicate whether I was using a pseudonym, I adopted a convention that I hope will prove clear but unobtrusive. If a woman gave me permission to identify her, I used her full name on first mention. If she asked me to conceal her identity, I introduced her by a first name different from her own (except in some of my personal recollections). In either case, I referred to her friends by pseudonyms, unless I interviewed them, too, and they agreed to be identified. If I used a woman's real name, I did the same for her current husband or boyfriend.

Although I conducted a handful of friendship interviews during 1992, almost all of those presented in this book took place between January and August 1996. The ages and occupations of the women I quote were those that pertained at that time.

Introduction

✢

Family therapist Barbara Ellman told me about a couple who came to her seeking help for their deteriorating marriage. The wife described her husband as emotionally distant and unsupportive. Ellman had heard that complaint often in her practice and frequently had found it justified. But in this case, the man had struck her as exceptionally empathic and caring, in touch with his wife's feelings and concerned about them.

A more traditional therapist might have kept her focus on the couple, investigating whether the woman was neurotically needy or whether the husband was a sort of Jekyll and Hyde figure, sometimes sensitive and supportive, sometimes cold and distant. But Ellman's sensibility and training prompted her to look elsewhere. She asked if the couple had experienced any changes in their lives recently. Yes, they'd moved to Houston just a year earlier. In fact, that was when their marital troubles had begun. What was different about life in Houston? Ellman probed. The wife replied that she'd left behind a very close friend, a woman she'd talked to at length every day, either in person or on the phone. "I could tell her *anything,* and she'd listen and understand," the woman said wistfully.

Ellman saw that the couple's marital problems lay with the loss of this intimate friendship. The husband was just as sensitive as he'd ever been; but without recognizing it, the wife now expected him to provide the validation she'd received from her friend. When Ellman showed the couple what had been missing, the woman burst into tears. She resolved to stay in closer touch with her old friend and to try to establish a similar friendship in Houston.

"Everything in our society had taught her to discount that relationship and her grief at the loss," Ellman told me.

As much sustenance and validation as that friendship had given Ellman's patient, nothing in her upbringing or in modern American culture had led her to consider it a primary relationship. From Freud forward, generations of social scientists have told us that the only human connections that really count are those between parents and children, siblings, spouses, and—by extension and recognized only recently—long-term lovers. Writing about what she called "the neglected relationship," sociologist Lillian B. Rubin noted:

> So blind have we been to the social and psychological meanings of friendship that anthropologists, trained in the art of studying alien cultures, have paid scant attention to these relationships . . .

Today, however, an increasing number of psychologists and sociologists on the cutting edge of women's development contend that female friendship *is* indeed a primary bond. Their research reveals that over the course of our lives, the ability to form and maintain solid, rewarding friendships with other women is essential both to our personal growth and fulfillment and to the health of our sexual and family relationships. Long-term friendships often outlast marriages. And with families scattered geographically, close friendships provide an essential buffer against isolation for elderly women, six out of ten of whom spend their last years without spouses. If women don't value and maintain friendships with one another, we risk dying alone.

Women today sense that we need female friendship more than ever. Our lives are moving so quickly, and everything from technology to the concept of what constitutes a family is changing so fast that we must we look to our women friends to provide both stability and a reality check: The companies we work for may vanish in mergers, our parents may divorce, we may find ourselves raising blended broods of children and stepchildren, but our closest girlfriends will remain constant, ready to tell us, whenever we need to hear it, that we're strong and good and equal to each new challenge.

About ten years ago, I began to notice how important my friendships with women had become to me. Their importance came to my attention in particular when my close friend Carol was diagnosed with breast cancer for the third time in the twelve years I'd known her. She'd entertained me with her off-the-wall wit, warmed me with her unconditional affection, opened my eyes with her on-target insights, and taught me—as much by letting me help her through her own crises as by supporting me in mine—not to be afraid of my anger and sadness. I'd always imagined us advancing together into eccentric old age. Now, I had to face the prospect that I might lose her to this insidious disease.

Another part of my awakening came when I moved to Galveston, Texas, leaving my dear friend Maida fifty miles behind in Houston. Separated by a little less than an hour of interstate highway, we could get together on weekends or for lunch when work took me up to the city; but I missed running with her at dawn three or four times a week, hearing the stories of her family and her law practice, stories she spun out artfully as we jogged along the bayou. And I yearned for her wise and nonjudgmental advice, offered whenever I asked, and only then. For me, no phone conversation could duplicate the intimacy of those early morning runs.

I realized that there was nothing peripheral about these two relationships, nor about those with three other close friends. They were near the center of my life. They helped define who I was, and they helped me become who I wanted to be.

This recognition didn't come easily. I'd grown up thinking that female companionship was a pleasurable distraction from the daily routine and a helpful source of practical advice and support, but that paying too much attention to what other girls thought of me might inhibit my growth as an individual. In those pre–*Thelma and Louise* days, everyone from my mother to movie characters told me that I could find intimacy and emotional fulfillment only with a man and, subsequently, as a mom. Romance and family were the sustenance of life; female friendships were the garnishes—the parsley sprig and orange slice, not the steak and potatoes.

Seventies feminism altered my attitude by helping me see other women as companions enduring the same unjust limitations and pervasive condescension that I did. But the political agenda so dominated the movement that I missed the emotional implications. Largely from the sidelines, I felt my consciousness rise and my respect for others of my sex expand. Still, although I experienced solidarity with women in general, I didn't experience a special bond with any one woman in particular.

In those days, when I did make a friend, it seemed like one of us would always move in a year or two, and the relationship would dwindle to an annual exchange of holiday letters, a hurried phone call or a shoe-horned-in meal when work took one of us to the other's town. If a Christmas card boomeranged because of an outdated address, I'd set it aside, intending to track the new one down; but I seldom did. I overlooked my female friendships the way I might overlook a dusty antique side chair in my grandmother's attic, not recognizing it as precious.

Confronting Carol's breast cancer years later, I wondered if my awakening to the value of my close friendships had more to do with the times or with my own age. I later learned that both were operating synergistically. Though the importance society has placed on female friendships has fluctuated, hitting a low point at the middle of this century, these relationships were becoming increasingly celebrated. At the same time, I was entering midlife, a period studies have shown to be particularly conducive to forging and deepening female friendship.

The example of my late mother-in-law, Kent Curtis, also taught me to recognize the richness and complexity of the bonds between women related by affection, rather than by genes. Kent was modest in economic resources but rich in friends. By the time we met in 1978, she'd been widowed four years. My husband-to-be and I lived in Houston, an hour from her green Dutch colonial house in Galveston. Once or twice a month, Tom and I would drive down to this quiet barrier island beach town. Sometimes we'd walk on the seawall or feed the gulls, but most of our visits revolved around Kent's kitchen and the lush semitropical garden onto which it opened. Until she retired in 1983, my mother-in-law owned and ran one of the two plant nurseries on the island, and she was her own best customer.

Saturdays and Sundays brought a reliable parade of friends through that kitchen and out onto the patio rimmed with ginger and oleander, plumerea and hibiscus. Most of these visitors were women, and most were in their sixties and seventies. Harriet, Alice, Jo, Jane, and Ada would accept the offer of a drink or iced tea, then would sit chatting leisurely about their children, the weather, or the mysteries of Gulf Coast horticulture. Often, they'd bring a plant clipping for Kent to identify or diagnose. Barbara, an accomplished watercolorist, would breeze in, announce that she was only stopping by for a minute, drop off some spicy condiment she'd made or picked up at a food import shop, and deliver an equally tasty insight into local affairs. Rose, an internationally recognized biomedical researcher, would stay for dinner, aiming her pointed New York wit at anything resembling conventional thinking. She and Kent had been fast friends since my husband and Rose's daughter Nancy were two years old. A generation younger than Kent's other friends, Jill, a speech therapist, and Marguerite, a rehabilitator of injured wild animals, were also frequent visitors. Jill would drop by with her little girl and Marguerite with Beowulf, a docile German shepherd almost the size of a Shetland pony.

As my mother-in-law's health declined because of chronic lung disease, these friends kept her involved with the outside world. At first, they'd cajole her into going out to dinner with them on Fridays, and they'd take turns hosting each other for drinks and hors d'oeuvres every Monday. Gradually, Harriet, who lived across the street, began doing Kent's grocery shopping. During the last two years of my mother-in-law's life, when she needed round-the-clock care and her physical universe had shrunk to a ten-foot radius, she asked her hired caregivers to mix the martinis and make the canapes. Kent's house became the sole venue for those Monday get-togethers, but they continued. Up until a few months before her death, those gray-haired women still gathered in that sunroom and spoke their minds, often bluntly and sometimes saltily, about the foibles of the grand and the humble, the direction of foreign and domestic policy, the accomplishments and failings of their children and grandchildren, and the challenges of raising roses and hibiscus so near the beach.

In those years after my mother-in-law "went in"—the Southern euphemism for an elderly woman's retiring into the confines of her home—her close friendships seemed, if anything, to increase rather than fall off. Trish, a thirtysomething woman who'd moved in next door, became a daily visitor, frequently bearing new towels, sheets, or other practical gifts no one else had noticed were needed. Betty, a biologist, began regular, week-long visits from Massachusetts, where she taught science at an art college. Decades earlier, Kent had supported Betty during a difficult divorce. Now, Betty was reciprocating, supporting Kent during her long illness and its inevitable outcome.

Of course, Kent had family who visited, too. But none of us could give her what her friends could. As I observed Kent's friendships, I recognized that each relationship was different. Each allowed her to explore or express something about herself, and each seemed to have its own rules and limits. Kent and Rose got enormous pleasure and intellectual stimulation from each other, and their bond had endured more than forty years. Yet, although each had lost a husband to a lingering illness and each had lost a child to suicide, they never discussed those experiences together. Kent saved those painful topics for Betty; and it was Betty—rather than Rose, rather than my husband or me—to whom she revealed her feelings about her own death.

I began to see patterns in women's friendships. There must be different kinds of female friendship, I thought, and it must serve different purposes at different stages of our lives. I wanted to learn about both. I also wanted to find out how women's friendships formed, why making and keeping friends was so easy for some women and so hard for others, and what women who were adept at friendship could teach the rest of us. And, as a journalist, I wanted to be able to share my findings. In other words, I wanted to write a book.

Of course, I wasn't the first. Carmen Renee Berry and Tamara Traeder had celebrated this special bond charmingly in their bestseller *Girlfriends.* Lois Wyse had pieced together a delightful quilt of anecdote and insight in *Women Make the Best Friends.* But neither these nor the rest of the recent crop of well-written and often inspiring books and articles on women's friendships answered my questions. Those were buried in the rich vein of research I uncovered on specific aspects of the subject. Most of it focused on children, adolescents, college students, and the elderly—populations easy to reach through schools, senior centers, and nursing homes. Some of the most thought-provoking findings appeared in unpublished dissertations and master's theses.

The deeper I delved into the subject of female friendship, the more fascinating I found it. One of the advantages of being a freelance magazine journalist was that I could indulge my interest by writing related articles. I did two for *Self*—one on keeping money differences from getting in the way of friendship, the other on ending a friendship without making an enemy. Both times, I was struck by how eager the women I interviewed were to discuss their friendships and how candid they were in their responses. When it came to understanding female friendship in all its complex variety, academic and clinical research might provide the conceptual skeleton, but the flesh and blood necessary to bring it to life would have to come from individual girls and women.

Attitudes and experiences vary from region to region, age to age, and ethnic group to ethnic group. Although I was more interested in similarities than differences, I realized that if I was going to write about female friendship in America (rather than, in my case, the Upper Gulf Coast of Texas), I was going to have to travel. I had some questions for the sociologists and psychologists whose work I planned to draw on most heavily, and I wanted their help with a few ideas that were taking shape in my own mind, particularly about the different forms of female friendship. Basing my itinerary on the locations of these twenty-seven social scientists and clinicians, I set up in-person interviews with 204 girls and women, from 8 to 90 years old, from Florida to Washington state. Some of them were friends or acquaintances of mine; some worked with people I knew. Others I contacted through churches, schools, or social service agencies. Two of the women I interviewed were serving in the U.S. Army in Panama; two were Roman Catholic nuns.

I conducted the interviews in person, all but a few of them in 1996, then had the tapes transcribed. In the chapters that follow, the age, education, relationship status, and other details I give for each person reflect her situation at the time of the interview. Each of the sessions lasted about two hours (though some ran several times that) and included a battery of standard questions (see The Friendship Interviews: Method and Questions), but our informal and unstructured discussions often extended well beyond that template.

I strove to make the mix of the women I interviewed as ethnically diverse as America itself. Their lifestyles varied as well: About half were married, a quarter each single and divorced. Thirteen volunteered that they were lesbians. And while most were middle class, a few were struggling to stay above the poverty line, and a couple had annual incomes in the millions. (For a more precise breakdown of my interview sample, see The Friendship Interviews: Method and Questions.)

Although I intentionally avoided choosing women with a particular facility for creating and maintaining female friendships, the diverse individuals I interviewed shared remarkable insights, along with their personal stories. Even women who considered themselves inept at friendship had wisdom to impart, and even those who knew they were good at it had questions. Time and again, they talked about the challenge and joy of building relationships with one another—relationships that would endure and help them become their best selves.

As I traveled the country, learning from the women I interviewed, the book started taking shape. I decided to begin by looking at what female friendship had meant to women in past eras and what it means to us today—its varied forms and functions, as well as how an individual friendship develops and how it can help *us* develop as individuals. The logical next step was examining how friendship operates at different seasons of our lives, from girlhood to our later years. Finally, I knew that I needed to delve into the challenges, both within us and outside us, that can strain and even shatter female friendships; and I needed to suggest some strategies for dealing with those challenges, so that the women who read this book would come away better able to form and maintain these growth-promoting, life-enhancing relationships—to become the best of friends and to enjoy the best of friendship.

Part One

❧

The Meaning of Female Friendship

I

～

What Our
Great-Grandmothers Knew

Yes'm, old friends is always best,
'less you can catch a new one that's fit
to make an old one out of.

—Sarah Orne Jewett,
The Country of the Pointed Firs

One day in 1957, when I was eleven years old, I asked my mother to tell me about her friendships. My mom and I were ironing together in the kitchen of our house in suburban St. Louis, where we'd moved when my dad's company had transferred him a year earlier. I'd left behind two close girlfriends, and I was having trouble replacing them.

My mother described several girls she'd known as she grew up in a mining town in northern Idaho, as well as young women she'd met in college and as a new bride in New York City. She spoke of them fondly, but dismissively. "Your father is my best friend," she concluded. "He's really the only friend I need."

Over the decades, we moved whenever my father's company asked. When we got to a new town, my mother would join the Episcopal women's guild, volunteer for the Scouts, and pitch in for other worthy causes. She did the socializing expected of a corporate executive's wife. Meanwhile, she corresponded with friends she'd left behind. Beneath her energetic involvement in the world around her, however, I sensed a wistfulness.

I also noticed that we didn't have a piano, even though we could well have afforded one. Whenever my mother talked about playing the piano as a girl, her eyes brightened. But if my father was such a close friend, why didn't he notice? Year after year, I kept expecting to find a spinet sporting a red bow next to the Christmas tree, but I never did.

When I was away at college, my father's career brought him back to New York City. My parents bought a house in a New Jersey suburb, where my mother met a woman named Gertrude. The two of them would go into the city to tour art museums and take in Off-Broadway plays, neither of which interested my father. They became confidantes—the type of relationship I don't think my mother had while I was growing up.

My mother still insisted that my father was her best friend, the only friend she really needed. But it was Gertrude who gave her the 1910 vintage piano.

❧ The History of Female Friendship ❧

My mother lived most of her adult life in a period that seriously undervalued female friendship. In the first few decades of this century, however, women considered close bonds with others of their sex a priority and a right, and they took these relationships seriously.

Throughout much of history, women—at least the middle- and upper-class women who left written accounts of their lives—were socially segregated from men. Except in the case of family members, women weren't allowed to see men alone. Husbands and wives expected loyalty, fidelity, practical support, affection, sexual gratification (at least for the man), and tenderness from each other; but they didn't expect to share interests or confidences.

Friendship as we know it today is a relatively recent concept. In the seventeenth and eighteenth centuries, the rise of individualism and idealism, concepts that grew from the modern notion of a self distinct from the obligations of family and society, brought to Europe and America the promise that a friendship with a kindred spirit could be the most fulfilling earthly experience. Writing in the mid-1600s, English poet Katherine Phillips echoed the sentiments of her era when she declared "Oh my Lucasia, let us speak our Love/ . . . I've all the World in thee." To Phillips's contemporaries, a woman becoming celebrated for her poetry may have been shocking, but her strong attachment to her female friends apparently wasn't. Far from finding close bonds between women threatening, people of the seventeenth and eighteenth centuries saw them as ennobling unions of the soul.

In *Surpassing the Love of Men,* Lillian Faderman wove a detailed tapestry of emotional bonds between unrelated women by combing through letters, diaries, and literature from the Renaissance forward. She discovered that by the mid-eighteenth century, the passionate, committed, but nonsexual attachment among women that became known as "romantic friendship" was "a recognized institution" in America. For the next 150 years or so, women sought, and found, in female friendships the intense warmth and mutual involvement the twentieth century has taught us to look for in love affairs and to cultivate in marriage.

This may be why one true-life romance that caught the late eighteenth-century imagination was the elopement of two young women—not with male sweethearts, but with each other—in 1778. Girlhood friends Sarah Ponsonby and Eleanor Butler were daughters of titled Irish families—the sort accustomed to marrying children off to unite land holdings. The first time the two ran away together, their families brought them back; but when Sarah and Eleanor escaped again, their parents decided to let them be and gave each a modest stipend. The pair settled in a cottage outside the Welsh village of Llangollen, where they tended a lovely garden and entertained such literary lights as Lady Caroline Lamb, William Wordsworth, and Sir Walter Scott. The Ladies of Llangollen, as they came to be celebrated in story and verse, had done what so many young women of their day yearned to do: They had escaped a dreary future to live a blissful, apparently nonsexual partnership of mind and heart.

Nowadays, two women living together in open love and devotion would be assumed to be lesbians. But the openness with which the Ladies of Llangollen and their admirers discussed their relationship indicated that at least on the surface, their relationship conformed to the conservative mores of the day. Of course, the popular wisdom of the seventeenth, eighteenth, and nineteenth centuries held that a nor-

mal woman had no independent interest in sex. If her character happened to be weak, a man might seduce her. But in a pair of women,
the era reasoned, there was no one to initiate sexual activity; therefore,
it wasn't suspected.

Side by side with references to prayers, biblical analogies, and expressions of spiritual zeal, friends penned letters pledging enduring
devotion, exchanged tokens of affection, and wistfully recalled visits
during which they kissed, gazed into each other's eyes, and even slept
intertwined. "How I love you & how happy I have been!" one such
woman wrote to a friend in 1861. "My darling how I long for the
time when I shall see you."

Our own era has struggled with what to make of these unabashedly
romantic friendships. Some scholars of eighteenth- and nineteenth-
century literature have decided that the period treated these close and
tender relationships so openly because it accepted the potential for sex
between women. Others have argued that the written evidence of ardor
merely reflects the Victorian penchant for idealizing relationships. Still
others have contended that these tender letters lent voice to genuine
commitment rarely, if ever, expressed sexually. Regardless of the role
sexuality played in these relationships, it seems clear that, in the words
of scholar Carroll Smith-Rosenberg, intimate female friends of that era
"assumed an emotional centrality in each others' lives." What Smith-
Rosenberg described as "the female world of love and ritual" included
a tradition of passionate friendship between women whose husbands
and families "considered such love both socially acceptable and fully
compatible with heterosexual marriage."

At this time, it was not uncommon for a woman to marry her
friend's brother, as Sue Gilbert wed poet Emily Dickinson's. Such
marriages bound two women even closer by making them sisters-in-
law. As historian Carol Lasser noted, novels and poems of the time
often presented female friendship as an idealization of the sister bond.
A few months after they met at college in 1846, Antoinette Brown
began a letter to Lucy Stone "My own dear sister." Their close friendship lasted forty-six years, and like Sue Gilbert and Emily Dickinson,
the two friends eventually became sisters-in-law, in this case by marrying two brothers. But the sisterly terms in which they couched their
relationship predated their weddings by a decade.

By calling a friend "sister," a Victorian woman invited her into her closest circle of acquaintance. The practice pervaded all classes. Female mill workers and even slaves adopted each other as sisters, pledging the same support and commitment they extended to their closest relatives.

Female friendship not only enriched the lives of those who engaged in it, it also altered history. As early as the mid-1700s, American women were forming alliances with one another to promote religious and social causes. British feminist Mary Wollstonecraft, who revolutionized attitudes about female education in her 1792 tract *A Vindication of the Rights of Woman,* was influenced by Thomas Paine, William Blake, and other brilliant, radical men she knew; but her primary source of emotional support was her dear friend Fanny Blood, who stuck by her through scandalous and often unhappy love affairs, the birth of a daughter out of wedlock, and an attempted suicide.

Not all women had such support near at hand. The letters and journals penned in the 1800s by women pioneers in the American West are full of poignant laments about missing the company of female friends and relatives. "For women who went West in nuclear families, one of the experiences of the frontier was the loss of the company of other women," historian Elizabeth Jameson told me. "The worst time for these women was the period we romanticize so much, which was the early frontier. What we see in their diaries is their hunger for other women."

The American West was a notable exception to the nineteenth century practice of separating the sexes. Ranches and farms were spaced so far apart that when married women went visiting, their husbands and children came along. Women did forge close bonds with one another, but like many of the friendships that developed back East between religious evangelists and social reformers, these formed around largely female efforts to establish schools, churches, and cultural societies and to transform rough boomtowns into outposts of gentility. Essayist Fannie Quain recalled middle-class life in Bismarck, North Dakota, when she was growing up during the 1880s:

> All through these early years a crowd of women who came here in the first years of settlement, worked together. They had seen the suffering and endured the hardships of the frontier and there was a bond as close as sisterhood among them.

Occasionally, a pair of adventurous young single women would even homestead together. In 1886 Bee Randolph and Mary Anderson homesteaded adjacent quarter sections, living together in a cabin straddling the property line. When Mary's wedding ended the arrangement a year later, Bee commemorated their last day of joint housekeeping with a wistful entry in her friend's autograph album: "We cannot be happier than we have been here, although we may have wealth and other great pleasures."

Back East, women who decided to pursue professional careers—callings incompatible with the role of a genteel Victorian wife—or women who otherwise rejected the prospect of marriage often set up housekeeping together. Perhaps because of their popularity among well-educated, urban New Englanders, these were dubbed "Boston marriages." By dint of work or inheritance, women in these committed relationships were almost always financially self-sufficient. Polite society treated them as couples. They entertained together and were invited to parties as pairs.

Late nineteenth-century author Sarah Orne Jewett enjoyed devotion and diversion in her Boston marriage to Annie Fields, widow of *Atlantic Monthly* publisher James Fields. Supported by this stable and caring domestic partnership, Sarah did some of her finest writing, capturing the provincial manners and pungent idioms of coastal Maine, and served as a mentor for younger women writers, notably Willa Cather. But after Sarah's death in 1907, as Annie Fields was editing her companion's letters for publication, her friend and biographer Mark De-Wolfe Howe recommended that she remove 80 percent of the expressions of affection between them to prevent "all sorts of people reading them wrong." Clearly, the attitude toward female friendship had undergone a dramatic change.

The tide of suspicion about intimate female friendship had begun to wash west from Europe. In 1892 *Psychopathia Sexualis,* the 1886 treatise by German physician and neurologist Richard von Krafft-Ebing, had been published in English, describing "inversion," or the adoption of interests associated with the opposite sex (for example, fishing for a woman or clothing design for a man), as a genetic defect. Five years later, British psychologist Havelock Ellis published the first volume of *Studies in the Psychology of Sex.* Six more followed. In this work, Ellis coined the term "lesbian," likening one of his wife's close female friendships to the passions of the ancient Greek poet Sappho, who lived on the island of Lesbos. Sigmund Freud's 1905 *Three Essays on the Theory of Sexuality* created a furor even before its 1910 translation from the German. Since 1869, German sexologists had been saying that there was something wrong with women who displayed masculine interests (the professions, sports, or business, for instance) and preferred the company of their own gender. But Freud added the disquieting contention that the human psyche suppressed both early emotional trauma and taboo impulses. In other words, a person could be influenced by forbidden urges, such as an erotic attraction to members of her own sex, without even knowing it. Unconscious sexual desires could manifest themselves consciously as more acceptable forms of attachment.

Suddenly, what had seemed innocent, even exalted, became tagged as unhealthy. Experiencing intense feelings of affection, yearning for another woman's company, exchanging tokens of sentiment, articulating commitment, even providing comforting embraces in times of sorrow became suspect.

Mary Grew of Providence, Rhode Island, in her 1892 response to a letter of condolence on the death of her lifelong friend Margaret Burleigh, summed up the attitude of her own century toward romantic friendship but also signaled the dawning psychological sophistication that would bring an end to this tender tradition in the next:

> To me it seems to have been a closer union than that of most marriages. We know there have been other such between two men and also between two women. And why should there not be.[sic] Love is spiritual, only passion is sexual.

During the 1910s and 1920s, women began to socialize with men in public; they got the vote, won expanded property rights, and enrolled by the tens of thousands in colleges and universities. Ironically, one of the great accomplishments of early twentieth-century feminism was one of the biggest contributors to the decline of female friendship. As a marital ideal, the rigidly hierarchical Victorian marriage gave way to a union between a man and a woman who, although they performed different roles, were equal partners. Implicit in what came to be called "companionate marriage" was the notion that women should direct all their energy into relationships with men. As historian Christina Simmons explained in an article for *Frontiers:*

> In this framework, traditional female friendship and interdependence took on an ominous overtone; resistance to men and marriage was perceived as a threat.

At the same time that the concept of companionate marriage was filtering through American popular culture, so, too, was the recognition that women had their own sexual drives. In this light, open physical affection between women began to seem dangerous, likely to arouse "unnatural" desires.

Some women, including some prominent feminists and intellectuals, refused to let the prevailing cultural wariness interfere with their friendships. Harkening back to the alliances forged in nineteenth-century reform movements, Eleanor Roosevelt's friendships made through the League of Women Voters gave her the emotional support and validation she needed to become a major force for social justice. English writer Vera Brittain's friend Winifred Holtby helped her transform her personal grief at the deaths of both her fiancé and her brother in World War I into persuasive pleas for global peace. Poets Marianne Moore and Elizabeth Bishop influenced and supported each other's work.

With the men off fighting, World War II gave American women the opportunity—in fact, forced them—to exercise their competence and intelligence and to validate one another. But the aspirations promoted for women after World War II focused on life in the suburbs, stressing the importance of the nuclear family above all else. While their husbands commuted to work, the women relied on their neighbors for help watching kids and running errands, as well as for companionship. They weren't supposed to look to each other for validation or intimacy. For those, they had husbands.

By the 1950s, women were told that they could expect to enjoy sex, but that they could only have it within marriage. As Brett Harvey pointed out in *The Fifties: A Women's Oral History,* the eroticized marriage became the ideal. Now, popular magazines proclaimed, women could find in marriage not only romantic love, financial security, and the joy of rearing children, but companionship, emotional support, and sexual gratification as well—everything in one convenient package.

At the same time, the importance society placed on female friendship dwindled. As Susan Faludi observed in *Backlash: The Undeclared War Against American Women,* women who'd buoyed one another up during World War II were encouraged to view one another as competitors for the returning men or for the few jobs remaining open to females. Of the six million women who joined the workforce to help America fight the war, 80 percent of those polled said they wanted to keep working after it was won. Nonetheless, four million were fired in 1946 alone in the campaign to send American women back to the kitchen.

In the 1950s and 1960s, middle-class women were encouraged to be cordial and helpful toward their neighbors and the wives of their husbands' colleagues, but not to develop friendships for their own sake. After all, close ties would only have to be broken if their husbands were transferred. Magazines hailed "togetherness" in the nuclear family, and women who wanted to convey that they had perfect marriages asserted, like my mother: "He's not just my husband. He's my best friend."

All too often, what those housewives were revealing wasn't marital success; it was emotional isolation.

Very few of the female rituals that characterized women's friendships in the nineteenth century carried over into postwar America. The planning and production of weddings remained the exclusive province of women, as did baby showers and debuts. As quilting bees, sewing circles, and other collective strategies for transforming chores into social events declined, twentieth-century women developed rituals for sharing leisure. Many spent hours each week playing bridge, canasta, or mah-jong. Although members within any one group tended to share the same background, the bridge club phenomenon crossed ethnic and economic lines. Dallas philanthropist Ruth Collins Sharp Altshuler belonged to a club that hadn't played cards in forty-five years but was still meeting regularly when I interviewed her in 1996. "That means an awful lot to my generation," she told me.

Gladys Simon, now seventy-nine, belonged to three of Galveston's dozen or so African-American bridge clubs simultaneously. "One played on Thursday, one on Friday, one on Saturday," she recalled.

"You went to different houses, and each person tried to outdo the other. You sent flowers to the hostess, and the place would look like a funeral parlor. We tried to outentertain each other and outdress each other. We dressed, darling. We dressed."

Women in these groups saw one another every week, but they didn't share their deepest selves. That would have meant revealing unmet longings, lending validity to discontent. Theoretically, these housewives, the mothers of the baby boomers, had it all—prosperity, security, a cornucopia of consumer goods, and the leisure to enjoy them. Above all, they had husbands and children, which, the psychologists of the time told them, were the sole ingredients of feminine fulfillment. If a woman wasn't happy under those circumstances, there must have been something wrong with her. So if she experienced the sense of anxious emptiness Betty Friedan dubbed "the problem that has no name," she didn't acknowledge it, often not even to herself.

For Kim Waller, the breakthrough came early in the summer of 1964. Like legions of other young Manhattan mothers, she had taken her preschooler to the neighborhood park. She recounted her vivid memories of that afternoon: "We were all watching them eat sand and throw sand. No one to my knowledge had confessed the horrors of motherhood to each other, because we were still all trying to be perfect. One woman sitting next to me, whom I had chatted with before—'Does he roll over yet?' 'Does he sit up yet?'—turned to me and said something like, 'Couldn't you just throttle them at four o'clock or toss them out the window?' I looked at her in awe and shock and couldn't believe that somebody was actually confessing that.

"That comment opened up to me the whole possibility that women could stop being competitive and perfect and really show each other the way that we were feeling. It made life a hell of a lot easier."

Still, like me, many young girls during the 1950s and 1960s grew up convinced that close bonds with others of our sex were unimportant. We had unwritten conventions: If you made plans to do something with another girl and a boy called for a date, you could justifiably break that plan—even on very short notice, and even if both you and your friend knew the guy was a jerk.

The civil rights, anti–Vietnam war, and environmental movements began to change women's conceptions of one another. Working together for these causes, women shared ideas, feelings, and validation.

The women's liberation movement took this a giant step further by insisting that we view one another as individuals with as much inherent value as males.

Artist and social activist Gertrude Barnstone, seventy, had grown up in the era before World War II with men for role models. "Girls seemed to represent this kind of fluff and nonsense—worrying about your makeup or your clothes or boys," she recalled. During the late 1960s, when she was in her forties and serving on the Houston school board, Gertrude went to Dallas to attend one of the first feminist conferences. "It was like the scales falling away from my eyes, to see women in a different light than I had seen them before," she said. "I suddenly realized that here were these wonderful creatures saying intelligent things, that I didn't have to compete with them. I didn't have to feel like there was a wall between us."

In the wake of those first heady conferences, women began coming together to raise their consciousnesses. By 1973, about 100,000 American women belonged to consciousness-raising groups, each usually composed of eight to twelve members who met weekly. As the movement's motto, "The personal is political," suggested, they believed that by sharing their experiences and feelings, women would recognize their oppression and be motivated to reform the culture and its institutions.

The purpose of consciousness-raising may have been to send women to the front lines for equal rights, but it also sent thousands of women back to their offices and schools, churches and neighborhoods trained to speak honestly about themselves and to listen empathically to one another. It taught them that when they made themselves vulnerable to other women, they could often expect support. This created a new template for female friendship.

"One of the greatest contributions of the feminist movement was getting women to talk to one another—to hear each other's stories and see ourselves in them," psychotherapist Barbara Ellman told me.

American women were yearning for that kind of connection more than ever. Studies have revealed a marked rise in signs of friendship deprivation among women between 1957 and 1976. Ironically, some of that loneliness was an indirect consequence of the gains made by feminism. Preparing for and taking on serious careers left women less leisure to form and enjoy friendships. And a woman now able and determined to move out into the world often had to leave old friends behind.

That's what happened to Betsy Alden, a fifty-three-year-old Methodist minister in Albuquerque. When she announced to her bridge group in the early 1970s that she planned to return to school and become ordained, she felt "dismissed." These were well-educated young mothers; most had met through the American Association of University Women. But all were focused on their homes and children. "I don't think they could identify at that stage with starting a whole new career and going off into unexplored territories," Betsy explained.

❧ Generational Ground Rules ❧

Betsy Alden experienced two kinds of dissonance in her female friendships. On the surface, her ties to the women she'd known were strained by the opportunities opening up to them. That tension among women who make different life choices continues today, as it may for the foreseeable future.

But something deeper was also disrupting Betsy's woman-to-woman relationships. Born during World War II, she belonged to an age group for whom the ground rules of women's friendships would never be clear. As I analyzed transcripts of my interviews, I noticed a generational split. Certain standards of conduct held constant across all ages. No one thought it was okay to betray a friend's confidences or have sex with her romantic partner. And most women dodged conflict, even when confronting it might have been better for the relationship.

However, I noticed that some of the rules of female friendship seemed to shift according to changes in the social landscape women experienced as young adults. In general, women born prior to 1940, who had entered their twenties before the upheaval of the 1960s, played by one set of rules. Women born after 1950, who had come of age during and after the first wave of modern feminism, played by another. And women born in the decade between them had to sort things out for themselves. Not every woman on either side of this divide conducted her friendships according to her generation's norms. But those who didn't tended to be conscious of breaking away.

For women who turned twenty in the 1950s and earlier, the following guidelines seem to apply:

- Don't discuss family or personal problems. Don't ask overly personal questions.

  Gladys Simon described the members of her bridge groups as "all pretty close, two or three of them closer than some." Yet, when her marriage was breaking up, she didn't confide in them. "I just stood it," she said. "We knew things that were going on with each other, but we didn't discuss them."

- Relationships with men and obligations to family always take precedence over female friendship.

  When Dallas publicist Julia Sweeney was in high school, she noticed that her girlfriends underwent a complete transformation whenever a boy appeared. "As soon as the boys showed up, you would get kind of coy and cute," she said. Even in her late middle age, Willie Ann, a friend from home whose acquaintance Julia had recently renewed, continued that pattern. When men were around, she immediately shifted her attention to them. "It doesn't matter who the man is," Julia explained. "She's going to flirt with him and try to get him."

- Whatever the norms of behavior accepted by one's peer group, friends must encourage one another to follow them. If a woman violates an important one, her friends are permitted, in some cases even obliged, to distance themselves.

  Barbara Tuttle, the only daughter of a Midwestern politician, recounted what happened when she once confided too much to her best friends at Stanford. Her fiancé, a premed student, had interrupted his studies to serve in the navy. While he was away for months on a destroyer, she became pregnant from a one-night stand and, with the help of her physician uncle, got a back-alley abortion. "When I got back to college, I told a few of my close friends and they turned against me," she recalled. For most women born after 1950, ditching a friend for such a reason would be unthinkable—even if they thought abortion was wrong.

- Encourage one another in traditional female virtues such as self-sacrifice and maintaining appearances.

  During the 1970s, when Dallas philanthropist Ruth Altshuler

was in her late forties, her late husband was suffering from Parkinson's disease. Under those circumstances, she put aside her generation's rule of reticence and expressed her frustration to her closest friends. The support they gave her in response affirmed their admiration for the way she handled the stress but indicated that they'd never doubted that she could cope with it.

"One of my friends said, 'You know, you always wore your lipstick,' " she told me. "Women of my generation always wore their lipstick."

- If a friend engages in self-destructive behavior, don't intervene.

   Several women born before 1940 mentioned being distressed by a friend's smoking or excessive drinking. Several even gave those as reasons for distancing themselves. Then, as a hasty aside, they added something like, "Of course, I couldn't tell her it bothered me. It was none of my business."

- Don't tell a friend how much you care about her, and don't ask how she feels about you. Limit physical expression to a restrained hug or a peck on the cheek.

When sociologist Helen Gouldner discussed female friendship with women of this generation, she found that they considered it "uncouth" to ask a friend for her assessment of their relationship. Women I interviewed of all ages mentioned that they were more comfortable hugging, kissing, or casually touching a platonic male friend than a woman—even if the relationship with the woman was much closer.

For women born after 1950, many of friendship's ground rules seem to belong to the world on the other side of the looking glass.

- If something important is going on in your romantic or family life, share it. If a friend seems troubled, ask if she wants to talk about it.

   This began as a necessity born of the 1960s sexual revolution. In those days, it was a rare college student who could go to her mother for advice on sexual matters. In that newly permissive environment, it took a friend her own age to help plot a course that avoided prudery on one hand and promiscuity on the other.

   Without rigid norms to define acceptable behavior, women who came of age after the 1960s still struggle to mesh their personal values with the challenges of contemporary life. Should a lesbian come out to her doting grandmother? How should a mom respond when her fourteen-year-old confides that she's sexually active? For empathy and relevant guidance, a woman at forty will turn to the same source she did at twenty—a female friend.

One reason women born after 1950 feel free to entrust one another with the intimate details of their lives is that they tend to make their friends independently—at work, at the health club, through an alumni group, on a trek in Nepal—not simply with their next-door neighbors or the wives of their husbands' coworkers. But some of this modern self-disclosure is a function of time pressure. Women juggling careers and families don't spend enough hours together to pick up the subtle hints of how each other is doing; so it's important for friends to be explicit about their feelings.

- Give the claims of close friendship the same priority awarded those of romance and family.

Among women in their twenties and thirties, sacrificing female friendship for a heterosexual relationship falls somewhere between bad manners and treason. "That's a big issue among most of the women I know," said Kiran, a twenty-four-year-old graduate student in New York. "To say about a woman, 'Oh, she's dating someone now. We never see her anymore'—that tells something about her character, like, obviously, she doesn't care about her friendships with women."

Chicago anthropologist Madelyn Iris, who studied women's creativity in mid- and late life, identified a major difference in attitude toward the rival claims of family and friends among women now middle-aged and younger. One cause was geographic mobility, she explained; another was the weakening of family bonds. "For my mother's generation, family was everything," she said. "I don't think that's true for a lot of people anymore."

- Even when a friend violates generally accepted norms of behavior or does something you consider morally wrong, stick by her.

As mid-century American society turned from the tenets of Protestantism to ethical relativism, tolerance, nonjudgmentalism, and loyalty ascended the shortened list of generally accepted virtues. Dropping a friend for a moral or social offense became justifiable only if it affected the relationship directly. A devout Catholic told me of accompanying a friend to an abortionist, in the days when abortion was illegal, waiting there for her during the procedure, then taking her home and staying with her until they were both confident she was all right. "I'd tried to talk her out of it, and I felt awful that I couldn't persuade her," the Catholic explained. "But once she'd made her decision, I knew I had to be there for her."

- If a friend engages in self-destructive behavior, intervene—or feel guilty about not doing so.

Several women of the post–World War II baby boom and younger told me that they felt bad because they hadn't done anything about a friend's smoking or drinking. Far from being none of their business, their friend's problems had partly become their own.

Not that the women on the receiving end of this well-intentioned interference find it easy to take. We're still trying to figure out an etiquette for intervention.

- Exchange exuberant hugs on meeting, even after a short separation, and avoid giving the impression of being uncomfortable with physical contact or verbal expressions of affection, even if you are.

During the course of the interviews I conducted, I asked whether and how female friends had helped each other through crises. As women described the support given and received through divorces, deaths, failed love affairs, and losses of jobs, those born before 1940 spoke of distractions ("You've been sitting in that house too long; let's go shopping."), while those born after 1950 talked about physical comforting ("She just took me in her arms and rocked me while I cried"). On happier occasions, younger friends hugged one another straight up, rather than bending forward, I began to notice, and they sometimes prolonged the contact by strolling from the car to the front door with their arms around each other's waists. Any discomfort seemed to stem not from the touching itself but from reluctance to be the first to disconnect.

Compared to their mothers and grandmothers, these women also were more fearless about stating their feelings for one another. Asked what they valued about a particular friend, several of them replied, "That she loves me, and she isn't afraid to tell me so."

❧ Class Variations ❧

Virtually all the women I interviewed would have described themselves as middle class if I'd asked them, but I didn't, because I wanted them to feel relaxed enough to discuss their friendships candidly. Talking about social class makes Americans acutely uncomfortable. Merely acknowledging its existence goes against one of our most cherished illusions: that we live in a meritocracy.

So when sociologists warned that I'd find class differences in female friendship, I wasn't sure what to expect. I'd been told, for example, that working-class women tended to have few friends outside their families and to regard those they did have as adopted kin. But my own interviews didn't bear this out. The number of close friends didn't differ from class to class, but the function of the friendships did. I found that for working-class women, practical help is a key ingredient of friendship. Social psychologist Karen Walker observed something similar, concluding that working-class female friendships emphasize "material and emotional interdependence," while those of the middle class stress "leisure and emotional support."

Maria Dillig, who bottled beer at a plant in Milwaukee, described her friendship with her coworker Agnes as a mixture of shared fun and mutual aid. "She's helped me out a lot at the house when I've had different projects to do, wallpapering or painting," she said. When Maria and her husband bought their house, a neck problem prevented him from participating in the redecorating or heavy lifting. "So Agnes and her brother came over, and they did it all," Maria explained. "In turn, I went back to her house and I wallpapered her two bathrooms for her."

If a woman lives at or below the poverty level, a strong network of female friends serves as a personal safety net. Friends can also make the crucial difference in her ability to rise occupationally. "Say one lady gets called for a job—she'll ask the other one 'Do you mind sitting my children while I go to the interview?'" explained Sylvia Castillo, the director of De Madres a Madres, a social service agency helping low-income Hispanic women in Houston. "Then if she gets the job, she may hire one of the other ladies to baby-sit her children."

At thirty-two, single mother Angela Gamble worked as a receptionist in a Chicago office to support her two children. Although her parents had been able to move out of the housing project where she'd grown up, they weren't much better off than she was; so when she needed cash to make it to the next paycheck, she turned to a female friend, a coworker with no kids.

"How deep is the love for each other?" Angela asked rhetorically. "It's about being there when needed. If you really want to know who your friends are, talk about money and living together."

For middle- and upper-class women, borrowing money from friends is virtually taboo. Once past college, so is borrowing clothes and cars. Only family can be counted on for that sort of assistance.

Incorporating material support into the concept of close friendship leaves low-income women vulnerable. Sometimes a friend will withdraw from the relationship because she can't repay a loan. Sometimes a woman in desperate circumstances steals from a close companion, a double betrayal. The theft itself stings, but so does the revelation that by taking what she wanted instead of asking for it, she showed that she didn't trust the other woman to share whatever she had with a needy friend.

Pinkey Rowe had met her friend Alva when they were in junior high school and were living in the same public housing project. They remained close throughout adolescence and early adulthood. Alva escaped the burdens of cooking and cleaning for her thirteen younger siblings by marrying first one abusive man, then another who became addicted to heroin. During Alva's serial crises, Pinkey pitched in with child care, a place to stay, and occasional loans, although as a cleaning woman and home health care worker, she never made much money.

Then one day, Pinkey got a call at work. A furniture store wanted to know when she was going to pay her bill. "What bill?" she asked. The store's representative insisted that she had one, that they'd delivered furniture to her house sometime back. Pinkey asked for the delivery address. It was Alva's.

"I was angry," she told me. "I had them take the furniture away, and I said, 'If you needed me to do that, you should have let me sign my own name.' She should have known that if she needed me to help her buy that stuff, I would have done it."

For middle-class women, frequent moves mold friendship patterns, especially during early adulthood. Even if a woman goes to college in her hometown, then finds a job and settles there, many of her friends will have scattered within a few months of high school graduation. Affluent women can afford plane tickets to visit one another, take cruises, or rent vacation houses together, and talk on the phone whenever and however long they want. But such occasional contact still can't replace the sense of connection forged over regular morning walks or the spontaneous pleasure of grabbing coffee with a friend after work.

For women of great wealth, as well as those who have become famous, female friendship can provide a sanctuary, a haven of comfort in which they can slip out of their personas as if these were a pair of stylish but confining shoes. But trusting that a friend values her for herself, and not for the enhanced status the association provides, may be a problem for a rich woman. She may miss out on one of true friendship's main benefits—the sense of being treasured as a unique and irreplaceable individual.

By being self-aware and sensitive, a woman who becomes rich or famous as an adult can keep connected to friends from her past. If she's an astute judge of character and can resist flattery, she can even make genuine new ones. But what about women born into wealthy, high-profile families? For these women, the best hope for true connection often lies in nurturing relationships formed early in life, before either girl became aware of the importance society attached to money and celebrity. When forty-five-year-old New York publicist Carol Edgar first met her lifelong friend Swanee Hunt at choir practice in a Baptist church in Dallas, they were both nine years old. Months passed before Carol's mother explained that Swanee's father was H. L. Hunt, the fabulously rich and famously eccentric oilman. To Carol, growing up in a middle-class neighborhood, that wealth had little significance beyond the fun of sleeping over at a big house and exchanging secrets on a log next to a private pond.

The two girls went to summer camp together, hashed out the big adolescent questions about boys and the meaning of life, and toured with their church music group. They stayed in touch even though Carol went away to college and Swanee lived at home and attended Southern Methodist University. As the decades passed, they remained close friends despite the pressures of families and careers—Carol's in media, Swanee's as head of her own charitable foundation and as the ambassador to Austria during the Clinton administration.

"She's been phenomenally attentive, especially considering the demands on her time," Carol told me. "During the dissolution of my marriage, she was right there. She even sent me flowers. I chose to live a rather private adult life, and she's chosen to live a very visible one. But I never feel excluded when I'm with Swanee."

❧ Ethnic Imprints ❧

A woman's financial fortunes may change in the course of her lifetime. Her ethnicity doesn't. And although minority women often have friends from other races, they need some from their own, too, who can affirm their experiences and empathize with their feelings.

"There's a shared experience that women of color have that white women don't, in terms of dealing with racism and the impact that that has on daily life," said Mount Holyoke professor Beverly Tatum, an African-American. "I certainly have white friends who try to empathize and identify and acknowledge the impact of racism, but it's not the same."

A white woman who believes in racial equality is bound to feel uncomfortable when she learns that she's been the recipient of certain privileges all her life, just because of her ethnic affiliation. That's why, for many of the African-American women I interviewed, the subject of race was off-limits with acquaintances or even friends who were white.

"One issue I stay away from almost entirely at work is anything to do with race," said Geena, a thirty-one-year-old reporter for a national magazine. "At this very moment, in the office, I have pals who are white, and I have pals who are black and Asian. There's a matter that's come up, and I told only my minority friends and had to say to them, 'By the way, this is in confidence. I haven't told any white people.' No explaining. We need not go any further than that. I think the blacks and Asians in the office do feel somewhat kindred in that way."

Most of the black women I interviewed (as well as most of the Hispanics and all of the Asians and Native Americans) named white women among their closest friends. These cross-race pairs shared intellectual and recreational interests, professional goals, senses of humor, and tastes in clothes and food. They liked, trusted, and nurtured one another. Yet, their connection would always lack one important element.

For women of color, the craving for ethnic empathy is often strong enough to pull them across social boundaries that normally keep white women apart. When sociologist Helen Gouldner interviewed middle- and upper-middle-class women about their friendships, she found that substantial differences in social status and education caused them to disregard people as prospective friends. A quick glance around a typical office just before noon bears this out. Everyone forms into lunch groups: secretaries with secretaries, junior management with entry-level professionals, upper-level executives with their peers. Americans honor rank in the workplace.

But not African-American women. "It's like it's us against the world, and so it doesn't matter what your status is," explained attorney Alberta Johnson, who frequently lunched with secretaries from her office.

The issue of ethnic empathy is compounded for women whose backgrounds are racially mixed. At two and a half years old, Renee Asofsky, a twenty-seven-year-old events coordinator for a nonprofit agency in Boston, was adopted into a white family. All her childhood friends were white. Lately Renee had begun to consciously cultivate friendships with other African-American women, but she felt that the connection was incomplete. "I have a black friend who does my hair, and we're close in a strange way," she said. "But because of my lifestyle and my family life, I've been kind of excommunicated."

In the course of my interviews, I discovered what appeared to be a generational shift in minority friendship patterns, particularly among Asians. Whereas many women now middle-aged had formed most of their friendships with women outside their own ethnic group, their daughters were actively seeking friends from similar backgrounds.

"When I was young, my friends were not Asian," said Kim, a forty-eight-year-old economist, who came to the United States from mainland China when she was a few months old. "In my daughter's generation, they have a lot more Asian friends."

At twenty-four, Kiran, a graduate student in international studies at Columbia, knew that she needed at least some female friends who were culturally Indian, like her. She was dealing with many of the same issues that other women her age dealt with: choosing a meaningful career and preparing for it, stealing time from her busy schedule to keep in touch with equally busy friends, and deciding whether—

and when—to marry and start a family. But she faced an additional challenge: striking a balance between the two sides of her identity. Kiran was both an ambitious young American professional and a member of a small ethnic and religious minority—Indian Christians. Although she had lived in New York since age four, she had been born in India, and many of her personal concerns were similar to those of other Indian women her age. Her closest friend, Anya, whom she'd met as an undergraduate at Yale, shared Kiran's intellectual interests, as well as her ethnic background. Although Anya's family wasn't Christian, they were Indian immigrants struggling with issues of identity and assimilation.

Kiran treasured Anya's friendship because they related to each other on two levels, both as unique individuals with distinctive interests, tastes, and personalities and as fellow members of a minority group. "One thing I've noticed about my relationships with other Indian women is we all have one issue that we can talk about—dating and marriage," Kiran said. "Like, would you marry someone who was not Indian? I have met almost no Indian women for whom it's not an issue. And they're the only ones who really understand what you're going through. So even if I have nothing else in common with the other Indian women, I can talk to them about this particular thing."

For Mexican-American women, family relationships remain close throughout life—so close that an adult *chicana*'s best friends will be intimately acquainted with her parents and siblings, if not in person, then as characters in an ongoing narrative. Family is so central to Mexican-American women's lives that when two friends meet after even a week's separation, the first thing they do is exchange status reports on their relatives, at least down to nieces and nephews. After years in New York, reporter Norma Sosa felt a special bond with Esperanza, another fortysomething South Texas Mexican-American who also worked at the *New York Times.* Because Esperanza's assignments kept her out of the office for long stretches, sometimes they went for weeks without seeing each other. Following those absences they always began their conversation with the traditional family litany, conducted in English but ending with *"Y las plantas?"*—"And the plants?"

"She says it as a joke," Norma explained. "It's not like she's asking me how my cactus is. But that's what Hispanic women eventually say to each other when they run out of family things to talk about. It's hilarious, but it's kind of an offhanded way of acknowledging that we're coworkers and acquaintances, but we're also something else."

That "something else" is *comadres,* the female incarnation of the more familiar term *compadres.* By becoming *comadres,* women adopt each other into their respective families, with the benefits and obligations that adoption implies. Literally, the term means "co-mothers," and it often does entail a co-parenting relationship. Two Mexican-American women become *comadres* when one agrees to serve as godmother of the other's child or when the daughter of one marries the other's son. But other kinds of adopted kin arrangements also count.

Even though Norma had no children, she considered Esperanza her *comadre.* Two thousand miles from South Texas, in a city where Mexican-Americans made up a minority even of the Hispanic population, Norma and Esperanza didn't need to be in-laws or godparents to feel that special connection. Their common background, age, and situation made them consider each other almost kin.

"If I needed someone to hold my hand at the hospital while somebody reset a broken bone or something, I'd call Esperanza," Norma told me. "It's a cultural thing."

Beyond needing each other to preserve the legacy of such female customs and to discuss such culture-specific issues as how to treat a grandparent or whether to date "out of tribe," black, Asian, Native American, and Hispanic women value close friendships with those who share their backgrounds for another reason: the validation and empathy that enable them to cope with belonging to an ethnic minority.

For women born in other countries, the immigrant experience amplifies the sense of being different, and the strangeness of the new country presents a further challenge to friendship. Until Graciela Perez was fourteen, she lived in pre-Castro Cuba, where women cultivated friendships begun in girlhood throughout their lives. Once a woman married, the new friends she made would be wives of her husband's friends, but those she made in elementary or high school remained separate and special. "There's a very clear demarcation there," she told me. "You trust the childhood ones more. You share more with them than you do with the ones that are basically couple friends."

Back in Cuba, her friendships had to survive the test of parental scrutiny. "Your friends were not only *your* friends," Graciela said. "Your family knew them. I had friends from the time I was born. When I was little, they would come over to my house. I would go over to their house. We would go to the movies together. My parents would take us to the beach."

All that changed when Graciela's family moved to Florida. "We were all in a strange country, and it was difficult to create those bonds," she told me. "The meaning of friendship was very different. It wasn't until college that I started again to have ongoing friends, but it wasn't the same."

Without the social guideposts that had been so obvious back home, Graciela and other Cuban teenagers couldn't decide whether another girl was a suitable candidate for friendship. "In Cuba, everybody knew their place," she said. "Here, all of a sudden, you were all together. So you had to separate who were those friends that you wouldn't have had if you were back there, plus figuring out among the Americans who was a nice girl and who was not so nice, in a culture that you didn't know."

For the 800,000 individuals who move to the United States every year, that uncomfortable sensation of not quite knowing the social score is a common experience. The challenge of becoming fluent in English, interpreting different nonverbal cues, and developing traits considered socially desirable in the new country can make forming friendships with Americans daunting. To compound the problem, immigrants to the United States, particularly women of color, often experience an initial drop in social status.

Even immigrant women who are happy and successful in their new homes feel a special bond with one another, especially if they come from the same country and speak the same language. Helen Kucharski left Poland for Chicago in her twenties. Now forty, she owned her own nail salon in the fashionable district known as the Gold Coast. Most of the young women she hired and trained had similar backgrounds, as did all three of her closest friends. "I always lean toward Polish women because it's the same culture," she told me as she gently pushed back my cuticles. "We deal with the same marriage problems. Our guys are different. Our lifestyles are different. That's why we have to stick together."

Being able to talk about common problems in the language of home was a huge relief. "We always speak Polish, not a word of English," she said. "I choose friends who are not ashamed of who they are."

Other immigrant women bring their country's style of friendship to the bonds they form in the United States. Monika Garrick, a Jamaican, described growing up in a culture that had never doubted the importance of female friendship. "We've always been open in lending a hand across the fence," she said. "It really does come from our moms and their moms before that. Like in a lot of cultures around the world where the men have failed women, women have not failed women. Even when the men don't show up for the kid's birthday party or the sitting by the bedside when a friend is very ill, the women do."

In the United States, just as in Jamaica, "Women really depend on other women for emotional support more than they depend on their husbands or their brothers," Monika said. "Between women, once an emotional connection is established, it takes over. The key is the connection."

Although women from different cultural backgrounds may rely on different rituals and different interpersonal cues in forging these connections, the friendships themselves are variations of one recipe. They are mixed together out of sharing, trust, respect, humor, loyalty, love, and talk—the single largest ingredient.

2

~

What Friendship Is— and Isn't

True happiness
Consists not in the multitude of friends,
But in the worth and choice.

— Ben Jonson, *Cynthia's Revels*

Recently, my husband and I went to two parties. The first, toasting the publication of a friend's book, mixed about forty writers, artists, and academics, most of whom we didn't know or knew only slightly. I had several engrossing conversations, and the mesquite-grilled eggplant transformed my opinion of that humble vegetable. Reluctant to quit such stimulating company, Tom and I stayed an hour later than we'd planned.

The second party celebrated the birthday of someone I'd known for eighteen years. Although none of the sixteen individuals who shared that spirited potluck supper with us ranked among my five most intimate friends, six had been good friends for almost two decades, three were casual friends who'd become nearer in the past year, and five were acquaintances I enjoyed encountering socially. Only two of my fellow guests were strangers. Once again, the conversations were invigorating and the food delicious. And once again, Tom and I stayed an hour later than we'd planned. But this time, I left wrapped in a deep, reassuring warmth, because I had spent that evening surrounded by people I knew and cared about—from close friends to more casual friends and, finally, acquaintances. At the first party, I'd felt stimulated but isolated; at the second, I'd felt connected. What was it about friendship, even in its casual form, that made being among friends so much richer than being among the most accomplished and interesting strangers? I decided to find out.

At long last, social scientists and therapists are starting to recognize the significance of friendships in our lives. "It's only just recently in our culture that the importance of friendship has been recognized," Helen Gouldner, coauthor of *Speaking of Friendship,* told me. "There are data now that indicate that even just one intimate will make a difference in emotional and even physical well-being."

Coworkers, neighbors, classmates, and fellow club members, the hairstylist who recommends a new jazz CD because you share musical tastes, the attendant at the dry cleaners who remembers that you prefer light starch, the woman who always smiles when you pass each other walking your dogs—encountering these people regularly, no matter how casual the interaction, helps us maintain a sense of social reality and stave off feelings of isolation in a largely anonymous world. Addressing the annual meeting of the Institute for Contemporary Psychotherapy, James S. Grotstein called friendship the "experience governing all intimate relationships" and declared that it was "more profound than sex or love." In addition, psychologist Beverly Minker Schydlowsky found that the women she studied placed close female friendship second only to health in importance to their lives.

Friends at different levels of closeness serve different functions. Asked whom they'd seek out to talk over a personal problem, most women name a friend they consider close. But asked whom they'd call on to help with a practical problem demanding on-the-spot assistance—say, having a car break down in a remote spot late at night—many choose a friend on the basis of special knowledge ("She really understands cars"), convenience ("She's divorced, so I wouldn't be waking her husband"), expectation of opportunities to reciprocate ("She knows she can drop off her kids with me at a moment's notice"), and proximity. A friend 1,500 miles away can help sort through a love or work dilemma but not through belongings damaged by a flood. For going shopping or seeing a movie or play, women often select a friend who shares similar tastes, even though their emotional bond isn't that strong.

Most of the girls and women I talked to told me they had between four and seven close friends. I was surprised to find that about 5 percent confided that they currently had no close friends. But because all but two of these women were in their thirties, I suspected that this decline might have to do with being in a phase of life when friendship activity drops off.

A few women told me they had fifteen or twenty close friendships or even that they had more close friends than they could count. When I probed a bit, they usually admitted that a few of these were nearer and dearer than others, but several did continue to number their close friendships in the dozens. I began to suspect that the latter actually had no close friends and so enumerated what I would call good friends instead. Indeed, when these women told me about their relationships, they revealed a sense of distance: "We only see each other at the office" or "I would never discuss a marital problem with any of my friends." Because all the women who spoke of these large arrays of close friends were over fifty-five, I suspected I'd stumbled on another phenomenon linked to life stage, or perhaps to that generation in particular.

As I conducted my interviews, I noticed that the old ways of looking at female friendship didn't fit. Women have varied and often complex webs of friendships—different friends to share different aspects of their lives. These relationships can't be easily pigeonholed with terms like "close," "good," or "best." Rather, they are fluid and uniquely life enhancing.

❧ The Essentials of Friendship ❧

Although human beings are social creatures, we often have trouble sifting friendship from the rest of our human connections. Our culture treats the term "friend" loosely. Some people use it to refer to everyone with whom they're on a first-name basis and don't actively dislike. They say "a friend of mine at work" to refer to a colleague about whose private life they know little more than what they gather from the photos on her desk.

One of the reasons we have trouble talking meaningfully about friendship is that it's what philosophers call a fuzzy concept. Unlike marriage or parenthood, friendship lacks sanctions set forth by society to describe its responsibilities. No natural event, such as a birth, or no public ceremony, such as a wedding, marks the start of the relationship. And yet there are some qualities we'd all agree are essential.

First, friendship is voluntary. We choose our friends, and they choose us. We aren't born into friendships, as we are into relationships with members of our immediate family. We don't acquire friends as by-products of other relationships, as we acquire in-laws and step-children by marriage. We aren't assigned friends, as we're assigned teachers or supervisors.

Because friendship lacks much of the external structure of other important bonds, it can rupture, fray, and wither more easily. Yet despite its fragility, we expect it to last. When we invest our time and emotions with a friend, we anticipate that she will be there for us in the future. Endurance may not be a quality by which we define or even judge friendship, but an expectation of endurance is.

Friendship is a personal, social relationship. Its purpose is human connection for its own sake. We may eventually become friends with someone we've cultivated as a client; but if business is the motive for getting together with her, our tie is something other than friendship.

Friends appreciate and value each other as unique individuals. That requires being well enough acquainted to have a sense of each other's interests, aspirations, and personalities—the things that set us apart. This mutual knowledge is one of the major features that distinguishes conversations between friends from those between acquaintances.

Of course, liking someone is a precondition of friendship. That doesn't mean, however, that we have to like everything about a friend. In fact, the way we deal with characteristics we don't like is a measure of friendship. Friends don't just know us; they accept us. One friend may dislike another's habit of chewing gum or disapprove of the way she pads her expense account and yet accept her as an individual. Friends expect us to have flaws, and they love us despite them.

Caring about the other person's welfare, hoping she achieves her fondest dreams and escapes harm, wanting her to get what she wants or at least what we think is best for her, being willing to assist, within reasonable limits—these are necessary but not alone sufficient for friendship. Commitment to avoid harming each other and to encourage other's well-being actively lies at the root of loyalty and other obligations of friendship. Trust is the corollary of friendship's personal goodwill. If we have a friend's best interests at heart and act accordingly, we expect her to trust us to continue to do so.

A relationship has to be mutual to be a friendship. We may like and admire someone, enjoy her company, and look forward to getting to know her better; but if she doesn't feel similarly about us, we aren't friends. Mutuality is so important that even if two women acknowledge each other as friends, the friendship may fracture because one considers it closer than the other does.

Mutuality manifests itself through reciprocity. What friends give each other needn't be identical. For instance, a woman returning from two weeks in Europe may bring a bottle of French perfume to thank a friend for looking after her cat and house plants. But if one friend feels that she's giving substantially more than she's getting, resentment will wither the relationship. Reciprocity of time and attention mattered far more to the women I interviewed than reciprocity of the material sort. One of the most frequent complaints I heard about former close friends went something like this: "She'd call me whenever she had a problem; but when I had something I wanted to discuss with her, she was always too busy."

Some level of positive emotional exchange occurs in any true friendship. We try to make each other feel good or, failing that, we try to make each other feel less bad. That doesn't mean that friends never experience irritation, anger, envy, contempt, or any other negative emotion toward one another or that a friend can't cause us to see ourselves as inadequate, wicked, or otherwise lacking. But overall the relationship should increase each person's balance of pleasure over pain. We not only take delight in a friend's company for itself, but the old adage also holds true: Sharing good experiences with a friend enhances the enjoyment; sharing bad ones with her makes them easier to bear.

One of the pleasant feelings friendship offers is comfort. Not comfort in the sense of relief from sadness, although friends often do offer that, but comfort that comes from being at ease. In the company of strangers, we mute and filter our responses. With friends we can let down our guards. Whether we reveal everything about ourselves down to our most secret vulnerabilities or choose to remain closer to the surface, we can be ourselves with friends.

Some things that have the appearance of friendship aren't. Far from being examples of friendship activities, for example, networking and related business-success strategies have confused and corrupted the notion of friendship. "One thing I react very negatively to is the idea of taking women's desire for connectedness and turning it to self-promotion," psychotherapist Barbara Ellman told me.

Although women who meet through structured business or professional networks occasionally do become true friends, those relationships must overcome obstacles that wouldn't exist if those same women met at the health club or at a party thrown by mutual acquaintances. Setting aside the ethical issue of valuing someone primarily for how she can advance our career, women's networks generally aren't appropriate venues for meaningful self-disclosure. No one is going to confide in a woman she hopes will recommend her for a job or become her client that her husband is an alcoholic or that she can't stand her boss.

Granted, we enter into friendships expecting to get something out of them—including what we get by giving. In fact, sociologists routinely divide what they call the "rewards" of friendship into two categories: utilitarian, which includes rewards like practical assistance and increased social status, and self-referent, which encompasses rewards such as the pleasure of enjoying a sunset with a friend or the relief of unburdening ourselves of our deepest fears. But the first and most essential element all true friendships share is valuing each other as unique individuals. Sure, a friend may help us achieve our business or professional goals, but she does so not by sending us clients but by supporting us in genuine friendship—by holding up a mirror that reflects a positive but not idealized vision of ourselves.

⤳ The Options We Seek ⤳

In addition to the qualities essential to friendship are those that are optional but important. Not all friendships have them, but the best ones have most.

One of those features is security. Of course, in all but the most volatile friendships, we feel secure that a friend isn't going to attack us physically or emotionally. But true security also implies confidence that a friend won't endanger or embarrass us by her behavior. Even a friend we treasure may make us feel unsafe, for example, if when we have an evening out together she drinks heavily then refuses to relinquish the car keys.

Security involves trusting a friend's judgment and consideration, not just her feelings for us. Again and again, women I interviewed told me about close friends with whom they felt a specific lack of security: They'd never discuss a sensitive work issue or personal problem with them because they didn't trust them to keep a confidence.

Women also seek empathy in friendship. Although we may tolerate a friend who's so self-absorbed that she can't imagine herself in our position, we place special value on one who connects with us emotionally. The primary way women express empathy toward each other is by listening attentively. We don't need to say we understand; eye contact and an occasional sympathetic nod, or their phone equivalents—silence during pauses, a well-placed "Then what happened?" or "You must have been furious"—will do. Focus is the key.

When I asked the girls and women I interviewed what they valued most in female friendship, one answer I heard often was "honesty." The popularity of this virtue surprised me, because many of these same women had praised their friends' tact. Clearly, honesty is an ideal we seek, though we have trouble dealing with it. If we're shopping with a friend, we don't want her to say, "Those slacks look awful. Go home and lose fifteen pounds," even if that's what she thinks. But neither do we want her to tell us they look great. A comment like "I think something with a pleated front would be more flattering" strikes an ego-protecting middle ground.

The tact with which women friends temper their honesty is a reflection of the ego support many of us give each other almost as a matter of course. "Women naturally create a holding environment for one another where one expects to be nurtured and cared about," explained social psychologist Joan Berzoff.

At its best, a friend's nurturing has the warmth of mothering, but without judgmentalism, interference, or reflexive guilt. It satisfies our dependency needs while providing something else we look for in friendship—respect.

For some women, respect is an absolute prerequisite for friendship. They restrict their friends to women who see them as people of good character, as role models for their children, as individuals with exceptional value to society in general. Because friends act as mirrors, those who reflect our strengths in clear focus, our weaknesses more fuzzily, bring out our best qualities. Those who magnify our shortcomings and blur our virtues encourage us to remain psychologically and morally stunted.

When I asked women what they valued about specific friends and what they sought in friendship in general, one answer in common was dependability. Virtually every friendship has limits. Few of us have a friend we'd feel comfortable calling at four in the morning except in a true emergency. Our feelings aren't bruised when a friend gets up from lunch at 12:45 in order to get back to the office on time; we honor the demands of each other's jobs. Married women, in particular, share a tacit understanding that the obligations of marriage and motherhood have precedence over those of friendship. But if a friend promises to do something with or for us, we expect her to come through. And we especially want to know that she's available—if not right this minute, then soon—to rejoice at our good news and commiserate at our bad.

Sometimes we seek out friends who can help us in specific, practical ways. A mother of two young children may be drawn to another mom in a similar situation partly because she wants someone with whom to trade parenting expertise and occasional baby-sitting. A recently retired woman interested in gardening may feel a special attraction for a neighbor with a showcase yard. If such pragmatic exchange is all there is to the relationship, it isn't a friendship. But many of us do appreciate a friend partly because she's willing to help us clean the garage or suggest ways to hone our résumé. Conversely, women also cherish friends who allow them to assist and feel useful.

Another practical function friendships can fill is providing status and affiliation. Maybe we don't consciously choose to befriend someone because she's an accomplished professional, has drop-dead taste, belongs to a fashionable clique, or for that matter, is well known for her moral courage; but the truth is that people do judge us, in part, by our companions. Several times I've reevaluated a superficially vacuous woman after learning that someone I admired counted her as a friend.

Solidarity is another quality women look for in their friends. Knowing that men have historically had more power forges a particular bond among our sex. Whether a woman experiences a keen sense of oppression or feels relief at not being expected to shoulder full economic responsibility for her family, she is in a position that only another woman can fully understand and appreciate. "We have always done what subordinate people do," explained Joan Berzoff. "African-Americans form close friendship ties. So do women, as a function of their lesser place in the social structure."

Perhaps because we experience inequity at work, in the market-place, and in the family, we seem especially sensitive to the power balance in friendship. Some women can't tolerate being in a voluntary relationship with another woman that entails assuming the less power-ful position—for example, being a protégé. If we sense that a friend has the upper hand in a relationship—that she always gets to dominate the conversation or choose where we'll eat—we may struggle to assert ourselves or may even withdraw.

Most friendships occur between individuals of roughly the same age and background. Some research has even suggested that people tend to seek out and support others who are genetically similar to them. But even for women who cultivate diversity in their friendships, similarity can be important. We need common ground on which to meet.

Women often seek out friends as companions with whom to share specific interests. Research suggests that friends working together per-form both decision-making and motor tasks better than acquaintances. Some activities, like bird watching and exploring restaurants, are more enjoyable when shared. Others, like tennis and bridge, require an-other person.

Sometimes we simply yearn for fun in our friendships. Our lives are so busy, so jammed with "oughts" and "shoulds," that the only way many of us can enjoy ourselves is to have a friend cajole us into joining her in some lighthearted pursuit. The friendships that work best in this regard are those that have a good measure of spontaneity. Sociologists Steve Duck and Paul H. Wright, two of the most prolific researchers on friendship, have noted: "It is the kind of spontaneity that leads a person to nonchalantly help her/himself to a cup of coffee while visiting a friend's house."

Even women who may be reserved about its overt expression want affection from their women friends. Lingering hugs and sentimental greeting cards make some people uncomfortable; a warm smile and a voice flavored with feeling seldom do.

An important quality many of us look for in a female friend is her ability to make us laugh. In my interviews, when I asked what initially attracted one woman to another, one attribute came up repeatedly: her sense of humor. That trait far outstripped kindness, intelligence, and appearance and ran a close second only to shared interests.

Women also look to friendship to provide opportunities for uncensored self-expression. With the right friend, we can recapture some of the zany delight we knew as little girls. We can ditch our responsible personas and be goofy and outrageous.

One summer night, after a casual dinner with a couple of friends from out of town and a local woman we thought they'd enjoy meeting, my husband and I suggested that we all go for a walk on the beach. With moonlight spilled across its surface, the Gulf of Mexico looked enticing. "I feel like going in!" announced my single friend Faith Lagay, who spent her weekdays writing university grant proposals and working on her Ph.D. in medical humanities.

When Faith shimmied out of her linen slacks and ran into the gentle surf, I followed her, stripping off my shoes and belt and splashing into the water in my tee-shirt and cotton pants. Although I'd often been tempted by the shimmer of moonlight on the Gulf, I never would have gone in by myself. I was too inhibited.

Female friendship is the one place women can indulge in that particular form of self-expression called girl talk. Hair, makeup, clothes, diets, whether a particular politician looks like she's had a face-lift or a given male movie star is too handsome to be attractive—we would never venture into these topics with a man (at least not a straight one) or even the wrong woman, lest we be taken for airheads. Sure, we know such subjects are trivial; it's their very triviality that makes them refreshing. With a woman who understands this, we can explore them in the right spirit.

Women often rely on their friends to provide a safe place to vent their hostility toward third parties. After studying the close friendships of married women, sociologist Stacey Oliker observed:

> Expressing anger to an intimate who is not its object permits a woman to experience her feelings without escalating conflict or using strategies she might ultimately regret.

It's one thing for a woman to tell a friend that she's so fed up at her husband's addiction to televised sports that she feels like divorcing him. It's quite another to say the same thing to her husband—with potentially lasting consequences. Complaining to a confidante that the boss is an idiot might relieve a woman of stress. Blurting out the same thing to her boss might relieve her of her job.

Many women couldn't imagine coping without a close friend to help them defuse such hazardous emotions. Some also seek secure ground for a different kind of self-disclosure—the sharing of our darkest secrets. We want to be loved for ourselves as we really are, not for some idealized version we construct for public view. It's true that few female friendships offer a safe ground for full self-disclosure; most have their limits. But being able to be ourselves and allow our friends to be themselves—seeing each other literally and figuratively without our makeup—is essential to the elusive bond of intimacy.

By its nature, intimacy must be mutual. A person may reveal everything she can dredge up about herself to her psychotherapist, but that doesn't make them intimate, since the therapist shows little or nothing of her own private side. Intimacy requires the willingness to let another person into our most vulnerable psychological space and a genuine interest in meeting her on that level as well. Desire for intimacy can result from either weakness or strength—from a desperate need to connect or from a secure sense of who we are that allows us to accept the risks this closeness entails.

In her studies of both women in therapy and women who identified themselves as having at least one female friendship they valued on a par with their marriages and their health, Joan Berzoff found that the women with the best-developed egos experienced the highest levels of intimacy. "If you think about it, what is intimacy?" Berzoff asked rhetorically. "It's the ability to dissolve those boundaries temporarily, knowing that you still have strong boundaries to go back to."

⤙ How Women's Friendships Differ from Men's ⤙

When Lionel Tiger's *Men in Groups,* the book that propelled the concept of male bonding into popular consciousness, appeared in 1969, it theorized that humans evolved a propensity for male-female and male-male bonds because these attachments conferred reproductive advantages—directly in the first case, indirectly in the second. Nowhere did Tiger, a professor of anthropology and sociology, mention a genetic tendency on the part of women to form strong ties to anyone but their mates and their young.

In ignoring the unique connection between females, Tiger had plenty of company. At the time, the conventional wisdom held that women were too competitive with one another for the attention of men and for the social and economic benefit of their children to be true friends. As recently as the late 1970s, some social scientists and therapists persisted in pronouncing friendships between women inferior to those between men. When, inspired by the women's movement, psychologists and sociologists began to reexamine the subject, they discovered that, if anything, the opposite was true: that female friendship was a closer, more emotional, more reciprocal bond, and that women valued friendships more than men did.

Paul H. Wright, one of the early social scientists to consciously put aside male bias in these comparative studies, described women's friendships as "face-to-face" and men's as "side-by-side." Many researchers have observed that men tend to share activities and women to share feelings. Others contend that the most frequent reason both genders get together with friends is to talk. But even when the primary purpose is conversation, the content differs. Men tend to stick to external topics. Women, on the other hand, interweave shared interests with revelations about their personal lives and discussions of relationships.

Women's friendships are generally more personal and empathic, based more on emotion, than men's. Women care more about giving one another understanding, acceptance, and support; men care more about having fun. Both sexes place a high value on trust, loyalty, and reciprocity; but men emphasize offering one another practical assistance, from helping a buddy fence his backyard to carrying a comrade off the battlefield, while women stress being there for each other in less tangible ways—with an attentive ear, with unfailing emotional support. What makes men and women uncomfortable in friendship differs as well. Women have trouble dealing with conflict and the healthy expression of anger, men with intimacy and self-disclosure.

"I think intimacy is greatly overrated as a friendship attribute," social philosopher John Douard told me. "What I want of a friend is someone I can relax with. Once you've revealed yourselves to each other in those kinds of intimate ways, you find it scary to be there for each other in practical ways."

Just because males in our culture don't consider intimacy a necessary or even desirable feature of their friendships, that doesn't mean that men don't care deeply for their friends or that they're insensitive to their feelings. But the emotional support women and men give their friends comes in different currencies. For example, on learning that a friend's spouse has demanded a divorce, a woman will respond with commiseration, inviting her friend to vent her grief and anger over a bottle of wine and a box of Kleenex. Faced with similar news from a male friend, a man will respond by offering distractions, suggesting a twenty-mile bike ride, an afternoon spent channel-surfing football games, or having a few beers and some good conversation—about sports, politics, business, anything but the deteriorating marriage. He might clap the troubled friend on the shoulder; but he wouldn't rock him and pat him soothingly on the back, even if he did become teary-eyed.

In the modern era, both men and women worry that a tender touch might be misinterpreted as a sexual advance; but between heterosexual men, the prospect of physical attraction is far more threatening than it is between heterosexual women. Some social scientists point to homophobia as the main reason that male friendships are relatively low on self-disclosure. Yet something else is operating as well: Most children of both sexes grow up with a female answering their cries, bandaging their scraped knees. But by the time a boy is out of the crib, the major male figure in his household praises him when he's brave and tells him big boys don't cry. Add to this early conditioning the competitiveness of the playing field, and it's no wonder that men feel that they are surrendering power when they reveal their vulnerabilities to one another. On the other hand, when women open up to one another, they expect nurturing, support, personal growth, and relief from whatever is bothering them.

Sharon Itaya, an Austin physician with two young children, described the differences between her friendships and those of her attorney husband like this: "Bob never shows any weaknesses to his friends that I can tell. They're always openly competing—on the tennis court or in terms of job, salary, wife, house, kids, car, the whole thing. With the women I know, one way we share is to share our problems and get help or advice. When we feel weak in a particular way, it seems to draw us together."

Differences in the patterns of male and female friendships start appearing in early childhood, becoming pronounced by fourth or fifth grade, when boys look for friends who can promote their status in larger social groups and girls seek out a few close chums for more intense relationships.

As human beings progress through the seasons of life described in Part Two of this book, the friendship patterns of the two sexes take on opposing rhythms. For men, the number of close male friends they have increases from adolescence until around age thirty, falling off thereafter. For women, some research has shown that the number of important friendships rises gradually over the lifespan, while other studies indicate a slump in early adulthood followed by an increase beginning somewhere between the late thirties and early forties—a phenomenon my own interviews reflected as well. From middle to late life, a man is less likely to have a close friend the older he gets, while a woman's chance of having at least one such friendship doesn't change with age.

We don't know for sure whether the contrast between women's and men's friendships is based in biology or in the different ways we're socialized. For 80 percent of its existence, our species lived as hunter-gatherers. Men went off together to track down game and make war—activities that demanded physical courage and long periods of silence. Even back at camp, where talk wouldn't alert an enemy or scare off game, recounting brave exploits helped the group bond and prepare for the next venture, whereas admitting vulnerabilities would have been bad for morale. Women, when they weren't gathering food and firewood, spent their time nursing and watching children, preparing communal meals, tending the sick and wounded, making baskets and pots, and performing other tasks in which sharing experiences and feelings would have helped. Reinforced by tens of thousands of years of evolutionary benefits, gender differences in friendship patterns may have become hard-wired into the human psyche.

But some research suggests that those differences have more to do with nurture than nature. A study of Polish university students revealed that unlike Americans, they considered intimate self-disclosure just as appropriate between male friends as between females. And when anthropologist Walter Williams looked at male friendship in American Indian and Asian cultures, he found "that intimate relationships among men . . . have indeed existed in many other times and places."

Whether hard-wired or programmed, gender differences in friendship patterns persist. But these are generalizations; they don't limit what's possible between any given pair of women or men. After speaking informally with men I know, I suspect that both men and women are capable of the full range of friendship forms set out in chapter 5, but that women tend to have more of some forms and men of others. That issue will have to wait for another book, however.

❧ Female-Male Friendships ❧

Nonsexual friendship between women and men not only is possible; it can be richly rewarding. But even the best of these cross-gender friendships can't give us the validation and empathy we get from our friendships with other women. For one thing, men don't have our bodies. They don't develop breasts, menstruate, bear babies, or go through menopause. For another thing, they haven't been raised as we have to attract rather than to act. Age, disease, and vanity are all different to them. And like husbands and brothers, men friends tend to feel responsible for the welfare of the women they care about. "When I bring something up, a male friend will want to fix it or give me advice," psychotherapist Linda Walsh said, adding that women seem to understand intuitively that simply validating each other's experiences can be enough.

Of course, sometimes women value men as friends precisely because the male concept of friendship emphasizes practical support. When I asked the women I interviewed whom they'd call in an emergency if their husbands or lovers weren't available, many of them named a man, even if he wasn't one of their closest friends. "I have a friend I have known since junior high, a man," said university administrator Sharon Goodwin, forty-seven. "We don't see each other a lot, a couple of times a year, maybe. But if I ever needed something, I know that I could call him, and he would be there."

Norma Sosa, a single forty-five-year-old newspaper reporter in New York, speculated that growing up with four brothers but no sisters might have led her to include a man among her five closest friends. "When I meet a man, I know some men are going to be quasi little brothers or big brothers, and others aren't," she said. "I think I immediately put Bob in the category of little brother because he's a few years younger." In most respects, Norma described her relationship with Bob as more similar to her close female friendships than different: "We have dinner. We go to shows. We cook meals with groups of friends. We do about the same things with maybe one exception: When it comes to drawing in very, very close and having a long conversation about man trouble, for example, it's probably Connie I'd want to compare notes with and get advice from and not Bob. But then, if I wanted to find out what this man might be thinking, it might be Bob that I would ask."

Although men and women can provide each other with this insider's perspective on the opposite gender, when it comes to empathy and emotional support, women tend to do more giving than receiving. In study after study, men have described their friendships with the opposite sex as more intimate and fulfilling than those with their own, while women have reported just the opposite. When psychologists Leigh Elkins and Christopher Peterson questioned a mixed group of 122 college students about their cross-gender friendships, they concluded that "friendships that involved at least one woman were more satisfying than friendships that did not."

In forming and maintaining a friendship with a man, a woman faces four unique challenges. One of the most daunting is adapting to the power differential. Even assuming that the two have equivalent jobs and he has done his best to overcome the expectation of dominance imparted by his upbringing, our society treats him as the one in charge. Not only do maître d's and car rental agents reinforce this inequity, but so, too, do the friends themselves by the way they interact. Take something as basic as offering advice. Her helpful suggestion doesn't diminish his status, both because she will probably deliver it sensitively ("When I don't know how many people might show up for a party, I've always found . . ."), and because he unconsciously knows that he can give it whatever weight he chooses. His advice, however, almost invariably puts her down, both because he is likely to couch it as a directive ("Look, call the guy who put in the radiator and tell him . . ."), and because she unconsciously feels that she ought to comply.

This pattern seems to be changing, however. Several women I interviewed in their twenties told me that they adopted a sort of big sister role with their men friends. "I have a lot of male friends," one said, "and in truth, I'm usually the bossy, advice-giving one. I think this is becoming increasingly common."

The second issue women deal with in their friendships with men is society's assumption that the relationship either is sexual or is likely to become so. Most of us find it annoying to hear the furniture sales-person say, "Your *wife* seems to like the couch," when you only came along because your buddy wanted advice on his décor. In addition, a close male friend may enable a woman to go dancing even if she lacks a romantic partner, but he may also make it harder for her to find one, since she appears to be spoken for.

Dealing with the reactions of other intimates can present bigger problems. If a woman is married or seriously involved, a friendship with another man may threaten her committed relationship. A hus-band might gripe when his wife announces that she has to dash across town at ten o'clock at night to comfort a woman friend, but he would have to be remarkably secure not to react more strongly if the troubled friend were male. The need to quell such suspicions limits where and how often opposite-sex friends can get together comfortably, even the amount of time they spend on the phone. This in turn restricts the friendship.

Determining the form of the emotional bond is the third challenge to female-male friendships, and it's an issue that is never completely resolved. Nostalgia might rekindle the sexual spark in a friendship that grew out of a brief affair. Or subsurface erotic tension might erupt on a business trip. Even if the temptation is mutual and they aren't otherwise committed, close friends may avoid acting on their sexual impulses. They decide, often tacitly, not to imperil their friendship for the sake of a fleeting romance.

A more delicate situation arises when one friend is looking for one kind of intimacy while the other wants another. Maybe a rejected suitor settles for friendship but holds out hopes. Maybe the breakup of a primary relationship prompts one friend to see the other in a new light. What makes this challenge to cross-gender friendship so problematic is that, in some cases, the very act of preserving the rela-tionship's original form can destroy it. However it's packaged, sexual rejection hurts.

The potential for such problems is one reason many women become close friends with gay men, who offer the benefits of cross-gender friendship minus the potential for misunderstanding. A woman can tell a gay male friend that she loves him, in words or through touch, with an openness she wouldn't dare with a straight man. And she can elicit a male perspective on her appearance or her romantic problems without worrying about being misinterpreted. "All my close male friends are gay," forty-five-year-old New York publicist Carol Edgar told me. "There's just that element of safety, and there's the absence of ambiguity."

❧ How Lesbians Handle Friendship ❧

Like all women, lesbians need nonsexual female friendship—bonds free of the dance of eroticism and of the earnest agenda of establishing and nurturing a life partnership. But except for the perceived inequity of power, lesbians face the same challenges in their friendships with women that women face in their friendships with men.

For many lesbians, though, drawing a line between friendship and romance can often be difficult. "It's very hard to separate out the friendship part of my primary relationship," said Jillian, a thirty-nine-year-old clinical psychologist. "I had an earlier significant relationship where I would not have said that the person was my closest friend. There was a clear demarcation: She was my partner, and I had other people who were my friends. It doesn't feel like that in this case."

The lesbians I interviewed told me of life partnerships growing out of friendships, of ex-lovers becoming their friends, and of ex-lovers becoming friends with each other. Cybil, a fifty-nine-year-old science professor, talked about a funeral she'd attended for a lesbian in her eighties. Three of the deceased's former lovers delivered eulogies. While supporting her in her final illness, these three had become friends. I heard similar stories often enough that I figured there had to be something to the notion that among homosexual women the boundary between friendly and sexual involvement was permeable in both directions. This permeability doesn't make the lesbian world a relationship utopia, however. A woman may become suspicious of her partner's friendship with an ex-lover, or a woman in a committed relationship may become romantically involved with a friend. And whether a lesbian has a partner or not, making a pass at a friend poses risks to the friendship.

Cybil, who came out after she'd been married and had two children, explained: "Usually, as they get older, lesbians will set aside the sexual dimension if they need to in order to maintain the friendship. That's not to say that you lose your sexual interest, just that your friendships get more important."

All the lesbians I interviewed counted heterosexual women among their friends, and when straight women mentioned that a particular friend was lesbian, they did so almost off-handedly. For someone just becoming aware of her homosexual orientation, a strong friendship with a heterosexual woman can provide essential support at a particularly vulnerable time. Often, the first heterosexual a lesbian will come out to will be a female friend, rather than a family member. But the biases of the dominant culture can be hard to shake, even for an individual innocent of conscious prejudice.

Jay Vanasco, a twenty-four-year-old university publicist, told me about a close female friend in college who became worried when Jay stopped eating and attending classes during her junior year. Far from being depressed, Jay was so involved in a happy love affair that nothing else interested her. Had the object of Jay's exhilarating emotions been a man, the friend, who was heterosexual, might have warned her not to sacrifice her future for what might be a transitory romance; she wouldn't have criticized her interest in men. But because Jay's lover was a woman, the friend blamed her sexual orientation for what she saw as self-destructive behavior. "She talked about how she didn't mind that I was a lesbian," Jay said, "but she thought that maybe this wasn't for me because it was too intense. I got very angry, and so we pretty much stopped talking."

On one level, the friend accepted Jay's sexual orientation. On another, she harbored old stereotypes—that lesbianism was unnatural and dangerous. Because she dismissed Jay's feelings as pathological, the bond between the two friends snapped.

⚬ What Friends Offer That Families Can't ⚬

Throughout our lives we teeter between belonging and individuation—the sense of ourselves as distinct, autonomous, complex individuals. Close friendship may be the one form of human interaction that strikes that balance perfectly.

"Women's friendships are extraordinarily valuable and a source of survival for women," said psychiatrist Jean Baker Miller, whose work demonstrating that females develop in connection with others revolutionized thinking about the psychology of women. And these female friendships, she continued, "can do something other relationships don't. Because you don't have the familial obligations or the old issues, you can start on a fresher basis, and you can be freer to be yourself."

With our families, lovers, and husbands, our roles keep getting in the way; with our friends, we're individuals. It's true that some elements of friendship can exist in marriages, in love affairs, and in relationships with parents, siblings, and children; and friendship lacks certain forms of intimacy and commitment that these, at their best, offer. But to feel true empathy with another requires having nothing at risk beyond the companionship and validation inherent in the relationship. As Houston psychotherapist Linda Walsh put it: "Friends love you, but they don't have a stake in the outcome."

Our families, by their very nature, seldom allow us to be completely open. We hesitate to reveal to our parents our deepest insecurities or nastiest feelings of vindictiveness, even toward third parties they've never met. They've invested too much in molding us to fit their ideals. When we consider sharing our true feelings or most sensitive secrets with our lovers, we fear compromising our desirability. A woman may fear that giving her husband a window into her soul may make him doubt her ability to be a capable life partner. We also feel an impulse to protect our children from our darker and weaker sides; we don't want to imperil their feelings of security or our credibility as good examples. Even our sisters are bound too tightly to us to permit us to be totally open. Because they're part of our original family constellation, siblings tend to remain in the roles each played in childhood, and encourage us to do the same.

These considerations aside, many women have no family members nearby. Geographical dispersion has always been a feature of American life, but it has increased dramatically since World War II. For two generations, contact with aunts and cousins has become the province of reunions, not of everyday life. Nowadays, mothers and daughters and sisters may be separated by so many time zones that even long-distance commiseration requires careful scheduling. They can't help us pick out a new suit for an important job interview, watch the kids when the baby-sitter cancels at the last minute, or pitch in to make two hundred hors d'oeuvres for a big party. The less support our traditional families are able to give us, the more we must rely on friends.

The issue of power always lurks in interactions between family members, even when both parties do their best to ignore it. Until the age when their capacities decline, and frequently beyond, parents have more power than their children. Siblings often continue to jockey for power throughout their lives. Conflict with parents and siblings, so prevalent during adolescence, can echo through sniping and bickering for decades to come.

Friendship is a matter of attraction, while family relationships always carry the taint of obligation. Despite this, some of the women I interviewed ranked female family members among their closest friends. I had no trouble accepting this in the case of cousins. Except for weddings, funerals, and other reunions, adult cousins in contemporary North America can choose the amount of contact they have with one another. Any rivalry or resentment baggage is strictly of the lightweight carry-on variety. Although sharing a set of grandparents serves as a childhood introduction, it doesn't confer continued close connection.

A woman's interaction with her immediate family raises issues of a different order of magnitude. At first, I disregarded the claims that sisters or mothers and daughters were friends. After all, these relationships weren't voluntary, so they couldn't be friendships. But something kept nagging at me: Women who had several sisters often would identify only one as a friend, even if they said they were emotionally close in some other way to the rest. And no one described these dual bonds off-handedly.

As I went over their interview transcripts, I realized that these women were telling me that their relationships with certain close female family members transcended biologically defined and socially sanctioned roles. A woman viewed and loved another not just, or even primarily, as mother, daughter, or sister but as a unique individual with her own separate needs, desires, and interests. She liked her and empathized with her, felt relaxed in and enjoyed her company, and the feeling was mutual. "We're a lot more friends than mother and daughter," said Heather Chapman, a Smith College senior whose parents split up before she was born. "We have a lot of fun together. We've driven across the country twice together and have made the most boring stretches of Oklahoma seem hilarious."

Unlike parents and children, sisters have their generation as well as their family in common, but before they can appreciate one another as individuals, they have to overcome two big hurdles—sibling rivalry plus, unless they're twins, the big sis–little sis power differential. "She's my best friend, but she used to be my worst enemy," artist Chula Sanchez, forty-six, said of her sister three years her senior. "We fought just like cats and dogs growing up."

Pam Canty, a forty-five-year-old accounts manager for a bank's collections department, also told me that she and her younger sister Lori didn't become close until they were adults. A joint trip to Lake Tahoe launched the new relationship in 1984, when Pam was in her thirties and Lori in her twenties. "She's a professional fund-raiser," Pam continued. "Nevada was part of her territory, and she knew how to tip the doormen at the shows so that we'd get seats right next to the stage. We were playing blackjack at three in the morning, and she'd try to explain to me over and over how to double down, and I'd never remember. It was like all of a sudden I saw her as a totally different person. She had grown into this beautiful, accomplished woman."

Because sisters shared our childhoods, they give us irreplaceable insights into the dynamics of our families. Pam recalled how Lori helped her understand why one particular color was banned from their wardrobes: "Neither of us wears yellow, because Mom always said we looked bad in yellow. Lori looked at me one day and she said, 'It's not that we looked bad in yellow. It's that Mom looked bad in yellow, so she would never let us wear yellow.' "

Whenever two sisters get together, their childhood selves are always present, along with the shadow of everything they've been between then and now. That's part of the limitation: A friend made in adulthood sees the vice-president for sales, the formidable racquetball player, the mother of two happy and accomplished daughters. Granted, a sister sees those, but she also sees the seven-year-old who ate so much birthday cake she threw up all over her party dress and the high school junior who sobbed all night when she didn't make cheerleader. Still, holding the unblinking reality of each other's early lives is part of what makes sisters irreplaceable.

"I feel like my sister is part of me physically, like she's my link to my mother," explained Chula, whose mother died when Chula was twenty-six. "I feel like we're symbiotic. If something's going on in her life that's not right, then my life's a mess. And whenever I have really, truly been in need, or just a little needy, she's always there. She senses when I need help emotionally or physically, jumping in and scrubbing floors or painting or cleaning windows—whatever it takes."

As close as Chula and her sister's connection or as distant as some of the hostile or indifferent sibling relationships described by other women I interviewed, sisterhood is a permanent, cradle-to-grave state. Asked how her relationship with her sister was different from her relationships with her women friends, Margo True, a single thirty-two-year-old magazine writer, told me: "I've gotten so angry at my sister, like a pulsing red wall of rage, and she still is around. There's not a lot I could do that would get rid of my sister."

The majority of the three hundred men and women psychologist Lillian Rubin interviewed for her book *Just Friends* said they could disclose much more about themselves to friends than to family because friends were less judgmental. However, they felt freer to show family members their negative sides, engage in conflict with them, and treat them with less sensitivity. Rubin concluded:

> For whatever our anger or disillusion with our own families, however we may have known the failure of love or understanding there, friendship, for most of us, is experienced as a conditional relationship, kinship as an unconditional one.

Compared to family ties, which can be damaged but not broken, friendship is a fragile bond indeed. That's why we often treat our close friends better than our close relatives: We know that we can lose them, through our actions, our reactions, or our simple inattention.

❧ Single Women and Friendship ❧

Even people who don't put much value on female friendship admit that a single woman needs friends, if only to have a partner for tennis or company at a movie. Since meeting in math class, Donna Freund, an eighteen-year-old freshman at Boston University, had a typical close college friendship with Brenda. "We had lunch today on the steps of the school across the street," Donna said. "We go out for coffee. We go see movies. We watch TV. We go out to dinner. We talk on the phone. We go dancing. We go shopping. We do everything together."

From the mid-twenties on, adult responsibilities intrude. But for a woman in her twenties, the better the quality of her friendships, the higher her self-esteem, expectations for achievement, and even personal independence are likely to be. Friends are much more than companions of convenience for single women. Often, they serve as surrogate families.

Terry Kwan, a fifty-year-old Brookline, Massachusetts, business consultant, had never had children; but through her close female friends, several of whom had become first-time mothers in their forties, she could participate vicariously in family life. Crowding her living room sofa, a menagerie of stuffed animals awaited young visitors. "I have three godsons," she told me proudly, "one who's almost finished college, one just starting grade school, and one who has just become a kindergartener."

Divorced, widowed, and single mothers often find friends better insurance against isolation than children. Because a friend's visit is a matter of free choice, it enhances a woman's self-esteem in a way a filial-duty visit can't.

"You don't feel alone when you have friends, and you aren't really ever very lonely," explained eighty-seven-year-old widow Sara Williams, a retired teacher in Marietta, Georgia. "They make the quality of your life so much better because they have time for you. Children have their own problems, and they have their own work to do, and you can't count on them for all this stuff."

Not only can a single woman ask her friends to help her run an errand or to accompany her to a movie; she also knows that she can ask them without setting in play the pleasure-killing dynamic of expectation and resentment. And she understands that those friends will get as much enjoyment out of her company as she will out of theirs.

⁀ Married Women and Friendship ⁀

Women who are married or in other enduring domestic bonds continue to need women friends. Even a strong, mutually satisfying life union occasionally requires outside perspective to help it reach its potential.

For example, no matter how equitably a husband and wife try to share parenting responsibilities, motherhood presents unique challenges that only another mother, with a child the same age, can share fully. After marrying for the first time at age forty, Bett had been retired from her job as a social worker for three years when her daughter was born. Through the little girl's kindergarten class, Bett met another mom, who was looking for a running partner. Although fitness was their original motive for getting together three times a week, they gradually became close friends. Without being conscious of it, both women needed another mother with a child the same age, in the same school. Bett explained that those early morning runs were "an opportunity to have a sounding board around parenting and school issues. I find myself sharing a concern or a frustration, and feel that she always offers good support and ideas."

When University of Wisconsin–Milwaukee sociologist Stacey Oliker studied the close female friendships of twenty-one married women, she found that these relationships supported marriage by giving women more power and at the same time encouraging their commitment to their families. More than half the women said their friendships with other women helped their marriages work more smoothly.

Women *listen* to their friends, and they return caring but objective reflections. To a married woman, a close female friend can serve as a safety valve for everything from mild irritation to white-hot rage. Surprisingly, women often express empathy for a friend's husband. Not that they take his side, but they may say something like "Joe loves you so much. He'd be devastated if you walked out." A woman may also praise a friend's husband, even at the expense of her own. "So he doesn't make a huge salary," she'll say. "At least he's a devoted father. My Harry is such a workaholic he never gets home before the kids are in bed."

Husbands may feel uncomfortable at the thought of their wives discussing their habits and flaws. But this discomfort also stems from the reality that men aren't as inclined to discuss their marriages with one another as women are. Perhaps because women are better than men at getting other people to open up emotionally, many husbands consider their wives their only confidantes, whereas married women tend to rely on their female friends for such support.

Female friendship also promotes strong marriages by keeping women from demanding too much from their partners. A husband may object to his wife's unloading the intimate details of their marriage to her female friends but be relieved not to have to listen to her complaints about a coworker or to a litany of her problems with her mother.

Without their own sex to turn to for empathy, wives are tempted to ask their husbands to understand things that they can't possibly relate to. No man can fully comprehend how a woman feels about a diagnosis of breast cancer or the pull women now in their forties and fifties experience between striving for success in the world of work and wanting to be taken care of, after being reared to view the latter as evidence of love.

While many husbands and wives share interests apart from family concerns, as well as sharing tastes, opinions, and values, a woman involved with a man who differs from her markedly in some of these areas nonetheless can still find her union romantically and erotically fulfilling. To keep discontent from eroding that relationship, however, she needs friends with whom to share the other sides of herself.

Cecile, a forty-five-year-old physician assistant in a public health clinic, counted on a friendship from her student activist days to give her a kind of intellectual and emotional stimulation her architect husband couldn't. "My husband is not political," she explained. "Those connections to that important period of time are really crucial to me. I've been trying to figure out what to do about it as opposed to just pressuring him to be different." Having a female friendship in which she could share those attitudes and memories enabled Cecile to reconcile herself to a marriage in which she couldn't.

Women friends help military wives deal with the anxiety of having their husbands sent off to combat. When Daphne Perkins's fighter-bomber pilot husband was deployed to Saudi Arabia during the Gulf War, leaving her behind at a U.S. Air Force base in England, two fellow teachers at the American elementary school kept her otherwise lonely weekends occupied. "They'd always ask me toward the end of the week, 'What do you want to do this weekend?'" Daphne explained. "If I said, 'Let's go to London,' they said, 'What time?'"

When catastrophe strikes a woman's life partner, friends can make the crucial difference between her coping or falling apart. In *Women Make the Best Friends: A Celebration,* Lois Wyse recounted how friends pitched in to help National Public Radio reporter Nina Totenberg when a slip on the ice left her husband, Sen. Floyd Haskell, with a brain injury requiring three operations. During the four months her husband spent in the hospital, Totenberg never ate dinner alone. Totenberg summed up how that crisis had taught her to appreciate the value of friendship:

> How could I have done all the things my husband needed during those months? How could I have kept his spirits up? Kept both my job and my house running if not for my friends? How could I have lived without that extra source of courage and support?

For a woman caught in a destructive marriage, a female friend can spring the trap. Meg, a science writer for a newspaper in the Southwest, was once married to a possessive alcoholic who insisted that she cut her ties with her women friends. To preserve the marriage, she reluctantly complied, then regretted her decision. "I was smothered," she recalled. "I was suffocated. It was like I lived in a walled city. But you know, I wonder if my husband had some sort of sense about how important women friends were to me and realized that cutting them off would make me a prisoner—because I really was a prisoner for five years." Without friends, Meg had no one to validate her experiences and her interpretation of them. "There was no reality check," she said. At last, Meg reached out to a female colleague: "I started confiding in her about just how bad my life was, and she opened up her heart and her home to me. She said, 'You know, if you leave, even if it's in the middle of the night, you should come over to my house.' " Three months later, Meg did just that. She and the colleague have been close ever since.

"She saved my life mentally," Meg explained, adding that it wasn't something even a loving, supportive family member could have done: "It had to be a woman friend. It's not that we sat and did male bashing or talked about how dastardly my husband was. It was nonjudgmental support, which I think women do give each other a lot. And I remember very vividly when I got out of that marriage, before I even thought of getting my apartment, I got back and renewed my friendships with my women friends."

Female friendships can give a woman the essential perspective she needs to free herself from a destructive relationship with a man; but it is not—as some men fear—a threat to a good, or even an average, marriage. When two female friends discuss their marriages, each receives, along with support and advice, a sense of where hers fits along a continuum extending from self-destructive through disappointing to satisfactory, reasonably happy, and ideal. These heart-to-hearts help women define and redefine marriage, focusing on attainable satisfactions rather than unrealistic fantasies.

In their separate research on married women, sociologists Pat O'Connor and Stacey Oliker found that friendships strengthen marriage rather than compete with it. O'Connor challenged the contention that each human being has a "fund of sociability" and that, therefore, if we have a lot of intimacy in one relationship we won't have the need or the resources to seek it elsewhere. If this were true, women whose husbands were close confidants wouldn't develop friendships to fill that role, and women with friends in whom they confided wouldn't develop that side of their marriages. Looked at another way, marriage and friendship would compete for intimacy. O'Connor found, instead, that women with close female friends were no less likely to confide in their husbands than women without. Perhaps people who need and are good at intimacy tend to foster it in all of their important relationships.

Oliker asserted that for the majority of women, the most important primary relationships aren't limited to our nuclear families and that close friendships both support women in their traditional roles and help them develop autonomy and become successful in the public sphere. One of the tender ironies of marriage is that a happy husband doesn't want his wife to change. He may take a dim view of her decision to explore another side of herself—to go to law school once her youngest child enters kindergarten, to quit a boring job with a plump salary to teach in an inner-city school, to climb the ten highest peaks in North America. For a caring but less self-interested sounding board, she needs a female friend.

While we can, and often do, grow in marriage and other domestic partnerships, in these structured alliances we are also trying to recreate and improve on the roles we grew up observing. We're dealing as well with society's expectations. Friendship, on the other hand, is more fluid. Within broad guidelines, we're free to design, in collaboration, relationships that can help us become our best selves.

~ The Productive Joy of Connecting ~

Female friendship is far more complex than we've been led to believe. Just because women are more comfortable being close to each other than men are, that doesn't mean that we're natural experts on friendship, that our openness to intimacy and our capacity for empathy translate into an almost instinctual ability to be good friends. That idealization is no more realistic than the notion that we're naturally good mothers. And when our friendships don't match the pictures we're been handed, we feel not only saddened, but flawed, ashamed. But when women friends connect, we experience a spark, part exhilaration, part affirmation, that is intensely pleasant.

Not only do women friends encourage us to develop the various sides of ourselves, explore new interests, try new things, dream our dreams and pursue them. As chapters 3 and 4 examine in detail, the very processes involved in initiating and maintaining—even in ending—a close female friendship help us grow psychologically. Stacey Oliker found that "women friends engender and reinforce *interdependent individual* identity" (my italics). And by providing this unique balance between belonging and individuation, women friends give one another a solid base on which to build productive, satisfying lives.

3

The Seven Stages
of Friendship

. . . A wish for friendship may arise
quickly, but friendship does not.

—Aristotle, *Nichomachean Ethics*

Friendships don't just happen. Like romances and, for that matter, like human beings, they develop through predictable stages, although we may not be aware of each stage at the time. Examining my own friendships and those that other women have described to me, I've identified seven steps: attraction, initiation, structuring, comfort, strengthening, testing, and commitment. Not all friendships reach the later levels—which is part of what distinguishes acquaintances from casual friends and casual friends from close ones. But even friendships that form on fast-forward pass through an abbreviated version of these stages.

✦ Attraction ✦

We meet people constantly—at work, at parties, while running errands. Waiting in line at the post office, we ask the woman ahead of us the age of the baby she's balancing on her hip. The woman who sets her step next to ours at aerobics class tells us that she's missed two weeks because her job kept her on the road. A friend's birthday party introduces us to five women we've never run into before.

For his 1961 Ph.D. dissertation for the Massachusetts Institute of Technology, Michael Gurevitch asked 17 people to keep diaries of everyone they knew by name and came in contact with at least twice during a hundred-day period. The totals ranged from around 175 for blue-collar workers to 600 or 700 for professors, with the average being 500. When I interviewed him thirty-five years later, Gurevitch, who taught sociology of media at the University of Maryland, told me that he would expect similar results nowadays.

Only a tiny portion of these encounters evolve into friendships. First, we have to recognize a person as a candidate for friendship. Then, we have to feel attracted to her. At its simplest level, that can be a matter of shared interests. If we have a baby the same age as hers, we may be on the lookout for someone who can provide a playmate for our child. If our job involves a lot of travel, we may want to trade war stories with another woman whose career does, too. If we appreciate spontaneous humor, we may want to get to know the woman at that party who peppered her conversation with fabulous one-liners.

Small talk helps sort out which individuals might make appropriate friends. Take complaining—not the kind directed at someone who can correct the situation, but indirect griping about the weather or the glacially slow line at the bank. University of Florida social linguist Diana Boxer found that people are most likely to engage in such grumbling either with close friends and family or with total strangers. In the first case, we're looking for empathy and affirmation. In the second, we're breaking the ice. "It's really a way to establish a connection," Boxer explained. "It often prompts the kind of self-disclosure that leads to people getting to know each other."

While interviewing seventy-five women for their book *Speaking of Friendship: Middle-Class Women and Their Friends,* sociologist Helen Gouldner and journalist Mary Symons Strong found that middle-class women limit the universe from which they choose potential friends directly and quickly to a "pool of eligibles." (So do working-class women, and their criteria are even narrower, often including only one ethnic group and one neighborhood.)

First, women exclude those with traits they dislike—whether those are superficial quirks like a braying laugh, attitude dissimilarities like pessimism versus optimism, value differences about issues like race relations or abortion, or character flaws like dishonesty or judgmentalism. One appeal of sports leagues, alumni associations, and political, professional, religious, and community groups is that, because membership is based on interests, backgrounds, or values, they provide a pool of potential friends screened to eliminate at least some disliked qualities. So do private clubs. These organizations also create an environment in which women can observe one another in a social setting before committing themselves to closer acquaintance.

Business entertaining also brings together women preselected for similar professional status, cultural interests, and educational background. Yet, surprisingly, acquaintances made under such circumstances don't tend to develop further. Gouldner and Strong discovered that women whose careers or whose husbands' careers required superficial socializing reported that they never considered women they met under those circumstances potential friends. The mores of the American upper middle class dictated that guests chat with as many people as possible without getting mired in conversation with any given person. Two women meeting at such a reception likely would be too busy playing their parts to notice their compatibilities.

Gouldner and Strong called this screening process "disregarding." Required socializing isn't the only circumstance that triggers this response. Convention dictates that we disregard the people passing us on the sidewalk, sharing the office elevator, and sitting around us at the movie theater.

Even if one woman indicates to another that she's interested in getting to know her, the second woman won't pick up on the cue if the first woman falls into her "disregard" category. That can happen either because the environment in which they meet isn't conducive to the purpose or because of a personal characteristic that, while not actively disliked, nonetheless seems to rule her out as a suitable friend. Age, ethnic, and class differences are cases in point.

Disparity in real or perceived social or economic status can lead women to rule out one another as potential friends. Heidi Knox, a twenty-seven-year-old at-home mother married to a motorcycle mechanic, met Lisa Taylor, a twenty-six-year-old professional singer married to a musician and computer consultant, at La Leche League, the breast-feeding support organization. They discussed forming a play group, which would provide regular socializing for both their toddlers and themselves; but when they exchanged phone numbers and addresses, Heidi realized that Lisa lived in a high-rise adjacent to Chicago's fashionable Gold Coast. "I just felt like it'd be harder to relate," Heidi said. "Then when I saw her the second time, she got out of the car and she was barefoot and her baby was barefoot. I thought, okay, maybe she wasn't how I thought she was." That second encounter blossomed into friendship.

Sometimes our "disregard" criteria permit us to make a stranger into an acquaintance but keep us from making her into a true friend. At eighty-three, Nonie Thompson had spent decades on the boards of nonprofit agencies. Through these worthy causes, she'd met scores of accomplished women, but none of them had evolved into close friends. Describing "sort of a line" that they didn't cross, Nonie explained that a woman met on a board might be "somebody you have great respect for, but you're not going to sit down and put your feet up with. You work together."

Many women similarly exclude people they meet on the job. "Women did not make close friends in the workplace," Helen Gouldner found in her research.

But not all women draw a clear "disregard" line around colleagues. Since we spend so much of our time at work, that's one of the main places we meet people. The structure of modern businesses throws women of similar ages, backgrounds, and aspirations together. Lunch breaks provide opportunities for casual socializing. Cooperating on projects builds feelings of solidarity and connectedness. The downtimes spent waiting for meetings to start or sitting in adjacent airplane seats on the way to a conference provide opportunities for candid talk. Sometimes the attraction is so strong and the circumstances so compelling that women do chance friendships with coworkers, but such relationships carry some of the same risks as office romances.

Amanda, a Silicon Valley staff development specialist, described her feelings when a coworker she ranked among her best friends criticized her job performance in a staff meeting. They'd worked together for five years—three of those as partners, shared personal revelations and (in a pinch) hotel rooms on business trips. They'd even been pregnant at the same time. "She took over the meeting and started lambasting my department," Amanda told me. "Everyone else in the meeting was floored." As for Amanda herself, she was heartbroken.

That's why women often stop at the level of congenial collegiality with women they meet at work—and why two women sometimes will become true friends only after one of them has left for another job. "I think friends at work should never be confused with friends from your outside life," said Geena, a thirty-one-year-old magazine reporter in New York. "It's very difficult to keep that in check because you're around them much more than you are your regular friends, so you have this illusion in the workplace that people are more bonded to you than they in fact are."

Becoming close, separate friends with the wife or girlfriend of your husband's or lover's friend carries some of the same risks. Couples typically do much of their socializing as duos. Two pairs may know each other for years. They may get together for dinner or a movie every week, go on family picnics with each other, even share a vacation house. But unless the women were friends first, they may never become intimate as individuals.

Couple friendships have their own implicit barriers. In general, if the women get along well, but not so well that they feel comfortable discussing their partners' flaws, they are able to defuse jealousy on both sides while maintaining the lines of loyalty. "Even closest couple friends tend to be less intimate than would be expected by the label 'closest,' " Lyn Beth Bendtschneider noted in her Ph.D. dissertation.

Sometimes institutions set up rules or informal policies discouraging individual friendships. When Donna Ambrogni, sixty-seven, joined the Grail, a group of Catholic women working to combat poverty, she soon learned that while getting along with her coworkers was encouraged, strong bonds between any two women weren't. "In the early years we worked in teams," she explained, "and there was a concern that developing very close friendships would be counterproductive." The group's leaders feared that if any two women on a team became close friends, they might exhibit favoritism toward each other, care more about being together than getting a task done, or make other team members feel excluded.

In the military, rank and the cautionary aphorism "Familiarity breeds contempt" delimit which people are considered appropriate for personal relationships. "My friends are captains and lieutenants and majors," said Capt. Charlene Guardia, a U.S. Army occupational therapist stationed in Panama. "I've never had a good friend who was a lieutenant colonel."

Certain professions frown on practitioners becoming friends with clients, on the theory that a personal relationship might distort the professional one. A person can base her decision to become friends with her C.P.A. on rational grounds, such as whether she'd really want to be bosom buddies with someone who knew every detail of her finances. Her attraction to her female psychotherapist, however, may be prompted by the unconscious psychodynamics of the therapy itself or by the affirmation she received from being listened to attentively. But what if that psychotherapist feels a reciprocal pull? No matter. Professional ethics dictate that the therapist, the one controlling the interaction, avoid blurring her role. In other words, she has to learn to disregard her patients as prospective friends.

Suppose one woman meets another who passes both the "dislike" and "disregard" tests. In order for the second woman to make the next cut, she must exhibit attributes that the first person likes, consciously or unconsciously. These attributes could be intelligence, warmth, or kindness toward those less fortunate, or they could be social and professional status, hair color, or resemblance to a favorite aunt. When I asked the women I interviewed what initially attracted them to their closest friends, three qualities predominated: Shared interests, humor and physical appearance, in that order. These traits outstripped genuineness, intellect, and consideration for others by at least two to one. Other characteristics, from daring to centeredness, from taste to creativity, ran even further behind.

I was surprised at the role appearance played in sparking one woman's interest in another. Some of the women I interviewed talked about a friend's presence or style. Others cited a specific feature—her height, her eyes, her hair. By any name, they were telling me that their first attraction to their friend was physical. To my surprise, that answer came more often from heterosexuals than from lesbians.

"I saw her moving in—she was carrying some stuff upstairs," said fifty-two-year-old Boston-area social work professor Carol Deanow. "And I said to myself instantly, 'We're going to be tight.' I don't know that I can explain it—her looks on some level, her obvious energy."

Sometimes, appearance reflects shared interests. "I opened this door and saw this person with really bright red hair," said Heidi Knox. "I thought, 'Wow, here's somebody who is really creative and different.'"

Half of the more than four thousand women who responded to *New Woman's* friendship survey said that they liked their best friends the first time they met them. Occasionally, two women feel an immediate, almost irresistible pull toward each other—an interpersonal magnetism so strong that some social scientists have dubbed it "falling in friendship." As Helen Gouldner described it to me: "There's sometimes this instantaneous attraction. I don't know what it is—chemical or common values. It's sort of like falling in love."

Along with disliking, disregarding, and liking, vaguer forces are at work in why women attract each other or not—how lonely or time-pressed two women feel, the expansiveness that comes with taking a new job or exploring a new creative pursuit. Each of us has what Gouldner and Strong call "her own personal budget of friendship" determined by the time and other resources available for friends balanced against the number of friends in our current network.

"She manages to have this huge network of hundreds of women friends," Flora Maria Garcia, a forty-three-year-old administrator of arts organizations, said of her friend Penny, an artist. "It's amazing. Usually I have one or two really good friendships, because to me, it requires so much energy and history."

Individuals vary in their desire for companionship and their need for intimacy, and those desires and needs change over the life span. As Part Two of this book explores, we crave different kinds of friends at different ages. As our circumstances shift, so do our friendships. One may be sprouting at the same time two others are becoming firmly established and a fourth is withering.

❧ Initiation ❧

Once two women register an attraction, the dance of friendship initiation begins. One strikes up a conversation. They search for common ground in general attitudes, then in specific life experiences. As they talk, they look at each other; their pupils even dilate. If things seem to be moving too fast, one will pull back. They'll talk about the weather or the quality of the coffee. Then the two will test the waters of connectedness again.

Embarking on a friendship entails confronting our fear of rejection, our difficulties setting boundaries, our problems dealing with conflict, and the limitations of our ability to empathize and nurture. At every step, one woman chooses to move toward connection, and the other chooses to meet her partway, to hold her ground, or to withdraw. Psychiatrist Daniel J. Levinson observed in *The Seasons of a Woman's Life:* "To initiate is to make a *choice.* . . . I start to make some investment of self in the relationship, often without a conscious sense of choosing."

One common misconception about relationships is that they begin by spontaneous combustion, that if two people with compatible interests and personalities are placed in proximity to each other under the right circumstances, a friendship just starts. In his book *Understanding Relationships,* University of Iowa sociologist Steve Duck noted that what sparks friendship is mutual behavior, as opposed to individual qualities.

Carol Safran and Janice Rubin met when Janice, a professional photographer and folksinger, gave a slide presentation on her recent trip to the Baltics. "After this thing, I went up to Janice and told her how interesting it was," Carol recalled. "She was a photographer *and* a singer. And traveled around the world—so impressive. So I walked her to her car. I was somehow attracted to her. I think it was because I thought of her as so competent and me as not so competent."

Carol and Janice called each other several times, trying to get together. For weeks, their schedules never meshed, but Carol persisted. Finally, they met for coffee at a French bistro—coincidentally, on Carol's birthday.

"We had a very nice conversation," Carol said. "We talked about family and lots of intuitive things. Then she did this wonderful thing."

Telling Carol that she had to arrange for the flowers for her upcoming wedding, Janice asked her to swing by the florist across the street and drive her to her car several blocks away. When Carol pulled up, Janice was standing in the street.

"I rolled my window down," Carol recalled, "and she threw a basket of flowers in and said, 'Happy birthday!' That was such a nice birthday gift from a person I didn't even know, that I felt this attraction to. Maybe she felt attracted to me, too."

The friendship initiation process can take hours, or it can take months. "Usually, after an initial attraction friendship develops very slowly, stage after stage after stage," Helen Gouldner told me. " 'Would you like to come over for a drink?' 'Why don't we have lunch?' "

Most women seem to have an intuitive sense of how far to go how fast. Unless the prospective friends met as neighbors, they are more likely to arrange to get together someplace public initially. Friendships germinate best under conditions which allow both women to control the closeness and duration of the interaction. As anyone who's been trapped on a long flight next to a compulsively confiding fellow passenger knows, circumstances that prevent a graceful exit can evoke emotional claustrophobia.

Certain traditions provide a formal structure for initiating social contact. For example, the custom of bringing food to a new neighbor offers an opportunity to express helpfulness while checking her out as a potential friend. Some people develop their own methods of initiating friendships. In an article for *Cosmopolitan,* writer Susan Jacoby quoted a thirty-eight-year-old museum administrator who sent notes to people she wanted to get to know.

The initiation stage of female friendship is crucial not just because of the content shared but because of how it's done. It gives each woman a chance to demonstrate her empathy and self-assurance, her ability to listen well, and her interest in developing the friendship. Minute by minute, each balances her own comfort level with the comfort level of the other and weighs the strength of her attraction against her fear of rejection. "I have two tickets to the opera tomorrow night," one woman says to another who rides to work in the same carpool. "Would you like to go?" It's a risk, but not too big a risk.

✧ Structuring ✧

If two women complete the initiation phase without either of them backing off, they've agreed to move from being acquaintances to being at least casual friends. The next step, structuring, involves defining the format of the friendship. This is the stage at which friends decide how often and under what circumstances they'll meet or talk.

Structuring also involves establishing ground rules, which include delineating personal boundaries. Sharing coffee in a coworker's office, a woman may gesture to the photos on her desk and say, "Cute kids." If the other woman says, "Aren't they? They're my sister's. But, listen, can you believe the way Frank dropped the ball on the Miltner contract?" she shows that she wants to keep the relationship confined to workplace issues, at least for now. On the other hand, if she says, "Aren't they? They're my sister's. I don't have any of my own, so she lets me borrow them twice a year. I'm taking them to Colorado with me next month," she invites her visitor across the threshold into her private life.

This stage of friendship involves a lot of contact and communication. By making carefully chosen disclosures about themselves and discussing other people and current events, women who are structuring a friendship work out which subjects are fair game, which are off-limits, and which might provoke conflict. For example, if one woman says to another, "Jane has great taste, but she's always talking about what things cost," she's signaling that she considers discussions of personal money matters taboo. If she expresses disgust at a celebrity's well-publicized affair, she's signaling that she might be sympathetic to another woman's anxiety about her husband's possible infidelity but not to confessions of her own sexual adventures.

Faith Einerson, a fifty-year-old computer systems analyst, told me that she'd learned with one friend early on that "you can't talk about sad things with her." This woman had shrugged off tragedy in her own family. "That's her defense," Faith explained. So during the nine years Faith had taken care of her own mother as her health had declined, and especially in the six months since her mother's death, Faith knew that when she felt down and just wanted to cry, she needed to turn to other friends.

❧ Comfort ❧

Once their relationship has a structure, women can relax and enjoy each other's company or turn to each other for empathy and support. The excitement of initial connection has passed, replaced by an easier, less anxious form of exchange. Friends move on to learning to read each other's facial expressions, anticipate reactions, and gauge the appropriate amount of physical contact. Friendships may spend a long time at this level, and they may never go beyond it—in which case, they remain casual.

"It's really been recently that we've started getting to be such good friends, even though we've known each other all these years," Dallas publicist Julia Sweeney said of a friendship currently moving through the comfort stage. "About a year ago, I invited her to lunch, and then a couple of weeks later she invited me to lunch, and then another week later, I invited her to lunch, and then all of a sudden, she said, 'You know, this is fun getting together every week.' I know there are parts of her life that she has never told me about, and I haven't told her everything, either."

Only when their relationship has navigated the comfort stage do two women feel utterly at ease with each other. Passing through it, they experience both the pleasure of discovery and the anxiety of potential rejection. Each new friend begins by presenting an idealized version of herself—the unflappable mother, the health-conscious athlete, the savvy businesswoman—then lays bare her more vulnerable or less attractive qualities gradually, checking the other's reaction to one before letting her see the next. Generally, we're most cautious about avoiding disagreement at this stage, although one of the stage's functions is to identify areas of potential conflict and negotiate ways around them.

Strategies that allow us to reveal our true selves indirectly have particular appeal during friendship's comfort phase. Shopping for clothes together, for example, lets us check out each other's tastes while we ease into communication about how we feel about money and our bodies—two of the hottest buttons on our emotional consoles. Seeing a movie together or reading the same book opens up opportunities to trade reactions toward the intricacies of the protagonists' lives, helping us decide which details of our own lives we can safely share. This process goes beyond the structural stage task of determining which topics are off limits and which might provoke controversy or conflict. At the comfort stage, two friends decide implicitly how personally they'll discuss these topics and how they'll handle any disagreements that might arise.

Although it often is trivialized and even demonized by the male-dominated culture, gossip helps women become comfortable with each other. Sometimes it's destructive of reputations, but it's not idle chatter. In her best-seller *You Just Don't Understand: Women and Men in Conversation,* social linguist Deborah Tannen observed that gossip "can serve a crucial function in establishing intimacy—especially if it is not 'talking against' but simply 'talking about.'"

By talking about third parties, we can safely test each other's attitudes and determine what support we can expect of each other. Houston psychotherapist Linda Walsh chose a zoological simile to explain the function of gossip: "It's like animals that have rituals when they meet: 'Do you smell the same as I do? Are you going to accept me if I show you who I am?' Gossip establishes the common ground and determines whether you're safe as a person."

When a group of Temple University psychologists studied members of a student sorority, they concluded that gossip had information and entertainment value, as well as influence on the way others perceived the person who was the subject of discussion. Far from the popular image of vindictive isolates who spread tales about others to earn approval, these gossipers were among the more socially successful women on campus.

Some women prefer to come right out with sensitive information about themselves early in a relationship. This strategy tests the waters of intimacy at the same time it protects against rejection at a later stage, when it would hurt more. Faith Einerson hadn't lost any friends because of either her multiple divorces or her former membership in the Socialist Workers Party, she explained, "because fairly early on I disclose my four marriages and my politics. So if anybody is going to be upset about it, now is the time, before there's a whole lot of attachment."

Because comfort is a subjective state, a lot of friendships are aborted at this stage. That's what happened with two members of the play group Heidi Knox, Lisa Taylor, and five other moms started in Chicago. At first, the women were guarded, but gradually they began to feel comfortable enough to reveal more about themselves. "I guess you just slowly mention a few things, then a few more things," Heidi explained. "We'd talk a little bit more, then talk a little bit more—about other friends in the group, about our relationships with our husbands, about our situations growing up."

One blustery day six or eight months after the play group began, they were sitting around at the home of one of the moms. "There was a little booklet from the far right out on the coffee table," Lisa told me in a separate interview. "I picked it up and I was reading it, and I was saying, 'This is pretty cool right here. This makes sense about putting your family first.' All of a sudden all the women were right there and we were all talking about our feelings about it. It got pretty explicit for a play group. Usually we're saying stuff like, 'Oh, Zack has the cutest little suspenders on today.' "

Then the hostess and one of the other mothers argued that America's major social problems sprouted from a decline in family values and that outlawing abortion was an essential step back toward the right path. When another woman ventured that even if the two moms would never have an abortion themselves, they shouldn't deprive others of that option, they "got really angry and spewed at her," Heidi said. "This was a woman who when she was twenty had this boyfriend that she thought she was engaged to, and it turned out he was married. She got pregnant and had to give the baby up for adoption. She just said that she wouldn't want somebody else to have to go through that."

Once that came out, the pair who had argued the conservative case were embarrassed that they'd yelled at her. The play group no longer was comfortable for them, so they dropped out. But that confrontation helped bond some of the other mothers as friends. They'd witnessed how one another handled conflict.

"I guess I sort of like the safety," Heidi said about her closest friendships. "I feel close enough that I don't feel like they would do anything to hurt me."

The point of the comfort stage is to arrive not at full disclosure but at a map of our mutual boundaries and at a sense that we can relax and be ourselves with each other. We enter this phase of friendship figuratively dressed in our public persona, with our hair and makeup just so. We exit it not naked, but wearing our favorite old clothes, with freshly washed faces.

ᴙ Strengthening ᴙ

Unless one of the friends is uncomfortable with what she's revealed to the other, or something like a fight or a move disrupts the relationship, a friendship involving empathy and self-disclosure strengthens of its own accord. This strengthening does take work, but at this stage the work is so pleasant and natural that neither woman may be conscious of doing it.

If two friends spend a lot of time together, if they are real and honest with each other, if they exchange emotional or practical support, and if each feels she's getting as much as she's giving, the relationship will become more durable and resilient. Simply sharing the ordinary details of their daily lives enhances female friendship and strengthens the bond.

In the comfort stage of developing a friendship, disclosing personal information helped each woman become more comfortable with the other—and the more comfortable they became, the more they disclosed. Now, rather than taking the relationship deeper, self-disclosure makes it stronger.

Sharing good times also can reinforce a bond. University of California sociologist Robert B. Hays identified "the amount of fun and relaxation experienced" as the factor most associated with how highly the undergraduates he surveyed rated the progress of their friendships. Fun helped strengthen the friendship between Tara Boland and her high school classmate Glynnis. They quickly moved from having lunch together to accompanying each other to football games and dance clubs. Tara remembered that instead of going to their homecoming dance, they went to hear the rock band U2. "That was my first concert," she explained. "We had front row tickets." Recalling such adventures helps cement friendships.

"We shaved our legs together the first time," Carol Edgar, now forty-five, said of Swanee Hunt, her close friend since age nine. "We cut ourselves a hundred times. There were little pieces of toilet tissue all over our legs."

Joint memories become part of the personal culture close friends create with each other. Every time old friends use each other's childhood nicknames or ask after relatives, they strengthen the bond between them. "Friends are often appreciated exactly because they share private understandings, private jokes, or private language," Steve Duck explained. By sharing their experiences, feelings, and memories, each friend makes the other's private world in some sense her own, and each incorporates the other into her inner life.

Gifts also strengthen friendship, especially if they go beyond fulfilling what Helen Gouldner and Mary Symons Strong dubbed "ceremonial obligations"—pro forma offerings at birthdays, Christmas, weddings, and baby showers. Presents can accomplish this by demonstrating intimate knowledge of the recipient, such as when a house guest brings a half dozen beeswax candles in the exact blue of her friend's best china, or by coming at an unexpected but meaningful time. When my friend Maida surprised me with a purse-size spray bottle of Shalimar the first time we got together after her trip to France, the gift had double value: It was my favorite perfume, and it showed that despite all the distractions of Paris and the Loire, she'd been thinking of me.

Certain special gifts become artifacts of a friendship, imbued with a value far beyond the generosity or even the insight they reflect. When a woman gives a friend a pin she inherited from her grandmother or an afghan she crocheted during a hundred hours stolen from busy days, she gives more than a thoughtful present; she gives something of herself. As I interviewed Carol Edgar, she brought out a scrapbook Swanee had made documenting their friendship. Guiding me through photos of choir trips and church bake sales, high school parties, and horseback rides, she mused, "This book is very special. It's like a relic."

Women bolster friendships by exchanging material resources—a sleeping bag for a camping trip, a roasting pan for a Thanksgiving turkey, cash to cover lunch at a restaurant that doesn't take credit cards. Friends also exchange practical services—a ride to the airport, an evening of baby-sitting, help cooking for a party. By the strengthening stage, a rough balance of favors will do. But one form of reciprocity still matters: what Helen Gouldner and Mary Symons Strong called the "equal time" rule of conversation between female friends. They noted that among the women they interviewed:

> Over the long run, each person was allotted time to talk and expected to grant some rough equivalent, although not necessarily an exactly equal, amount of talking time. In addition, a woman frequently was attentive to what was being said by another woman, did not interrupt, and stored the information in her memory.

One task of this friendship stage is accepting each other's faults. Gouldner and Strong discovered that many of the women they talked to admitted they found some of their friends' attributes and habits irritating or even morally repugnant. Yet these hadn't kept these relationships from developing. A flaw may not show up until the friendship is well established. Or the annoying trait may have been obvious early on but was more than compensated for by the friend's virtues.

Once a friendship progresses through the strengthening stage, its survival isn't dependent on how much time the women spend together or how often. Strengthened friendships become what Helen Gouldner and Mary Symons Strong called "banked for life." They can endure years of separation, then be resumed, either by chance or because of a change in life circumstances that makes one of the women feel she needs the other. Gouldner and Strong found that many women maintained these "friends in escrow." So did I. Dozens of the individuals I interviewed told me of durable friendships sustained by no more than annual holiday letters, with visits spaced years apart. As Chicago anthropologist Madelyn Iris explained it: "You carry people around in your heart, even though they're not any longer part of your life. You might not see them for years, and then when you do it's like it was yesterday. Nothing's changed."

These friendships are important, not just as mental constructs but in terms of enduring rapport. They are the bromeliads of intimate relationships, seemingly able to survive on nothing but sunlight, air, and mist.

↞ Testing ↞

Over time, things happen to test any friendship. These may be a matter of the individuals' growth or change. One of the friends is transferred to another city; the other has a baby. The test may constitute limitations built into the relationship. For instance, a knee problem forces two running partners to find a new venue for meeting or risk drifting apart. Or the test may involve something that a friend does or doesn't do. One woman drops everything to take care of her sick friend's toddler. Another decides it's too much trouble to drive two hundred miles to attend her best friend's third wedding.

Certain ordinary life events—among them moves, marriage, and motherhood—pose classic tests to female friendship (chapter 13 is devoted to them). After all, anything that makes once-easy contact difficult tries the bond. But once the friendship has matured through the strengthening stage, it has the potential to endure such challenges.

Often two women undertake some joint activity that tests their friendship. Monika Garrick, a forty-year-old partner in a Manhattan public relations firm, knew that Elsie considered her a close friend when Elsie asked her to make her wedding dress. Monika's hobby was designing clothing, which she would either make herself or have made by someone in New York or in her native Jamaica. Feeling honored, Monika set to work. Since this was a fall wedding, she designed the entire dress and train to be covered in autumn leaves done in cutwork—the lacy, white-on-white embroidery that was a Jamaican specialty. But a hurricane hit Jamaica while the embroiderers were in the middle of working on the gown.

"We were thrown together because of that adversity," Monika explained. "We shared what most friends would not have had the opportunity to share, this anxiety. What were we going to do to get her a dress in a couple of days if that one didn't come in from Jamaica?"

Elsie's wedding dress did arrive in time. "But that was only after we had spent many waking hours together praying and planning and finding all the alternatives there were," Monika said. "It proved to me what a really good friend she was. Other people would have turned on me and said, 'Monika, why isn't the dress here?' or 'You'll have to fix it somehow.' "

That test tempered the friendship, giving it the strength and resilience it needed to handle a more serious crisis—the birth of Elsie's first and only child, a little boy with Down's syndrome. "That was a devastating experience," said Monika. "She's a very strong person, but of course, it's always good to have somebody to share that type of experience with."

Moving in together also tests female friendship. If the potential roommates know each other little or not at all, it can be a casual matter. They may become friends, or they may remain distant cohabitants of the same space. If the arrangement doesn't work out, they lose time and maybe money. However, if two close friends decide to share living quarters, they put much more at risk.

For a lesbian, "coming out" poses a major test for any friendship.

Jay Vanasco, twenty-four, and her friend Carla met when they were juniors in high school and working at a bookstore. They both loved literature. Between customers they talked for hours, weaving their conversations back and forth between what they were reading and what was going on in their lives. "She was completely shocked when I came out," Jay told me. "Not that she thought it was bad, but because I flirted so much at B. Dalton. I'd dated men in her life. But it was one of the few friendships that changed not at all."

Nothing tests a friendship more profoundly than a friend's terminal illness. With their contemporaries, elderly women recognize death as a third party, like a waiter at a restaurant, always present but only sporadically intrusive. Though seldom easy, support in the last months becomes an expected function of friendship. For women middle-aged and younger, however, the news that a friend has only a few months to live presents a premature challenge. In an essay for *New Woman,* novelist Elizabeth Berg described her response to her best friend Kate's terminal breast cancer. She and Kate's other friends took shifts running errands, cooking for her, keeping her company, helping her and each other laugh. One day, Elizabeth took her to what turned out to be her last movie; appropriately, it was *Fried Green Tomatoes.* On the way back, Kate asked her to drive through the cemetery. Elizabeth recalled:

> "That's my spot," she said, pointing to a place by the water. . . . "I'm not too crowded in. And there are two trees near me that will flower in the spring." "Oh great," I said. And then I put my head down on the steering wheel.

Any test of friendship involves a choice: We can respond in a way that brings us closer together, or we can respond in a way that pushes us apart. A single friendship may be tested numerous times, and each test can either strengthen, change, or break it. Some friendships disintegrate when they're tested. Others experience a hiatus. Those that survive either increase in intimacy and importance or go back to the structuring stage to be rebuilt as virtually new relationships.

ᴙ Commitment ᴙ

Retired Catholic lay worker Donna Ambrogni met Diedre, a Methodist minister, through the ecumenical movement in 1963. After four

years of shared interests and deep conversations, they moved in together. During their year and a half of joint housekeeping, they entertained as a pair, made mutual friends, and helped each other explore
the spiritual dimension of their lives. Donna's midlife marriage tested
the friendship. "When we asked Diedre to perform the marriage, she
was taken aback," Donna explained. "It was disrupting our way of
living, and she wasn't married, so there was that kind of challenge
for her."

Working through the issues, rather than withdrawing from them,
involved making a clear commitment to the friendship. Since then,
the relationship had withstood several other tests—repeated moves for
both women, Diedre's marriage to, and divorce from, a man with
whom neither Donna nor her husband felt rapport. Each time, by
making the effort to stay connected, Donna and Diedre committed
themselves to their friendship. "We're much closer, because we've
gone through a lot," Donna said.

Once a friendship has passed its first serious test, the natural next
step is for the women involved to commit to it as an important relationship. They may do this through an open declaration, saying something like "I'll always be there for you" or "I think of you as a sister."
Or they may do it by coming through in a way that's beyond what
we normally expect of a friend. That could be something heroic—
anything from Louise in *Thelma and Louise* pulling a gun on the man
who tries to rape her friend to a woman risking embarrassment to
stand up for a friend under verbal attack.

"I was in Colleen's office one time, and she said something about
somebody that she doesn't speak to anymore," Faith Einerson recalled.
"One of her coworkers said, kind of archly, 'The number of people
you don't speak to anymore must be getting pretty high.' You could
tell that got to her, and being the honest person she is, she immediately stopped and thought and counted, and she said, 'Well, that one
makes three.' And I said, 'Oh, hell, Colleen, I've got more ex-husbands
than that.' Everybody laughed, and it broke the tension. But she told
me later that she felt incredibly defended." Using humor at her own
expense as a weapon, Faith defended her socially wounded friend, and
Colleen responded. Faith had demonstrated her commitment.

The expression of commitment also could be something more traditionally nurturing: One woman I interviewed drove two hundred miles
to wait outside the operating room while a friend had a hysterectomy.

Berkeley psychologist Jane Burka and her friend Jodie met during graduate school. "She and I were often the only two with a sense of humor in the whole class," Jane recalled. The friendship moved into the comfort zone when Jane brought Jodie flowers while she was at home recovering from surgery to remove uterine cysts. A joint vacation to Hawaii strengthened the bond, especially since it involved dealing with areas of conflict. Jane explained: "She's much more careful about money than I am, so we had to negotiate all kinds of things, like how much we were going to spend."

Although the two had taken several other successful trips together, Jodie's expression of commitment to their relationship had nothing to do with travel. "One of my cats was run over in the middle of the night," Jane said. "I never did see his body. But when I looked in the street where he had gotten hit, I could see the bloodstain. I couldn't stand it. I wanted it gone, but I wasn't capable of getting rid of it myself. So I told Jodie, and she volunteered to come wash the street. I didn't watch. But when I came out of the house, the bloodstain was gone.

"It was on July Fourth in a busy street. She would have to go and scrub and run to the curb and go and scrub. That's somebody you can count on."

Sharing intense experiences speeds a friendship through its developmental stages. Armies have always relied on this phenomenon to bond individuals so tightly that they will risk their lives for one another. "It's an automatic camaraderie," U.S. Army Capt. Charlene Guardia said. "You have to get up at five and go to physical training. You have to wear this uniform. You have to do all these things, and you're doing them together. Because of that, you bond."

Once the commitment is made, the friendship relaxes into a richer level than it ever enjoyed in the comfort stage. The two women may even restructure the relationship, altering the ground rules to allow more intimacy. A deep, lasting friendship may go through repeated reevaluation and realigning in the course of two women's lives. It may even become so profound that the distinctions between the two individuals begin to blur.

"There were people who had deeper than close friendships; they were really on the level of the soul," clinical psychologist Lynda Marie Behrendt said of some of the long-term, intimate friendships she studied for her dissertation. "They felt that they could trust this person with their life and they could disclose *anything*. There weren't a lot of boundaries."

Joan Berzoff, director of the Smith College School of Social Work, uncovered a similar phenomenon. For her dissertation about the effect of valued female friendships on psychological development, she identified sixteen women with at least one such relationship as important to her as her marriage or her health. In the course of the interviews Berzoff conducted, four of the women mentioned what she called "merged self-other boundaries."

One woman, a musician, described it as "almost like entering into an altered state." Comparing it to an experience she had had playing in her quartet, she explained, "I was not any longer aware of the separate sounds of each individual instrument. After a while there is a click and it comes together as one quartet."

Traditional psychological theories would have predicted that this woman and the others reporting similar experiences were afflicted with weak senses of self. Instead, these women had scored highest on the standard test of ego development Berzoff had administered.

"It really makes sense when you think about it," Berzoff told me. "What is intimacy? It's the ability to dissolve those boundaries temporarily, knowing that you still have strong boundaries to go back to."

Not only are psychologically strong women capable of the closest friendships, but, as the next chapter explains, the very process of building a close, committed female friendship also helps build psychological strength.

4

Becoming Our Best Selves: How Female Friendship Encourages Our Development

> We know ourselves as separate only insofar as we live in connection with others, and . . . we experience relationship only insofar as we differentiate other from self.
>
> —Carol Gilligan, *In a Different Voice*

I ntimate friendships with smart women brought Eleanor Roosevelt out of her shell and gave her the savvy and self-confidence to become perhaps the most effective First Lady in history. In 1921, when she was thirty-seven, she met lawyer Elizabeth Read and publicist Esther Lape through the League of Women Voters. The house Read and Lape shared in Greenwich Village pulsed with the intellectual excitement of New York between the world wars. As Doris Kearns Goodwin noted in her Roosevelt biography *No Ordinary Time,* the "community of women" they brought together gave Eleanor Roosevelt "the strength and encouragement . . . to explore her own talents, to become a person in her own right."

At first, Eleanor was awed by her friends' careers, but soon they helped her recognize her own insight, judgment, and organizational abilities. Goodwin noted:

> In the space of two years, with the guidance of her female colleagues, Eleanor emerged as a major force in New York pub-

lic life . . . sought after for statements in newspapers, chosen to serve on all manner of committees.

Although few people have the advantages of position and prominence that allowed Eleanor Roosevelt to have such an impact on the world, female friendship can help any woman realize her potential for leading a constructive, satisfying life. On the most obvious level, women friends serve as role models and encourage our growth. Beyond that, as a friendship progresses through the seven stages described in chapter 3, the work we do in building the relationship strengthens us as individuals.

✣ Deep Influences ✣

Ever since Freud, the nature of women's psychological development has been a hot topic for debate. Freud took male development as the norm. Little boys, he explained, begin life fused with their mothers. If all goes well, they emerge at school age as autonomous miniature men. As compensation for loosening his possessive attachment to his mother, a boy gets to identify with his powerful father.

Freud equated emotional development with a journey from attachment to separation. Because girls and their mothers are the same sex, Freud said, that disengagement is never complete. A woman may transfer her attachment to a husband or children, but she will remain dependent, overly concerned about what other people think and feel. She will have trouble making decisions, especially moral decisions, which demand an understanding of the concept of justice, which centers on ideas of rights and responsibilities, rather than on the impact one person's actions have on another.

Following in Freud's footsteps, twentieth-century psychologists first dismissed the importance women place on relationships as evidence of dependency and weakness. But in the late 1970s, feminist psychologists began to reexamine Freud's assumption that separation from others equaled emotional maturity. After all, the detached loner, unable to make commitments or form close ties, was no model of mental health. Maybe psychological maturity consisted of the ability to maintain a strong sense of self within the context of intimate relationships. Today, psychologists recognize that female friendships, rather than propping up a faltering ego or serving as substitutes for other "primary" bonds with mothers, sisters, and children, are independently important and help us develop into stronger individuals.

Harvard developmental psychologist Carol Gilligan articulated the priority women place on relationships. In her groundbreaking 1982 book *In a Different Voice,* she explained that women speak "in a relational voice: a voice that insists on staying in connection and most certainly staying in connection with other women . . ." We understand interpersonal relationships, and we understand their importance. But it isn't just our insight into the dynamics of relationships that helps us grow, morally and otherwise. It's our relationships themselves.

In 1976, psychiatrist Jean Baker Miller published *Toward a New Psychology of Women,* a slim volume challenging Freud's definition of psychological maturity as completed separation. Like Freud, Miller drew her theory from her experiences with patients. But as a woman, she had a different interpretation of what constituted healthy psychological development. The ideal for women wasn't the male model of solitary autonomy, as Freud and his followers had attested. It was a productive, mature connectedness. In *Toward a New Psychology of Women,* she explained that females' development takes place in the context of their relationships with others, that those relationships can promote growth on both sides, and that rather than being evidence of an ego stunted by dependency, concern with connectedness could be a sign of maturity and authenticity.

⁓ The Power of Connection ⁓

In women's lives, relationships assume a central position. We delight in them, worry about them, nurture them, and focus our creative and intellectual energy on them. Even when they don't involve us, they form a favorite subject for conversation, for books, and for movies.

"Women really do take the responsibility for everyone's relationships," Jean Baker Miller observed. Women also take the responsibility for other people's psychological growth. In the common everyday activities women perform—nurturing, guiding, and teaching children, caring for the sick and elderly, working cooperatively in factories, fields, offices, and marketplaces—they participate in the development of others. And doing so, they themselves can grow. The authors of the new batch of feminist fairy tales have gotten the message. As Jack Zipes noted in *Don't Bet on the Prince,* rather than take on a solitary quest: "The female protagonist becomes aware of a task which she must complete in social interaction with others to define herself."

Nancy Chodorow, a sociologist with psychoanalytic training, agreed that girls want to grow up to be autonomous *women,* not men. In 1978, two years after Miller's book, Chodorow's *The Reproduction of Mothering* explained that for both men and women, the earliest psychological development occurs in relation to our caregivers. Because these caregivers are almost always women, little boys learn to renounce this connection; little girls don't have to. As a result, Chodorow explained, "Feminine identification processes are relational, whereas masculine identification processes tend to deny relationship." In her subsequent book *Feminism and Psychoanalytic Theory,* she elaborated:

> The selves of women and men tend to be constructed differently—women's self more in relation and involved with boundary negotiations, separation and connection, men's self more distanced and based on defensively firm boundaries and denials of self-other connection.

Chodorow explained that because of this crucial difference, women seldom, if ever, find the connectedness they seek in relationships with men; that's why they place such importance on bearing and raising children. But Phyllis Gillman, now a Los Angeles psychotherapist, challenged Chodorow's theory by showing that even women with young children felt a special need for connectedness that only female friendship could fill.

"Women's friendships are crucial to women's development," Gillman explained when I interviewed her. "When I see someone who doesn't have friends, it says so much about her. It says that she's shut down emotionally. I wonder about her relationship with her mother. I wonder about her capacity to relate at all."

Chapter 12 addresses the issue of why some women find it so hard to make and keep female friends. But whatever the cause, one effect is clear: By avoiding close female friendship, a woman avoids her own growth. Women can grow in relation to their parents, their children, their siblings, their lovers, their husbands, their colleagues, and their clients, but the most fertile ground for development is female friendship.

"Because you don't have the familial obligations or the old issues," Jean Baker Miller explained, "you can start on a more mutual basis, and you can be freer to be yourself."

In 1978 a group of female therapists began meeting in Miller's kitchen in the Boston suburb of Brookline. Miller and Irene Stiver, a senior psychologist at McLean Hospital, exchanged ideas with Judy Jordan and Jan Surrey, a generation younger. All of them were having trouble accepting the time-honored tenets of psychology that branded as dependency the penchant for caring and cooperation they observed in their female patients—and in themselves. Building and elaborating on the work Miller had done for her book, they explored how women grow through interpersonal connection. Miller's group examined this dynamic process in theory, in their professional practices, and in their own relationships with one another.

Instead of equating psychological growth with developing autonomy, which implies independence from relationships with others, the theory group took four attributes as its yardstick:

1. initiative, creativity, and responsiveness
2. clarity of perception and desire [knowing what we experience, feel, and want]
3. capacity to act with intentionality [the ability to establish goals and work toward them, to be conscious of what we do and understand its impact on others and on ourselves]
4. capacity to effect change

The discussions, while serious, weren't without humor; for example, Miller's group dubbed psychology's fondness for using separation as a yardstick for maturity "the Lone Ranger ethic."

That ethic doesn't even work for men, although they're raised to consider it an ideal and to fear attachment, Irene Stiver told me. "People grow in connection and not in separation," she said. "If in the process of a mutually empathic encounter, you can begin to risk showing more of who you are, you will become more effective in the world."

Jean Baker Miller identified five growth-enhancing things that happen when two people connect. The first is a pleasant spark she called "zest"—the back-and-forth flow of energy we experience during a good conversation with a close friend. Because it feels good, zest reinforces the connection. Stiver enumerated the rest of Miller's "five good things": Second, two people in connection become more able to take constructive action in their lives. "Usually when we're alone with a painful thing, we feel immobilized," Stiver explained. "When we can join with someone, we can begin to mobilize ourselves." Third, talking together about their fear, guilt, sadness, anger, and other complex feelings helps women clarify them. Fourth, when one woman connects with another, she feels more self-worth; somebody is listening to her, so she must be worthwhile. And she feels like a better person because she's listening to someone else. Fifth, having one positive relational experience like this makes a woman want more of them. "These five wonderful things are what we call mutual empowerment," Stiver concluded. "Women do this all the time."

Three years after the theory group began meeting in Jean Baker Miller's kitchen, Wellesley College invited Miller to direct its new Stone Center for Developmental Studies and Services, founded to promote mental health among the college's all-female student body. To help psychotherapists and other professionals working with women understand the role of connection and to incorporate their experiences and insights into the theory, she established a series of colloquia at which papers on topics related to women's development could be presented and discussed.

One of the subjects these colloquia have allowed Judy Jordan to explore is something she calls mutuality. "Mutuality doesn't mean 'I'll scratch your back, and you'll scratch mine,' " she said when I asked her to explain the concept. "It means taking mutual responsibility and having mutual respect and what we call mutual empowerment." Compared to family and romantic relationships, female friendship creates an ideal environment for mutuality to flourish. "There isn't typically the power differential," Jordan explained. "There aren't the role constraints."

This equality of power may be why Phyllis Gillman's research contradicted Nancy Chodorow's theory that most women get their needs for connectedness filled through relationships with their children, rather than through close female friendships. No matter how devoted to each other a mother and her child may be, the mother holds the power. Furthermore, a 5-, 10-, or even 15-year-old can't *reciprocate* an adult woman's empathy or wisdom, developed over decades. For true mutuality, no one can beat a friend.

⚘ Daring to Be Ourselves ⚘

When the women I interviewed for this book told me that one of the things they valued most in their friendships was "honesty," they didn't mean blurting out the blunt truth without regard for a friend's feelings. What they were talking about was the quality Miller's theory group called "authenticity" —a term borrowed from Existential philosophy and signifying, roughly, the opposite of phoniness. Female friendship both promotes authenticity and thrives on it.

"The more you can bring yourself fully into connection with someone else, the more that sense of zest, that sense of vitality, that sense of expansiveness develops," Jordan explained. "You're not just doing it to enhance the self. You get intrinsic pleasure out of participating in the development of another person and a relationship."

Clinical psychologist Kerry Ann Moustakas interpreted her own research on nine close friendships as showing that the intimate bonding these relationships entailed promoted the growth of both individuals, as well as of the relationships. She wrote in her dissertation:

> The experience of intimate bonding in friendship offers a unique opportunity for self-discovery and self-actualization. The bonding that occurs between friends creates a powerful emotional, spiritual, and intellectual surge of energy and meaning. Each partner becomes known through the sharing of mutual values and interests and the removal of barriers to bonding.

When we disclose our true selves, reach out for intimacy, or acknowledge conflict, we always face the chance of losing the relationship and of damaging our opinions of ourselves. But that risk taking in itself is a source of personal growth.

Each of the seven stages of friendship entails growth-enhancing risks. Even that first pull of attraction makes us vulnerable; we want the other person to feel drawn to us as well. Making the first move in establishing a friendship risks rejection; responding to another's initiation risks embroiling ourselves in a relationship we might not be able to handle. To structure a friendship successfully, we have to communicate what we want from it. The comfort stage entails self-disclosure, which the strengthening phase takes to a deeper level. Experiences shared along the way challenge our empathy, assertiveness, and flexibility. Whatever tests the relationship tests the friends as well. Finally, committing to a close friendship makes us vulnerable to profound disappointment and betrayal.

In return, every time we negotiate one of these steps, we become more in touch with ourselves, as well as with our friend, and we become stronger, because we have exercised our emotional courage.

"Most women are always thinking there's something wrong with them because they feel scared or they're mad or they feel they don't know what they're doing or they have no idea what to say," Irene Stiver explained. "Friendships are based on being able to expose that vulnerability and find out that you're not alone, that there's nothing wrong with you for having the feelings that you have."

On the other hand, a friendship that requires that one person alter her experiences or remold her personality to meet the other's needs inhibits and distorts development. Instead of fostering growth in both women, it can become what Cambridge, Massachusetts, social worker Karin Schultz described as "an exchange of selflessness." "Women's friendships are often marred by excessive responsibility for the friend's needs and feelings," she asserted.

If we alter our true selves or hold back our feelings in an effort to preserve a valued friendship, we may inadvertently destroy the genuine connection that makes it so worthwhile. "In order to stay in the illusion of relationship, we keep large aspects of ourselves out of our relationships," Jordan said. "We have a very easy time connecting around similarities in experience. There's that great feeling sometimes when you've felt like you're all alone with some experience and you share it with a friend and she says, 'Oh, my God, I felt that way, too!' Then there are times where you're in a different place, and those require empathy across difference. That's harder, but it's also one of the ways we grow the most."

As psychotherapist Christine Hejinian pointed out in her dissertation, by revealing her true self to a friend, a woman confirms her identity, her values, and the choices she's made in her life without sacrificing her sense of connection to others. She receives support for being and expressing who she really is.

Discussing those findings in her San Francisco office, Hejinian explained: "When women are willing to risk their desire to be close, to risk saying things about themselves that are not pretty or nice, that are humiliating and embarrassing, when women are willing to acknowledge anger or discomfort or conflict with their friend—then that friendship really can carry some developmental value in and of itself."

Venturing into such vulnerable areas puts the relationship itself at risk—something many women find scary. Initially, Hejinian assumed that friendships that incorporated the three forms of risk she'd identified "would turn out to be long-lasting." That was true in the majority of the cases she studied, but not in all. "The friendship may not survive it," she said. Even so, she explained, taking these risks would still allow the women to grow.

Conflict makes women especially uncomfortable, partly because it threatens relationships, even though it has the potential for strengthening them as well. Facing conflict in friendship requires courage—not the macho denial of fear, but what Judy Jordan described as "the capacity to act meaningfully and with integrity in the face of vulnerability."

I grew up in a family so conflict averse that the only time I ever heard my parents disagree was when they were hanging pictures. "Half an inch to the right," my mother would say. "No," my father would insist, "it's fine where it is." Or "It's tilted to the left." "It is not. It's straight." In fact, my mother once claimed to me that she'd never experienced anger.

So I learned to sidestep conflict, even when doing so meant erecting a wall between me and the people I cared about. Then, in 1980, I became involved in the Women's Professional Association, a group being formed in Houston by graduates of the historically female Seven Sisters colleges. Most of us were in our twenties and thirties, relatively new in town, and looking to meet other well-educated working women like us. At one of our first sessions, I volunteered to serve on the program committee.

The chair was Carol Safran, who'd gone to Barnard. Her sharp New York wit and Brooklyn accent reminded me of some of my favorite classmates at Vassar. After she responded positively to some

of my suggestions for keynote speakers for the group's monthly dinners, I liked her even better; so I was pleased when she called to
arrange lunch.

We spent more than an hour getting to know each other, filling in
our sketchy impressions of each other's families and careers. Then, over
coffee, Carol explained that she wanted me to send each speaker a
thank-you note. Carol didn't type; she assumed that, as a journalist, I
did. I could be of most use to the Women's Professional Association
if I took on that task.

I was stunned. I'd envisioned her asking me to do something related
to my rarer skills—say, trying to drum up media coverage for our
events. But although I felt undervalued, the best I could do was argue
weakly that thank-you notes should be handwritten, to which she replied that the club president thought typewritten letters would be
more businesslike. I accepted the folder of addresses, complete with
its scrawled draft of the desired text. Carol may have intended that
rough draft to be helpful, but it merely deepened my sense of insult.
She didn't even trust me to think of something appropriate to say.

For weeks, the folder sat in my "in" basket. Every time I considered
opening it, I got angry. What made the situation worse was that I
found Carol so compelling. That lunch had been an initiation of
friendship. We could have restricted our conversation to committee
business; instead, we'd plunged eagerly into each other's lives. But I
had no idea how to express my anger without severing the connection.

Carol didn't give me much choice. After calling several times to
find out if I'd sent the notes, she asked what my problem was. And I
told her. My heart galloped, and I had to lean my elbow on the desk
to keep the receiver steady in my hand, but I told her exactly how I
felt and why.

"Really?" Carol responded, sounding surprised, even slightly in-
trigued. "I had no idea. You should have just said you couldn't do it.
I'll get someone else. Now, do you want to do lunch next week? Or
would coffee be better?"

Warmth, relief, and gratitude flowed through me. For the first time
I could recall in an adult female friendship, I'd risked anger, ventured
conflict. Rather than rejecting me, Carol had expressed a desire to
continue developing our relationship. I've loved her ever since.

And from that day on, I've been better at handling conflict.

↜ Our Mothers, Our Friends ↜

For women without sisters, lifelong female friends can serve as sister substitutes. "Women are always working on their relationships with their sisters and their mothers—if they didn't have a sister, creating a sister, if they had a negative sisterly relationship, creating a different kind," explained Joan Berzoff, head of the doctoral program at the Smith College School for Social Work. "Likewise with their mothers—reexperiencing friends in terms of the best of what they had with their mothers or having friends mother them and mothering friends in ways they couldn't be mothered."

With friends, though, the nurturing flows in two directions. "I really do feel that friendship is mutually mothering," Los Angeles clinical psychologist Phyllis Gillman said.

If a little girl's mother listened with genuine interest to accounts of her activities, if the mother applauded her accomplishments and delighted in her creativity or intelligence, then that child may grow up to seek out friends who will do the same, Joan Berzoff explained. That woman may also look for friends who embody qualities she admired in her mother—competence, empathy, style.

And if a woman's mother fell short, female friendship can help repair the damage. "Even women who have had very difficult and painful relationships with their mothers can have friendships," San Francisco clinical psychologist Christine Hejinian noted. "But when friendships are close, all the things that Mother wasn't, that you couldn't get with Mother, get pushed in the friendship. I wouldn't necessarily say that the friendship will heal the relationship with the mother directly. But it has the potential to heal the issues, the woundedness."

The theme of maternal reparation winds through some of the most popular British novels of the late nineteenth and early twentieth centuries. For her dissertation, Janice Bowman Swanson studied the motherless heroines of Jane Austen's *Persuasion,* Charlotte Brontë's *Shirley,* George Meredith's *Diana of the Crossways,* and Virginia Woolf's *Mrs. Dalloway.* To deal with the trials life sets before them, each protagonist seeks guidance from a female friend. When the friend acts like a controlling mother, the heroine feels smothered, Swanson observed, adding: "But when a healthy maternal interest develops, heroine and friend nurture each other toward a complete expression of self."

A female friend can never replace a mother, but she may be able to replace some of what mothers often have trouble giving: nurturing that affirms us as individuals, connection that is close without binding.

⤳ Mirrors and Models ⤳

By providing insight and empathy, women friends create for each other what developmental psychologists call a "holding environment" —a secure base that supports our individual growth. But they also help us become our best selves by serving as our clearest mirrors and our most positive models.

By mirroring our feelings, friends put us in touch with what's going on inside us, at the same time helping us accept what we might have been taught was unacceptable. A woman tells her friend that her boss refused to give her a raise, even though he thought she deserved one, because if he did he'd have to give a raise to everyone else in her department.

"You must have been furious," her friend responds even though the woman's tone of voice had been hesitant.

"Well, I guess I was," she admits, a little surprised at herself.

"I'll bet," her friend says. "I would have been, too."

Reflecting the other woman's anger in this empathic way makes it visible to her and, at the same time, lets her know that far from being shameful, it's appropriate. The interchange leaves both friends feeling more connected and more powerful.

"My best friends are always able to help me be aware of things that are going on in me that I'm not willing to face or confront," said Betsy Alden, a Methodist minister.

Female friends act as mirrors in another way: They can reflect the best parts of ourselves, qualities that we may doubt or ignore. "I know you're anxious about that presentation tomorrow," a woman acknowledges to her colleague. "But you know your material so well, and you're so attuned to your audience. You're going to do a great job."

Or a woman tells a friend who's dating a divorced man, "I'd be worried about meeting his kids, too. But kids love talking about themselves, and you're such a good listener."

Studies by psychologists and sociologists demonstrate that female friends often make women feel stronger and more capable. Women especially value their friends' reflected confidence in their ability to handle problems.

"Women friends reflect parts of the self that one can't necessarily see," explained Joan Berzoff. "There's also tremendous identification that goes on between women in terms of identifying with a valued attribute, with some part of another which gets taken away as a part of ourselves, and that is a way in which we grow. It's true of my own friendships."

One of the most important things one friend can do for another is support her sense of herself as an individual apart from her function in her family. Clinical psychologist Christine Hejinian observed that friendship both reinforces the importance of a woman's identity and gives her the leeway to try on different personas—the creative artist, the vivacious fun lover, the competent professional, the wickedly witty critic.

Families act as distorting mirrors. The images they show us reflect the script passed down from generation to generation. For the family to preserve *its* identity, someone has to inherit the role of the martyr, someone else play the flighty coquette. To develop fully as individuals, however, we have to rewrite our parts in the script.

By the very act of interacting with us as individuals, apart from our family roles, friends give us relief and perspective even when they don't serve up direct insight. We don't need to use all our time together to dissect our problems in order for friendship to help us grow. A lunch spent speculating on the other people in the restaurant, an afternoon beachcombing, an hour laughing about a shared misadventure back in high school can serve as a vacation for our emotions. Friends do each other good merely by helping each other put some of their problems aside and simply enjoy themselves.

Sometimes, though, we want to change—not to please others, but to please ourselves. When that happens, we look to friends as models. We may even be attracted to another woman in the first place because she possesses some attribute we admire and would like to develop in ourselves. Maybe she radiates self-confidence. Maybe she's so well organized that she always seems to get things done with time to spare. Maybe she speaks three languages fluently. Maybe she communicates well with her teenagers. We can pick up tips from her, even if we don't ask her how she does it, even if we aren't aware that we're emulating her.

Another way female friends help us grow is by accompanying us in activities that stretch us, developing and expressing new sides of ourselves. Whether it's training for a marathon, learning Spanish, picking up watercolor painting or going back to graduate school, these new steps produce more pleasure and less anxiety taken in tandem. Even if a friend doesn't join us, she's likely to do the next best thing— encourage us and applaud our progress. Female friendship provides a secure base from which we can explore both the world and emerging parts of ourselves. Married women in particular rely on female friends for support when their husbands find such ambitions threatening and discourage them.

If it weren't for Emily Dickinson's female friends, her poetry might have languished unpublished in an Amherst attic. When she first submitted her poems to male editors, their condescending reaction inhibited her work. But her women friends made a more appreciative audience. With their encouragement, Dickinson kept writing—in her own voice expressing her own vision. Eventually, one of those friends, fellow poet Helen Hunt Jackson, persuaded her to venture into the broader literary world again. This time, Dickinson found a publisher who recognized her extraordinary talent.

Sometimes, even when our gift isn't great, a friendship allows us to explore and express that part of ourselves uncritically, simply for the joy of it. That was one of the things Johey Crawford, a forty-year-old nurse in Toledo, Ohio, valued most about her friend Shaneesha. "It's crazy," Johey said. "I love to sing, and I don't have much of a voice. But she lets me sing with her. She has a beautiful voice."

Some friendships develop one side of us; others embolden us to delve into another. Some repair damage done by earlier relationships; others provoke us to change the way we relate. Female friendship takes different forms at different stages of our lives. But each variety, at each age, has its own way of helping us become our best selves.

5

☙

The Ten Forms of
Female Friendship

Each friend represents a world in us . . .

Anaïs Nin, *The Diary of Anaïs Nin*

One of the basic truths of female friendship is that it takes various forms. Our friends don't duplicate one another; each has her own way of fitting into our lives. Examining my own friendships and those of women I knew well, I noticed that these relationships seemed to fall into categories according to what drew friends together initially, how they interacted, what they did together, and even what strained or ended the connection.

Other writers who have examined friendship have also noticed that it comes in several varieties. Sociologist Lillian Rubin distinguished between "friends of the road," or temporary companions who *do* things together, and "friends of the heart," or enduring intimates who can just *be* together and whose closeness defies even long separation. In *Speaking of Friendship,* Helen Gouldner and Mary Symons Strong identified three types of female friendships: talking, activity centered, and work centered. Irish sociologist Pat O'Connor divided close female friendships into four forms: confidante, nurturant, companionable, and latent—friends who felt close to each other even though they got together infrequently. In addition, clinical psychologist Joel Block and his co-author Diane Greenberg described five kinds of women's friendships: special interest, convenience, business, crisis, and intimate.

Although each of these taxonomies offered insights into the diverse nature of female friendship, none struck me as adequately describing its rich complexity. In some cases, the categories seemed too broad. In others the criteria shifted: What attracted the individuals defined some forms; the conditions under which they met defined others. I thought that a more specific and consistent classification could help women better understand and even improve their friendships.

The pattern that emerged from my own observations had nothing directly to do with the closeness of the bond. Instead, it reflected the sides of herself that a woman wanted to explore, express, or recapture and the kind of support she needed to heal old wounds or meet present challenges. Different friendships resonate with different aspects of our personalities, our varying moods, our diverse identities. In the intricate tapestry of female friendships, I saw ten basic forms: soulmates, lifemates, companions in crisis, nurturer and nurtured, workmates and playmates, allies, complementary opposites, mentor and protégée, history friends, and ensemble friends.

Each of the ten varieties brings out part of the best in us. Unfortunately, though, woman-to-woman relating also has its dark side. Some of these ten positive kinds of friendship have evil twins. Apparent nurturers can be foul-weather friends, and women who attract nurturing can become draining. Some playmates are enablers. And the flip side of a soulmate, lifemate, or crisis friendship is a relationship whose point is betrayal. Rather than helping us grow, these friends are bad for us.

Friendship's basic categories exist apart from any scale that might run from "best friend" to "distant acquaintance." Although some types of friendship lend themselves to intimacy better than others, any one of them can vary in closeness, importance, or strength of attachment. A musician might feel a stronger bond to a woman who plays in her quartet than she does to a friend from high school.

We don't all have one friendship from each category; in fact, few of us do. Some of us are more comfortable with certain sorts of friendships, some with others. Although I've focused on female friendship,

I suspect that both men and women are capable of having all types, but that some forms (allies and workmates and playmates) are more common among men and others (soulmates and nurturer and nurtured) among women.

Viewing friendships from this perspective helps explain why some last while others, just as close or even closer, seem to evaporate. By their very natures, some friendship varieties endure only a while, and others are fragile. Being able to recognize what type of friendship she's in helps a woman nurture it and will lessen the pain if it dies a natural death. It may also help her save the friendship by changing it from a temporary or fragile form to a more abiding one.

~ Soulmates ~

Within a few hours of meeting, Karen and I were friends. I was on a travel writing assignment; she worked for the tourism office of the small resort community I was visiting. Her job was to show me around, but I found her a lot more interesting than the sights. Karen's wicked wit would have made her entertaining company no matter what, but the attraction went beyond that.

Both of us kept remarking on how much we had in common. We were close to the same age and came from similar backgrounds, with Irish ancestors and retired corporate executive fathers. Karen had grown up in the Mohawk Valley, one city over from Rome, New York, where my father ran a wire and cable plant for two years of my childhood. She and I even looked similar; she was taller and thinner, but we both had auburn hair and fair skin prone to freckles.

What brought on the real rush of connectedness was our identical reaction to the current event everyone was talking about. We met in mid-December 1978. A month earlier, the Rev. Jim Jones, who'd brought his People's Temple flock from San Francisco to the jungles of Guyana, had led more than nine hundred of them in a mass suicide. On his orders, parents had fed their children cyanide-laced grape Kool-Aid and then had downed doses themselves. The media seemed unable to fathom how people could do that. Karen and I were horrified, but we understood their actions. Shortly before the mass suicide, some of the Jonestown men had shot and killed San Francisco Congressman Jim Ryan, who was investigating the cult at the request of its members' families. In the wake of that shoot-out, Jones had warned his followers that the U.S. government would be sending troops to take over the compound, and both children and parents would be tortured and killed.

Karen and I agreed that if someone truly believed such an atrocity was about to happen, a quick death by poison would seem attractive by comparison. Under such circumstances, a mother might kill her child, believing that she was protecting that child from a more agonizing fate.

This is amazing, I thought as we talked. For the first time in my life, I've found someone who sees and reacts to the world the way I do.

We were soulmates.

The soulmate bond is one of the deepest and one of the most fragile forms of female friendship. Because it's sparked by often uncanny similarity between two women, it provides one of friendship's greatest gifts—validation—abundantly and almost effortlessly. Soulmate relationships both require and reinforce narcissism: Loving ourselves, we seek someone like ourselves. And finding someone like ourselves boosts our self-love.

All women are outsiders, explained Houston psychotherapist Barbara Ellman. Many of us feel doubly so because of some exceptional quality. We may be from a tiny town in Arkansas or from an alcoholic family; we may have lost our mother to cancer when we were twelve. When we meet another woman who shares this characteristic, we feel an immediate bond similar to what we experience on encountering a fellow American in a foreign country. If we find that we also share opinions, responses, and tastes, the attraction quickly develops into intimacy.

In *Girlfriends: Invisible Bonds, Enduring Ties,* Carmen Renee Berry and Tamara Traeder described what they called a "soul connection":

> Sometimes you become so connected with a friend that other people mistake you for each other. Perhaps they have merely linked your names in their minds because you are with your friend frequently, or perhaps there is a more ephemeral reason: when two people share an intuitive link, other people unconsciously pick up that link.

Soulmates needn't have all the particulars of their lives in common. This kind of friendship is distinguished instead by the shared sense of seeing the world the same way and reacting similarly.

After retiring as director of a senior center, Pat Taylor, sixty-nine, embarked on a career as a bank trust officer in Evanston, Illinois. She told me about her soulmate friendship with a woman named Edith. "She could buy me anything any place in the world, and I know it would be something that I'd really like," Pat explained. "She came over for dinner one night. She walked in with this necklace on that was so good-looking that I said, 'Oh, how wonderful.' And she said, 'Well, it's yours. I got it for you a couple of years ago, but I wasn't sure you'd like it.' She made me take it in the bathroom and put it on, and of course, I loved it. I came back out, and she had another necklace on, so I believed her."

Pat and Edith were tuned in to each other on an almost other-worldly level. "Our lives are different and our backgrounds are different, but we're very much on the same wavelength," Pat explained.

What makes soulmate friendships fragile is that they're so dependent on the sense of the other as a second self. Any significant difference carries the destructive power of a major disillusionment. Fueled by long letters, occasional phone calls, and even less frequent visits, my closeness with Karen lasted through her marriage to a man who was longer on charm than on truthfulness. But instead of weakening our bond, her troubled marriage strengthened it; I'd recently extracted myself from a similar situation when we met. But the friendship began to cool when Karen took a more important, more visible job in tourism and married an old boyfriend in the business. Her letters, faxes, and conversations all carried the same refrain: "No one who hasn't lived in a small, politically sensitive resort community can possibly understand."

I hadn't, and so, try though I might, I didn't understand her situation. And if I couldn't possibly understand, we weren't soulmates anymore.

⚬ Lifemates ⚬

When Judythe Wilbur, a computer systems designer, told me, "My best friend now is a woman I met in Lamaze class," she echoed what

I'd heard from other mothers. The physically and emotionally de-manding experience of pregnancy and childbirth and the separation from adult company that comes with caring for a young child prompt women in similar circumstances to seek each other out. A woman who's been through it already and can give sage advice won't do; what we yearn for is one who's right where we are right now. What we want is a lifemate.

The lifemate form of friendship may be the most basic one for women. Certainly, it has served a survival function since the dawn of the species. In a hunter-gatherer culture, if a new mother couldn't produce enough milk, another lactating mother might be able to wet-nurse her infant. While one woman was out foraging for berries or setting traps for small game, other women looked after her children, along with their own. Emotional bonds would have strengthened an arrangement decreed by circumstances.

Like motherhood, starting college, beginning a new career, going through menopause, or experiencing any key milestone can bring on the desire for a lifemate. And lifemates are among the easiest friends to make. Whatever it is that we're doing, it usually puts us in contact with other women who are doing the same thing.

Of course, we don't single out for friendship every woman we meet who is roughly our age and in similar circumstances. Nursing a baby prompted Cathy Arden Kaats, a writer in suburban New York, to seek out lifemates. After her first lactating friend left town, she sought out another, but she quickly proved incompatible. Finally, Kaats found a comfortable fit, as she recounted in *New Woman*:

> We actually looked at each other when we spoke and talked to each other first before we talked to each other's baby. When we met one afternoon that week and laughed together, talked about life *before* baby as well as life *with* baby, I rejoiced.

Lifemates help women survive and thrive in their careers, too. At the time I interviewed Toni Dewey, sixty-eight, she had retired to Boulder, Colorado, where she was busy presiding over the launch of the Museum of Women in the West. Challenging though the project was, the demands didn't compare to what she'd faced back in Chicago as a vice president of Motorola, among the first women to hold such a position in a *Fortune* 500 corporation. "One of the things that was so difficult in those days was the isolation in the workplace," she told me. "It was being in a total wall-to-wall world of men from morning to night."

Having pushed open the doors of opportunity in the early 1970s, other executive and professional women in Chicago discovered the same loneliness once inside. No male executive, however sympathetic, could understand what it was like; no female middle manager, however bright and promising, could either. So Toni and a handful of her peers founded the Old Girls Club. Unlike the women's business and professional networks that came along later, its purpose was validation, not profit. Members exchanged war stories rather than business cards.

Lifemates both help us sort out our experiences and help us respond appropriately. "Mothers are always sharing problems about their children," said Sharon Itaya, a physician and mother of two. "Is my child normal? Is my child getting along, doing okay in school? In a way it's kind of neurotic, because we end up just talking to each other about all of our anxiety, but in another way, it's tremendously self-affirming to have somebody say, 'Oh, yes, I have the same problem.' "

Lifemate friends often have a knack for pitching in with practical help—just what we need just when we need it. If things don't work out between a thirty-year-old woman and her live-in boyfriend, another thirty-year-old single female knows to say, "I'll borrow my brother's pickup truck and be over at ten o'clock Saturday. We can go around to junk stores and Pier One and find stuff to replace what was Joe's." The woman enduring the breakup doesn't have to ask; the lifemate knows to offer.

In her work with young adults in New York City, social psychologist Susan Bodnar found that many friendships formed because of shared change. Nancy Uscher, a violist from New York, met Betty, a teacher from England, when they were living in Israel. Both women were thirty-two or thirty-three, only four months apart in age, and single. And each had just begun what she considered her first real, interesting job—Nancy as a musician for the Jerusalem Symphony, Betty as an instructor in cultural studies at a university in a nearby town. "We were both in the same place, not home, and were both there for a finite length of time," Nancy told me. "Meeting Betty was just a godsend."

Women of color have a special need for lifemate friendships. Beverly Tatum, who taught psychology and education at Mount Holyoke College, observed: "The value of relationships with women of the same background is that the mutual empathy which is growth producing is more likely to be present, because that person really does understand your experience."

The experience of poverty can bind women to one another even after the poverty itself has passed. "A lot of it is the similarities in our backgrounds," forty-year-old nurse Johey Crawford said about her friend Shaneesha. "I've been in the food stamp line; I've been a single mom, with the humiliation you went through. That was basically what started us talking. 'This is what it felt like to me. Well, you've been there.' It's like a secret club."

A kindred chemistry unites individuals marked by similar trauma years after the event. In *Motherless Daughters,* Hope Edelman, who was seventeen when her own mother died, wrote about the bond between women who've experienced early maternal loss:

> When four or five motherless women sit together in a room, . . . the camaraderie is nearly instantaneous. *Finally,* they say. *Others who understand.* Like veterans of the same war, the unmothered are drawn to each other.

Because they're built on common experiences, lifemate bonds tend to weaken or dissolve when the friends' lives diverge. "You have different friends at different times in your life," said forty-six-year-old Maria Dillig, who worked in a beer-bottling plant in Milwaukee. Both Maria and her once-close friend Edna Mae were in their mid-forties, divorced and remarried, with grown children. But unlike Maria, Edna Mae had started a new family with her second husband.

"Our lives differ now," Maria noted. "My husband and I can come and go as we please. He's retired. We have a trailer up north, and we like to travel, where Edna Mae, with her two kids, they take their vacation once a year."

↝ Companions in Crisis ↝

Crisis friendship is a bond forged by sharing the same stressful but temporary experience—something unusual and troubling enough that it makes us sure that no one who isn't going through it too could possibly empathize with us. If not for the extraordinary circumstances that bring them together, companions in crisis might never notice each other, let alone become close friends.

At 9:02 on the morning of Wednesday, April 19, 1995, a van packed with explosives blew up on a downtown street in Oklahoma City, taking with it most of the Murrah Federal Building. Within forty-five minutes, Tina Fellows, then a twenty-six-year-old state park ranger, had volunteered with the Red Cross to provide logistical support to the rescue workers, mostly firefighters, risking their own lives to free the trapped and injured and to recover the remains of those not so fortunate. The 168 who died included retirees who'd been waiting in line at the Social Security office and children in the day-care center provided for federal employees.

Tina likened her eighty days as a full-time Red Cross volunteer to her service with the National Guard in the Gulf War. "You have to be friends during that time period," she said. "That person knows what's going on and how you're reacting to it. If you would have met that person on the street, you might not have ever thought of being their friend."

Tina normally lived on her family's farm about an hour from Oklahoma City, but the volunteer work demanded such long hours that the Red Cross put her up in a hotel near the bombing site. Almost immediately, Tina and her roommate, Angela Hillian, bonded. Fourteen months later, as I interviewed them together at an all-you-can-eat buffet restaurant along the interstate, they kept glancing at each other and nodding in obvious rapport, two women united despite their divergent backgrounds. Angela was a nanny five years Tina's junior. Her path had been rough and full of sharp turns: interrupted high school, a series of low-paying jobs. Tina's life had followed a more orderly course: a college degree in biology, a stint in the military, then a career as a park ranger. If not for the bombing, Tina and Angela probably wouldn't have met, or if they had, wouldn't have recognized each other as potential friends. But talking and crying together in their room after fourteen or fifteen hours of dealing with other people's tragedies forged a deep connection.

"We called it our debriefing period," Angela said. "We'd tell each other what was going on in our outside lives and what was going on right there, at headquarters, and what we thought about it. We shared a whole lot." Those late-night sessions relieved the stresses of each day enough to allow the two friends to face the next. "Otherwise, we might have gone crazy," Tina said.

During the day, they tried to help each other maintain emotional equilibrium, but the reality of the horror would break through unexpectedly. "We were making up the list of the victims, so we could get them any kind of aid that they were needing," Angela said, twisting a paper napkin. "I was reading the names for her to type into the computer, just name after name. I only got three-fourths of the way, and I lost it. I started bawling, realizing how many had actually lost their lives."

Describing experiences like these to family and outside friends was never as comforting or validating as discussing them with each other. Even Tina's mother, who'd always been understanding and supportive, couldn't understand. "With my other two friends, saying, 'Hey, look what I'm going through' wasn't working out," Tina said. "You have to develop a new friend, someone who shares the experience and knows what you've been through."

Crisis friendships become very close very fast. Two women meet in the waiting room of the intensive care unit, in a support group for people laid off by a corporate merger, in a high school gymnasium converted into a hurricane evacuation shelter. Immediately, they open up to each other, cry together, give each other practical help—looking after one another's children, cleaning up after the flood.

After studying the people who lived near Mount Saint Helens when it erupted violently in 1980, Janice Vermiglio-Smith concluded that the more support a victim of a natural disaster received from friends, the less anxiety and disruption that person experienced. But the crises most of us endure are more personal—the death of a parent, the loss of a job, the breakup of an important relationship. Existing friends can lend support, but not the same kind we can get from someone enduring a similar trauma right then.

"We both got divorced at the same time more or less, so we really got to be close," psychologist Jane Burka recalled of her friendship with Sheila, a university professor.

When I interviewed Jane, she and Sheila had been friends for twenty-one years. But many crisis friendships evaporate as suddenly as they begin. Speaking of their range of friendships, several of the women I interviewed said something like, "I don't know what happened to my friendship with Anne. We were so incredibly close, and now I never see her anymore."

What killed the friendship probably wasn't anything either woman did. It died because by their very nature, crisis friendships don't last. As the crisis passes, so do they.

Crisis friendships may go through the first six stages of development described in chapter 3—from attraction through testing—in a matter of days. They sprint in a few sentences from attraction to initiation to structuring (in this case, predetermined by the circumstances) and can race on to comfort in a couple of hours. When strengthening comes by way of a brief series of related extreme experiences, rather than a parade of less intense ones over months or years, a friendship can withstand tests that are related to the crisis and yet fail those that aren't. To companions in crisis, commitment, if it does come, is of the moment. As the emergency fades, the unspoken contract expires.

Like a ceramic dish snatched from the oven and plunged into cold water, a crisis friendship can crack if its environment suddenly shifts. We may be eager to put the unpleasant incident behind us, along with everything and everyone who reminds us of it. And while some women may be close and nurturing during an emergency, when the situation improves, they may withdraw, often because they're uncomfortable with intimacy. Finally, crises bring together people who otherwise might not socialize with each other. Once the emergency is over, differences in background and interests may get in the way. Lifemate friends require several qualities in common; crisis friends need only the crisis.

Crisis relationships differ from lifemate relationships in another way: The shared experience is short-lived—not one of life's predictable passages. Even if it results in a permanent change in our circumstances, once we adjust to it, that change is no longer a crisis. Losing a mother to illness is a crisis from the terminal prognosis until a few weeks after the funeral. After that, missing her becomes a sad fact of daily existence.

For the right individuals in the right circumstances, a friendship begun in crisis can mellow into a lifemate bond. The test of whether Tina's and Angela's friendship would endure came two months after the bombing when Tina's brother died of heart disease. "Angie took care of me," she explained. "She was there from the time I found out."

One act of intuitive kindness touched Tina particularly. "She was there with me when I ordered the flowers," Tina told me. "I went to buy a great big heart for my brother made out of red carnations. But I couldn't afford the carnations, so I got yellow mums."

Later, Angela persuaded the florist to substitute the flowers Tina had wanted, but she kept it to herself. "At the funeral home, I'm just sitting there, and in comes the delivery guy with a heart done in these red carnations," Tina recalled.

She burst into tears.

"Nobody else understood why I was crying," Tina continued. "I knew then that she was going to be my friend forever."

✤ Nurturer and Nurtured ✤

Unlike crisis friendships, nurturer-and-nurtured friendships develop between two women in different situations: One needs support, and the other is moved to give it. Any close female friendship involves nurturing by both parties. What distinguishes these particular friendships is that nurturing is the essence of the bond.

On the surface, caregiver friendships may seem to be one way, but a closer look reveals a complex web of reciprocity. It is obvious what the nurtured partner gets from this kind of friendship. The nurturer, on the other hand, receives the ego boost that comes with being needed and being affirmed as capable. Nurturer-and-nurtured friendships give women the opportunity to be good mothers—and good daughters.

Some women can't tolerate nurturer-and-nurtured friendships. Others need to be on one end or another of this dynamic throughout their lives. "I seem to attract people that for one reason or another I have to protect," Renee Asofsky told me. "It's my role."

In a nurturer-and-nurtured friendship, both parties may confide in each other about their lives and feelings, but this intimacy has one important limitation: Although the nurturer or rescuer may have troubles of her own, she can never reveal that she feels emotionally weak. Indeed, when she's with her friend, she may always feel strong and confident, no matter how she feels when they're apart.

When Fran decided to move from New Jersey to a warmer climate, one of the first friends she made in Florida was Suzanne. Fran and her husband had hired a builder to make modifications to the house they were buying. Suzanne, his girlfriend, spent a lot of time at the work site. Despite the eighteen-year difference in their ages, Fran liked her immediately, but the friendship really deepened when Suzanne started having trouble with her boyfriend, who was physically and emotionally abusive. Fran spent endless hours listening to Suzanne's woes, urging her to leave him, reminding her that there were other guys out there.

Then Fran found a lump in her breast. "I told her, 'I think I have breast cancer; I've got to go have it biopsied,' " Fran recalled. "And she said, 'Oh, that's too bad. It's probably not.' "

Rather than calling right after the biopsy, Suzanne waited two weeks. Fran continued: "She said, 'How did you make out? You just had the lump removed?' I said, 'No, I've had a breast removed.' And she said, 'I just thought it was a lump.' This is how concerned she was about me. Did this hurt? Oh, big time!"

Given the form of their friendship, it couldn't survive the reversal of roles.

"I became the nurturee," Fran said. "I was in a bind. But she was absent. Did she call me after that? No."

Although Suzanne may have abandoned her when breast cancer struck, Fran had another friend, Dolores, who poured on the practical, emotional, and even spiritual support. As Fran first described Dolores and how she'd come through in a pinch, I pegged their relationship for a strong nurturer-and-nurtured bond, with good potential (given Fran's friendship style) for role reversal down the road. But a year later, I learned that once Fran's cancer went into remission, so did her relationship with Dolores.

When Fran realized that the lump she'd noticed in her breast could be life-threatening, Dolores was the first person she told. "She came right over," Fran recalled. "And she said, 'I'm gonna be here until you contact the surgeon. I will take you to the doctor, but you're going to call *right now*.' And I did."

Dolores phoned daily for updates on Fran's physical condition and state of mind. Instead of withdrawing in the face of Fran's need, she drew closer. Any help Fran asked for, Dolores gave enthusiastically.

"She had her church praying for me," Fran said. "It was the first time in my life that I really felt the power of someone else's prayer. I felt comfortable, and I felt safe."

But two years after the cancer diagnosis, this important relationship had cooled. Now that Fran's cancer was in remission and her life was back to a pleasant normal, Dolores, so close and constant when Fran had needed her so badly, had withdrawn.

The relationship faded not because of anything Fran did or didn't do, but because she stopped being needy. Although Fran recognized it only in retrospect, Dolores was a foul-weather friend—a distortion of the nurturer-nurtured bond. True nurturer friends provide emotional or practical help when needed, but like good mothers they also support and celebrate their friends' efforts to develop strength and independence.

Foul-weather friends, on the other hand, only care about other women when they're in trouble. They can't join in on the good times. The need to dominate turns some women into foul-weather friends. Others develop this twisted relational pattern because envy keeps them from being able to enjoy anyone else's good fortune.

In her book *The Best of Friends, the Worst of Enemies,* Eva Margolies described a typical foul-weather friendship: Jackie, who had left a destructive marriage, initially found her friend Donna's solicitude comforting. But within a few months, she began to feel smothered. When Jackie mentioned that she was considering going into business for herself, Donna urged her to hold on to her secure job instead. When Jackie announced that she was ready to start dating seriously, Donna warned her that she was too emotionally vulnerable. Margolies observed: "The more time that passed, the more Donna started looking like a doting mother rather than a friend."

The danger of foul-weather friends is that they encourage us to focus on our troubles in order to stay in the relationship. Instead of fostering our growth, such relationships inhibit it.

Just as a foul-weather friendship can damage the person on the receiving end, another destructive cousin of the nurturer-and-nurtured form threatens the caregiver. Even the best nurturers can be sucked into a draining friendship. A draining friend's well of need can never be filled—nonetheless, she expects her friend to fill it. As the friendship progresses, the needy friend becomes needier. In a healthy nurturing relationship, by contrast, the nurtured friend's needs remain fairly constant; she may even become stronger thanks to her friend's support.

Writing anonymously, one woman told *Good Housekeeping*'s "My Problem" department how her time was monopolized by three draining friends. She listened patiently to their problems, even to the detriment of her relationships with her husband and her daughter. In addition to their disregard for her own feelings and obligations, these draining friends shared one characteristic: Their lives never improved. The woman finally concluded:

> [T]hey were all in the same spot, still telling me the same complaints as before. I realized they were just using me as a sounding board, a sympathetic ear willing to listen as they played their "tapes" over and over again.

Getting sucked into a draining friendship is easy. Few things are more seductive than having someone come to us for help and advice. The lure of instant validation can be almost irresistible. In that pleasant glow, we let the initiator of the friendship set up its one-sided structure—all take on her part, all give on ours.

If draining friendships seem to be increasingly common, it may be because of what Janice Raymond, author of *A Passion for Friends,* called "therapism." This "tyranny of feelings" includes the tendency some women have to take the relationship between patient and psychotherapist as the model for any female bond. Of course, good female friendship *is* therapeutic, both directly and indirectly. But expecting a friend to double as a psychotherapist is a burden both to her and to the relationship.

At first glance, the friend being drained may appear to be in the stronger position, but in reality, the needy woman dominates the relationship. "Complaining all the time is a controlling kind of thing," observed Albuquerque artist Felice Locano.

Anita's friendship with Cleo didn't start out as draining. They met through the P.T.A. in 1976, when both were in their mid-twenties and had seven-year-old daughters. They were soulmates as well as lifemates. "I would be thinking something really lousy. She would say it," Anita explained. "We were really, really close. Mostly, we would sit around and talk."

Then, when both women's children were on the verge of independence, the friendship changed. With her youngest in high school, Anita enrolled in classes to finish her B.A. and went back to work in her husband's retail operation. She managed the grocery store, and he ran the seafood shop across the street.

"Cleo was having problems with her husband, big problems," Anita explained. "They were talking about getting divorced, and she got all upset that I couldn't be there for her all the time, because I was working."

Cleo had been married to Andy, an angry, unsupportive, and occasionally violent man, for two decades. Anita had listened to the same complaints for years, but Cleo never took action. The more attention and compassion Anita gave her, the more Cleo seemed to need. Despite the talk of divorce, she stayed in the marriage and even allowed Andy to talk her out of going back to school for additional nurse's training.

Draining friends may seem pathetic on the surface, but underneath, they are narcissists who control their close relationships by jealously keeping the attention focused on themselves and their problems. And as long as they get that attention, drainers can avoid making the changes that would improve their lives.

Eventually, like Anita, the nurturer in a draining friendship may pull out of the relationship, confirming the needy one's worst fear—that she'll be abandoned. But a caretaker may be so determined to be a "good mother," so bad at establishing limits, or so intimidated by emotional blackmail that she remains in the friendship to her own detriment. Drained by demands she can't possibly meet, she may neglect other, more rewarding relationships and sink into depression herself.

Another sort of draining occurs when one woman tries to usurp the identity of her friend. Mimicry and adulation replace empathy and reciprocity. The bond may be intense, but it ultimately exhausts itself, not to mention diminishes the friend being imitated. Imitating a friend's admired qualities is healthy; attempting to *become* her isn't.

One of the women Joan Berzoff interviewed for her dissertation on valued female friendships described such a case of blurred boundaries:

I came to love her obsessively. . . . She thought I was just fantastic, creative, wonderful, and beautiful . . . I got into a position of being so obligated to her that I lost my strong sense of self.

Flattered by the ultimate compliment—"I want to be you"—the woman no longer felt she owned the very qualities that her friend so admired. She saw them in that adoring mirror, but she couldn't find them in herself.

⋈ Workmates and Playmates ⋈

The variety of woman-to-woman friendship that comes closest to traditional male friendship is the bond formed around enjoying the same activity. It doesn't matter whether the friends run together, are bridge partners, join each other every June for a trip somewhere exotic, or collaborate on creating advertising campaigns or designs for office buildings. The relationship offers a similar blend of pleasure and affirmation.

"When you want to play tennis, you need to have somebody to play tennis with," said Kim, a forty-eight-year-old Chinese-American economist. Her favorite partner was another Asian woman, a top player who tied for club champion. They "clicked" from the first time they played, Kim told me.

Kim relished the challenge of her partner's skill, enjoyed their shared enthusiasm for the game, and liked her company. But during the whole summer, they saw each other only once off the courts, for a lunch date that Kim's partner initiated.

Focusing conversation on the game and taking pleasure in having companions with whom to share it fit Kim's relational style. Intimate disclosure made her uncomfortable. "I guess I do put up this invisible barrier, this little space around me, where I don't want you to intrude," Kim explained. "I have certain reservations about how much I want to give of myself."

Different people prefer different types of friendship. Women who, like Kim, might describe themselves as reserved or private, often favor relationships based on their pet pursuits. Cheering for the same team, discussing politics, sailing offshore, reading contemporary German novels, or practicing law—any mutually enjoyed activity can provide the basis for the bond.

Take shopping.

"I *love* shopping," said retired Motorola corporate vice president Toni Dewey, whose favorite shopping friend, Maureen, had been a top editor at one of Chicago's two major newspapers. "I love clothes—not so much for the buying as for the theater of it all. Some of the best times I've had have been shopping days."

First thing Saturday morning, Toni and Maureen would hit the shops. Maureen knew the best ones—not just the high-profile merchants along Michigan Avenue, but the smaller, out-of-the-way boutiques. And her foraging skills complemented Toni's. "Maureen has a great eye, different from mine," Toni explained.

Working for Sears in Queens, New York, Cheryl James and Sandi Denton shared a taste for funky music and a distaste for their telemarketing jobs, so they quit and paired up as Salt-N-Pepa, a phenomenally feminist duo in the otherwise misogynistic landscape of rap. When *Bazaar* contributor James Servin caught up with them three successful albums later, the two were still fast friends, sharing the exhilaration and stress of performing before packed arenas night after night. Servin wrote:

> [T]he thing that drives the S-N-P machine is still the tight friendship between the two women. . . . As they walk . . . to their trailer, laughing and holding hands, there's a sense of what they must have been like before all the screaming crowds and grueling schedules.

Women needn't be partners or even work for the same employer for a workmate bond to form. "Dora also works in health care," Marguerite Salmon, a thirty-five-year-old case manager at a San Francisco medical clinic told me. "I can say, 'I had this client today and blah, blah, blah,' and she'll know exactly what I'm talking about. It's nice not having to translate."

The two friends were able to give each other this support and perspective even though they were personally dissimilar. "We have cultural and racial differences; we have style differences," Marguerite noted. "She is much more traditional than I am. She's African-American. Dora is really interested in job stability, hooking up her retirement, kind of a safe person. I'm more of a loose cannon, a risk taker."

To be a real friendship, a workmate or playmate relationship must provide more than just a partner in a pursuit that is impossible, impractical, or simply less fun alone. It must support our development and allow us to express ourselves, at least where that activity is concerned.

Meeting women in similar fields through civic clubs, professional and academic societies, and business networking groups can lead to workmate relationships, provided the women involved are willing to discuss how they feel about what they do, rather than simply promote themselves to each other.

"To know that there are other women who struggle with these things makes an enormous difference," said Boston area psychiatrist Irene Stiver. "Of course, these women would connect more effectively if they could show more vulnerability, if they were able to say, 'You know, I'm scared to death; I have this new venture, and I'm really terrified that it's not going to work,' and somebody else could say, 'I've been there.' "

The more the relationship acts as a catalyst for mutual growth, the better it is likely to make us feel, and the stronger the bond itself is likely to be. Workmates and playmates offer criticism, but they offer it in ways that don't bruise each other's egos. "That lamp's gorgeous, but I think it's too big for the end table you have in mind," one woman might say to her shopping friend. Another might tell her tennis partner: "You were hitting the ball a little high on your backhand today. Maybe you should check your grip."

Such friendships can teach us to compete with people we like, to deal with the disappointment of defeat, and to channel our aggressive impulses so that they don't destroy relationships. This is one friendship lesson that women can learn from men.

Unlike most playmate or workmate friendships between men, these relationships among women tend to move to a closer level. When Debbie Maury, a lawyer in Greensboro, North Carolina, met Paula, they were thirteen and sixteen, respectively, with a shared passion for horses. Thirty years later, they still enjoyed riding together, but they also had become lifelong confidantes.

The transition from sharing activities to sharing our unguarded selves is generally gradual. My friend Maida Asofsky and I began our relationship literally as running buddies. Together, we could take a scenic greenbelt trail that would have been risky for a woman alone. Meeting before dawn three times a week, to pass the miles we began talking about current events, plays and operas, travel, restaurants, and books. Once we established common ground, our conversations shifted to the personal. Eventually, Maida became one of my closest friends.

A workmate or playmate friendship can be relatively casual, or it can be profound. What makes it endure in its form is that the pleasure of the shared activity remains a central element.

Enabling friendships are the evil twin of workmate-playmate bonds. When we share a healthy and enjoyable activity with a friend, we tend to engage in it more often than we would otherwise. That increased frequency combined with social reinforcement helps us become more physically fit, better bridge players, or more discerning judges of food and wine.

Unfortunately, the same dynamic comes into play if we share an unhealthy compulsion with a companion. Enabling friends encourage us to drink, spend, or gamble to excess. They allow us to remain in denial about our addictions; we can look at each other and think, I'm not drinking any more than she is, so I must be drinking normally. Worst of all, when sober reality does break through and we decide to straighten up, an enabling friend will try to tempt and wheedle us back into our destructive behavior, not just to keep from losing the companionship but also to avoid facing what she's doing to herself. When her friend turns her own life around, an enabler must either join her or pull back from the friendship.

Sharing a self-destructive experience occasionally doesn't make a friendship an enabling one. But when those activities are the focus of the friendship, when the closest and best feelings come when the two friends are indulging in the behavior together or reliving it uncritically, then it is.

When I was in my mid-twenties, I had a friend my age who worked in the office next to mine and had a similar job editing teacher's manuals. Zoë had style, brains, and an outrageous sense of humor; she also had a well-developed taste for expensive clothes. By the time we met, I was already spending a disproportionate percentage of my modest salary on my wardrobe. Zoë let me in on a dangerous secret: You could develop a favored-customer relationship with a salesclerk, so that when she spotted something she thought you'd like, she'd hold it for you. My office phone began ringing with calls from the designer salon of a local department store and from Zoë's favorite boutique, neither of which I could afford on my salary. Since both lay within a few blocks of our office building, we visited them together at lunch. Saturdays, we'd hit the malls.

We egged each other on. If I liked a skirt that came in brown and navy, Zoë would say, "Why not buy both?" If she spotted a pair of fuchsia and electric blue platform pumps with a price tag half her weekly paycheck, I'd tell her, "Get them. Otherwise, you'll kick yourself later," even though I knew they went with only one dress she owned. We both overspent recklessly, especially when we were together. By taking each other as benchmarks, we were able to continue this self-destructive pattern, conning each other, and ourselves, into considering it normal behavior.

It was too bad, not just because we were accumulating debt when we should have been laying down foundations for financial independence, but also because we had better material on which to build our friendship. If we'd concentrated on being workmates, we could have helped each other move on from our boring editing jobs to the magazine writing to which we both aspired. If we'd focused on our lifemate potential, we might have helped each other sort out our family and romantic relationships. We could have just had fun together, as playmates, cooking spaghetti dinners or watching old movies, spending a hundredth of what we did. Instead, we structured our relationship around our mutual addiction. After Zoë moved to another city, we lost touch.

An enabler friendship can be intimate. Studying young adults who used illegal drugs regularly, psychologists Denise Kandel and Mark Davies found that on average their friendships were at least as close as those enjoyed by nonusers, but that their friends tended to be involved in the same deviant lifestyle. This was both a matter of selection and of influence: Drug users sought out each other as friends; and as friends, they encouraged each other's drug use. As I read the Kandel and Davis paper in the journal *Criminology,* I recognized that they were describing the dynamic that had operated between Zoë and me. We'd given each other affirmation, and like all affirmation, it had felt good. But we had affirmed each other's weaknesses, not our strengths.

An enabler bond also can form around a shared situation that limits growth. Take two women in abusive marriages, each encouraging the other to stick it out by calling on misguided notions of loyalty or persuading the other that she'll never be able to support herself.

In *Friendships Between Women,* Irish sociologist Pat O'Connor discussed studies that explored how some women use friendships to maintain separation between social classes. To the extent that this restricts a woman's ability to relate to others from different backgrounds or discourages her from pursuing the education she needs to develop her potential, these, too, are enabling friendships.

Another, though rarer, type of destructive relationship can initially look and feel like a workmate and playmate friendship or even a lifemate or soulmate bond. Although women engage in far fewer of these betrayer relationships than myth has it, they do exist. These are truly false friendships—not friendships hobbled by neuroses, but a nasty pattern of power plays masquerading as friendship. Linda Tripp's misalliance with Monica Lewinsky is merely the most notorious recent example.

Early in her career, Matilda, a program analyst, shared many intimate revelations with a coworker she thought to be a friend. When a higher position opened up, the coworker lied about Matilda to their supervisor. Because the two women appeared to be friends, the supervisor believed the betrayer. Many years later, at age forty-seven, it was clear to Matilda that the coworker had entered into the "friendship" primarily to gain an advantage over her. "It hurts," she told me. "So I've toughened."

Treacherous "friends" build themselves up by diminishing others. They enter into close relationships with other women in order to secure an advantage over them.

In a weak or angry moment, a true friend may betray another—at the time, that promotion seems more important than anything else in her life or her friend's husband really is devastatingly seductive or she's had a couple of drinks, and that story told in confidence seems too good to keep to herself. A treacherous "friend" makes a habit of this kind of betrayal; everything else in the relationship is bait for the trap.

⭯ Allies ⭯

Physician Sharon Itaya said wistfully: "There was a feeling of camaraderie in college and medical school that sustained my friendships with some women for a long time—having big issues, like the war for safety and health, uniting with the poor people and the oppressed whoever against whomever. There was always a sense of finding common political enemies and political goals—this common purpose of fighting the bad guys in the street."

Few bonds are as affirming as those between women working for a cause they both care about deeply. And these friendships thrive between women fighting to make abortion illegal just as they flourish in pro-choice feminist groups. What distinguishes these friendships from the crisis variety is that the shared effort lasts longer and involves something bigger than the two women and their families.

Paradoxically, this the-enemy-of-my-enemy-is-my-friend bond is both one of friendship's strongest and one of its most fragile forms. Solidarity can feel like love. Commitment to a shared cause can prompt women to risk economic disaster, physical injury, jail, and even death for their allies. But their relationship may strain or even shatter because they disagree on some fine point of ideology or strategy.

Furthermore, friendships among allies can survive power tussles and honest disagreements over approach only to evaporate once the goal has been reached or the enemy vanquished. This isn't much danger with some causes; a mutual commitment to global environmentalism can last a lifetime. But winning shorter campaigns—say, defeating a school board proposal—may soon leave allies with nothing to share, at least nothing that equals the intensity of that shared cause. Often the friendship simply fades as life circumstances change.

Women of color have a special need for allies, both within their own ethnic group and with members of the dominant culture. "In my own experience, if I have a friendship with someone whom I consider to be a white ally, there are things that that person will do which will make life easier for me," said Prof. Beverly Tatum. Tatum recalled being part of a statewide meeting including several hundred people. Participants were asked to review some documents to be used throughout Massachusetts. Tatum quickly noted that these failed to address ethnicity or racial diversity.

To discuss the documents, the participants broke into groups of five or six. Tatum found herself in one that included two white acquaintances whom she knew shared her perspective. When the time came to make suggestions and pose questions to the entire meeting, she left that to the two like-minded white members of her group.

"When a black person stands up and says, 'How come there's no reference to issues of racial diversity in any of these materials?,' it's very easy for other people to dismiss it," she said. "When a white person stands up and says, 'How come we're not addressing this issue?' it legitimizes it in the eyes of the other white people. That is the role of the ally. If you have a friend who understands that role, then that person can do the appropriate thing."

Allies needn't be lifemates. They can be decades apart in age, come from dramatically dissimilar backgrounds, and have completely different tastes and interests—aside from the cause that brings them together. Once the battle is over, what separates the women can become more significant than what united them, unless there's some other basis on which they can reformat their friendship.

Because they already share important values, allies may become soulmates. Johey Crawford, a forty-year-old nurse, and Faith Einerson, a fifty-one-year-old computer systems manager, met in the mid-1970s in Toledo. Working in tandem leading consciousness-raising groups, they discovered links beyond their devotion to the women's movement.

"It was like a series of giant clicks," Johey said. "It was finding out that of all the people I've ever met in my life, she is the most a part of my spiritual being."

On one level, their relationship centered on their political beliefs; on another, it centered on the validation and emotional support they gave each other as activists, as mothers, as women. Nine years before our interview, Faith had moved to Texas to take care of her aging mother. Strengthened, tested, and restructured to a soulmate bond, the friendship held firm. Although they'd visited each other several times, for the most part they sustained their relationship through phone calls, and relatively infrequent ones at that.

"Since she's been gone, I've had acquaintances but nobody I would call a friend until about the last year and a half," Johey said. "I think it was because I was always looking for somebody just like her. I wanted another Faith, exactly."

⤳ Complementary Opposites ⤳

"Angela works in the fashion industry, and she is the opposite of me," Carol Edgar told me. "When we go out, I feel like I'm silver and she's gold. She's glamorous in a very open way, and I lean more toward understatement. If I'm yin, she's yang. We're very, very different; yet we complement each other very well. What I love about Angela is the differences, the differentness that she brings to our friendship."

Such friendships between apparent opposites give women the opportunity to sample vicariously lives very different from their own. They extend the realm of our experience. That's one reason adolescents seek out pen pals and E-mail correspondents in other countries. But in addition to enabling teenagers to learn what it's like to live in, say, Hong Kong versus Atlanta, such relationships also allow them to explore the universal components of growing up. What sets us apart from each other throws what we have in common into high relief.

Complementary opposites are some of the most intellectually stimulating friends women can have. Growing up in a Brooklyn neighborhood of Eastern European Jewish immigrants, Carol Safran was drawn to individuals from different backgrounds. "I always sought out Christians and Muslims," she said. "If I could find a Hindu, boy that was exciting. I finally did in graduate school."

Although the appeal lies in the differences between the two friends, for complementary opposite friendships to work, the two women have to share some traits—temperament, taste, education, early family experience, or some other point of connection. Carol encountered her Hindu friend in a graduate school course, not at a bus stop.

I met my friend Marta Benaglio when I was working on a magazine story in Veracruz, Mexico. Except for a brief sojourn to New York for college, she'd lived in Veracruz all her life. Marta's father had been a doctor; she was a writer. We were no more than a few years apart in age. We gave each other glimpses into what our lives would have been like had we been born into families of the same socioeconomic status but in our different respective countries. It was the blend of differences and similarities that made our friendship work.

Along with some shared traits, complementary opposite friendships must include two other ingredients: First, the friends must be willing to discuss their differences openly. Second, they must feel comfortable with and respect the distinctions that made the friendship exciting in the first place.

Like exotic spices artfully blended, ethnic differences seasoned the friendship between African-American writer Audrey Edwards, editor at large for *Essence,* and her white college roommate. Edwards described the twenty-five-year relationship for the readers of the *New York Times Magazine*:

> As roommates, we shared not just living space but perspectives, culture and race secrets. . . . [W]e've been true and honest friends long enough to know that the grass is never really greener on the other side but rather, like us, just differently shaded.

If we're reasonably happy with our lives, complementary opposite friendships may actually affirm our choices. For example, I interviewed a happily married mother of two who found herself becoming increasingly close to two single women, both with active and turbulent sex lives. Participating vicariously in her confidantes' romantic adventures relieved the restlessness and desire for escape the married woman sometimes experienced; it also reminded her of the loneliness, anxiety, and grief her single friends felt when their short-term love affairs ended. The single women, for their part, heard about the financial worries, time constraints, and unending responsibilities burdening the mother, as well as the sense of comfort, emotional support, and continuity she got from a committed relationship with a man.

✨ Mentor and Protégée ✨

Elberta James, eighty-four, and Jody Miller, forty-seven, lived three blocks from each other in Eugene, Oregon. Despite the difference in their ages—or maybe because of it—they were close friends. "We talk about some of the things that she doesn't even talk to her mother about," Elberta mused.

Most forms of friendship assume equality. But some women bond because one is more experienced or successful and the other offers validation by being eager to learn and eager to imitate. Typically, the younger or less powerful woman chooses the mentor, rather than the other way around. When social psychologist Priscilla Roberts studied four famous female mentor-protégée friendships, she found that these relationships helped the protégée clarify her occupational dream, introduced her to the world of that occupation, compensated for lacks in the marriage of either partner, and provided the companionship, support, loyalty, and trust common to all varieties of friendship.

Mentor-protégée relationships are most obvious as such when they occur on the job, but in that setting they may be prevented from developing into full friendships. A woman embarking on a new career, having a first child, or moving to a new city often will seek out another woman who has mastered the ropes and is eager to share what she knows. Both nurture and support each other, but they do so in different ways. The protégée receives practical help and the verification that she has capabilities worth developing. The mentor enjoys the boost to self-esteem that comes with being admired and emulated.

Mentoring is a timeless tradition. Before written history and formal schools, it was the way knowledge, skills, and advice were passed on. In her dissertation, sociologist Lee Campbell observed, "[N]ot only have women's relationships often had mentoring elements but women's shared past continues to influence mentoring today." Campbell went on to identify personal history, particularly a woman's relationship with her mother, as "a central influence" on the character of her mentor-protégée relationships.

In fact, being a mentor or a protégée gives us a chance to continue the positive aspects of our mother-daughter relationships and to work through the negative ones—a process developmental psychologist Joan Berzoff has identified as one of the ways female friendship helps women develop. "Women do what mothers have traditionally done," she told me. "They teach each other how to take care of children. There's a whole teaching component to women's friendships."

Many cross-generational female friendships fit this pattern. Some of the deepest, most rewarding mentor-protégée bonds form between middle-aged and elderly women, like the characters played by Kathy Bates and Jessica Tandy in the movie *Fried Green Tomatoes*. But a younger woman or a peer can serve as a mentor if she has more experience.

When Erin Jo Jurow's husband, Martin, who co-produced the film

Terms of Endearment, developed Parkinson's disease, her long-standing friend Ruth Altshuler, three years her junior and already a blend of lifemate and playmate, added the role of mentor. Ruth's first husband had struggled with the same ailment for five years.

"Erin Jo and I were in New York two weeks ago," Ruth told me over our breakfast interview. "I thought, She has not left Martin one night in two years. So I called and I said, 'Let's go to New York for two days.' I knew enough to know she needed three nights off. I don't know that I would have known that if I hadn't been there myself."

The poignant side of mentor-protégée relationships is that no matter how close they are, they don't often last. If the protégée proves disappointing or disloyal, the mentor will abandon her. But if the protégée is worthy of the other woman's nurturing and modeling, she eventually will outgrow it. However, provided the mentor is willing to relinquish the power of her superior position, the relationship may evolve into another form of friendship. Because women tend to care more about connecting than they do about dominating, woman-to-woman mentorships (unlike those that involve at least one man) have a fluid quality that enables them to make this transition.

ᰃ History Friends ᰃ

Some friendships are strong and close simply because they've endured so long. These relationships that we start early in life and carry with us are irreplaceable. If a thirty-year-old woman has remained in touch with a playmate from elementary school, they feel a special bond of affection and stability. No one else now in her life was there when she won the broad jump in second grade or transformed the kitchen into a candidate for disaster relief while trying to bake a birthday cake for her mother.

When Colorado-reared psychologist Nancy Busch studied friendships among women in and around New York, she was surprised to find so many long-standing bonds among women leading very different lives. "People just don't move away from this area, so their friendships are often with their girlfriends from high school or college," Busch explained. "They may have taken very different career paths, in the larger sense, like marriage and motherhood. I'm amazed that their friendships can continue. New York has taught me a lot about the longevity of friendships and the history of friendships being important."

Even though history friends may not have much in common with each other as adults and might not even become friends if they were to meet for the first time now, the long duration of a history relationship is its own glue. In her mid-forties, Beth, a writer for national magazines and the author of several books, still kept in touch with Maria Dillig, her friend since elementary school. I interviewed Beth and Maria separately—Beth in her house in an affluent Houston suburb, Maria in her more modest home in an older middle-income neighborhood in Milwaukee.

"We really have very little in common except our past," Beth told me. "She's putting caps on bottles in a brewery. But I always look forward to seeing her when I go home to Milwaukee. When we get together, it's almost as if no time has elapsed."

That quality of being able to pick up right where we left off that Beth and so many other women I interviewed mentioned is a major, though not exclusive, feature of history friendships. So is the recognition that as witnesses to each other's pasts, we affirm the reality of who we were in the face of who we have become.

"Beth lived right around the block from me," Maria recalled. "We went to kindergarten together. We went to catechism class together. We made our First Communion together. Beth had this little funky haircut. I think her mom had just cut her hair right before the Communion, and it was really short."

Maria's family fascinated Beth as a child. "Maria's parents are from Germany," she explained. "So they did a lot of Old World things. Like, I'd go over to the house and her mom would have the dumplings on the stove kind of steeping in broth. I really thought her parents were pretty exotic."

Throughout elementary school, from First Communion to first crushes, the two girls were inseparable. Just before the seventh grade, Beth's family moved a few miles away, which put her in a different junior high and high school. "We didn't see each other that much until we were seventeen or eighteen," Maria said. "I had gotten married, and she was planning to get married. Then we both wound up in the hospital together having our kids. We stayed up until four in the morning. Our sleeping pills wore off. The nurses couldn't find us. We had a good time. We were laughing and joking all night."

Having babies the same age cemented the already strong lifemate bond. "We saw each other quite a bit," Maria told me. "We did things with the kids and took the kids with us when we went someplace. A lot of times, I'd come over and she'd immediately make chocolate chip cookies and let the kids help her. She was just really good with kids. A lot of times, if I had a problem, I would go over there and talk to her. She always knew what to say and how to make you feel better."

The great gift of history friendship is its affirmation of our own sense of continuity. Twenty years before our interview, Beth had moved to Houston. Even though that meant that the two old friends saw each other in person only once a year when Beth went back to Milwaukee to visit her parents, and even though they were no longer lifemates, the sense of being custodians of each other's histories made the relationship irreplaceable.

"I never feel as if I have to explain anything to Maria," Beth said. "If I talk about something with a friend I've made since moving to Houston, I might say, 'That drives me crazy, and it reminds me of when I was twelve years old.' Maria was there when I was twelve years old."

Because we generally have a say in how much contact we have with cousins, we can develop genuine friendships with them, uncompli- cated by the multiple bonds that tie us to closer family. And since we usually meet our cousins early, they tend to become history friends. At forty-seven Sharon Goodwin, who grew up in a refinery town south of Houston, remembered summers with an Alabama cousin. "We did a lot of things together growing up," Sharon said. "We laugh about when her stepmother moved out and took pretty much everything they had. We would take turns sitting on a blanket and pulling each other through the house, because they had these wood floors and you could just slide all over."

History friendships are double-edged: A friend from an earlier era of our lives helps us hold on to that reality, but she also views us through the screen of that past. As sociologist Lillian Rubin observed: "Most people who see old friends from time to time complain that, like family, these friends tend to see them as they were rather than as they are becoming. . . ."

Nancy Nadler, director of training for a high-tech corporation in California's Silicon Valley, met Lois and Trudy when they were all sixth-graders in Phoenix. Although they hadn't lived in the same city since they were sixteen, they kept their history friendship alive through regular phone calls and annual visits. But the friendship almost self-destructed four years before I interviewed Nancy.

To celebrate Lois's fortieth birthday, the three women planned a weekend together at an inn on the California coast. Nancy would meet Lois and Trudy at the San Francisco airport, and they'd drive down together to Carmel.

Trudy was married, Lois was single, and neither had children. Nancy and her husband and three-year-old son were in the process of moving. "Instead of moving the week before, we ended up moving the weekend I was going to be gone," Nancy explained. "On top of that, my little boy had had strep throat the week before, so I got behind in what I had committed to do. When Lois and Trudy called me the night before, I said, 'I'm going to need a couple of hours. How about if you guys come and help me finish up?' And they said no.

"The problem with them is they haven't seen my adult competence. They think of me as a little kid who takes twice as long as I should to do anything. I was angry at them the whole weekend. We had a terrible time. I felt like they had let me down, and they felt like I had let them down."

Fortunately, the three got over it. When we lose a history friend, we lose more than a companion; we lose a part of our past. Writing about the death of a close friend she had known since infancy, a friend she'd envisioned rocking in tandem with her on a sunny porch in old age, Mary Cantwell wrote in the *New York Times Magazine:*

> Today I can scarcely bear the terrible singularity of my memories. No one but I knows what it was to be chased around a bandstand on an autumn afternoon by two little boys bent on kissing us. . . . No one but I remembers how at midnight after lobster dinners we would surreptitiously hurl the empty shells into the harbor. Returning them, we intoned, "to the deep whence they come." Yes, I remember. Sometimes I even laugh. But I laugh alone . . .

History friends may exasperate us; they may embarrass us; they may even shake our confidence by making us painfully aware of the gawky girl we once were. Nonetheless, nothing can replace a close friendship cultivated and carried throughout life. Young women who don't recognize what a treasure such friends can be often find themselves at midlife wishing wistfully for what they let slip away. Their pain may be more muted than Cantwell's, but behind her eloquently expressed grief shines the remembered joy of that connection.

⤳ Ensemble Friends ⤳

Sometimes four or five women become friends with each other without any two of them being close separately. They meet often, do things together, and share their feelings, but not one-on-one.

In group friendships women usually take on functions or characteristics, as they do in families. One will always suggest outrageous adventures; another will be the perennial voice of prudence; a third will be a romantic, a fourth a cynic. These ensemble relationships are frequently characterized by a happy regression to adolescence, a sense of playfulness and levity—pressured professionals laughing uncontrollably over bad jokes and mediocre pizza. And there's often a deep sense of solidarity.

As military wives know, ensemble friendship provides distraction from anxiety and support in managing the day-in, day-out stress of raising young children alone. During the early 1970s, Maria Dillig was married to a Navy Seabee assigned to an aircraft carrier out of Quantas Point, Rhode Island. Thanks to the four other Navy wives in her apartment building, Maria remembered those days fondly.

"We were all in the same boat," she recalled. "Our husbands were on the ship—they were gone a lot—and everyone had little kids. Every morning, someone different had coffee, and we also made cinnamon buns. And the kids would play. They were all under school age. We just had a good old time going with the kids to different places and shopping and playing cards.

"When someone needed help with one particular thing, we'd all pitch in. If one of us went to the grocery store and she lived on the third floor, the others would be waiting to help carry the bags up."

Ensemble friendships aren't established; like any other form, they develop. Some begin spontaneously: Five salesclerks on the one-to-nine shift start going out for beer after closing out their registers. Six soccer moms begin sitting together and chatting while their daughters practice.

That was how the suburban kaffeeklatsches so prevalent in the 1950s through the 1970s arose. Thanks to home appliances and packaged mixes, housewives had the leisure to socialize for a few hours after getting their husbands off to work and their kids off to school.

"It was never that formal," explained Beth, who got together regularly with three neighboring moms when she was in her twenties. "People just tended to migrate to each other's homes. You talked about your kids, and that's where you found out whether what your kid was doing was bizarre or whether it was perfectly normal. There was a lot of community there that I don't think young women have nowadays. I look at my daughter: She works full time, and there's not time in her life for those kinds of relationships that I had."

Given the tightly packed agendas we carry around nowadays, many women lack the luxury of allowing a congenial group to accrete gradually—except in the workplace. Professional networks, activity-based clubs, and support groups for women dealing with similar problems provide opportunities for collective friendships to germinate and grow, but they aren't ensemble friendships in and of themselves. For her dissertation in women's studies, Jennifer Lee Grimes of the Wright Institute examined three women's friendship groups. She identified six factors that distinguish friendships of this kind from those organized around politics or career interests:

(1) Women's friendship groups tend to be subgroups of larger groups. (2) Group meetings are attended by members only. (3) These groups are leaderless. (4) These groups meet in domestic settings. (5) Topics of conversation focus on personal and interpersonal affairs. (6) Members must share feelings of trust, equality, and affection for women's groups to be successful.

The historic legacy of this female bond flows from quilting bees to consciousness-raising groups. Today, book groups have replaced bridge clubs as a popular medium for ensemble friendships. In addition to adapting better to time-scarce contemporary life, reading clubs have another advantage: They create a secure structure for dealing with discomfiting issues. "I can talk about things in a safe environment through books," explained market researcher Rhoda Kaufman Ferris, who made time in her hectic work and family schedule to participate in two reading groups. "You learn a lot about a person from the way she sees literature."

When the reality of life becomes all too serious, ensemble friends can buffer tragedy. Facing a crisis like terminal illness, a woman needs more than one friend, and her friends need one another to coordinate their support and to stave off despair. When forty-two-year-old Susan Farrow discovered that her rare cancer of the salivary glands had metastasized to her spine, where it would first paralyze and then kill her, she assembled a group of friends and asked them to help her cope with her illness. Until her death three-and-a-half years later, these twelve women ran her chores, dealt with her doctors, and even assisted in her daughter's wedding. In a *Good Housekeeping* profile, her friend of seventeen years, Sheila Warnock, admitted feeling relief that Farrow had reached out to other friends, not just her, for support.

Sometimes by acting as a group, ensemble friends can bring us out of deep denial about troubles we're having. As chair of her state legislature's environmental committee during the 1970s, Marlyn, a sixty-five-year-old university vice provost, had learned the value of group support. Since 1981, she'd gotten together once a week for lunch with five other managerial and professional women. Their discussions ranged from public policy issues to their daughters' divorces.

The test of the ensemble friendship came when the supervisor of one of her noon companions called Marlyn to confide that he was worried about the employee's drinking. He'd started documenting the times he had to send Jo home because she wasn't functional, but he valued the contribution she made when she was. Knowing that Jo belonged to the lunch group, he hoped they'd intervene.

"I started going over to Jo's and suggesting that we go out for lunch," Marlyn recalled. "Pretty soon, I realized that she was in trouble. So I called Estelle and said, 'Estelle, we're going to take Jo to Serenity Lane,' which is an alcohol treatment place. We actually kidnapped her. It was very exciting. She had gone to the store with her husband, and we waylaid her. We told her that we had come to take her to treatment, and she said, 'You know, I've been thinking about that, but my husband says we can handle things ourselves.'

"We were like Dorothy and the Tin Man and the Scarecrow in *The*

Wizard of Oz. Estelle took one arm, and I took the other, and we went skipping into the hospital. The doctor told us she was in bad condition; her liver was enlarged. She was waiting for somebody to do this, and it would not have happened without us. It was an example of where women's friendships probably saved a life."

Other forms of friendship almost always flavor ensembles: Women who get together to share books, television shows, or bridge are collective playmates. Like kaffeeklatschers, soccer moms who chat regularly at practices are lifemates, too. History can forge a particularly strong group bond.

Some women who have difficulty opening up to other women one-on-one find group friendships especially supportive. When they express some off-the-wall observation or deep anxiety, even if one of their cohorts gives a puzzled or disapproving look, chances are others will nod or say, "I know just what you mean."

In 1973 when Carol Barden was in her mid-twenties, she and seven women her age began a monthly potluck dinner. Ostensibly, the purpose of the group was to learn and practice gourmet cooking, but it soon gave way to self-disclosure and validation.

"We were looking for a way to get out of the house and escape *Monday Night Football*," she explained. "I can remember the first few times that members of that group started letting things out of the bag. It was very, very timid at first, and we were usually a little drunk. When somebody would share something intimate and deep and revealing, you felt that much closer to that person. A connection was forged, we bonded, and the next month something else would come out. And as each person shared more and more, the others felt freer. We agreed that you could not tell anything that you heard around that table."

The Gourmet Group referred to that rule as the Amnesia Door. The secrets that door enclosed could have life-shaking consequences. Being able to reveal them to one another brought relief, even when it didn't bring solutions.

"That group always knew, long before anybody else, that there was going to be a divorce," Carol said. "That group always knew when someone was having an affair. That group always knew when there was some kind of abuse, when there were problems with the children. All the secrets."

Decades later, the group was still getting together. They'd given up fancy cooking and recipe trading years earlier; most brought take-out. Carol had moved two thousand miles away, but she still timed her family visits to coincide with Gourmet Group Mondays, so she could participate.

One drawback to ensemble friendships is that they can be pleasant but remain superficial, like the interactions among the four women in Terry McMillan's novel *Waiting to Exhale,* who commiserated over their problems with men but didn't delve deeper. Another is that ensemble friendships can let us down in a pinch, because no one person has a special commitment to our welfare. When we lose a job, go through a divorce, or face another serious crisis, the collective encouragement of a group can buoy our spirits. Yet, that sense of support soon deflates if no one ever calls to ask what she can do to help or even simply to see how we're doing. The best, most life-enhancing ensemble friendships are those in which every member truly cares about every other member.

✦ Changing the Form, ✦
Maintaining the Bond

Taking the first steps of friendship, we may feel like we're responding to another woman as a separate individual ("I want *you* in my life"), then designing the relationship to fit a mutually agreeable pattern. But that response is triggered as much by our characteristics as by hers. Like atoms, we have valences—potentials for attachment. Atoms' valences depend on the number of available electrons; ours are keyed to our interests, emotional needs, temperament, and stage in the life cycle.

The boundaries between the ten forms of female friendship aren't firm. Some friendships described by the women I interviewed contained elements of several varieties, although one predominated; others were hybrids; many had evolved from one species into another. During the structuring stage described in chapter 3, friends determine the initial form of their friendship—usually without being aware that they're doing so. If they want or need to modify it later, they return to that stage, restructure it, and build from there. Even though they may not consciously identify it as restructuring, reestablishing comfort, restrengthening, retesting, and recommitment, this process requires work and determination on the part of both women involved. But the reward is a relationship that endures, even as they change—true friends for life.

Sarah Scott, a forty-five-year-old lawyer in New York, and Gretchen, a psychotherapist in Little Rock, met as juniors at their Kansas City high school. As their school's first female debate partnership, they began as a blend of workmates and playmates.

"Our main goal in debating was to go on as many bus trips as we could," Sarah said. "That's how we got to know each other."

Gretchen's approach to life added a zany zest even to relatively tame excursions. "We went shopping at this ritzy shopping area with fountains and pools all over the place," Sarah recalled. "We were walking along and talking, and Gretchen was so interested in the conversation that she stepped down into this fountain still talking and then up the other side. That's just the kind of person she was."

As they both came of age in Kansas City during the 1960s, Sarah and Gretchen became as much lifemates as playmates. "It was a highly conformist society," Sarah said. "There were a lot of terrible attitudes toward girls and women. We went to a very competitive school, and yet it was the craziest double standard in the world. We would be exhorted to work very, very hard and then told in the next breath that it was totally meaningless."

After they graduated, Sarah allowed the contact to lapse. She went to the University of Kansas, Gretchen to the University of Hawaii. Maintaining a playmate bond demands doing things together; sustaining a lifemate relationship requires sharing similar circumstances, either in person or through regular communication. Their friendship had to change forms or die.

As is often the case, one friend's persistence saved the relationship. "She wrote me steadily, and I wrote her, but you know," Sarah said with a shrug. "I traveled around the country quite a bit when I was in my early twenties, had my own adventures. I stopped answering the letters. Gretchen took it upon herself to stay in touch with my father and kept trying to get me to respond. Finally, at one point, it dawned on me that I wanted to keep this friendship. Then I responded, and she came."

Gretchen visited her every few years, and whenever Sarah went to

Kansas City to see her father, she and Gretchen got together. As they reminisced about their high school days, their relationship took on the qualities of a history friendship, complete with its own rituals and lore. Decade by decade, the friendship strengthened by adding the most positive qualities of a history bond. About thirteen years before our interview, Sarah realized how much the relationship meant to her when Gretchen flew up to New York to ask her advice. At the time, both women were childless thirty-two-year-olds facing the prospect of declining fertility. Sarah was married; Gretchen wasn't.

"She was thinking of having a baby," Sarah explained. "She had been married, but the marriage hadn't lasted, and I think that she knew that she wasn't going to marry again. Her mother had been ill for a long time, and her father was dead.

"I usually do not favor single motherhood, because I know it's very rough. But I felt like she was so extraordinary that she could do it. So I said, 'Gretchen, I don't see why not,' because I felt like she would be a very good mother. She just had so much warmth to her."

If Sarah hadn't understood, through similar experiences, shared as they occurred, just what motherhood meant to her friend, she might not have answered with such confidence. And if Gretchen hadn't known that Sarah held her history in her heart, she might not have asked. "She came all the way to New York just to ask my opinion," Sarah mused. "I was very touched. I was very honored.

"It all worked out. Her mother died sometime later, but the baby was born, and she got to see the grandchild. Then a year later, I had a baby of my own. Her child's a boy. My child's a girl. The two children are now good friends."

Maintaining that friendship over the decades hadn't been easy. It could well have disintegrated, as so many girlhood bonds do, after the two friends left for college. But Gretchen's persistence and her willingness to meet Sarah more than halfway had preserved enough of the connection through those vulnerable years to allow it to be restored, stronger than ever, a resilient, primary relationship evolving from form to form to support both women as they themselves evolved.

Part Two

❧

THE SIX SEASONS OF
FEMALE FRIENDSHIP

SOME FRIENDSHIPS GROW WITH US, like trees, changing in size and shape but bringing us pleasure and comfort year after year. Others are like flowering annuals, with us for a single season but no less beautiful for that.

When I began thinking about writing a book on woman-to-woman friendship, one thing became obvious to me right away: The nature of female friendship changes over the course of our lives. It takes certain forms and serves certain functions at twenty-seven, others at forty-three, and still others at seventy-two. I could see that phenomenon in my own experience and in the experiences of the women around me. By the time I reached my middle forties, I'd begun to recognize how important my women friends were to me. I'd begun to spend more time with them and share more of myself with them. I'd also added several new friends, and I noticed that as I did, I felt particularly drawn to women anywhere from a few years to a decade or so older than me.

Apparently, my experience wasn't unusual. Social scientists had noticed a surge of female friendship growth among women in their forties; they tended to explain it as a function of free time suddenly available when the oldest children left home and the youngest started school. Yet I was seeing it in friends who'd postponed childbirth until their early forties and in those who were just hitting the height of their careers and who lived by their tightly packed appointment calendars. Somehow, these women were managing to carve out time to develop new friendships and resuscitate old ones. I suspected the phenomenon had more to do with age than with obligations.

Psychologist Beverly Schydlowsky's research seemed to confirm this. When she queried women in midlife, Schydlowsky found no clear relationship between either their family or their occupational status and the number, importance, and content of their female friendships.

Meanwhile, I'd been observing my mother-in-law and her network of supportive friends, which I described in this book's introduction.

Her friendship patterns were different from mine, and I suspected that the difference had as much to do with where we were in our lives as it did with our individual personalities and the distinctive characteristics of our generations. Women my own age confirmed my theory indirectly: They talked about how different their daughters' friendships were from their own.

As I interviewed girls and women from ages eight to ninety, the details of the picture began to emerge. Even the friendships that had lasted for decades had changed form as the women aged. Some women recognized that essential evolution. "You have different friends at different times in your life," said Maria Dillig, the brewery worker in Milwaukee. "You can have the same friend, but at different times in your life that friend plays particular roles."

Could it be only a coincidence that the friendship surge I'd noticed in myself and in the women around me corresponded with the Midlife Passage that Gail Sheehy (no relation to me) lobbed into mainstream American culture in her 1976 best-seller *Passages*? I'd read that book when it first came out. After I'd almost completed my friendship interviews, I went back to it, this time with a greater appreciation for her contention that adults, like children, go through predictable stages of psychological development. At the same time, I also delved into two books by late Yale psychiatrist Daniel J. Levinson, whose research had inspired *Passages*. In *The Seasons of a Man's Life*, published in 1978, Levinson had divided male psychological development into four overlapping eras: preadulthood from birth to age twenty-two, early adulthood from ages seventeen to forty-five, middle adulthood from ages forty to sixty-five and late adulthood from age sixty until death. Levinson didn't mean, however, that every man entered a new developmental stage on his twenty-third or forty-fifth birthday. But that range was no more than "about two years above and below the average."

Levinson extended this concept to females in *The Seasons of a Woman's Life*, posthumously published in 1996. He wrote: "To my surprise, the findings indicate that *women go through the same sequence of eras as men, and at the same ages* (italics his).

Separating each of Levinson's eras was a transition—one at ages seventeen to twenty-two, another at ages forty to forty-five, and a third at ages sixty to sixty-five. These transitions could be smooth or tumultuous, depending on whether the individual was relatively satisfied with the life structure that preceded it or wanted to change it dramatically.

I was struck by how closely what women told me about their shifts in friendship patterns followed Levinson's ladder of development. The first two transitions corresponded to the ages at which so many of the women I interviewed reported strengthening, deepening, and increasing their friendships. The third ushered in the age at which the road seemed to fork: After sixty-five some women enjoyed, valued, and nurtured their female friendships as much as, or even more than, ever, while others allowed theirs to dwindle and atrophy.

Then the explanation for this convergence hit me: One of the functions of female friendship is to help us grow and develop as individuals. When we get ready to expand or change, we seek out new friends who can aid or inspire us in the task at hand, or we draw existing friends closer. I realized that I'd begun to find myself attracted to slightly older women because I was looking for mentors to teach me how to make my middle and later years vital, productive, and enjoyable.

What especially impressed me about Levinson's model was that his eras and transitions were defined in terms of developmental tasks, not by such personal milestones as marriage, childbirth, and retirement. That construct matched what I'd observed in my interviews. Marriage, jobs, and motherhood presented practical limitations, but they had surprisingly little influence on what female friends meant to these women. Therefore, I decided to use Levinson's map of human development to guide my exploration of the ages of female friendship.

6

~~

First Bonds Beyond
the Family: Ages Eight
to Twelve

In daring to challenge the unknown with me, she became my
first friend.

—Maya Angelou, *I Know Why the Caged Bird Sings*

Two weeks shy of her twelfth birthday, Alison Melville sat in the living room of the apartment she shared with her mother in New York's Greenwich Village, telling me about her friend Kirsten, whom she'd met at eighteen months. "The setting was pre-preschool," Alison explained. "It was called Sue's House, but some people called it Sue's Zoo, because there were like twenty kids running around and jumping and all that stuff—happy chaos.

"One day, Kirsten and I said, 'Let's get toilet trained today.' So we did it."

Although when we spoke Alison was only on the threshold of puberty, she already understood that shared history mixes with shared interests to make strong, resilient relational glue. Together, she and Kirsten had passed through the developmental steps of toddlerhood and early and middle childhood. As they had grown and changed, so had their relationship. It had progressed from playing together under close supervision to confiding their deepest thoughts and feelings and taking on tandem adventures.

A few months before our interview, Alison and Kirsten, with help from their mothers, had thrown a party to celebrate the tenth anniversary of their friendship. "We did a dance to one of my favorite songs," Alison said, showing me a snapshot of the duo hamming it up for the camera. "We toasted with ginger ale and then, by accident, Kirsten made me laugh and I spit it all over."

Fortunately for Alison and Kirsten, their parents recognized their friendship as a valuable bond worth encouraging for its own sake. Until recently, psychologists have looked on close friendships, or "chumships," between young girls as significant primarily as warm-ups for marriage. After learning to be intimate with a chum and sensitive to her moods and needs in late childhood, the reasoning went, a girl could transfer those skills to a relationship with a man once the hormones started flowing.

But lately, social scientists and clinicians have begun to recognize that early female friendships, especially close ones, do much more than serve as the opening act for heterosexual pairing. For starters, a bond like the one Alison and Kirsten shared supports a girl's healthy attempts to establish her own identity and deal with the aftershock of recognizing that her parents aren't perfect. "[B]est friendships in pre-adolescent girls are developmentally significant as the first important relationships beyond the family," University of San Francisco developmental psychologist Alyse Danis noted in her dissertation. Her interviews with eleven- and twelve-year-old girls revealed that these early bonds had six qualities in common:

> (1) The ability to share and keep secrets, (2) the development of altruistic concern for one's best friend, (3) the experience of correcting one's own faulty behavior in order to be a better relationship partner, (4) the growth of mutual sensitivity, (5) the lessening of difficulties of preadolescence as well as problems specific to each girl's home, and (6) the growing ability to seek compromise and offer forgiveness in the face of conflict.

Female friendship can do all this because, unlike a child's other relationships, it is a bond between peers. A young girl may love her parents, admire a teacher, and hero-worship an older sibling or feel protective toward a younger one, but with a girlfriend she can feel the empathy that forms the basis for female moral development. In order to remain emotionally connected to a particular friend that (unlike her parents or siblings) she could drive away, she begins to consider what effect her words and actions will have on that friend. Parents teach what's right and what's wrong, but it is friends who give a girl the opportunity to practice these principles, along with the social skills that will serve her throughout her life.

Friendship even spurs children's intellectual performance. In a study that demonstrated this with surprising clarity, Marie-Josephe Chauvet and Peter Blanchard of the University of London Institute of Education divided thirty seven-year-olds into three groups—one selected randomly, one according to math ability, and the third based on friendship. Then the children took on a series of tasks related to mathematics. Rather than distracting one another, the friends stayed more focused on the work at hand and outperformed both other groups.

Close, reciprocated friendship—the kind where the two parties feel roughly the same about each other—also builds self-esteem and serves as a buffer against anxiety and depression in the face of such stressful experiences as the loss of a parent to death or divorce. Having at least one true, reciprocal friend is particularly crucial for children growing up in troubled households.

But not all friendships are reciprocal. "A reciprocal friendship is when you identify someone as your best friend and they also identify you as their best friend," explained University of Miami professor of child development Sharon Vaughn. "You may say, 'Isn't that always the case?' And the answer is 'Absolutely not.' "

One study of fourth- through sixth-graders showed, for instance, that when asked to pick out his or her best friend, only 45.5 percent of the children chose each other. In other words, fewer than half of these best friendships were reciprocated. A nonreciprocal relationship shortchanges a girl on close friendship's major benefits. When both friends feel similarly about each other, they not only enjoy their time together more, they also give each other more empathy and emotional support, and therefore, do more to help each girl develop as an individual. And they feel far more secure in the relationship, at a time of life when such security can steady them as they make their first steps into the world.

Even a girl who is generally disliked can have a rewarding reciprocal friendship. Studies have found that some children who are rejected by most of their classmates have best friends, while some popular children don't. Just one mutual friendship can protect a girl from the lasting psychological damage inflicted by social rejection. "When girls are disliked, actively rejected, it bodes unfavorably for the kinds of social relationships they're going to have when they're older," Sharon Vaughn told me. "However, the one factor that seems to immunize them is a reciprocal friendship. So if they have one friend with whom they have a mutually satisfying relationship, it seems to serve as a buffer."

Having a few close friends is within the reach of almost all young girls, whether or not they are pretty or smart or good at soccer. "And I think it's important, because it's so necessary for success later on," Vaughn said. "When you don't have a single best friend when you're very young, you get left out of the opportunities to practice all of those skills that make you more and more socially proficient as you get older. When they don't get to practice social skills when they're eight and build on them when they're nine and extend them when they're ten and get more proficient when they're eleven, when they are fifteen, seventeen, twenty-five, and forty-two, they're dysfunctional. They're dysfunctional in the home; they're dysfunctional in the workplace."

Parents place too much emphasis on trying to help their daughters become popular, Vaughn observed. She noted that unpopular girls with one or two satisfying mutual friendships grow into psychologically healthier women than girls who are generally well liked but have no close chums. Forget extravagant birthday parties designed to raise a daughter's social status. Providing the time, space, and transportation for a girl to get together, one-on-one, with her closest friends is a far better investment in her current and future well-being.

⚘ Early Roots ⚘

I chose eight as the earliest age for my exploration of female friendship because children younger than that have to be observed rather than interviewed; they tend to tell adults what they think the adults want to hear. Initially, I'd also been guided by the time-honored assumption that full-fledged friendships didn't emerge until well into the elementary school years. Before that, the accepted wisdom held, peer relationships were arrangements of convenience: Put any two little kids the same age together, and they would play contentedly, provided neither was aggressive. And those two children wouldn't form an attachment. When they were separated, they wouldn't give each other a second thought.

But child psychologists have begun to recognize that social life begins as early as thirteen months and that children are capable of forming genuine friendships much sooner than previously recognized. By the time they're a year and a half, toddlers in day care, where they have a variety of companions to choose from, begin showing preferences for particular playmates.

By two, children start developing a sense of what's socially appropriate, beginning with understanding the difference between dominance and cooperation. Studies have shown that very young children choose playmates who have similar social skills. Kids who know how to share toys pick each other; kids who are good at expressing themselves verbally seek each other out. In addition, girls maintain these earliest friendships better than boys. Even this young, girls recognize the value of connection.

Between ages three and five, children's relationships take on a new dimension. Frequent playmates start helping each other make sense of the world. Over a fifteen-month period, developmental psychologist Roberta Shreve observed drawings made by two preschool girls who'd chosen each other as companions; as time passed the interests and themes they expressed in their artwork became more alike, suggesting that the two children were beginning to share a common view of reality. Friends this age often collaborate on creating scenarios drawn from the adult world or from movies and television. The closer the friendship, the more likely two preschoolers are to engage in this kind of play.

As school age approaches, children begin to develop a concept of friendship as a relationship with its own rules of conduct. When Robyn Holmes of Monmouth College asked five-year-olds to make a picture of themselves with a friend and with a stranger, they drew the friend closer. By age four or five, children understand that talking about highly personal matters is appropriate with best friends, but not with acquaintances. This practice of secret sharing seems to emerge around age four. Even this young, girls already disclose more of their private thoughts and feelings than boys.

Embryonic though they may be, these early intimate friendships are important. They help young children cope with stresses ranging from the arrival of a younger sibling to the dangers of growing up in poverty. When a close friend moves away, even children as young as three years old feel the loss.

Friendship plays such a crucial role in early development that young children who don't have friends often invent them. These imaginary companions serve as buffers against loneliness and as idealizations of themselves. If a little girl is shy and fearful, her fantasy best friend will be outgoing and brave. If she is awkward, her imaginary chum will excel at sports or ballet. Having a fantasy friend not only offers a child the illusion of company during solitary hours; by giving her a model for characteristics she might want to develop, it also helps her grow.

✤ From Chumship to Friendship ✤

During the first few years of elementary school, both girls and boys learn the rudimentary rules of friendship, such as the need to be dependable and to share with others. By age nine or ten, kids say they're willing to shoulder risks to help a friend; by age ten or twelve, they expect friends to bolster their feelings about themselves and include them in activities; by age twelve or thirteen, they can distinguish between close and casual friendships. They understand that manners—being careful about taking turns, reciprocating small favors—matter more with acquaintances and that bigger issues like loyalty are what count with true friends.

Ten-year-old New Yorker Eva Kuhn already possessed a grasp of the distinction between intimate and casual friends. "I'm going to sleep-away camp with my friend," she told me. "Susan's not really close. She's like a friend to play with at recess."

When I asked what kept Susan from qualifying as a close friend, Eva explained: "She just has different interests than I do. She has a different idea of what's a good time."

Even though children may need another year or two of social judgment to identify them, deep friendships begin to emerge around age eight or nine. Whether or not these relationships were exclusive, the girls I interviewed used the term "best friend" to refer to what child psychologists call "chums"—those first intimate partners outside the family. In his 1953 classic *The Interpersonal Theory of Psychiatry*, Harry Stack Sullivan used "chums" to denote a particular early form of close friendship, rich in secret sharing and heightened sensitivity to each other's feelings. Sullivan described these intense relationships as the beginning of "love" as psychiatrists construe it—that is, one individual caring as much (or almost as much) about another's happiness and well-being as her own.

As early as preschool, girls tend to select girls for their closest friends and boys select boys; and this preference intensifies steadily from ages three to nine. Just how much of this phenomenon has to do with natural affinity and how much with imposed sex roles is open to debate.

Like most of the adult women I talked to for this book, the seven girls aged eight to twelve I interviewed each named between four and seven close friends, although the number of individuals within that inner circle fluctuated much more, year to year, than it did for women. Only two girls included boys on their lists. Olivia Cory, eleven, told me that three of her four closest friends were boys. Boys were "definitely different kinds of friends" from girlfriends, noted another eleven-year-old, Robin Harris, who lived in Austin and included one boy in her roster of seven close friends.

Girls ages eight to twelve have already noticed that boys' friendships differ from their own, especially when it comes to intimacy. "They're not as affectionate as girls would be," ten-year-old Eva Kuhn told me.

Developmental psychologists have noticed the same thing. After studying 198 third-, fifth-, and seventh-graders, M. L. Clark and Monnie Bittle of Virginia Commonwealth University concluded: "Girls . . . expected and received more kindness, loyalty and commitment and empathic understanding from their best friendships."

However firmly rooted the gender distinctions in children's friendships may be, the way girls and boys talk to their best friends differs dramatically. In her best-seller *You Just Don't Understand: Men and Women in Conversation*, Deborah Tannen compared how two pairs of sixth-graders expressed their mutual commitment. The boys spoke briefly about doing everything together and being willing to defend each other in fights. The girls discussed the length of their relationship, the absence of conflict, and the sense of being there for each other. Tannen noted:

> All the girls' talk is about friends, friendship, and feelings; they orchestrate this talk at a level of subtlety and complexity that is not seen in the sixth-grade boys' talk.

Difference in conversational style is one factor that makes preadolescent boy-girl friendships relatively rare. When boys disagree, they tend to be direct to the point of bluntness. Girls adjust their conversational styles to accommodate one another and their relationship, as well as the task at hand.

Sabrina Hall-Little, an eleven-year-old in Sausalito, California, prevented conflict with her close friends by leavening negative comments with humor. "We give each other constructive criticism in a joking way," she told me. Take when one of them asked the other for an honest opinion on her unflattering outfit. "We take quotes from our favorite movie, which is *Clueless*," Sabrina explained. "We're like, 'Do you prefer "fashion challenged" or "fashion disabled"?' "

From elementary school on, talking and listening are essential ingredients of female friendship.

↜ Emerging Forms ↜

Talking to the girls I interviewed, I was struck by how many of the elements of adult female friendship already were in place. Granted, these seven girls don't constitute a representative sample, but the matter-of-fact way in which they described their relationships told me that they, at least, didn't consider their patterns unusual. One thing that surprised me was that, like adult women, these girls sought different companions to help them explore different sides of themselves.

Eleven-year-old Alison Melville tottered out of her room wearing Rollerblades. When I asked how many close friends she had, she replied: "A lot. I have Kirsten, who's my major friend. I've known her for a long time. And then there's Lynn. We've been friends ever since the first day of kindergarten. But she goes to a school on the Upper East Side now, so we don't see each other that much. There's Ilona. She's the one that I'm going Rollerblading with. I've known her since kindergarten, and it's been kind of an off-and-on friendship. We're pretty close friends now. Then there's Megan. I met her this year. She's my fashion friend. We like talking about fashion and clothes and all that stuff. And then there's Erika. She's like my other fashion friend. She really cares about what I like to think about. She listens to what I say, so I talk on the phone with her a lot. And then my other majorly close friend is Dawn. I've known her since first grade. We go to Bible study together."

Since children can play together even before they can talk, the first peer relationships toddlers develop are playmate bonds. And that form remains popular throughout childhood.

At this age, playmates almost have to be lifemates as well, because children develop so fast that two years' difference in either direction adds up to vastly different interests, depth of experience, level of judgment, and dependence on adults.

Even a year can make a difference. Of ten-year-old Eva Kuhn's four best friends, one was six months older than she was, one six months younger, one closer to her own age. They saw each other for individual and threesome play dates, but seldom as a foursome, because the age difference between the oldest and youngest friends was too great.

Of course, the structure of most schools facilitates meetings between agemates. Girls spend their days in class with twenty or thirty other children born during the same twelve-month period. But even in mixed-age classrooms, most pairs of close friends tend to be close in age, as well. In cases in which these nontraditional classrooms do spark mixed-age friendships, these relationships are often less intense than those between children the same age.

As adolescence looms, even girls with birth dates a few months apart find themselves on different rungs of the developmental ladder. "A lot of people in my class are still kids, and I'm not very much friends with them," Alison Melville told me.

One casualty to development had been her friendship with Lynn, whom she'd known since kindergarten but now saw only every two or three months. "We don't have that much in common anymore, because she's still that kind of elementary school kid, even though she goes to junior high school," Alison explained. "But I still enjoy being around her, because I like being an elementary kid once in a while."

Partly because they had developed in synch, Robin Harris hadn't had that experience with her lifemate Justine. "As far as I can remember, it was Justine, because our moms were friends before we were born," she said. Robin and Justine were confidantes, but not soulmates. They saw the world "not extremely differently, but not very much the same, either," Robin noted.

"We both have a love of animals and math," she said. "We both write poetry, and she has a little sister who's about my little brother's age, so she's one of the closer ones to talk to about siblings."

Sharing the experience of being a sister—its joys and especially its frustrations—is an important form of validation lifemates give each other. "With my friends, siblings come up a lot," Robin said.

Trading secrets and fantasies, young girls quickly identify potential soulmates. In her autobiography, *I Know Why the Caged Bird Sings,* poet Maya Angelou described her first close bond with someone outside her family. It was clearly a soulmate friendship. Angelou was ten years old when she got to know Louise Kendricks. Seeking refuge from a church picnic, where they'd been given the choice of playing games with the younger children or cleaning fish with the women, they'd both discovered the same clearing. That afternoon, they developed their own game: Holding hands, they leaned back, stared up at the sky between the treetops and spun faster and faster. Angelou wrote:

> After a few near tumbles into eternity (both of us knew what it was), we laughed at having played with death and destruction and escaped. . . . In daring to challenge the unknown with me, she became my first friend.

That adventure brought the two girls together, but it was the way they attached the same meaning to it that forged their friendship.

Some young girls find themselves already developing nurturer-and-nurtured friendships. They can reach out to a child who is less outgoing socially, and they can help one who is less capable academically. Her friendship with Nina gave Robin Harris, a gifted student, an opportunity to do both. "Nina's kind of quiet and kind of strange, but I always seem to befriend that kind of person," Robin explained. "I like to teach things, and Nina has trouble in math. A lot of times our teacher lets us help somebody, and I can help her, and she's appreciative."

Both girls grow in this form of friendship, as well as in mentor-protégée relationships, where an older girl adopts the role of big sister to a younger one at school or camp.

Friends from different backgrounds, with different strengths, stimulate each other's growth. That may be why some of the closest girlhood friendships are between opposites.

"We often choose friends based on things we have in common, interests we share," psychologist Sharon Vaughn explained. "But we also choose them looking for ways to help compensate for things we don't feel very good about. Then we think our friends can help us."

When I asked Olivia Cory, who lived in an ethnically diverse neighborhood in Brooklyn, what attracted her to her friend Dee, she replied: "She wasn't exactly like me. She's part Mexican, part American, and part Chinese. She speaks English excellently, and she speaks two other languages pretty well. She can fix just about anything. She comes over to my mom's house and fixes all our radios and VCRs."

Comparing her to her soulmate Inez, Nancy Kelton wrote in *Parents* magazine of her friend Cindy, whom she met in the seventh grade, "Cindy was less my kindred soul. I saw in her the things I lacked: sophistication, unconditional acceptance from the sharp crowd . . ." That friendship carried benefits of association, but it offered something else as well: Nancy would have a chance to observe close up and imitate the social skills that made Cindy popular.

Courage is another quality girls this age look to friends to model. "It seemed to me she wasn't scared of anything," Eva Kuhn said, telling me what had drawn her to Melissa four years earlier. "There was this boy in our class I was afraid of. He stole your markers and stuff, and he grabbed what you had for dessert at lunch. And she did things to him that I wouldn't even dream of doing. When he sat down in her seat once, she shoved him off. She called him a bully."

Sometimes a young girl learns a different kind of fearlessness from a friend, like overcoming stage fright well enough to sing a solo in the school pageant or mustering the bravery to speak her mind when she sees another person, or group of people, treated unfairly. By modeling and mirroring these sorts of courage, girls literally encourage one another to develop strong character.

In addition to their one-on-one friendships, eight- to twelve-year-old girls gravitate to groups. Often comprised of intersecting and over-lapping best-friend pairs, these ensembles help young girls develop psychologically and socially.

Although Alison Melville had several close chums, she followed the pattern of more general socializing. "I always go everywhere in huge, huge groups," she told me. "You don't go with a friend; you go with friends," she said, extending the "s" sound for a good three seconds.

Young girls' ensembles exert group pressure to conform in every-thing from sock color to attitudes. This has its downsides, as it does when the child of a cash-strapped single mom feels miserable because she doesn't have the shoes everyone else is wearing or when a girl who really likes school pretends she doesn't because her friends say they don't. But although some preadolescent girls relinquish their judg-ment to the group, the research suggests that the majority don't. In fact, it is in the context of these early ensemble friendships that a young girl learns how to navigate between belonging and being her own person.

ᴥ More Than Child's Play: ᴥ
What Girls Do Together

One area where the friendships of the eight- to twelve-year-olds I interviewed differed from those of adult women was in the variety of things they did together. Late childhood is an age of exploration, of extending intellectual and artistic capabilities, of developing physical competence, of learning the social ropes. At this age, close friends help one another grow both by sharing challenging activities and by providing the motivation for acquiring and honing interpersonal skills.

Young girls are still developing the art of conversation. Like adult women, they engage in long, intense talks; but to sustain the interper-sonal connection, girls often need the pretext of an activity, such as playing dolls or Monopoly. Yet, however it takes place, mutual self-disclosure is a major feature of preadolescent female friendship. In ad-dition to offering a caring, independent perspective on family or school problems, shared soul-baring helps develop empathy and the ability to be a good listener. However, these come at a price: Girls this age tell their closest friends what they really think and feel, unedited and uncensored. This intimacy leaves them tremendously vulnerable, and they know it. Recognizing this vulnerability in each other spurs growth in still another area—the ability to keep confidences.

Friendship at this age helps creativity to blossom. Girls enter late childhood adept at fantasy play. At least with close friends, self-consciousness has yet to inhibit their imaginations, and they now have the skills to augment them with whatever props are at hand. By encouraging each other's inventiveness, friends help each other sustain the natural creativity of childhood and begin to apply it to the real world, where it may lead to a life-enriching career or avocation. Building a backyard playhouse with a friend may give a child her first inkling that she might want to become an architect. Concocting elaborate scenarios with two chums and a trunk of castoff clothes may lead to lifelong involvement in theater.

Friendship can make the difference between whether a young girl develops into an active adolescent or a couch potato. Studies show that companionship motivates children to participate in sports and that preadolescents find being taught a sport by their peers more fun than being taught by an adult. My own interviews bore that out. "When I started fourth grade, I had no idea how to play sports," Sabrina Hall-Little of Sausalito confessed to me at age eleven. "Melinda took it upon herself to inform me exactly how to play baseball, football, soccer, and volleyball. By the end of the school year, I could pretty much play them all."

Doing things with a close friend, especially one-on-one, girls can learn how to navigate the waters of disagreement without destroying connection. Shopping together is one way girls help develop taste that's both their own and acceptable to their peers. Reading the same books and discussing them offers a safe way to test out ideas and learn to manage differences of opinion. Robin Harris and her longtime friend Justine see eye to eye on some books but not on others. "*Little Women* was a very nice one, because we had slightly different views about it," Robin told me. Through the medium of books, she was learning not merely to tolerate difference, but to enjoy it.

As they progress through late childhood, girls become better able to identify the qualities they value in their friends. Eva Kuhn told me what she liked best about Marilyn was her imagination. "When we were littler, we used to play 'Pretend,' " Eva recalled. "She would make up the stories, and I always envied her because I didn't know how she could make up such an adventurous story."

Speaking generally, Charlotte Wood, at age twelve, said that what she appreciated in a friend was "being polite, being friendly," and keeping secrets. Alison Melville looked for a combination of loyalty and honesty.

The girls I interviewed also valued different qualities in different friends. When I asked whom they'd call to talk over a personal problem, Eva replied: "Melissa, because Melissa's a better friend to talk to but Eleanor's a better friend to play with."

Robin Harris responded that she'd call her friend Justine, "because she's kind of level-headed but still very understanding and also one of my closest friends. I'd probably tell her a lot of stuff if I had anything bad. She always calls up when their hamsters die or something."

For a friend to share a movie, Charlotte Wood told me that she'd pick Annette, "because she's quiet. She wouldn't get all rambunctious and start making loud noises and knock over her popcorn and knock over her soda."

As young as they were, these girls already had developed an understanding of the different ways different friends enriched their lives.

❧ Friendship's Early Enemies ❧

However a friendship begins, its course isn't easy. "Friendships are really challenging for everyone," University of Colorado psychologist Beth Doll told me. "They're especially so for kids, because kids don't have the equipment to deal with them that adults do." When I interviewed her in February 1997, Doll was in the process of developing a curriculum to teach children the rudiments of friendship: making time to have fun with friends, noticing when friends need something and helping out, staying loyal to friends and standing up for them, figuring out what friends do well and telling them, and resolving conflicts.

Even for eight- to twelve-year-olds, finding time to be with friends presents a problem. What with after-school sports, clubs, music lessons, and the like, many of today's young girls juggle calendars as tightly scheduled as their mothers'.

Sabrina Hall-Little told me that she got to see Ada, her friend since preschool, only once every two or three weeks. Just two months earlier, they'd played together weekly. "I've been very busy, and she's been very busy," Sabrina explained.

In addition to conflicts in scheduling, conflicts in affections can strain girls' friendships. Often, one close friend simply doesn't take to another. That means the girl has to see them separately. Even worse, a girl's best friend can befriend someone the girl herself can't stand. "Ilona made friends with a girl that I didn't really like," Alison Melville told me. "That kind of tore us apart, but we're now good friends again."

Friendships survive under such circumstances only through mutual effort, and the girls who go to that trouble seem to appreciate how much a good chum can mean. Some forms of psychological trauma—particularly the loss of a parent through divorce or death—can deepen chumships as the bereaved girl turns to her friend for comfort; but others can disrupt the development of friendships and, in extreme cases, prevent a girl from having even one reciprocal intimate friend.

Moves rank among the most common culprits. Many girls manage to form close friendships in the face of repeated geographic dislocations, but the loss they feel is real and profound. For Tara Boland, a twenty-one-year-old college student at the time I interviewed her, the pain of separation from her childhood chum Joanna Winslade was still palpable. "I don't think I realized how strong a friendship we had until I moved from Galveston to Boston after eighth grade," Tara said. "It was devastating for me to leave her and my other girlfriends."

When a girl moves, she has to reestablish herself with a whole new set of kids, and they might be less than welcoming. That's what Sabrina Hall-Little discovered at the first school she attended when she arrived in Connecticut at the start of the second grade. "They were really mean," she told me.

At the smaller school she switched to, the children accepted her. "It was just like a family," Sabrina explained. That nurturing environment allowed her to develop a close friendship with another girl her age, Leah. After moving back to California, Sabrina was trying to maintain this important relationship long-distance. Fortunately, her parents encouraged her efforts.

"I talk to Leah every month or so," Sabrina said. "We talk about what's going on at her school and what's going on at my school. And then, when it gets toward the summer, we arrange what we're going to do when we see each other, because my parents promised me that every single year we would make a trip to Connecticut."

Sometimes parents help girls develop and maintain friendships, but sometimes they interfere, often out of concern for their daughters' welfare—an impulse to protect them either from direct harm or from bad influences on their health or character. However, psychologists and sociologists are still debating how peer pressure operates and are even investigating how it often steers children away from—rather than toward—what can hurt them.

Smoking is one destructive behavior that parents worry about their daughters picking up from friends. But a recent study of seventh-graders demonstrated that children who lacked reciprocal friends ran the greatest risk of being initiated into smoking. If a girl has even one or two close friendships, she may not be tempted to take up a harmful habit to gain a looser, and therefore less satisfying, connection to a whole group.

The anxiety and ambivalence parents feel toward their daughters' friendships may spring from one simple, unassailable fact: These first close outside bonds dilute parental influence. In one sense, an outside friendship challenges the family bond, because the two girls see, and value, each other as unique individuals, not as anyone's daughter or sister.

Even young children question parents' right to forbid them to associate with certain friends. When psychologists Marie and John Tisak of Bowling Green State University questioned 126 second-, fourth-, and sixth-graders, they discovered that the younger children thought such restrictions were okay *only* if the parent explained that the friend endangered their safety or morals. The older children were even less inclined to consider themselves bound by their parents' attempts to control their associations. Sixth-graders ruled out safety concerns as legitimate objections. "By sixth grade, they think they have the maturity not to copy unsafe behavior," Marie Tisak told me.

But sixth-graders did agree that their parents had the right to prohibit a friendship on moral grounds—for instance, if the other child stole. Hearing her parents' concern that she might become the thief's victim and that other people might mistakenly accuse her of shoplifting because she was in the company of a shoplifter, an eleven-year-old will tend to acknowledge that the rule against associating with her light-fingered friend is legitimate.

❧ Sunshine and Shadow ❧

Despite all the good that intimate friendship does for young girls, it also has its dark side. Intense chumships can involve tremendous vulnerability, jealousy, and pain. Adults watching the drama often wonder whether all that turmoil is healthy. In extreme cases, it may not be. One study has shown that when it came to bringing on depression or anxiety, friendship difficulties could do as much damage as parental divorce.

One of the features of early female friendship that mothers told me bothered them most was its apparent instability. Girls notice that, too. Those that I interviewed described classmates who were best friends one week, not speaking to each other the next, then tight chums again by the third.

Friendships tend to get less volatile as girls near adolescence. "I liked Leta, and then I didn't like her, and then I liked her, and then I didn't like her—because in fourth grade we had so many fights," Alison Melville recalled from her sixth-grade perspective. "Fourth grade was just like the fighting year. And this year, nobody hates anybody."

As girls get older, they also learn to enter into friendships more slowly and selectively, to avoid getting too close to children with annoying habits or clashing temperaments. Since moving back to the San Francisco Bay Area after four years in Connecticut, Sabrina Hall-Little had reconnected with friends she'd made in first grade and earlier. But she was also trying to establish new ones, going through the process of sorting through prospects. From the start of school in September to the time I interviewed her in May, every girl she'd considered had turned out to have a major flaw. Since none of these relationships had progressed beyond the casual level, Sabrina could disentangle herself without precipitating a major rupture. A split between best friends, on the other hand, can be agonizing—both for the children themselves and for the adults who love them. Even so, it's more likely to promote psychological growth than psychological damage. By making mistakes, either in the friends we choose or in how we conduct our friendships, we eventually learn to initiate and build friendships that last.

Seeking to protect their daughters from similar pain in the future, some mothers respond by cautioning them to avoid conflict at all costs.

That's a mistake. "Conflict is what gives kids a chance to realize that they're different from other kids," psychologist Beth Doll explained. "It's how they get to know themselves."

And dodging disagreement can create lifelong problems: A girl afraid to speak her mind may grow up into a woman who doesn't know hers. Only if she's willing to take on the risk of conflict can her early friendships teach her how to assert herself without severing connection. By the time they reach puberty, girls can distinguish what's worth fighting about from what isn't. As they develop impulse control, they learn to sidestep spats; as they develop more subtle social skills, girls learn how to get over them.

Competitiveness can strain girls' friendships, especially because our culture still teaches females that competing openly with one another isn't nice. "The problem with Megan is she always gets better everything than I do," Alison Melville told me. "Her report card was ninety-six, ninety-seven, ninety-five, ninety-six, ninety-eight—something like that. And mine was ninety-five, ninety-five, ninety-five, ninety-five, ninety-nine. I pretend to be very happy. Like, 'Oh, it's so great.' And I don't mind it that much. But she likes to jump around when she gets good grades. When I get a good grade and she gets a bad one, I keep quiet, because she doesn't want to hear about it."

I noticed in my interviews that girls who peg their self-worth on where they rank relative to their peers can turn commonly cooperative activities into win-lose situations. Even griping can be a competitive sport. Sabrina Hall-Little told me that whenever she complained to her friend Ada about a problem, Ada one-upped her. Sabrina gave an example: "I could say, 'Oh, I really twisted my ankle.' And she would say, 'But you know what? The other day, I tripped on something and really got a lot more hurt.'"

Another negative emotion afflicts young girls' close friendships in particular. In the years immediately preceding puberty, jealousy plagues female pairs in a way that it never does later. I remember at ten having two girls pressure me to declare one or the other of them my best friend. I couldn't. I liked them equally, for different reasons: Karen was the more imaginative. Like me, she loved to read. Also like me, Kathy enjoyed swimming and hiking and combing the local lake shore for fossils. I found her mother, a Scottish war bride, marvelously exotic, both for her accent and because she'd been so traumatized by German bombing that she still hid under the bed during thunderstorms.

Having Karen and Kathy each want to be first in my affections was enormously flattering, but having them fight openly over me was excruciatingly uncomfortable. I had no idea what to do to defuse the tension. In the middle of sixth grade, my family moved halfway across the country, and I lost them both.

If only I'd used Sabrina Hall-Little's approach, I might have been able to quell that distressing possessiveness with honesty, well expressed. When I asked Sabrina whether two of her close friends had ever been jealous of each other or asked her to say which she preferred, she replied: "There was a lot of that in fifth grade.' Do you like her or me better?' I would just say to them, 'I don't think of it that way. People are different, so I can't really compare them.' "

But the issue hasn't gone away for girls, especially when one best friend can claim clear seniority over another. Alison Melville admitted that her lifelong friend Kirsten sometimes got jealous. "Whenever Kirsten and I were on the phone, I'd be talking about what Rhea and I had done together because Rhea was basically my life," Alison explained. "She came over every day after school. There was nothing I could do without Rhea being around, so I guess Kirsten was jealous."

Sometimes jealousy is a natural reaction to being left out. "Denise wanted to play with somebody else, and I didn't have anybody to play with," Charlotte recalled of an incident at camp. "So she got all mad at me and I got all mad at her."

Feeling excluded is one of childhood's most painful experiences. For Cecile, a forty-five-year-old physician assistant, the memory still stung. "It happened in the fifth grade," she recalled. "Suddenly, there were the popular kids and the nothings. For reasons unknown to me, the popular group took me up as a member. One of the key boys in the group thought I was cute, and we became sort of boyfriend-girlfriend for a brief period. Then, like all fifth-grade boys, he developed an interest in somebody else. Once he lost interest in me, the whole group decided I was not worth much. I became bewildered by the whole process. It was a terrible sort of ostracism."

As puberty approaches, the blurry boundaries of childhood ensemble friendships become clearer and more rigid. Permeable networks become closed cliques. Girls begin to be concerned about who's in and who's out, to bar the gates against outsiders, and to care about where their group ranks in the pecking order. Status and power loom over the landscape of friendship.

"The big issue in school now is friends," Alison Melville told me. " 'I have a friend; you don't.' 'My best friend is really popular. Yours, nobody knows her name.' It's that kind of thing."

When it comes to guarding a group from interlopers, girls' strategies can be long on inventiveness. By forming their own rock band, Olivia Cory and her friends were creating their own private culture: members only. "This kid Donald was in our band for a couple of weeks, but then it was, 'So long, Donald,' because we got fed up with him," Olivia said. "He's just annoying, and he's not that good a pianist."

For a parent trying to pass along values of inclusiveness and compassion, what seems like the most mean-spirited of melodramas can be agonizing to watch. But "that's the way girls bond," Sharon Vaughn noted. "You might not like it, but it's necessary for them. It's a way for them to say, 'We're special.' You can't be special when everyone is included."

When a girl is actively disliked by all or almost her peers, Vaughn noted that there may be a good reason. One trait that nearly guarantees rejection is aggression. Girls have little tolerance for either the direct nonverbal kind (hitting, biting, kicking) or the direct verbal kind (yelling, name calling). But the variety that they dislike most is indirect—sneaky acts like concocting and spreading lies or swiping the pens and pencils from a classmate's desk, so that the teacher scolds her for not having what she needs to do an assignment.

With help from parents and professionals, many girls who begin childhood as outcasts can learn to control inappropriate behavior well enough to have at least one or two mutual friends, even though general acceptance—let alone popularity—may elude them. For preadolescent girls, popularity is power. The chosen few float on a sea of affirming adulation. The pariahs flounder in corrosive rejection. For the girls in between, the pretty-well-liked, this melodrama offers real opportunities for growth. Being excluded by some cliques and included in others can teach them empathy. In the long run, the girls who benefit most from the preadolescent popularity game are those who don't win it.

7

Challenges and Changes: Ages Thirteen to Seventeen

[G]irls' development in adolescence may hinge on their resisting
not the loss of innocence but the loss of knowledge. . . . To seek
connection with others by excluding oneself is a strategy
destined to fail.

—Carol Gilligan, *Making Connections: The Relational Worlds of
Adolescent Girls at Emma Willard School*

In the year since I'd attended her bat mitzvah, the Jewish rite
of passage for girls, fourteen-year-old Sara Heller had sprinted
from puberty to adolescence. Her friendships had evolved as
well. Of the seven or eight girls she considered close friends, Meredith was the closest; and their friendship, which began in third
grade, had matured as they had. Initially volatile, it had mellowed
to a reliable relationship as both Sara and Meredith developed social
skills and sensitivity.

Now Sara could trust Meredith with secrets, something she hadn't
been able to do before. "She was one of those people who told secrets
to be cool," Sara said. "But now she tells me pretty much everything,
and I tell her pretty much everything."

Sara and Meredith inhabited the ambiguous world between childhood and adulthood. The boundaries of adolescence blur at both ends.
Setting its beginning at a girl's thirteenth birthday is as arbitrary as
setting its close at her eighteenth. Yet, since society's institutions and

expectations shape this metamorphosis, these traditional dates make as much sense as any.

At the cusp of her teenage years, a girl needs the friendship of other girls and of unrelated women more than ever. She enters adolescence as a child of her family and emerges five years later as a woman of her culture. In this short time, she must decide not just who she is but how to conduct herself—as a student in the classroom, as a daughter and sister in her family, as a female partner in romantic relationships, and as a friend. The exquisite discomfort of trying to integrate her own contradictory attributes peaks in middle adolescence, but by the time a girl turns seventeen, the inner conflict normally subsides. Meanwhile, her relationships with others, and even with herself, change continuously, as if she were racing through a funhouse in which the floors tilt at crazy angles and each mirror reflects a different distortion of reality.

Yet it is in these changing relationships, particularly in those with her girlfriends, that she structures her emerging identity. Female friends her own age help her keep her balance by validating her experiences, reassuring her she's not the only one who feels the way she does, communicating her generation's norms, and offering a safe space for venting unruly emotions. Older women smooth this transition by providing nonjudgmental nurturing, offering insights into the larger culture, affirming her unique worth, and serving as role models.

University of Colorado developmental psychologist Beth Doll observed that during adolescence, children "recognize the interrelationship between being authentic and being a friend." In the sense psychologists use it, "authentic" means the opposite of phony and then some—a genuineness anchored in an awareness of one's own feelings, a willingness to be oneself. When Sara noticed that Rhonda, her friend since elementary school, seemed to fall short in authenticity, she cooled the relationship. "Rhonda changed so much when she was around certain people," Sara explained. "I just couldn't be friends with her, because I didn't know who she was."

Adolescent girls don't like imitation, even when it's imitation of themselves. Sixteen-year-old Marcia Winslade complained of her best friend Julie: "She feels like she needs to be like me, or something, when other people are around. It's just uncomfortable, and tension develops."

Forging and maintaining authentic connections is tricky, even for grown women. Because adolescents are still developing a sense of themselves, a knowledge of their culture's conventions, and a mastery of negotiation and other interpersonal skills, they live in a state of chronic social anxiety. Agonizing about having zits, dropping a book in the school corridor, or saying something stupid all comes down to fear of rejection.

Trying to avoid disrupting relationships, a girl may shy away from saying what she thinks or expressing what she feels. But by succumbing to this temptation to silence herself, she destroys, rather than protects, her connection to others. The greatest danger of such self-censorship is that the girl will lose touch with her own observations and emotions. As developmental psychologists Jill MacLean Taylor, Carol Gilligan, and Amy Sullivan pointed out in *Between Voice and Silence,* concerns about being too outspoken inhibit even poor and working-class girls, who generally aren't saddled with the injunctions to be ladylike that burden their middle- and upper-class peers. When the authors asked the twenty-six ethnically diverse girls in their study to complete the sentence "What gets me into trouble is . . . ," more than half answered "my mouth," often "my big mouth."

But if she's lucky, a girl will have a friend to whom she can say what she thinks.

❧ The Top Priority ❧

Teenage girls understand the importance of relationships. In fact, many of them rank all other aspects of their lives a distant second. In a landmark study of female development, twenty-three students at the Emma Willard School—a girls' school in Troy, New York—were interviewed once a year beginning their sophomore year. Each time, the interviewers asked the girls to describe themselves, and each time the responses included twice as many statements about their relational style and skill as about their achievements, the runner-up for most-mentioned.

"I definitely think, especially for this year, that it's been more important that I meet friends and that I have a place for myself in the high school than that I get good grades," Sara Heller said. "My parents freaked out when I got a C in bio. I didn't get a C in friendship."

Besides, she explained, the prospect of spending time with friends actually helped her academic performance. "Last year, I never wanted to do homework, because I didn't have any friends," she said. "Now I have friends, and it's like I've got to get this done so I can talk to my friends."

Research, too, suggests that adolescents with friends do better in school. Developmental psychologist Richard Alan Spurling interviewed inner-city students at risk of dropping out and concluded that friendship was among the most important ingredients in a successful transition from eighth grade to ninth. Other studies demonstrate that prodding from friends is often what gets dropouts to return to school.

On the other hand, trouble forming and maintaining intimate friendships seems to spell trouble elsewhere. Although close friends can be a crucial source of support for an adolescent girl, the anxiety and hurt feelings that plague unstable friendships can spill over into the rest of her life. The overall importance of being able to maintain friendships has spawned efforts to teach social skills to adolescents who have trouble making and keeping friends. One program, developed in the United States and in Israel, works like group therapy, but with a specific focus: Participants practice initiating friendships, expressing emotion, and giving constructive criticism with others in the group. Another program, devised in Australia, involves a group discussion of friendship issues in which the adolescents must apply what they learn to their real-world relationships and report back.

Helping girls ages thirteen to seventeen become better at friendship seems to be worth the effort. Positive adolescent friendships offer benefits that last long after adolescence itself has passed. Ego strength—a firm sense of who one is—is essential to psychological health. And establishing individual identity is the major developmental task of adolescence. This becoming a person doesn't happen in isolation. It occurs in social context; and female friendship, with its mutual sharing and caring, its freedom from set roles, can provide an ideal environment for this growth.

᚛ The Big Betrayal ᚛

Just at the point when girls need each other most, they get a countervailing message: It's time to set female friendships aside in order to focus on boys. Women who had gone through their teens before 1975 told me that this message had come through loud and clear from their families, schoolmates, and the media. Even if you had a long-standing date with your best girlfriend, convention allowed you to—even encouraged you to—cancel it on short notice if a boy asked you out.

This practice may have been socially acceptable in the past, but many adolescents and young women I interviewed told me it wasn't any longer. With divorce so common, they knew that landing the right man didn't guarantee that you would live happily ever after.

"I never let a guy get between me and my friends," fourteen-year-old Marley O'Leary told me. "Guys are second. Friends are forever."

That doesn't mean that many adolescent girls don't still neglect their female friends when boys enter the scene. In fact, a 1995 study reported that both girls and boys involved in romantic relationships were less intimate with their friends of the same sex. But girls today no longer accept this shift of loyalties as right and natural.

✦ When Family Ties Bind ✦

For girls, as for boys, adolescence is all about declaring and achieving independence. As chapter 4 explained, throughout women's lives, psychological growth takes place in the context of connection. We become stronger and more independent by connecting with others, not by severing ties and marching off on our own. Teenage girls aren't pushing their families away so much as they're pushing themselves up, while trying to stay connected. But it often doesn't feel that way, either from a girl's side or from her family's, particularly from her mother's. Tears, shouting matches, bitter arguments, and icy stares invade what had been pleasant and virtually trouble-free relationships only a year or two earlier.

As a child, Sara Heller had looked forward to the time her family spent together at their second home in the Berkshires, a couple of hours from their residence near Boston. Now, as an adolescent, she pleaded with them to leave her in the city.

"My parents went to the Berkshires last weekend, and my dad just didn't understand why I didn't want to go," she told me. "And I didn't want to go because mainly I just wanted to see my friends. I don't want to spend time with my parents at this age. I need my parents. But I just don't want to be around them."

This is the stage of life when girls turn to each other constantly for validation and are more likely to confide in friends than in mothers or sisters. Girls enter adolescence facing an issue boys work out by kindergarten: defining themselves as individuals independent of their mothers. From the mother's point of view, the impulse to hold on, to protect, to validate herself by molding a copy of herself can be overwhelming. From the daughter's, the temptation to remain blended, to become an extension of her mother, is so strong that the emerging young woman must resist it if she is ever to become her own person. Although she desperately needs female nurturing and advice to help her through this passage, her mother may be the last person to whom she feels comfortable turning for those imperatives.

Even the most devoted mothers and daughters find themselves at odds during the teenage years. For girls who've had problems relating to their mothers all along, adolescence only widens the communication gap. The simplest discussion can quickly degenerate into a battle of wills.

Maternal conflict aside, girls often have trouble talking to their mothers about their aspirations for the future and even about their ideals. Women now at midlife grew up in a world with different expectations and opportunities, and different concepts of feminine virtue, from the world their daughters now face. Adolescent girls know that they can expect to be employed outside the home from the end of their schooling until retirement age and that no matter how hard they work at it, they can't count on a lifelong marriage.

One topic many adolescents feel they just can't discuss with their mothers is sex. For a girl growing up in a family that espouses strict religious or cultural mores, the issue of sex poses particular problems, especially if sex outside marriage is considered a serious sin or if her virginity is viewed as a matter of family honor. If she were to reveal to her mother that she was having sexual feelings for her boyfriend, even if she was resisting the temptation to act on them, she might find herself forbidden to see him. Faced with such possible sanctions, naturally she would be wary of seeking maternal advice.

But even girls from more tolerant backgrounds feel uncomfortable revealing their most private thoughts and feelings to their mothers.

When I interviewed fourteen-year-old high school freshman Dotria Rowe, a petite, stylish African-American, she told me that she'd discuss a problem regarding her boyfriend with her best friend, Mareesha, rather than her mother.

"I used to talk to my mom a whole lot, but as I got older, I kind of kept things to myself more," Dotria said "My mom is my best friend; she's easy to talk to. But if I had anything that was real, real personal, I'd probably talk to Mareesha."

Stung by the rejection of themselves and often their values, parents often feel betrayed and blame this natural distancing on the "bad influence" of their daughters' companions. This becomes increasingly tempting, because the number of friends a mother doesn't know generally increases as a girl enters her teens. Sociologist Lillian Rubin observed that parents often view adolescent friendships as "outlaw relationships"—as threats both to the family's authority and to its central position in their daughter's world.

⟿ Hanging Out, Hanging Together ⟿

In the three weeks since Marley O'Leary had moved from San Jose, California, to Galveston, Texas, she and Ariel had become best friends. They went to the beach and to the movies; they slept over at each other's houses and stayed up half the night talking—doing at fourteen the same things they might have done together at age eleven.

During early adolescence, female friendships struggle under the same practical limitations that restrict those of young children. But an American girl's sixteenth birthday ushers in new possibilities for social interaction: A driver's license gives her mobility, and a part-time job offers spending money and the chance to meet new people.

"Your activities are really dependent on your age," said eighteen-year-old Joanna Winslade. "Sixteen is a major liberty point. Until you have a car, you have to have a planned activity before you can go somewhere, because you are dependent on your parents to drop you off here, pick you up there at this time or that."

That liberty propels teenage girls closer to friends and takes them farther from parents, literally adding wheels and fuel to a process that was occurring naturally. Cars introduce an element of spontaneity. A girl with a car can go to one friend's house and, after an hour of listening to CDs, head off together to another friend's or to see a movie. Family rules may require that she alert her parents to the change, but that's a far cry from expecting them to drop everything and provide transportation. Best of all, a girl with a car doesn't have to cut short a heart-to-heart conversation because Mom, Dad or an older sibling has arrived to take her home.

For adolescent girls, even more than for adult women, intimate talk is the currency of friendship. If they can't share the details of their days in person, they do so by phone, awing adults with their ability to spend hours discussing "nothing." But through this apparently trivial talk, friends help each other develop psychologically. Research shows that one of the most popular topics is gaining independence from parents. Whether the exact content of the exchange is as mundane as griping about a curfew or as profound as questioning the family's religious beliefs, the subtext is "I am becoming my own person, and this is who I am."

And at this age, girls really do tell their friends just how they feel, exactly who they are—at least at that moment. Adolescent girls reveal so much of themselves to their intimates at a time when they're so vulnerable, it's no wonder that many of them consider trust the quality that distinguishes friends from associates. That trust cuts two ways: A girl has to be able to trust her girlfriend to keep secrets, and she has to be able to trust her not to lie about herself. "You need trust in a friendship more than anything," Sara Heller said. "If you can't trust somebody, it's not worth even pretending you are friends."

Sara had experienced both kinds of breaches of trust. After learning that Nora was using her confidences to improve her own social standing, Sara no longer considered her a close friend. Sara broke with another friend, Rena, because she faked some injuries to get attention. After that, Sara decided that she didn't know what was the real Rena and what was fabrication.

↝ Forms That Flourish ↝

Like the adult women I interviewed, the adolescent girls I talked to displayed the range of friendship types I described earlier. But certain forms predominate at this age. Childhood bonds that survive the turmoil of puberty become history friendships, and girls easily make playmate friends as they hone their interests in specific activities. Several studies of female high school athletes suggest that friendships often get girls involved in sports, that friendships stimulate players to do their best, and that girls bring their emotionally supportive interpersonal style to the playing field.

Marcia Winslade had cultivated friends for two of her favorite activities—night swimming and dancing at ska clubs. She was prudent enough not to plunge into the lake behind her house or the nearby Gulf of Mexico alone after dark. And the club scene was best experienced in a group. Although Marcia enjoyed the friends she hung out with, she didn't count them in her inner circle. They were companions, not confidantes. These relationships were different from the one she had with her closest girlfriend, Julie.

"We don't spend a lot of time together, but we understand each other," Marcia said of Julie, whom she'd known since second grade. "I've known her for so long, we can say things to each other and understand what we mean by what we say."

From ages thirteen through seventeen, a girl has an urgent need for soulmates, lifemates, and mentors, as she first begins to consider her adult prospects and as she explores relationships with boys—nowadays, in an environment that pressures her to be sexually active.

Marley O'Leary told me she'd never had a fight with her new best friend Ariel. When I asked why she thought that was, Marley replied, "It would be like fighting with myself."

Although she didn't use the term, Marley was describing a soulmate friendship, a form that has special appeal to teenage girls. A soulmate's uncanny understanding and unfailing support serve as a refuge from a world that seems quick to criticize but slow to comprehend. In a study of eleven- to nineteen-year-olds advertising for pen pals, Israeli psychologist Shmuel Shulman found that more than half wanted to correspond with someone almost exactly like themselves. What they were looking for, he explained, was a relationship "in which each friend finds his or her lost self in the other." Not surprisingly, more than three-quarters of the adolescents placing the ads were girls.

Girls tend to choose friends who are like themselves in personality and intellect, and both girls and boys tend to pick friends of the same race. That phenomenon may indicate lingering racial prejudice and the reaction to it, but it also reflects the importance of having a life-mate during adolescence. Black, Latina, Asian, and Native American girls have a special need for lifemates because they face challenges that only another girl from the same background can help them meet.

Any girl who's an outsider will feel a bond with another girl her age who's in the same position. Marley was drawn to her friend Dana because of the way she dressed and acted. "She was different, and I was different, and we were different together," Marley explained.

Because an adolescent must make the transition from girlhood to womanhood at the same time she is declaring her independence from her mother, she may turn to an older woman outside her family to give her the guidance she needs. Marley chose a friend's mother as her mentor. "I had a two-year-old sister that I took care of," Marley told me. "I would just take her over to Kristen's, and Kristen's mom would help with the baby. They just kind of took care of me over there. I loved it, and I felt so at home. Her mom was my mom."

Some adolescent girls find themselves drawn into a nurturer role themselves; but because they lack experience setting limits, these friendships often become draining. That happened to Sara Heller. "There is this one girl, Nora, who says, 'You never call me,' " Sara said. "She is one of those people who need attention, really bad, like they don't know how to survive without it."

Research may show that most bonds between adolescent girls are founded on similarities. But forming a friendship of opposites—one with an agemate who's different in some significant way—can help a girl learn tolerance and explore emerging sides of herself.

At the time I interviewed her, Susan Baker Olsen was a forty-six-year-old family court judge, but she still saw Ina, the friend she'd made the summer between her sophomore and junior years in high school, when they'd both worked behind the candy counter at a local movie theater. Despite their similar situations, the real attraction lay in their differences. "Ina is very opinionated," Susan said. "She decides right away whether she likes somebody or not. I am not that way, because I wasn't raised with the freedom to do that. My mother is English. If you can't say something nice, you don't say anything at all. And here I am friends with this woman who immediately says, 'Oh, I can't stand him.' " Ina exemplified being open and direct—qualities Susan wanted to explore and make her own.

Friends help teenage girls sort out who they are—and who they aren't. To become themselves, girls need other girls—to serve as models, to nurture them, to dare them to scale the walls of convention. And to become fully themselves, they need to set limits with and define themselves independently of those friends.

Teenage girls do this one-on-one with their close friends and en masse in ensemble friendships and cliques. During adolescence, cliques are defined according to interests, aspirations, and poses. By adult standards, the qualities that characterize adolescent groups range from the laudable to the ridiculous to the frightening.

Whether a girl is drawn to the cheerleading squad or a gang, the impulse is the same: the longing for affiliation. Erik Erikson explained the dynamic this way in *Childhood and Society:*

> Young people can . . . be remarkably clannish, and cruel in their exclusion of all those who are "different" . . . It is important to understand (which does not mean condone or participate in) such intolerance as a defense against a sense of identity confusion.

Social crowds carve up huge high school populations into manageable interpersonal chunks. Some girls choose all their close friends from within their affinity group; others cross the boundaries. Some set great store by their group identification; others resist being categorized.

Despite parents' worries about peer pressure—and their perennially dismayed reactions to teenage clothing and hair styles—their fears about the negative influence of friends are often exaggerated. As sociologist Lillian Rubin observed, the tug-of-war between individuality and conformity that characterizes adolescent friendships is an outward manifestation of the struggle each girl goes through internally as she develops into her own woman. Not only is the resulting tension to be expected; it's healthy.

~ The Dangerous Passage ~

That doesn't mean that teenage girls don't face real and serious dangers. Adolescence is a treacherous time. According to figures compiled by the U.S. National Center for Health Statistics, as girls move from the five- through fourteen-year-old to the fifteen- through twenty-four-year-old category, they become two-and-a-half times more likely to die and become almost eight-and-a-half times as likely to become victims of accidents and homicides. Even more sobering, the chance that a girl will die at her own hand increases eightfold.

Adolescents are at risk in part because they are risk takers. The urge to try something new, even though they know it might be damaging, is irresistible.

"My parents want me to get these great grades, and I have all this curiosity about what it would be like to be somebody who skips all their classes and doesn't get good grades and doesn't study," Sara Heller told me jauntily. "Obviously, I know that that is not worth it later on in life. But it's like little babies: They touch everything. They eat everything to check it all out. You want to check everything out."

Scores of studies on the use of tobacco products, illicit drugs, and harmful quantities of alcohol focus on early adolescence and the effect of peer influence. Much of the evidence from this research suggests that young people tend to choose friends with similar predispositions, not friends likely to pressure them into doing something they don't want to do. Selecting friends and conforming to fit in with them also operate synergistically. Smokers pick other smokers for friends, who in turn encourage them to keep smoking; nonsmokers hang out with other nonsmokers, who discourage them from picking up the habit.

Even though the influence of peers increases throughout adolescence, parents retain significant power in shaping their children's behavior. In fact, adolescents who have strong relationships with their parents tend to imitate their drinking behavior. If a girl feels close to her mother and her mother abstains or drinks moderately, she'll be inclined to follow her example. She'll also emulate her mom if her mom is an alcoholic.

When it comes to the use of illegal recreational drugs, the issue of peer influence remains murky. Adolescents who have a lot of drug-using friends are more likely to do drugs themselves. But that doesn't mean that their friends cajole them into starting. After interviewing thirty-seven high school students, Harvard educational psychologists Randy Kafka and Perry London found no support for the common belief that kids do drugs because their friends pressure them to.

Adolescent girls face another risk as dangerous as drug use: depression. Granted, a certain amount of what psychologists call "depressive affect" is normal for teenage girls. Sulks, mood swings, and bouts of grief over broken friendships and romances are so common at this volatile age that serious emotional problems can be difficult to spot. But the tendency among girls to experience genuine clinical depression rises during the sophomore and junior years of high school.

A close, caring friend can help a girl defeat depression, but only if the two can stay connected. Serious emotional problems wreak havoc with friendship, and sometimes the bond doesn't hold. "I have no idea why, but Elise became really depressed and anorexic at the end of seventh grade," Sara Heller told me. "I tried to be friends with her again, but she was in her own little world because of her depression."

Friends often know when an adolescent girl is in serious emotional trouble before the adults around her do. A senior participating in the study at the Emma Willard School faced the dilemma of whether to tell a counselor that a freshman friend was seriously considering suicide. Although bringing in the counselor meant breaking a confidence and possibly losing the friendship, the older girl decided she couldn't risk keeping quiet. What finally convinced her to intervene was the thought of how she'd feel if the younger girl did try to kill herself. "I'd just feel like garbage," she said. "I'd rather she be alive and never want to speak to me than be dead and not have the chance."

In 1995, the most recent year for which statistics are available, 1,890 Americans fifteen to nineteen years old took their own lives. And that figure includes only the deaths officially ruled suicides. Failing a note or similar evidence of intention, when a seventeen-year-old driving alone fatally slams her car into a bridge abutment or when a sixteen-year-old consumes a lethal cocktail of barbiturates and vodka, the National Center for Health Statistics groups her with victims of "accidents"—the official cause of death for 3,529 American women age fifteen to twenty-four.

Between a quarter and a third of all adolescents think about killing themselves. A study of 409 Virginia high school students revealed that roughly the same percentage had a friend who tried or talked about committing suicide in the past year. Describing hopelessness as "the critical link between depression and suicide," the psychologists who conducted that survey noted that research suggests that suicidal adolescents are less likely to have a close friend than their nonsuicidal peers.

But providing that support can be hazardous. Suicide threatens not only girls who try it; it may also do serious emotional damage to their friends. In fact, almost a third of the friends and acquaintances of adolescent suicide victims are likely to suffer major depression, as opposed to normal bereavement, and friends of adolescent suicides run an increased risk of suicidal behavior themselves.

~ Getting Better at Friendship ~

Having a depressed friend puts a girl herself at risk, but it can also teach her two valuable lessons: to accept responsibility for the conduct of her relationships and to consider the potential consequences of her actions and words. By puberty, girls grasp that friendship has certain rules and parameters—keeping secrets, listening to each other's problems, not leaving each other isolated on the playground or at a party. But adolescents go a step further, replacing this concrete notion of friendship as a contract with an abstract sense of it as a web of mutual support and commitment.

In fact, deep down, the friendships of teenage girls are a lot like those of adult women, with one essential difference: The girls in them are still developing an authentic sense of themselves. Because they're not quite sure of who they are, they have trouble creating an interdependent, as opposed to a dependent, connection. That's why adolescent girls often get immersed in their friends' needs and neglect their own.

After finding that the adolescents with the strongest, most satisfying friendships were those who scored high on both identity and intimacy, Australian developmental psychologists Susan Moore and Jennifer Boldero concluded:

> [F]riendship may lead to developmental gains, or those who are more mature may be more likely to form and sustain meaningful friendships. The most likely possibility is a two-way street . . .

Early adolescent friendships can be just as stormy as those of late childhood. Quarrels flair over nothing and subside just as quickly.

Such small spats disrupt but don't necessarily damage a close friendship. As girls develop impulse control and communication skills, they learn how to avoid them.

"I used to blow up at my friends when I was younger, just because I had a really bad temper," Sara admitted. "But I learned that it's not really worth fighting with people. When I get mad at somebody, I don't keep it inside me. I tell them, and we talk about it and pretty much work it out. When somebody gets mad at me, I make them tell me why, and I tell them exactly what I think, and we talk about it."

Simply acquiring basic social skills, such as being on time and conducting a conversation, eases adolescent friendship. As a girl learns to listen to her friends—really listen not just to the content, but to the nuances of what they say, she begins to develop the empathy that characterizes adult female friendship.

To experience empathy, a girl first must be able to read accurately the thoughts and feelings of others—to see from body language, facial expression, or tone of voice that a friend is nervous or sad or hurt. But a girl can have this intellectual capability, which developmental psychologists call "social cognition," without its emotional sequel, the ability to share the experience vicariously. It's the difference between seeing that a friend is embarrassed and feeling embarrassed for her.

Empathy enables older adolescents to give each other support in real crises, but younger girls often haven't fully developed this ability. Jennifer Lee and her friend Adrienne had been just fourteen when Adrienne's father died; Joanna Winslade was seventeen when her friend Elsa experienced a similar loss. The difference in their responses reflects their difference in maturity.

Although Adrienne's father had been seriously ill for nine months, Jennifer wasn't prepared for her friend's call from the hospital. Jennifer recalled: "She said, 'Oh, hi. It's me.' It didn't sound like anything was wrong, and I had no idea where she was calling from. And I just said, 'Well, I'm kind of walking out the door. What do you want?' She was quiet for a second, and I realized that she was crying. Then she told me, 'He died.' I was just stunned. I'll always regret the fact that I had that attitude when I talked to her. But then, we were only fourteen."

Joanna and Elsa were halfway through their senior year when Elsa's father died of an asthma attack. Because the death was unexpected and Elsa was alone when she discovered his body, the circumstances were more traumatic. But Joanna felt in retrospect that she'd given her friend appropriate support.

"She found him in the middle of the night," Joanna explained. "The next day, a few of us who were her close friends spent the day at her house helping her deal with everything."

During all kinds of family crises, adolescent girls turn to their friends. Chronic turmoil at home exaggerates the normal shift away from family and toward peers. A girl whose parents are divorcing, for example, will turn to her soulmate for comfort but also seek out new friends—crisis friends among girls going through the same trauma, lifemates and mentors among girls who've learned to live as children of divorce. Even though these new friendships may be fleeting (as crisis friendships are by their nature), they help the girls in them work through their feelings and resist becoming intensely attached to their mothers, which could undo the identity-building work of adolescence.

☙ Friends Forever? ☙

At sixteen, Marcia Winslade knew that building an important friendship meant risking the pain of its loss. She'd experienced that with Nola, a girl she'd met while studying in France the previous year. "She was seventeen and a very charismatic person," Marcia said admiringly. When Marcia decided that she couldn't stand living with her host family, she confided in Nola, who responded with uncritical support. "She took me out, spent the day with me, and just talked, let me say anything I wanted," Marcia explained. But a few weeks later, Nola returned to Spain. "I got one letter from her, and that was it," Marcia told me wistfully. "I think she was just glad to forget about France."

Nola's apparent lack of interest in continuing the connection hurt Marcia in two ways: She felt the pain of loss, and she was reluctant to expose herself to similar pain again. Even though she had tasted empathy and now missed it, she seemed wary of intimate friendship.

But for adolescents, the pain of separation is often the price of true friendship—the bill that comes due when lives diverge. As girls become women and take different directions, they often do drift away from the girlfriends who played such a large role in their lives during childhood and adolescence. Sometimes, they manage to stay connected. Sometimes, they reconnect.

"There were three years that we weren't in contact at all," recalled Ronnie, thirty-five, of her high school friend Helen. "We just grew apart. In college, we went in the opposite direction."

Then, in their early twenties, Ronnie and Helen rekindled their friendship. Ronnie's first job took her to New York, which gave Helen an excuse to visit her. And when Ronnie flew back to Portland, Oregon, to see her parents, she usually made time to see Helen. "She's still so honest, and I can be really honest with her," Ronnie replied when I asked what she valued about their enduring friendship. "She knows all the ins and outs and all the craziness in my family and vice versa."

This is the kind of friendship many adolescents dream about—a connection that doesn't end at high school graduation but continues down the decades. Sara Heller observed: "I think that it is better to be friends with someone your whole life—and they will go to your funeral and you will go to their funeral—than to have twenty friends that you will see through high school and that will be it. You'll be looking at the yearbook fifty years later and say, 'Yeah, I sort of remember that person. I think that she was one of my best friends.'"

By recognizing early the irreplaceable value of lifelong friends, girls like Sara are already well on their way toward having them.

8

Flourishing amid Firsts: Ages Eighteen to Twenty-two

We met, and it was a complete connection. . . . It felt that I had found the other part of the person that I needed to be.

—Ronnie, thirty-five, on her closest college friendship

As I interviewed women in college and older women recalling that period in their lives, I heard tale after tale of close, life-affirming friendships, full of empathy, insight, shared discovery, and sheer fun. What was it, I wondered, that made college, at least for many women, female friendship heaven? And what about women who didn't go to college right out of high school—did they miss out on the bonding?

College is a transitional period between adolescence and adulthood in which women seek out emotional closeness and support to ease them through their new circumstances and replace some of the nurturing their mothers gave them at home. A young woman this age is in a unique position: She's on her own, and yet (if school is paid for by her parents and especially if she lives in a dorm or a sorority house) she is not burdened with full responsibility for her survival. Apart from her studies, she's free to focus on her social interactions with her peers and on the task of separating psychologically from her family.

"There's a huge difference between being in college and being in high school," observed Joanna Winslade, who grew up in Galveston, Texas, and had just finished her freshman year at Yale. "I consider myself an adult now, which I really couldn't do at this point last year, because I hadn't been away from home ever. Once you leave home, that's the first you can start feeling you are part of the real world."

She also felt an exhilarating sense of abundance. "Although I went to a large high school, maybe there were 120 people in my classes who would be likely candidates for friends," she said. "Now there are five thousand. And nobody knows you ahead of time. I can erase the things about myself that I don't like."

At no other stage in her life does a young woman meet so many others with at least age and education level in common. They engage in late-night bull sessions and share idealistic causes. They embark on adventures such as packing up right after the last final exam and driving nonstop from Massachusetts to Florida.

College is an ideal venue for this type of bonding, but it's by no means the only one. Middle- and upper-class Americans traditionally go away to college, where they remain financially dependent on their families but free of daily parental scrutiny. Working-class girls, who often contribute to the family finances through part-time jobs during high school, may keep living at home after graduation but chip in for rent and groceries as they work full time, even if they continue their educations. Many Hispanic families, whatever their social status, expect their daughters to leave home only when they marry.

Whether she's away at school, enlisted in the military, or embarking on an entry-level job, from ages eighteen to twenty-two a woman finds herself surrounded by potential lifemates, playmates, and intriguing opposites. The close friendships she forms help her deal with a succession of life's firsts—leaving home for college or first jobs, first marriages, first children.

"At this point in my life, I'm an adult," said Tara Boland, a twenty-one-year-old senior at Flagler College in Saint Augustine, Florida. "Part of that is learning about being an adult woman."

Because her mother had died when Tara was eight, Tara looked to her close female friends to teach her. "As far as my sexuality is concerned, as far as my womanhood is concerned, the only way for me to find that in me is through other coming-of-age women," she explained.

~ Antidotes to Loneliness ~

Cast into an unfamiliar environment when they are beginning to experience adulthood's heady power but before they must shoulder its full responsibilities, women eighteen to twenty-two are especially open to new experiences and new people. Like intense love affairs, college best friendships can form and flourish quickly under these conditions, then fracture and disintegrate just as fast. Propelling both the intensity and the fragility are the exhilaration and anxiety of leaving the nest.

Even surrounded by others her age and sex, a young woman away from home for the first time is vulnerable to loneliness. Her mother may not have understood her taste in music, but she knew, and cared, when her daughter was coming down with a cold or worried about a test. At college, no one nags a young woman, but no one considers her well-being her top priority. That first disappointing grade or bout of flu freshman year can bring on the sinking sense that no one really cares.

By serving as surrogate families, sororities promise protection from loneliness. That's one reason why, after being rejected as elitist and conformist by the first wave of baby boomers, they returned to favor. Between 1973 and 1995, membership in college fraternities and sororities increased more than 45 percent.

Sororities break a large university down into manageable social portions, and they also preselect women who are similar in interests and backgrounds. This provides a ready pool of prospective friends; but it also limits the prospects, and that limitation keeps some women from joining.

"I actually began to pledge," said Marissa Heller, a twenty-one-year-old senior at Columbia. "I got a bid from the one that I wanted and then decided it wasn't for me, because I could never imagine saying this is the type of girls I would like to be friends with. I like all types."

Some college women who already have close friends on campus join sororities to expand their social circles. "When we were choosing which sorority we wanted to pledge, Brenda and I didn't really want to be in the same one," Donna Freund, an eighteen-year-old freshman at Boston University, said of her best friend. "First semester, we only hung out with each other. We didn't really make other friends, and we wanted to do a sorority just to meet other people—not to make a new best friend. It ended up we both liked the same sorority, and we were a little hesitant about how that was going to be. But if anything, it's brought us closer."

By providing a sense of affiliation, the sorority gave Donna and Brenda a sense of fitting securely into university social life. By offering a ready pool of more casual friends, it gave their close friendship room to develop without being burdened with meeting all their needs for connection.

⤳ Forms That Flourish ⤳

One of the appeals of going away to college is the potential for finding a true soulmate. The size of the field of new candidates greatly increases the likelihood of meeting a good fit.

"She's smart, hilarious," Ronnie, thirty-five, responded when I asked what initially attracted her to her best friend from college, Kate. "We have the same tastes in music. At that time it was Joni Mitchell, Simon and Garfunkel, all the old sixties stuff.

"We met, and it was a complete connection. I had found the other part of the person that I needed to be. I'd just discovered literature that freshman year, and she and I would stay up till all hours talking about books and ideas. She wrote fiction, and we talked a lot about that. We read for each other and encouraged each other and acted out scenes. We also went out and danced like crazy. It was like a love affair without sex. It was a real, true female friendship."

Ronnie and Kate created their own interpersonal culture, complete with inside jokes. "We even have a name for our friendship that we made up, because no one could get the kind of connection we had," Ronnie told me. "We called it 'beachla.' "

Of course, not all college friendships are soulmate relationships. Heather Chapman, a senior at Smith, told me that Cathy, whom she described as her "closest friend besides family," was in many ways her opposite. "We lived across the hall from each other freshman year," Heather told me. "We were basically connected at the hip from the day we met. It was weird. We just clicked. We were so different. I was this bouncy, cheerleaderish California girl, and she was a Nebraska farm girl—something that I had never encountered. But we'd start talking about old boyfriends, and one could tell half the story and the other one knew what happened."

Women ages eighteen to twenty-two get more than just intellectual stimulation from opposites friends; they get a chance to explore different attitudes, values, and lifestyles. From the time they met during freshman orientation, Marissa Heller recognized Nan as her opposite. Both were from the Boston suburb of Brookline, and both were Jewish, but the similarity ended there. Marissa had gone to public schools, Nan to private. Politically and socially, Marissa embraced the liberal point of view, Nan the conservative. Nan's goal in life was material success, something Marissa considered unimportant.

From the start, the friendship between Marissa and Nan had thrived despite disagreement. Even vigorous arguments about philosophical issues didn't distance them from each other. If anything, these debates brought them closer. But disputes about personal issues were another matter.

"Nan is a self-centered, almost selfish person," Marissa observed. "It's a product of the way she's been raised. There are times when she can't advise me without her best interests at heart, rather than mine. In terms of my going to San Francisco next year, she screamed at me, told me she would be furious if I went. She wanted me to be in New York, because she is going to be in New York. I don't feel comfortable talking to her about my further plans with San Francisco now, which is a bummer."

The things that bothered Marissa about her relationship with Nan are common complaints among college-age female friends. During these years, the issue of whether one friend is attuned to the other's needs, or only to her own, is crucial to the quality of the friendship. In fact, in a study at the University of Texas at Austin, the more responsive one friend was to the other's needs, the more favorably the other ranked the relationship and the more stable it seemed to be.

Not all female friendships forged between ages eighteen and twenty-two are intense interpersonal connections. Marissa distinguished between her closest friends and what she called "social friends," or what I describe as playmate relationships. She partied with two, played lacrosse with a third.

Although ensemble friendships don't dominate social life in college the way they do in high school and earlier, they remain a popular interpersonal form. Donna Freund and her best friend Brenda had made friends separately with another Boston University freshman, Darlene, and the three of them regularly hung out together with several other classmates. "We all eat dinner together every night, just to see each other," Donna said. "Then we go to the library together. The nights that we're going to go out, we go out together."

Lifemate friendships also thrive, although at college, in the military, in an entry-level job, or in an apartment complex packed with newlyweds, women at this stage of life are surrounded by so many others in similar circumstances that forging a lifemate bond takes something more—coming from the same town, sharing similar family backgrounds, majoring in the same subject. Jennifer Lee decided early in her career at the University of California–San Diego to major in ethnic studies, although it was one of the school's smaller departments. Jennifer liked the program even more than she'd expected. After she talked it up to her dorm mate Jeri and Jeri decided to major in ethnic studies herself, they drew closer. "It was so great," Jennifer said, "because there were so few of us, and we all bonded."

ᴗ Shedding High School Friends ᴗ

"There were six of us, and you didn't go out unless we were all going together," Marissa Heller said of her high school ensemble. "Aside from Celia and me, I don't think anyone speaks to anyone else in that group of friends anymore. And I think it says something about what was real and what wasn't."

The period from age eighteen to age twenty-two is a time when lifelong friendships start, but it's also a time when friendships that once looked like they'd be lifelong end. High school graduation is a true watershed—a point where even the closest friends' lives diverge. Although Donna Freund and her best friend from high school vowed that they wouldn't let going to colleges in different cities disrupt their relationship, it did.

"I thought I would never, ever find anyone who would be able to compare with Freda," Donna told me. "Freda is still one of my best friends, but I've moved on with my life. I've changed, and so has she."

Staying connected is challenging enough when friends head off to different universities. But when one goes to college and the other doesn't, something more than miles separates them. That's what happened to army physical therapist Capt. Charlene Guardia.

"I'm not even in touch with my best friend from high school anymore," Charlene said wistfully. "That's a strange one, because out of everyone that I've been friends with, she was my closest friend ever. When we both graduated, I went to college. She didn't. We just started to drift. When I would come back from college, we would have conversations, and we were just not on the same wavelength anymore."

Sometimes it's the less intense adolescent friendships that survive the eighteen-to-twenty-two transition. Chrystal Hunter, a twenty-one-year-old junior at Southwest Texas State University, hadn't found anyone in college she felt nearly as close to as Anne, her friend since sixth grade. Going to different high schools didn't damage their friendship; neither did going to different colleges.

"We don't have the kind of friendship where we're constantly calling each other," Chrystal explained. "But when we do call, we are very supportive of each other. I know if I have a problem, she is there to listen and to give me a true response to the situation, not just tell me something that I want to hear."

⤳ Affirmation and Other Gifts ⤳

Anne gave Chrystal affirmation. One of the most valuable gifts of female friendship throughout a woman's life span, affirmation is especially important as she passes from adolescence to adulthood. By affirming her feelings, responses, and insights, friends mirror a young woman's emerging adult self, helping her identify which qualities she wants to discard and which she wants to keep.

Nonjudgmental affirmation was one of the main things Donna Freund treasured about her best college friend Brenda, too. "A best friend is someone you should be able to tell everything to, no matter if it's something that you feel is wrong or you're embarrassed about," Donna said. "With my best friend from home, I felt like there were certain things that I couldn't confide in her, because she wouldn't approve."

Wit and charisma attracted Marissa Heller to Pamela, but it was Pamela's knack for affirming Marissa's experiences that made them close friends. "She is charismatic and quirky and hilarious in a way that nobody else is," Marissa told me. "I guess I was drawn to her first for that. But then I was going through a really tough time, and I started talking to her about all the things I was going through, and she listened. She was there for me like most other people weren't. When they got fed up with me, she stuck by me. And she got it. She understood. I think she really connected to me, and I've loved her ever since." With Pamela, Marissa felt loved and appreciated for her true self.

As it does throughout life, female friendship also helps college-age women cope with personal loss. For example, parents whose marriages may have been in trouble for years sometimes wait until their children are away at college to divorce. Not only has a daughter in this position left home; the home she left no longer exists. When that happened to Charlene Guardia, her best friend's mother and father offered themselves as a surrogate source of stability.

"When my parents got divorced, Emily's family became more family to me than my family," she noted. "This was from college on, and it's still that way. That's kept me and Emily real close."

Friends also can be crucial to helping a young woman deal with a parent's death. Developmental psychologist Kirsten Jan Tyson-Rawson studied twenty female undergraduates whose fathers had died. She found that what she called "sustaining" friendships helped the bereaved daughters choose paths of "behaviors, beliefs, and attitudes" that enabled them to resolve their grief.

The transition from adolescence to adulthood heightens the importance of female friendship to a young woman's personal development. That's why conflict can be almost as great a gift as affirmation, provided two friends engage in conflict in a way that promotes growth. When two friends voice disagreement, then work through it rather than retreating, both the friendship and the women in it emerge stronger.

At ages eighteen to twenty-two, women are uniquely ready to engage in constructive conflict. They have the social and communication skills they need to express their own feelings and listen empathically to another's; yet they are still idealistic enough about relationships that they have little tolerance for artful dissembling and evasion. In fact, they tend to feel betrayed if a friend holds back something important, good or bad, that's going on in her life.

When I interviewed twenty-two-year-old Jennifer Lee, she was re-evaluating her relationship with Adrienne, her best friend since second grade. They were lifemates. Both were only children. Both had grown up Chinese-American in a largely white neighborhood in Southern California. After they went to different colleges, they'd stayed in touch by phone and E-mail. But something disturbing had been going on in Adrienne's life, and she'd kept it to herself.

"For over a year, this guy was stalking her, and she never told me about it," Jennifer said. "Being private, the school decided to handle it according to their own system. But they never did anything about him."

Adrienne lived in an old, coeducational dorm. Although pushbutton locks secured the individual doors, overhead crawl spaces used by the maintenance staff linked the rooms. One day, her boyfriend had just left her room when Adrienne walked over to her closet and happened to look up. There, staring down at her through a barely shifted ceiling panel, was a pair of eyes.

"That was the time that she actually called to ask me for my advice," Jennifer told me. "I said, 'This has been going on for over a year?' I was kind of upset with her."

But rather than complain, Jennifer got right to the point: "Stop fooling around with the residential life people. Go to the police. I don't want to hear about you ending up dead one day."

Jennifer may have been overly idealistic when she assumed that Adrienne would let her know as soon as she suspected she was being stalked, but that sort of idealism has an important practical side. Living alone, a young woman is vulnerable. By letting her close friends know the details of her life and telling them when she feels threatened, she gains a genuine measure of safety. Rather than encouraging dependency, friends who look after each other's well-being in this way help each other become, and remain, independent.

❧ The Roommate Connection ❧

Despite all Marissa Heller and her friend Pamela shared and how deeply they cared about each other, becoming roommates challenged their friendship. "When we first started living together this year, I got a little annoyed with her," Marissa admitted. "Every single thing that she does—'Is that wrong?' 'Do you think I should do that?' 'Are you sure I should have done that?' Her questions are ceaseless. She's a beautiful girl, and she's intelligent and all of that. She just needs constant reassurance."

Pamela was communicating her anxiety and insecurity, but at least she was communicating. One of the important lessons young women learn from having roommates is the essential role communication plays in enabling people to live together comfortably. It's a wonder not that roommate arrangements often don't work out, but that they often do. Consider the typical first roommate experience: Two young women who've never lived with anyone besides their immediate families find themselves sharing a cramped dorm room or apartment with someone they've met only briefly at orientation.

The roommate relationship is a unique hybrid. It has some of both the positive and the negative aspects of the sibling bond, but without the permanence. Two women share their personal space, undress in front of each other, listen to each other snore, overhear conversations with parents and lovers, witness each other's test anxieties, and share head colds. As a now-famous Israeli study conducted by Aron and Leonard Weller revealed, roommates even tend to synchronize their menstrual cycles. Yet they're not necessarily friends, although they can help each other grow in ways that friends who don't live together can't.

"Having a roommate allows you to learn things about yourself that you never had a chance to learn before," observed Faith Lagay, a graduate student in her fifties, who was in the process of resuscitating a friendship with her college roommate from three decades earlier. "You're used to having your brother or sister tell you you're inconsiderate," she explained. "You just blow it off. But when someone you're not related to tells you the same thing, you listen."

The mirror roommates hold up to each other may not be flattering, it may not even be kind, but its frank reflection makes self-awareness difficult to dodge.

✦ Surviving Romance ✦

Nothing challenges a young woman's female friendships like falling in love. A wise woman will spend enough time with her girlfriends to maintain those bonds, and a wise friend will recognize that sooner or later her smitten pal will integrate the new romance into her life and become available once again, even if on a reduced schedule. As sociologist David Lee Mitchell explained, sexual bonding takes place in the context of an individual's entire social network. Once two lovers establish a relationship, they restructure the rest of their interpersonal lives to accommodate it.

Early in her senior year, Marissa Heller had formed her first serious relationship with a man, and that had affected all her friendships, including the one with her lifelong best friend Nicole, who went to college in another state.

"This is definitely by far a more serious relationship than I ever knew existed," Marissa told me. "Darren is my best friend, next to Nicole, I would say. He looks out for me in a way that nobody else ever has. We have a connection that I think is really unique, and really phenomenal and amazing."

Darren hadn't replaced Nicole. In fact, Marissa and Darren planned to move to San Francisco for a year after graduation in part because Nicole would be living there, too. But the love relationship raised issues in the friendship, issues Marissa had never had to deal with before. For instance, Marissa didn't know if she should move in with Nicole or Darren in San Francisco.

When one close friend starts to build a serious romantic relationship, envy and jealousy often disrupt the friendship. The woman who doesn't have a partner may envy her friend's good fortune, especially if her lover is particularly desirable. At the same time, she may feel excluded and resent the attention her friend now lavishes on him, rather than her. Some of this is appropriate. Lovers do spend a lot of time alone together, excluding their friends, and the affair can so absorb a woman that she wants to talk about nothing but its joys and problems—and wants to listen to nothing but congratulations and comfort, no matter what's going on in her friend's life.

But when envy and jealousy make one friend unable to affirm the other's happiness or respond supportively to her anxiety or sorrow, the friendship is in deep trouble. A woman who can't discuss with an intimate friend what she considers, at least temporarily, the most important relationship in her life will withdraw. A serious affair challenges and tests a female friendship; envy and jealousy can destroy it.

❧ Facing the Future ❧

Jennifer Lee had managed to maintain her friendship with Valerie, whom she'd known since junior high, even though Valerie went to college a continent away. "We E-mailed when we could, or wrote or called," Jennifer said. "And when everybody was home for vacation, we got together."

Surprisingly, Jennifer's decision to finish her bachelor's degree in three years rather than four had brought her even closer to Valerie and her other friends from home. "Since I was graduating, everybody was anxious to see what I wanted to do with my life," said Jennifer, who was about to marry her high school sweetheart and start graduate school in ethnic studies.

Plans for the future are a main topic of conversation for friends aged eighteen to twenty-two. Traditionally, college provides a four-year grace period between adolescence and adulthood, with the real world always looming. As the end approaches, anxiety can overshadow eager anticipation. Female undergraduates report feeling even more stress than their male counterparts. Some of this has to do with concern about the changing role of women in society: Should she get married now or after medical school? Should she take a job in Europe or one close to her family? But research shows that part of the stress results from worries about the disruption and potential loss of close college friendships.

College women recognize graduation as a social turning point. They know that the connections that were so easy to maintain when everyone lived on the same campus will require hard, persistent work when they scatter. They sense that telling close friends about their lives will feel very different from living them together. They understand that only the closest, most life-enhancing of their college friendships will survive the challenge. And they suspect that even some of these may not.

9

Real-World Drift: Ages Twenty-three to Thirty-nine

Early adulthood is the era in which we are most buffeted by our own passions and ambitions from within, and by the demands of family, community, and society from without. Under reasonably favorable conditions, the rewards of living in this era are enormous; but the costs often equal or exceed the benefits.

—Daniel J. Levinson and Judy D. Levinson,
The Seasons of a Woman's Life

When Bett graduated from the University of Oregon, she knew exactly what she wanted to do: move to San Francisco and put her new degree in social work to use. Her closest sorority sister, Diane, thought that sounded like a great idea. So did another female classmate. They could share an apartment, get their first real jobs, and enjoy being young and single in what they all agreed was the most exciting city in the world.

Everything was an adventure—riding cable cars together, furnishing their two-bedroom apartment with castoffs, driving down to Carmel for a weekend, watching the reaction of dates to eating dinner off a Ping-Pong table.

"It was our first experience in the big world," Bett said.

The living arrangement lasted only a year and a half. When one roommate left for four months in Europe, the trio gave up the apartment. But during their brief cohabitation, the three young women smoothed the entry into adulthood for one another, providing empathy, companionship, practical help, and protection while they got their bearings.

As housing costs have risen and women have postponed marriage, a period of living with financially self-supporting but emotionally supportive girlfriends has become an American rite of passage. But as many women recognize, this arm-in-arm step over the threshold of adulthood is often a short one. If a romantic relationship doesn't dissolve the roommate arrangement, job opportunities in other cities or rising incomes and the desire to establish one's own space may.

⁕ Diverging Lives ⁕

Early adulthood is life's physical prime, the years when the body's systems are at their peak, able to meet the demands of bearing and raising young children. In Daniel J. Levinson's model of female development, which I described in the introduction to Part Two, this season begins with a five-year transition from adolescence starting at age seventeen and closes with a five-year transition to midlife starting around age forty. In between are three overlapping stages. From age twenty-two to age twenty-eight, a young woman tries out what Levinson called an "entry life structure for early adulthood"—embarking on a first career, committing to a marriage, or enjoying the freedom of single life. As she nears age thirty, she begins to see the limitations of whatever path she chose. By age thirty-three, she's made her adjustments and settles into the life she has built.

The thirty-nine women I interviewed between the ages of twenty-three and thirty-nine reflected this pattern. Those in their middle twenties were trying things out; those in their middle and late thirties had committed to a life course, sometimes even feeling stuck in it. Those in between were reevaluating everything, including how they related to other women. As women approached their middle thirties, their lives were changing constantly—and at different paces. This was playing havoc with their friendships.

Young women may enter the adult world intertwined with their female friends, but the rapid flux that marks the years from twenty-three to thirty-nine snaps some bonds. So much is going on in a woman's life that old friendships that do survive typically shift character, often several times. With adolescence officially ended, she becomes responsible for supporting herself or becoming part of a self-supporting domestic partnership. Even if she goes to graduate or professional school, society expects her to use loans and fellowships to pay her bills, rather than to rely on her parents. For a young woman on a starting salary, going out for a beer or a movie becomes a major decision. If she becomes a stay-at-home mom, she has to manage a household on one paycheck. Married or single, she shoulders the responsibility for her shelter, food, transportation, and health. Meanwhile, she faces the daunting tasks of establishing an adult identity.

Jean, a thirty-six-year-old horticulturist and triathlete who lived on the Hawaiian island of Oahu, told me that over the last several years she had begun to turn inward. "It is a realization that you have to figure out how you are going to make it in this world," Jean explained. "You're in your thirties now, and you can't just go off and do whatever you want anymore. You've got to make some decisions and stick with them, be it a career, marriage, or a relationship. So I think that you become a little more self-absorbed, maybe even selfish."

When I asked Jean how many close female friends she had, apart from her sister, she told me none. Of the 204 girls and women I interviewed for this book, only 7 gave that answer. Of those, four were between the ages of 23 and 39. (Of the others, one was 79, another was 90, and the third, who was 47, was battling multiple sclerosis.) In fact, 10 percent of the 39 early adult women I talked to lacked even one intimate female friend.

"I don't know that I have any close friendships right now," said Marti, a thirty-nine-year-old environmental scientist in San Francisco. "There are a lot of people that I get together with and consider good friends. But it makes me think about what the expectations are for a friendship and whether that has changed."

Whether a young woman goes to graduate school, enters the work force, or stays home to raise children, her friendships tend to decline in both number and intensity during this stage of life. At thirty-seven, Sally Good spoke wistfully about her girlfriends from college and the years right after. Now divorced, she was back in school, working on her doctorate in English, and rearing two daughters, ages nine and ten. She was down to one close friend and only tenuously holding on to a few others who used to be her intimates.

"A couple of them I probably talk to on the phone once a year, and we send Christmas cards," she said of her old roommates. "I have one friend who is in the process of moving to Denmark. Her husband's in the military. We've just made E-mail contact, so that's kind of nice. We can stay in touch that way."

Despite Sally's efforts, most of these friends had drifted out of her reach, the connection broken. "When I lose contact with a really close friend, I have a hard time turning her loose," she confessed. "I do everything I can to reestablish the friendship. I saw on a talk show that there was a friend-finder service that would find people that you had lost touch with. I even considered calling that."

When it comes to the drop in friendships in early adulthood, research confirms that overbooked lives are more to blame than lack of interest. Comparing women ages twenty to thirty-nine with those ages fifty to sixty-nine, social psychologist Kathleen Sullivan Ricker found that although the younger group reported more intimacy with their female friends, they also reported more difficulty keeping them.

"I've been losing a lot of friendships this year," twenty-six-year-old Renee Asofsky told me. "I'm getting tired. I used to exhaust a lot of energy keeping up with all my friends, making them all know that I was always there. I'd be out late. There was no night that I could just go home and relax. This year, I found out going home and relaxing is a good thing."

Loosening some of her formerly close connections left Renee feeling relieved, rather than bereft. But for many women, instead of fading away, the connection between friends snaps.

"Marietta was one of my best friends post-college," said army physical therapist Charlene Guardia. "Everyone else was married, and we were single. We were in first jobs; we had money; we had our first apartment. That was a very fun time of life."

When Marietta got married, Charlene gladly agreed to be a bridesmaid—even though the dress and travel cost her more than $800, and using her leave to come to the wedding meant Charlene wouldn't be able to see her fiancé for three months. A year later, Charlene was getting ready for her own wedding. But when she asked Marietta to be in it, she declined, citing the cost.

"We had a very big fight over that," Charlene told me. "I made this big sacrifice, and now she's telling me a year later that she can't come because of money."

Stunned that her best friend wasn't willing to extend herself to participate in something so important to her, Charlene ended the call. "She should have wanted to come and found a way," Charlene explained. "That was my thought. Maybe it was immature of me, but I just couldn't get past that at that point."

Shortly thereafter, a ten-page letter arrived from Marietta. "She said how sorry she was and how she didn't want to risk our friendship," Charlene recalled. "Then she just told me every reason financially why she couldn't make it."

A year after the wedding, Marietta wrote again. "She said her year had been just terrible, ever since our friendship broke up," Charlene told me. "They had to move for her husband's job, and she didn't have a whole lot of work where they moved. She was four months pregnant. She'd never been so financially unstable."

Enclosed with the letter was a $150 check—a belated wedding present. Charlene returned it. "With all these problems in her life, there was no way I could take the money," she explained. "I sent a real nice card and said, 'Please don't take this wrong. When you're financially stable, send it back, but right now I would feel so guilty taking this.' I haven't heard from her since."

This valued friendship had suffered major damage, which Charlene and Marietta might have been able to repair had they been able to sit down together and talk through their feelings. But living thousands of miles apart and facing the competing demands of early adult life, they were unable to reconnect.

⁓ Dilemmas of Time and Distance ⁓

Although early adult women may not be able to maintain their close friendships from earlier life stages, that doesn't mean they don't value them and mourn their loss. Roberta, a twenty-eight-year-old editor in New York, told me wistfully: "There was a period when I could have told you who my five best friends were, but that period has faded. All of my really vital relationships are in the past."

When I interviewed Sherri Jayson, she was a twenty-one-year-old college senior, working on a term paper about female buddy movies. *Thelma and Louise, Boys on the Side,* and the other films she was analyzing depicted iron-strong bonds between women, but Sherri wondered how to make such friendships last a lifetime.

"Women have their childhood friends, and they go to college and have their college friends, and then they move on," she observed. "They have their married friends. When they start giving birth, they have other friends that they know from having children the same age. What I want to know is, Why don't they hold on to some of the previous friends?"

Sharing change is what makes early adult friendships form and remain close. But sharing implies being there—if not in person, then through frequent two-way communication. Going through similar experiences independently isn't enough.

Moving, one of the most serious challenges to friendship, is an inescapable fact of early adulthood. The twenties are the most mobile decade in women's lives. In any given year, about a third of Americans age twenty to twenty-nine change their primary residence. If a woman this age doesn't move, chances are one of her close friends will. Many women move several times before they turn thirty.

For Kiran, who'd graduated from Yale two years before our interview, letters were the threads that knit her together with her far-flung friends. Taking a job as a reporter for a newspaper in Jacksonville, where she knew no one, she spent her free time writing to her college friends, who had scattered around the globe. Those who wrote back became closer; those who didn't faded. One friend, Jennifer, who was living in Moscow, made a particularly gratifying correspondent.

"Really, I think that was one of the ways our friendship deepened, because I got to see a more thoughtful side of Jennifer," Kiran said. "Her personality tends to be very bubbly and enthusiastic. But in her letters, when she was sitting down and thinking about what was going on in her life, I got to really appreciate her."

The mobility that separates friends also can reunite them. After a job offer at *Gourmet* magazine shifted her from Houston to New York at age thirty-two, Margo True rekindled two friendships from her California college days. Neither had been especially close then, but circumstances made them so now—at least potentially. Because she lived in Margo's neighborhood in Hoboken, Kitra, a photo editor at *Good Housekeeping,* was close geographically as well. Margo had learned that the distance factor was crucial in New York.

"This city really makes having friendships difficult, unless you live three blocks from each other," Margo complained. But even though she and Kitra did, they saw each other on average only every six weeks. "She's really busy, and so am I," Margo said, echoing a refrain I heard repeatedly from women aged twenty-three to thirty-nine.

Distance and time restraints disrupt female friendship, but they needn't destroy it. In fact, if both women in the relationship are flexible and expend the effort to stay connected, these challenges that test the bond can actually strengthen it, as I described in chapter 3.

❧ Work: Cutting Two Ways ❧

At thirty-five, Katrina Garnett was one of the hottest entrepreneurs in Silicon Valley. She had just launched her own software company, CrossRoads, bankrolling it with $15 million in private capital, $3.5 million her own and her venture capitalist husband's, made from the stock options they had negotiated from their previous employer. She had a dream career, a devoted husband, a two-and-a-half-year-old daughter and another child on the way, and the prospect of great wealth and influence, but only one good girlfriend—a classmate from college. "She's as hard-working and career-driven as I am," Katrina remarked when I interviewed her.

Although Katrina met other high-powered women through her business, none of those acquaintanceships developed into close friendships. "I couldn't tell you the last time I went shopping with a woman," she said. "I can't justify it, because I'd rather be with my kid. You have your company, your family, your house, your pets. It's hard to do something that's just social."

Whatever career they choose, women twenty-three to thirty-nine are chronically short of time. Myhang Nguyen, a thirty-three-year-old Carmelite nun who immigrated from Vietnam at the age of eleven, taught music in a Catholic school during the week and served as director of religious education at a cathedral on weekends. She also played the piano, sang, and conducted at church and school functions, and she shouldered her share of the housekeeping duties at the convent where she lived with thirteen other Carmelites. Apart from her sister, her closest friend was a married mother of three, who was deeply involved in church activities.

"Because of her different lifestyle, she with her busy days and I with mine, we don't talk that much," Myhang said. "When we get together or when we start talking on the phone, we can go on forever. We are very open. To a lot of people, a close friend is someone that you contact all the time. But I don't consider a close friend as that. I would say close friends are friends that you can be yourself around."

Myhang's experience illustrates what developmental psychologist Carol Goodenow found in her research for her dissertation on friendship patterns of adult women: Although full-time employment reduced the amount of contact between friends, it had no effect on the quality of their relationship.

Jobs limit the time available for friends, but they also increase opportunities to meet new ones. The promise of connection can be so alluring that many women choose monotonous, low-status, low-pay positions over staying at home, even if the wages barely cover the costs of bus fare and child care. After studying Mexican-Americans in a California cannery, cultural anthropologist Patricia Zavella concluded:

> [E]ven seasonal cannery work, under degrading conditions, has meaning for those women who are bored with the isolation of home . . . or who seek friendship with other women.

Work is where early adult women make most of their friends, because that's where they spend most of their waking hours. In 1997, more than three-quarters of American women between the ages of twenty-five and forty-four held jobs.

"If you work in the financial industry, your friends are in the financial industry," said twenty-three-year-old New Yorker Mali List. "They're the people you see at two in the morning while you're still working or at five A.M. because you're dealing with the international market. You end up getting an apartment together, because those are the people you meet. It's the same with law. If you're a lawyer just starting out, you work long hours, and most of your friends are the people you go to lunch with."

Lunch is only one of the built-in, almost institutionalized opportunities for social interaction afforded by the modern workplace. Co-workers encounter one another at the coffeepot, celebrate one another's birthdays, and, if they smoke, share their banishment to just outside the front door. Especially for time-pressured women simultaneously launching careers and families, the distinction between cordial colleagues and intimate friends can blur. Some relationships can translate from professional to personal life, but many exist solely within the office environment.

Office friendships present some of the same problems as office romances. For one thing, the power differential among employees limits interaction. And even two women with equal positions and equal salaries may not be equally able to pursue a friendship with each other. Professional and businesswomen with working husbands generally don't consider money a limiting factor in what they do with friends. But single women, especially single mothers, feel a financial pinch on their social lives even if they make above average salaries.

Despite the challenges on-the-job friendships present, the support that women give one another in their work can be crucial. Gail Penrice, a twenty-six-year-old artist teaching art part time, met Aja, another African-American artist, at a craft festival. Their friendship grew as they shared their feelings about their own work and their insights into each other's.

"I think we're both alike in the sense that we're not so sure about ourselves and our creativity," Gail explained. "We can't see what people are experiencing when they see our work."

Work is a subject that arises with friends made outside the workplace, too. Kiran, the twenty-four-year-old who'd traded her newspaper job for graduate school, described how she and her friends helped one another keep their careers in perspective. "An issue that comes up with a lot of women my age is, Do you go all out for your career or do you compromise a little bit to be nearer your family or your friends or your boyfriend?" she said. "It's a big issue for every woman I know who's working."

When a woman is unhappy in her job or suspects better opportunities lie elsewhere, friends who aren't coworkers often supply better affirmation and insight than those who are. Suzette, a thirty-five-year-old deckhand on a ferry, turned to her friend Cher for support and advice concerning an all-too-common problem: sexual harassment.

Cher encouraged her to file a complaint. And when the lawyer for her employer made Suzette feel as if she were the one who'd done wrong, Cher enjoined her to be strong. Suzette won her suit and kept her job.

Whether a working woman faces a crisis like Suzette's or merely the day-to-day stresses that come with most jobs, she needs female friends to encourage her and affirm her value, both in and outside the workplace.

❧ Marriage and Motherhood ❧

Nowadays, women marry at every age, but for first weddings, the early twenties remain the most popular time. Despite this trend, the U.S. Census Bureau projects that by the year 2010, a third of all twenty-five-to-thirty-four-year-old Americans of both sexes will never have been married. More and more women are choosing to remain single, and those who do so by choice tend to consider themselves exceptionally competent and socially desirable.

But despite the rising acceptance of the single state as a potentially fulfilling lifestyle, marriage is still the most popular option. In 1995 only 19 percent of American women between thirty and thirty-four had never married. However, the bonds formed by the other four-fifths often don't last. The 1990 census revealed that by ages thirty-five to thirty-nine, 34.1 percent of women had been divorced, 65 percent of those had remarried after divorce, and 28.5 of *those* had divorced. Such statistics demonstrate the flux in domestic status that early adult female friendships must endure.

When I interviewed her for this book, Rene Kealey was thirty-three and had been married for three years. Since ninth grade, Claire had been one of her best friends. In their early twenties, they shared some hilarious times. But then, while Rene was single, Claire married twice. The first union had little effect on their friendship, but the second challenged and changed it.

"When she was dating her first husband, we did a lot of things together despite their relationship," Rene explained. "Sometimes it was a threesome. Or he would do something while Claire and I did something.

"They got married and divorced really quickly. After that, we went out every Thursday, Friday, and Saturday night. Then she started dating George, and I felt I didn't have enough time with Claire anymore. I was maid of honor in their wedding. But my relationship with her has definitely changed. We're still very good friends, but she has her own life and her own friends now."

What was unusual about Rene's experience wasn't that the friendship changed after Claire's second wedding, but that it didn't after the first. For one thing, single women like to get together with friends during the very times their married counterparts set aside for their families. For another, the responsibilities of marriage, coupled with the assumption that these always come first, can be so constraining that many married women have to content themselves with the idea of a friendship rather than regular contact. "I know she's there for me," I heard again and again from women at this life stage. "But I haven't talked to her in three months."

Changes in friendships begin well before the wedding. Many women in committed relationships stop going out with their female friends or at least tone down what they do together: Careening around together in a convertible at midnight gives way to sharing a bottle of wine and an hour or two of conversation in a respectable café.

Often the intensity of female friendship fades even before a serious candidate for matrimony is on the scene. During early adulthood, many women who hope to marry focus their social time and energy on finding a mate. Though women's growing economic independence has lessened the frenzy of this search, it has also extended its duration. Single women who hope to wed keep looking well into their thirties; those whose first marriages don't work out feel pressured to find another husband while there's still time to have children.

At twenty-seven, Hollis Grant had just gotten used to having her first roommate; Amy Runyon, like Hollis, was an older-than-average student at the world-renowned Culinary Institute of America. In fact, Amy had become one of Hollis's closest friends, on a par with two girlfriends she'd had since childhood. Then Doug came along. The Culinary Institute's regimen didn't allow much free time, and what little Amy had, Doug was getting.

"I had gotten used to having her there all the time," Hollis said. "Then all of a sudden that was not happening because of him."

The phenomenon isn't limited to heterosexual women. Selena Wells, a twenty-seven-year-old lesbian artist and designer in Berkeley, felt excluded when her friend Violet fell in love with a woman named Merle. Although Selena hadn't been lovers with either, she was jealous because she was left out.

"Violet had gone through plenty of other girlfriends and boyfriends since I'd known her, but I don't think she'd fallen in love with any of the other people," Selena told me. "That was the difference. She really fell for Merle and became distant."

Before Violet and Merle got together, Selena typically found herself at Violet's two or three evenings a week. Now it was more like once a month. And Selena *liked* her friend's partner. All too often, that isn't the case.

Even friendships that survive the disruptions of marriage may founder when babies start arriving. Although a childless woman may understand intellectually that infants and toddlers require nearly constant adult attention to survive, she may still feel hurt when her best friend cuts her short in the middle of a heart-to-heart talk because the baby cries. The new mother may care as much about her friend as ever, but she's simply not as available emotionally.

Reliable, readily available contraception has increased the numbers of friendships that experience this strain. Before the middle of this century, women the same age almost always had children the same age. Now, although most American babies still are born to mothers twenty to twenty-nine years old, an increasing number of women postpone starting their families until their thirties. Between 1980 and 1994, the number of births to women over thirty more than doubled, and the number of *first* births per thousand women over forty rose by 50 percent in just six years—from 1990 to 1996.

Imagine four young women who become friends on their first jobs. Ten years later, one is single, another is married but childless, the third has a fourth- and a first-grader, and the fourth, a new baby. Even if these women remain in the same city, their paths have diverged at such sharp angles that the connection may snap.

When social psychologist Julie Carbery compared the friendships of women ages twenty to thirty-five in three categories—single, married but childless, and married with children—she found that, although on average the number of friends they had didn't change, the time they spent with friends declined progressively across the three stages. So did the amount of companionship and nurturing they were able to provide.

While experts agree that the intensity of female friendship reaches its lowest point right after a woman marries or moves in with a romantic partner, it's less clear how motherhood affects friendship. Sociologist Stacey Oliker found that "[m]others of young children have fewer friends and are especially likely to be socially isolated." But British sociologists Linda Bell and Jane Ribbens argued persuasively that far from being isolated, mothers of young children had ample opportunities to interact with others.

Two-and-a-half years before our interview, Lisa Taylor, a professional singer who had just given birth to her second child, had moved from Texas to Chicago. Despite that dislocation, she told me: "I have more close friends now than I've ever had. I'd say I probably have five to ten here in town and then probably another five out of town."

She'd made all of those new friends through the La Leche League—the support organization for breast-feeding moms. "I had a real urge to hook up with other young mothers," Lisa explained. "Like Laurel. She looked very, very happy and was very intelligent. She would verbalize a lot of things about motherhood that I was thinking or feeling but couldn't quite put into words. Also, her daughter was just a picture of beauty and health. I felt: 'What's her secret? How does she do this?' "

When I asked the difference between her friendships before she had children and those she had now, Lisa answered quickly: "A lot more information sharing."

Two decades ago, feminist sociologist Nancy Chodorow argued that female friendships dwindle once women have babies not because the women are busier, but because the children fill their emotional needs. But Los Angeles clinical psychologist Phyllis Gillman found something quite different when she studied the *closest* friendships of women between twenty-five and fifty: The friendships among mothers with preschoolers actually were stronger than those of childless women.

These women communicated with their friends primarily by telephone—a technology that allows a mom to concentrate on an adult conversation because she can supervise her youngsters without having to give them her full attention. A mother has a better chance of an uninterrupted heart-to-heart by phone—while the baby naps, while the toddler watches *Barney,* after the kids are in bed—than she does face-to-face at McDonald's with her offspring in tow.

When twenty-nine-year-old Lisa Gray agreed to be interviewed for this book, she suggested I stop by her apartment on a Saturday morning. In those familiar surroundings, she explained, her eleven-month-old daughter might nap. No such luck. The baby was wide awake and eager to be the center of attention, but Lisa and I managed to converse, albeit in fits and starts. She was looking forward to a week-long reunion with Donna and Gloria, two friends she'd made in college. Now the three were scattered from Massachusetts to Texas, but they'd all agreed to rent a beach house for a week on the Carolina Outer Banks.

The three friends had become pregnant within three months of one another. By phone and by E-mail, they'd compared pregnancy symptoms and traded theories on fetal and infant development. Now they were into teething. Having children at the same time had knit the women even tighter. When one's child did something cute or took a developmental step, however small, the other two friends applauded. And when one was troubled about her baby, the other two eased her anxiety.

For example, at a recent well-baby exam, the pediatrician noticed that Lisa's daughter grabbed things with her right hand, instead of reaching for them with both hands, as most children her age did. To make sure nothing was wrong with the girl's left arm, the doctor made an appointment with a specialist.

"I was of course terrified that it might be a neurological problem," Lisa recalled. "And Donna and Gloria were saying, 'We've seen the baby, and there is nothing wrong with her. Pediatricians feel they have to cover all their bases.' "

The specialist proved Lisa's friends right.

Lisa's experience illustrates why mothers need mothers as friends. Simply by acknowledging that being a mother is a difficult and important job, moms give one another support and recognition they may not get elsewhere. When one woman with children reassures another by sharing what she's learned, both gain—one from the information, the other from the affirmation.

Even women who get recognition for what they accomplish in other areas of their lives need other mothers to support them in their maternal role. Developmental psychologist Carol Goodenow told me about a psychotherapist she knew who treated a lot of highly successful business and professional women. "They would be desperate to find somebody else they could talk to about their kids, because at work, they were supposed to be working," Goodenow explained. Besides, female managers might not want word of their children's problems circulating around the office.

Vida, a thirty-six-year-old writer of continuing medical education materials, had recently moved to a new town. As she scoped out day-care centers, she had two goals in mind: The first was finding a center in which her two-year-old would thrive. The second was sizing up the other parents as potential friends.

University of Iowa sociologist Steve Duck noted that having a son or daughter start school automatically expanded the parents' friend-ship circle as they met the mothers and fathers of their child's class-mates. This, in turn, made the child "happier, more secure and better adjusted—possibly from having a good model to observe."

Angela Gamble's experience supports that hypothesis. As a single mother, she depended on her friends both for practical help and for affirmation of her competence. "Without my friends' and family's sup-port, I would not be able to be as strong as I am," she acknowledged. "And my children have also become strong."

Although the demands of family and work make friendship espe-cially challenging for young mothers, the effort pays off—not just for the woman herself, but also for her children.

❧ Forms That Flourish ❧

Although early adult women explore and enjoy all varieties of friend-ship, this season is prime time for lifemates. When she was in her mid-twenties and single, Liz Foreman hung out with a woman she met at work. "Matja was the only other single woman where I was working," Liz told me. "So we would go to these happy hours on Friday, and everybody else would have to leave, and Matja and I wouldn't.

"We became really close. We just loved to do the same things. We liked to go out. We liked to drink and dance, liked men. We were even living in the same apartment complex."

Then Matja introduced Liz to Jay, the man she first lived with and then married, and Liz and Jay introduced Matja to the man who be-came *her* husband. Now they were couples friends, as well as lifemates and playmates. But they still felt comfortable discussing their mar-riages frankly.

Matja wasn't Liz's soulmate. She was a bit more cautious than Liz, and that was part of the appeal. "I have a lot of girlfriends who are a lot of fun," Liz said. "But Matja is the one I feel safest with. She's fun, but she isn't dangerous."

For practical as well as emotional support, single women in their twenties and thirties rely on their lifemates. When I asked thirty-nine-year-old Carla Lowery what she valued most about her female friends, she replied: "Those minicrises that come up, we are there for each other, immediately. If a car breaks down or something, she's there."

As much as women who are single or married but childless need lifemates, mothers—especially first-time mothers—may need them even more. The mothers I interviewed reported feeling an almost mystical tug toward women with children the same age as theirs, and that pull began even before the babies arrived. Lisa Gray was only one of many moms who told me of bonds formed or strengthened with friends who were pregnant when they were.

The more life circumstances two mothers share, the more immediate the attraction. Woman after woman described initiating a friendship the day she moved into an apartment building: In the elevator, she would meet a neighbor who had a child the age of hers, had made the same choice about working or not, and was married to a man with a similar job. They must have been fated to be friends, these women told me. Never mind that they had such different temperaments and tastes that they might have ignored each other if they'd met, say, on a college campus. With motherhood, friendship priorities change.

Whether or not she has children, sometimes the combined support of a cluster of lifemates is what a woman needs. Even less intense lifemate ensembles help women in their twenties and thirties develop as individual adults, and in a crisis, a lifemate ensemble can be a literal lifesaver, or close to it. When Beatrice, an office manager for a real estate firm, was in her early thirties, she got a message on her answering machine from Catherine, a close friend she'd met five years earlier when their children were in kindergarten. "Her voice was very funny," Beatrice recalled. "I called her back and said, 'What's wrong? Are you alone?' No, her therapist was with her. At this point, I didn't realize she had any problems."

The therapist got on the phone and told Beatrice that Catherine was hallucinating and needed to be hospitalized. Summoning two other members of the ensemble, Beatrice rushed to her troubled friend's house. They bundled Catherine into the car and drove to the hospital.

Beatrice met with Catherine's children's teachers to explain that she'd had a nervous breakdown. The three friends took turns taking care of the kids after school and helping Catherine's husband with grocery shopping and other chores. And they visited Catherine every day of her hospitalization. Those three not only cared about Catherine, as lifemates they knew what she needed.

In early adulthood, women need female friends. But because the very changes to which friendship is most vulnerable—moves, mating, and motherhood, not to mention job jumps and divorce—proliferate during this stage, by their middle thirties, many women conclude that female friendship is fickle, an attachment of convenience.

Yet other women know that the potential for connection can be as great as ever during this time. Heidi Knox felt an immediate attraction to her friend Stella. The La Leche League had sent Stella to Heidi for tips on breast-feeding. When Heidi opened the door, she saw a young woman with artificially bright red hair cradling an infant in a long Victorian baby dress and crocheted bonnet.

Heidi instantly recognized that she and Stella shared similar, unconventional attitudes about child rearing. She told me, "People say, 'I'm having a baby. I need to have a crib and a walker and all these objects.' And we're saying, 'You really don't need all of that.' Neither one of us had cribs."

Heidi and Stella were more than lifemates; they were soulmates as well. Many of the twenty-three-to-thirty-nine-year-old women I interviewed spoke wistfully of the soulmates of girlhood and adolescence—connections treasured in memory. And the few women who did have current soulmate friendships cherished them.

Since moving to the New York area a year before our interview, Margo True had made two soulmates. Margo was a single woman dating a man half a continent away. Her two new friends were a lesbian couple. Yet the three of them held uncannily similar outlooks and opinions. "I like them because they are just like me," Margo said. "They really seem to be the same sort of person that I am, except they're gay. They're loyal friends, too."

Many of the women I interviewed spoke of having different friends with whom they shared different activities. For instance, twenty-seven-year-old Albuquerque massage therapist Deanna Batdorff told me: "I would go to a movie with Marcella; I wouldn't go to a movie with Roxanne. I'd probably drink with Roxanne. She and I drink together, and we eat together. Marcella and I have tea parties, and we do movies, and we go to parks. And Demi and I go wherever our minds wander, and we always end up somewhere strange."

But the primary glue between Deanna and each of her three closest friends was something other than the diversions they enjoyed in common. In fact, few of the women aged twenty-three to thirty-nine I interviewed described true playmate friendships. Among the exceptions, though, were those who played sports.

Lola, twenty-five, found Tammy a perfect fit as a running partner. With a similar stride but slightly faster pace, Tammy challenged Lola enough to make the training productive. "The important part is the support and encouragement that we give each other," Lola said. "I think that motivated me to get out there."

Other women loosen their hold on adolescence gradually or want to retain some part of that earlier era, often a favorite activity. A playmate friendship can help them do that.

Until Heidi Knox's two children were born, she and her husband would go hear live music four nights a week. Now adult responsibilities—and adult satisfactions—commanded her attention. But through her children's play group she had met Jenine, a woman with whom she could at least appreciate listening to the same music, albeit in its recorded form.

Friendships that began earlier in life as playmate bonds often change as women move through their twenties. Sally Good and Lucy started out as playmates when they were undergraduates at the University of Texas at Austin. "What we had in common was boys and going out and dancing," Sally recalled.

Lucy had been phenomenally successful with men. "One year on Valentine's Day she got seven arrangements of flowers," Sally told me. "She had many beaus, and I have never had a lot of boyfriends. That's always amazed me that other women can manage to attract so many at a time."

But Lucy had major personal problems, too. Her father had been missing in action in Vietnam. Her mother had disowned her. One night, when they were in their twenties, Lucy called Sally and told her that she'd just been raped. Sally rushed over to her apartment to call the police and stayed at her side while she gave her account, filed charges, and underwent the physical exam necessary to gather evidence.

Though this was an isolated and truly terrible incident, Sally recalled that, over the years, she always seemed to provide the shoulder Lucy leaned on. The friendship had settled into a classic nurturer-nurtured pattern.

Helping a friend who chronically needs it can be especially satisfying to a woman in her twenties or thirties, because it affirms her own recently acquired adult competence. When thirty-two-year-old Deneen Mickens's friend and cousin Kwaneesha, six years her junior, moved into her own place, Deneen gave her some of her furniture and charged her almost nothing for the rest of what she needed to set up housekeeping. And when she asked for advice, Deneen gave it cheerfully. "I enjoy helping her," Deneen said.

But early adulthood is also a time when a long-standing nurturer friendship can begin to feel draining. Sometimes the demands of the nurtured friend increase; sometimes the nurturer's other responsibilities rise, restricting the emotional energy available for her friend. Often, both happen simultaneously, as they did to Ronnie when she had her first baby.

"It really threw her for a loop that I had my daughter," Ronnie said of her best friend from college. "At the time I thought, 'Deal with it. I have other concerns.' One of the most important things in my life had happened. I was completely emotionally and physically spent, and she was worried about if I could take care of her anymore. I was furious."

Even if Ronnie's had been a lifemate or soulmate friendship, her daughter's birth might well have strained it. The greatest challenge to female friendship comes when life patterns diverge, which they tend to do during the turbulent twenties and thirties. One friend marries; the other doesn't. One has a baby; the other can't. One young mom stays home; the other goes back to work. Even between women who've been friends since elementary school, the gap can be unbridgeable.

But some women in their twenties and thirties take pains to maintain or even actively seek out friends living very different lives from their own. Opposites friendships can give childless women a chance to participate vicariously in parenting. "I don't want to be pregnant," explained Deanna Batdorff, who had several friends with infants. "I'm glad everybody else around me is doing it, because I don't want a baby."

Of the thirty-nine women I interviewed in this age group, only one described a current ally relationship. On the eve of the 1992 Republican National Convention in Houston, Lola had helped form the Women's Action Coalition to protest the GOP's efforts to roll back abortion rights. Lola and one of the coalition's other founders, Eileen, bonded almost immediately.

"I think we were very energized by the activities that we had, the events we had," Lola said. "There was a group of us that had a shared vision."

Women in early adulthood gravitate to women with whom to share similar experiences, but they also feel a special pull toward women who have already been there. When Liz Foreman was twenty-two, Carol, a fiftyish office manager for a medical school neurology department, hired her as a secretary. Carol and Liz developed a mutually supportive mentor-protégée friendship that lasted long past the six years they worked together.

Liz hadn't gone to college. Now, working in an academic environment, she recognized that she wanted and needed her degree. Carol encouraged her to go for it and offered her part-time work so she could. To help pay the tuition, Carol even passed the hat, raising $400 from the doctors in the department.

Carol's reflections on the hardships of early adulthood gave Liz the courage to meet them with good humor. "You know, you learn things from older women," Liz said. "How do you learn to have a marriage? Certainly, you learn it on your own, you and your husband, but you also learn it from the ladies at work. You tell them stuff you wouldn't tell your mother. If you're mad at your husband, your mom is going to say 'That rat!'—completely overreact, never look at him the same way again. The ladies in the office are on your side, but they don't have the same relationship with you. They didn't give birth to you."

Because Liz's own mother had died when Liz was twenty, she may have had a heightened need for this form of friendship. But other women twenty-three to thirty-nine described how important a mentor was to them at this life stage. When a woman is learning the ropes— of marriage or serious romantic relationships, of motherhood, of the workplace—she needs the encouragement and perspective of a woman who is older, wiser, and unrelated.

Examining the close female friendships of working-class married women ages twenty to forty-two in London, Irish sociologist Pat

O'Connor found that these bonds either had formed around their shared roles as wives and mothers (in other words, they were lifemates or possibly mentors) or during their own childhoods or adolescences. Lifemates share the daily challenges and joys of whatever path a woman takes in early adulthood; mentors offer example and sage counsel. But history friends, who correspond to O'Connor's second category, do something neither of the others can: They serve as custodians of our pasts.

Of all the forms of female friendship, the history bond is the only one to enjoy something close to institutional acknowledgment: For women without sisters, naming the longest-standing close female friend as maid or matron of honor has become a custom for American brides. When Lola married, she felt torn between her childhood friend Janet and her newer friend Amalia, whom she'd met three years earlier.

"At the time, I wasn't sure about who should be my maid of honor—Amalia or Janet," Lola recalled a year later. "I care for them both very much. Janet and I have this sense of history that extends back to the seventh grade. But I was really closer in a lot of ways to Amalia, because Janet and I don't share a passion for politics. We are very, very different."

Since the wedding was to be tiny (the guest list numbered ten), Lola had to select a single attendant. Citing the claims of history friendship, she chose Janet. But fate helped her have it both ways. On the December evening set for the ceremony, the weather was so bad that Janet's flight was delayed. So Amalia stood up with Lola after all.

Friends from childhood and adolescence keep us connected to our pasts; yet that very benefit can be a limitation. In her mid-twenties, Heidi Knox moved back to Chicago, where she'd lived as a teenager. She could share memories with friends from that earlier life stage, but she had trouble reconnecting with them in the present.

"They didn't really know me as an adult, so I felt like they were still acting like I was fifteen or sixteen," Heidi said. "And here I am with two children."

For history friendships to provide more than nostalgia value at this life stage, the women in them have to get to know and appreciate the adults their childhood friends have become.

✿ Coping in Connection ✿

Within a few months of moving from Florida to New York, Kiran had hooked up with several of her female classmates from Yale. They all seemed to be dealing with the same issues—in their careers and in their relationships with men and with their families. They were lifemates.

"We do the same things that we did together in college, like we have a meal and sit and talk or go to a movie and sit and talk," Kiran said. "But just the experience of not being in school and working has brought so many new issues that we all have to deal with."

Finding the time and emotional energy for female friendship is more difficult during the years from twenty-three to thirty-nine than at any other life stage, yet women this age need friends as much as ever. As a thirty-three-year-old elementary school teacher, Rene Kealey recognized that. The sense of connection she experienced with her three closest girlfriends was unlike anything she shared with anyone else, even the man she'd married.

"The relationship I have with those three is on a whole different plane from the one I have with my husband," she explained. "It's so much more earthy. We discuss what life is all about, and it's such a nurturing thing."

Research suggests that many early adult women rely on their female friends for the type of intimacy that only another, unrelated woman can provide. Clinical psychologist Leslie Smith studied the female friendships of sixty women in their twenties—forty single, twenty married—and found that marriage changed the functions these relationships filled, but not the sense of intimacy. When three generations of Anglo and Hispanic women were asked to list the members of their social networks, the younger women included more friends and fewer family members—and said they got more support from friends—than their mothers and grandmothers.

The women I interviewed told me of adapting their important friendships to moves, marriages, and motherhood by "visiting" with one another by phone, rather than face to face. For instance, Hollis Grant, who was single and lived in Poughkeepsie, New York, described how she and her friend-since-childhood Carolyn, who was married, had an infant son, and lived in California's Silicon Valley, maintained their ritual of watching the Academy Awards together every year: They turned on the TV, then picked up the phone and traded comments on what the actors and actresses were wearing, which movie deserved which award—the same sorts of remarks they'd made during the years they'd viewed the presentation from the same living room.

Women twenty-three to thirty-nine are relatively new to adulthood. Especially in the first half of this life stage, they may not know what their limits are, what they need, and that they have a right to what they need. Specifically, they may not recognize how much they need one another. Swept along on a flood of opportunities and responsibilities, they may push female friendships aside.

But for some women, female friendship blossoms, rather than fades, during the years from twenty-three to thirty-nine. "I became friends with a girl three years ago," Neiman Marcus saleswoman Tray, thirty-five, said. "And she would always say things like, 'I can't believe we've become such good friends. I had always thought you met your friends early and late in life.' "

As women move through their twenties and thirties, they often decide that they may never tell absolutely everything to a particular friend, even a dear one. When I asked Ronnie, thirty-five, how many close friends she had currently, she replied: "I would probably say about six, if not more. I have a changing definition for 'close.' That's part of the difficulty in answering that. Maybe I'm close to them, but there are certain things that we don't talk about. I feel that I don't need to be able to talk to them about everything."

In early adulthood, women don't talk about sex and romance in as much detail as the men in their lives may fear, but they do turn to each other for advice, reassurance, consolation, and the chance to simply vent about affairs of the heart. Occasionally a young woman needs a friend who isn't in the same place romantically as she is. Margaret Wu, a twenty-six-year-old attorney in San Francisco, had been friends with Sylvia since first grade. Even though they lived half a continent apart, when Margaret decided to tell her friends and family that she was a lesbian, Sylvia was one of the first people she wrote.

"It was no big deal," she told me. "I got a letter back from her saying she never thought I was a lesbian, but it didn't surprise her. She thought it was great and that I sounded happy in my life. Basically very supportive and positive."

Margaret needed that support. Her sexual orientation ran counter to both traditions in which she'd been reared—Chinese-American and Catholic. Although her parents didn't reject her, they disapproved of her decision to act on her inclinations. A long-standing, heterosexual friend's matter-of-fact affirmation meant a lot.

A female friend often is the first place a woman will turn when a romance doesn't work out. Three days after the wedding, Rene Kealey's friend Claire called her and said her new husband didn't want to be married. "She didn't tell her family for like a month," Rene recalled. "I was the only person who knew."

Rene listened. She commiserated. She kept Claire's secret.

Early adult women rely on their girlfriends to help them through all sorts of challenges—not just broken romances and shattered marriages. Five months before our interview, Lola suffered a miscarriage. "This was a surprise pregnancy, but we were certainly looking forward to the baby," she explained. Two women friends—one older, one closer to her age and pregnant herself—helped her deal with her disappointment and grief.

The thirties are the first decade when losing a parent to death becomes relatively common. Speaking of her friend Claire's mother's death, Rene noted: "It was a milestone: Like, now that we are really adults, we are moving on this path of growing older ourselves. These are always times you take stock of what life is about, who your friends are, that you're really happy that you have lifelong friends."

These crises are true tests of friendships, and some don't pass. Jillian, a thirty-nine-year-old Houston clinical psychologist, was completing her training three hundred miles away from home when her mother was diagnosed with terminal lung cancer. Over the phone and during frequent weekend visits, she noticed that Rita, one of her closest friends, seemed increasingly distant. When Jillian confronted her, Rita blamed their separation: Seeing each other every three weeks or so they couldn't expect to have the rapport they'd had as part of each other's daily lives. But after Jillian returned to Houston, the relationship didn't improve.

"It kind of limped along for about six months," Jillian told me. "I called her on it and never could get a direct answer."

But Rita finally did say, "You need too much."

"We'd called each other best friends," Jillian said, outrage and disbelief still lingering in her voice. "We celebrated the anniversary of our friendship. And she said I was too needy. My mother had just died after being sick all this year. So I thought: What is 'too needy' in this situation?"

If, instead of withdrawing, Rita had worked at staying connected, she would have been able to support Jillian in this crisis and would have strengthened both the friendship and herself. Remaining close to Jillian during the death of her mother would have helped Rita prepare for the eventual loss of her own mother. As it was, Rita abandoned both a valuable relationship and an excellent opportunity for personal growth.

❧ Companions in Continuing Quests ❧

As women move through early adulthood, they change, and so do their female friendships. "A lot of my earlier friends were Asian," Margaret Wu remarked. Now, she had unconsciously redrawn her circle of friends to include more people whose backgrounds differed from hers. As Margaret's sense of herself had clarified, other points of connection had become more important than ethnic identity.

Those changes often mean shedding friends from earlier eras. "People that you meet as an adult, they really know who you are as a person," Jillian observed. "It's not based on some old image of who you are."

As a child, Jillian hadn't liked tomatoes. Although she'd outgrown that antipathy long ago, she could count on her family to express shock every time she ate tomatoes in front of them: "You're eating a tomato!" Her parents made the same mistake with her friendships.

"Of course, they knew my friends growing up," Jillian said. "And my mother would ask, 'How's So-and-So?' We're talking friendships from junior high and high school, people who are not important to me anymore. Yet the people that I was closest to as an adult were very hard to integrate into my family in the same way that those old friends were. I always thought it was so interesting, because the people I was friends with as adults are truly connected to me, and they're not connected with the child."

Whether women marry or not, whether they have children or not, whether they work outside the home or not, they face a common challenge during their twenties and thirties: establishing themselves as adults in their families. What that comes down to—first, last, and foremost—is renegotiating their relationships with their mothers.

"As much as I love my mother, I have a harder time talking to her a lot of the time than I do to my friends," Hollis Grant confessed. "It's funny: When I talk to her on a woman-to-woman level, it's much easier. But when one or the other of us lets a mother or daughter thing creep in, it puts up a wall."

Hollis's mother was guilty of a common breach of boundaries: Sometimes she'd call Hollis's friends and ask what Hollis had told them about this or that experience. From woman after woman, I heard the same complaint with only slight variations: Their moms were trying to live their lives. These adult daughters were glad to give their mothers love, respect, and gratitude, but not the details of what went on in their jobs, their romances, their relationships with their kids. Those minutia they reserved for their girlfriends.

Early adult women also seek rapprochement with their own bodies. Women in their twenties and thirties continue to struggle with body issues, and they turn to their girlfriends for support.

Deanna Batdorff was what my mother would have called statuesque. She was about five feet seven inches tall, with lushly rounded breasts, a trim waist, full hips, and firm muscle tone. But I could understand how the sixty-five pounds of additional weight that she'd carried in high school would have made Deanna self-conscious. Losing those pounds had reduced that discomfort in one way but added to it in another: It had left her with stretch marks.

"As far as relationships and all kinds of things, I am very inhibited by my stretch marks," Deanna admitted. "I don't want anybody to see them. I feel scarred in my heart, just from the scars I have on my body. It's something that I'm working on every day, and it gets better."

And her friend Roxanne was helping.

"Roxanne is very thin and has this beautiful body," Deanna said. "She started taking me to these Japanese baths. It was just all women, and everyone would get naked and go in the steam bath and sauna and the whole thing. Pretty soon I got so comfortable with her seeing my body that I started getting comfortable with my body."

A lover couldn't have healed those emotional scars. If he left, or even if his interest faded, the wounds would have reappeared, maybe deeper. But the mirror of acceptance, held by a female friend close to the physical ideal herself, had the power to effect a lasting cure.

Women in their twenties and thirties struggle with spiritual issues, too. They may not feel comfortable with the faith in which they were reared; even if they do, they may want to reexamine its role in their adult lives. Or they may feel an urge to explore questions of meaning and ethics outside the boundaries of organized religion. For companionship in these quests, women often select one particular friend— someone who also takes the subject seriously, who shares a similar sense of wonder, someone who, above all, understands that for some women, disclosing their innermost thoughts on spiritual matters makes them feel more vulnerable than opening up about any other topic.

For delving into the spiritual side, Roberta, a twenty-eight-year-old editor, called her best friend from college, Beryl. "I can't have those conversations with anyone else," Roberta explained. "No one else has quite the same spiritual mix. She's struggling to be a very devout Episcopalian, and I'm a lapsed Catholic, quasi-pagan, agnostic. I vary from day to day, but I do have strong spiritual feelings. Yet we are able to communicate about spiritual subjects despite the serious differences we have. I just don't have that same kind of vocabulary with other people, the same core spiritual values that almost transcend category."

All the quests of early adulthood come down to a single search: the quest for oneself. With increasing self-knowledge comes increasing discernment, and that leads to stronger, more satisfying, more enduring friendships.

10

Friendship's Second Flowering: Ages Forty to Sixty-four

One of the pleasures of middle age is
to *find out* that one WAS right, and that
one was much righter than one knew at say
seventeen or twenty-three.

—Ezra Pound, *ABC of Reading*

At my fortieth birthday, my approach to friendship began to change. I remember looking around the table at the Thai restaurant where my husband had gathered ten of our friends and recognizing that, as much as I enjoyed these people, I had almost no separate relationships with any of them. Two of the women were primarily my friends; so was one of the men. But we always got together as couples. I felt a sudden longing for some friends of my own, especially female friends.

Later, as I researched this book, I learned that my craving had not been unique. Interviewing women between the ages of forty and sixty-five, I heard the same thing again and again: Sometime around age forty, they decided they needed more women in their lives.

Some took steps to meet and make new friends. "I've been thinking lately that I didn't have enough friends," said Susan Baker Olsen, a family court judge in Galveston. "I thought if I ran into someone who had similar interests to mine, we might just take that step to be friends."

So when a lawyer seeking a court appointment noticed a poster for a mystery Susan had written and mentioned that she, too, wrote as a sideline, Susan suggested they have lunch. In six months, that invitation had blossomed into friendship.

Other midlife women mentioned taking better care of existing friendships. "I notice as I get older, I treasure my friendships a lot more, and I work very hard to preserve them," said Polly, a sixty-three-year-old San Franciscan. "I think it's just a natural course for me to be taking."

Still other women I interviewed transformed long-standing acquaintances or casual friends into intimates. Miranda, a forty-year-old Los Angeles actress who looked twenty-five, told me that she'd just recently started to develop a close friendship with a woman she'd met at a theater workshop four years earlier. "I was not yet able to have friends at that point," Miranda said.

I heard scores of stories from middle-aged women who had rekindled friendships from previous decades. For Cat, a fifty-year-old poet in Buffalo, Wyoming, reconnecting with old friends had proved even more rewarding than she'd expected. "You pick up not only where you left off, but a little deeper," she told me.

The midlife surge in friendship activity can even overcome lifelong shyness. Mary Ruth, fifty-two, a teacher in Allentown, Pennsylvania, told me that she'd noticed her friendship pattern changing. In the past, she'd waited for people to choose her. "I was very quiet and introverted," she explained. But since she reached her early forties, she'd begun initiating friendships.

My search of the professional literature revealed that social psychologists had noticed this midlife friendship surge, too. Martin Fiebert and Kimberly Sue Wright of California State University at Long Beach found that women in midlife rated their current close female friendships as more important than those earlier in their lives. And a study of eighty-nine women between the ages of thirty-seven and fifty-nine conducted by Beverly Schydlowsky of the Fielding Institute showed that the importance they attached to these friendships declined from adolescence to early adulthood, then rose steadily thereafter.

ᴥ Going Where We Want to Go—Together ᴥ

Even women who haven't felt a strong urge for female connection previously seem to understand, consciously or not, that they need the company of other women to make the years from forty through sixty-four an era of growth, rather than decline. In his map of the human life cycle, Yale psychiatrist Daniel Levinson introduced this particular season with a five-year segue he called the Mid-life Transition. In reality, the entire two and a half decades are a transition for women. We enter it at forty, physically not much different from what we were at thirty. Yet, despite everything we might do to fight or hide it, "after about forty . . . biological senescing begins its inexorable predominance over adolescing," as Levinson put it. For our bodies at least, decline begins to win out over growth.

Genes, habits, affluence, and—yes—the quality of our relationships influence the speed and pitch of the decline. Nonetheless, by her sixty-fifth birthday, a woman will have gone through menopause, either have seen her youngest child leave the nest or have confronted the finality of childlessness, and have evidenced visible signs of aging. Unless she is very lucky, she will also have lost one or both parents. In a society that prizes youth, she will have found herself at the threshold of old age. To get there refreshed and invigorated, she needs the company of other women on her journey.

Conscious that the years ahead are limited, women at midlife take stock of themselves and their lives and make changes while they still can. Developmental psychologist Zoya Slive posited the concept of "unfinished identity" to explain the themes that arose repeatedly during the in-depth interviews she conducted with thirty middle-aged women. Slive noted "the woman's need to 'complete' her identity at midlife before it is 'too late.'"

Berenice Fischer, a sixty-year-old professor of educational philosophy at New York University, told me she "had had a long life as a single, actively heterosexual woman" before recognizing in her forties that she was a lesbian. Her friend from her college days, Roberta Galler, helped her meet the challenge of coming out. Although Roberta was heterosexual, Berenice knew that she wouldn't withdraw from their friendship.

"Roberta was actually the first person I started to talk with about this," Berenice said. "It enabled me to go through a life transition that I needed support for and from somebody who knew me well."

For many women, the fifties can be a vibrant decade, a chance to realize postponed dreams. That was certainly the case for Marjie Rynearson. Recognizing that, to fulfill her potential as an actress and playwright, she needed to live in a city with vital theater, she moved from Temple, Texas, to Chicago. Once there, she found herself developing far more than her dramatic abilities. In Chicago, Marjie's self-confidence grew, and she began winning friends who both appreciated her for the traits she possessed and modeled the traits she wanted to develop. One such friend was Nan Kilkeary, a fifty-two-year-old public relations consultant with wit and vitality to burn. "She chose me," Marjie said. "She's really bright, and confrontational, and loves life and makes the best of it, and she just doesn't take crap from anybody."

Women in midlife often seek out and maintain friendships that challenge them to change. One of the friends fifty-three-year-old graduate student Faith Lagay valued most was the one who made her the most uncomfortable. "Cath has a way of not letting me get away with bullshit, of naming what I'm doing in a way that is painfully recognizable to me," Faith told me.

Pat Tate, the fifty-five-year-old director of a neighborhood revitalization program in Galveston, and her best friend tried to encourage each other to live up to the ideals of their religions. "I am Episcopalian, and she is Baptist," Pat said. "But we have a tendency to stumble sometimes. We try to keep each other conscious of the fact that we should try to lead lives that would be pleasing to God."

For many women, midlife is a season of spiritual exploration and reawakening. Some, like Pat, renew their commitment to the religion of their childhood. Others, who may have abandoned the faiths of their parents in their teens or twenties, now search for a better fit. University of Colorado English professor Claudia Vangerven, reared Mormon, became a Wiccan after friends introduced her to the neopagan goddess-oriented tradition. Her coven met twice a month. "On the full moon, we give thanks and make wishes, and at the dark moon we banish things we want to get rid of," Claudia explained.

Wherever a woman's midlife spiritual journey takes her, the company of female friends helps her on her way. Author and lecturer Rabbi Lynn Gottlieb of Albuquerque told me: "Women my age are looking for authenticity, to look beyond or through the conventions and understand ourselves in a more profound way, so that we can liberate our creative spirit and support each other and not be shamed in the world."

Another kind of rebirth happens to women between forty and sixty-five: a spurt of creative inspiration and productivity. While studying women fifty-five and older who had put aside early dreams of becoming visual artists to take office jobs and raise families, Chicago anthropologist Madelyn Iris found something that surprised her. She'd expected these women to pick up their brushes or sculpting tools after retirement. Instead, they reported succumbing to a creative urge much earlier. "Most of the women I've spoken to have come back to art in their forties, not their sixties," Iris told me.

Whether this wellspring of early midlife productivity has its source in hormonal changes or in a well-seasoned sense of self-worth, women artists need companions in creativity. At forty-three, Yreina Cervantez was a successful painter and printmaker in Huntington Beach, California. Her two closest friends were a poet and a filmmaker. "I think I'm friends with them because they're on similar paths," she said.

But women artists also need friends who aren't artists, to keep them in touch with the other sides of themselves, which provide fuel for their creativity. Lilith, whose articulate, haunting paintings grappled with issues like the relationship between individuals and technology, made a point of making friends outside the art world. "It's an old saying that artists work in isolation," she said. "It's true. Part of what makes me feel real, part of what grounds me, are these friendships."

In interview after interview, middle-aged women described cultivating different friends to resonate with different aspects of their selves. "I am really fortunate because I have a lot of friends in different areas of my life," said Gabrielle Cosgriff, fifty-eight, editor of a hospital's magazine and co-author of *Chicks on Film,* a woman's guide to video rentals. Gabriel had friends in the media, friends for sharing movies and operas, friends who belonged to the same Unitarian church. "And then there are people I meet at parties and we strike up a conversation and end up being friends," she concluded.

Like adolescent girls, midlife women are suddenly game for trying new things—and they forge and deepen friendships in the process. Sometimes that entails putting adult responsibilities to the side. At forty-three, Kim, an economist, joined two women friends at Club Med in Puerto Vallarta. "The three of us left all of our families, with the laundry and kids and stuff, at home," she said, smiling as she recalled the adventure.

Sometimes it means taking on new responsibilities. In her early forties, Anita, a Cherokee Native American, enrolled in the University of Oklahoma's doctoral program in anthropology and soon became fast friends with a fellow graduate student a year older. Each supported the other emotionally in ways that only another middle-aged woman facing those particular challenges could. Anita was there for Rae when Rae, in the midst of her comprehensive exams, learned that her daughter was pregnant—six months before the wedding date. And when Anita had to defend her dissertation, Rae was there for her, literally: Throughout the ordeal, she waited right outside in the hallway.

Anita was only one of many women I interviewed who took on new careers, or renewed their commitment to old ones, between forty and sixty-five. Almost instinctively, they scanned their workplaces for compatible women of similar age and status who could be companions in the challenge. Martha Holstein, fifty-five, was just finishing her doctoral dissertation in medical humanities and had recently taken a position with a Chicago agency exploring public policy toward the elderly. After she received the offer, Martha went around the office, talking to the people who would be her colleagues. With Sally, a lawyer and social worker, she felt such rapport that she made up her mind to say yes.

"I just knew right away that this is a person I can be friends with," Martha explained. "There's wonderful laughter and a wonderful spirit, and yet she's quite serious and has enormous depth. If something goes on at work where I feel like I need to check out my feelings, she's the one I go to."

From their forties through their sixties, women experience an often overdue measure of respect at work, but they frequently have to face the facts that their careers may have fallen short of their dreams and their workplaces are flawed institutions. A female colleague who is also a good friend can help keep disappointment and frustration in perspective.

"It keeps us honest in a way," Cal State Los Angeles philosophy professor Sharon Bishop, fifty-seven, said of her friendship with a close workmate. "It keeps you focused on why your profession is meaningful and what you want to accomplish."

And because female friends made in the workplace tend to connect with each other as whole people, not just colleagues, these friendships also help a woman continue her own broader development, making her more effective in her work and in the rest of her life.

❧ Facing Up to Aging ❧

Just as female friends help each other go in the directions they want to go, they also ease the journey they wish they didn't have to take. Employee benefits consultant Beth Madison, fifty-one, put it this way: "I'd rather be fifty than thirty. I enjoy being older, except for the fact that the ultimate progression is that you're going to be really old."

To accept that inexorable reality with good humor and make the best of these years in which her creativity and personal power are at their height, a woman in midlife needs the friendship of female contemporaries. When Cleo Berkun studied sixty women aged forty to fifty-five for her doctorate in social work from Berkeley, she discovered that those "who had maintained contacts with other middle-aged women . . . exhibited the most positive attitudes and optimistic moods."

Younger friends may make us feel younger temporarily, as they help us tap back into our youthful energy and optimism. But this strategy doesn't always work. "Having been the precocious one who hung out with the older people, now I'm suddenly the older people, and I don't like it," said Vicki Jo Radovsky, who wrote for entertainment magazines in youth-obsessed Los Angeles.

Most of the women Vicki Jo met through her work were much younger than her forty-three years. "I've been where they are, but they haven't been where I am," she noted. By contrast, talking to friends her own age, even if they were married mothers when she was single, was "manna from heaven." She explained: "She may not be in my place, but we're the same age, so we have the same basis of experience to draw on."

Sharing fun with friends exorcises anxiety about what may lie ahead. The right friend can help a middle-aged woman shrug off the heavy cloak of maturity and play again. "It's a good feeling to know that when you are with this person, you can act like you are teenagers," said Sylvia Castillo, the fifty-one-year-old director of a nonprofit group assisting low-income Hispanic mothers.

But getting older has its joys and satisfactions, too, and good mid-life friends encourage one another to anticipate them. Several women I interviewed had participated in some version of the ancient female rite of passage called croning. Now a derogatory term, the word *crone* once denoted a woman free of the demands of child rearing and able to use her wisdom for the benefit of the entire community. When she was fifty-eight, NYU professor Berenice Fischer called together her female friends from academia, politics, and the other facets of her life for a ceremony. "I was trying to find a way to help myself move on to accepting myself as an older woman," she explained.

For women in their forties, and especially in their early sixties, genes, environment, luck, and lifestyle blur the apparent ages of women born the same year. This can sometimes strain longstanding friendships. At sixty, psychologist Marilyn Schultz could easily pass for forty-five. That caused tension in her friendship with Julia. "There's some jealousy there," Marilyn said. "She used to be very beautiful. She's gotten very heavy, and she's been very depressed. She feels very old, and she looks very old."

Trim and casually stylish at fifty-one, Karen Hyatt not only looked a decade younger, but her attitude matched her appearance. Sometimes that combination put a strain on her friendships with other women her age. "The few female single friends that I have are old, not chronologically, just the way they think," she complained. "It's like, 'I'm fifty. I shouldn't be doing that.'"

As a woman progresses from age forty to age sixty-four, her chances of developing a life-threatening disease rise. If she does, her female friends can make an enormous difference in how well she copes. Almost from the hour that Polly, sixty-three, learned she had cancer, her friend Hazel was there for her. "I came into this house alone feeling just totally devastated, and she called me at that moment and we cried together," Polly said. "She kept up with me all through the operation."

Polly recovered, but many people with cancer don't. Having a dear friend die of natural causes becomes increasingly common in middle age. When Houston attorney Alberta Johnson was forty-three, Bertha, her close friend since they roomed together in college, died of lupus. "It's hard to get over something like that," Alberta said. "She was exactly my age within three months."

Building strong female friendships in midlife helps dispel some of the inevitable anxiety that comes with facing, in a new and immediate way, the certainty of death. Because their relationship was so deep and caring, fifty-three-year-old graduate student Faith Lagay told me that if she became incapacitated, she would trust her friend Ellie Porter to make end-of-life decisions on her behalf. Faith said: "I would be extremely willing for Ellie to say, 'No, she wants the plug left in for three more days' or say, 'Faith would not stand for this. Pull the plug right now.'"

During the years from ages forty to sixty-four, a woman is more likely to have her husband die than to die herself. The support of friends makes an enormous difference in a woman's ability to cope with his final illness and death. Medical administrator Sharon Healy was forty-nine when her husband succumbed to AIDS. "We knew for a long time that he was going to die, but he was only really sick for six months," she told me. "My good friends were a whole part of the process. I believe that my relationships are stronger now than they were before, because we all traveled through that period of time together."

But being widowed so early had thrown Sharon out of synch with other women her age. A woman's social adjustment to widowhood depends on when it occurs. If it happens at eighty, she has plenty of company. If it happens at forty-five, she is likely to be the only widow in her crowd.

For fifty-four-year-old Brooklyn museum executive Bobye List, widowed four-and-a-half years before our interview, one of the problems making friends with other single women her age was that most of them were divorced. They either were hunting for husbands, eager to do it right this time, or felt so wronged that they rejected all men. "I'm finding that I'm somewhat unique, because I *had* a whole marriage," Bobye explained.

While widowhood may be relatively rare in midlife, having a parent die is common. With the average life span in the United States hovering in the mid-seventies, a woman born when her parents were twenty-five can expect to lose them when she's about fifty. Yet, it is one of the most traumatic events in a woman's life, especially when the parent she loses is her mother. In a study of middle-aged women whose mothers had died within the past two years, sociologist Julia Gamble Kahrl found them "surprised at the depth of their grief." Kahrl explained that these women had lost "a link with the past" and "a relationship which had provided an arena for self-definition since birth."

Often, years of physical and sometimes mental decline precede a mother's death. A second renegotiation of the maternal relationship, different from the one that took place in early adulthood, happens now, driven by the mother's frailty rather than the daughter's bid for independence. When death does come, it brings on a third renegotiation, during which the daughter accepts and honors her mother's traits that she wants to make her own and discards those she doesn't and forgives her mother for them. If a daughter doesn't work through this, she risks a lasting sense of estrangement—from her mother and from herself. By hearing and affirming their feelings about their mothers, female friends help one another through each step of this poignant process.

As their mothers die, middle-aged women learn to rely on their friends for maternal nurturing. "I'm at the point where you really need your friends to be like your family," said forty-nine-year-old Berkeley clinical psychologist Jane Burka, who'd lost her mother less than a year before our interview. "You break your ankle, and your friends help you. It's beyond emotional support."

Marcie Freedman, fifty-eight, director of marketing and public information for the American Society of Aging, belonged to a group of eight middle-aged women called the Wandering Menstruals. For the past seven years, they'd joined each other on semiannual retreats and had gotten together once a month to talk about issues in their lives, particularly those involving aging. When one of the Menstruals learned that she was HIV positive, the others pledged to take care of her if she developed AIDS.

"Our relationships with one another outside of the group are different," Marcie explained. "Some are absolute closest buddies, and some not at all. But the commitment that I have to the group as a whole is one of the strongest of my life."

These women had given each other the affirmation and empathy they needed to help them keep growing psychologically throughout midlife. Now they were consciously pledging to give each other, in addition, the practical help they would need to sustain that growth as their physical capacities declined. And because this was an all-for-one, one-for-all commitment, they could make this promise securely, without worrying that any single member of the group would be overburdened. For women with the good fortune and foresight to form similar ensemble friendships in middle age, the prospect of growing older looks almost inviting.

❧ Forms That Flourish ❧

Envisioning close women friends accompanying them into their later years helps take the sting out of aging for women ages forty to sixty-four. For Galveston artist Chula Sanchez, the fantasy was especially vivid when she was at her sister's beach house with their mutual friend, Jan. "I can see us there when we're eighty," Chula said. "We're going to be doing the same thing we've been doing for the last thirty years—playing Scrabble right here on this porch in these baggy bathing suits that somebody left here."

Chula was anticipating the lasting pleasure of history friendships, a form women rediscover with renewed zest in midlife. When I called for an interview with Kathleen Ownby, who directed a program for utilizing Houston schoolyards as parks, she told me that by coincidence, her annual reunion with five friends from her high school all-girl drum and bugle corps was the following weekend. The get-together would start with lunch at one woman's house, then turn into an all-night slumber party at the Omni Hotel. Would I join them for the first part?

I gratefully accepted. Over low-fat chicken salad, they explained how the tradition had started. To celebrate their fortieth birthdays, Kathleen had brought them all together for a weekend at her family's beach house. They discussed their marriages and divorces, their kids, and their jobs. "There was quite a difference in what each of us was doing," said Pam Traylor, who ran a bed-and-breakfast. "And yet we were still friends."

As I interviewed middle-aged women, one after the other spoke with affection and pride about her history friends. At forty-five, Tucson science writer Liz Maggio borrowed a simile from her profession to describe how she felt about them. "I am so proud that I have friends that go back to when I was three years old, from every stage of my life," she said. "It's almost like geologic rock strata."

Because history friends have shared earlier seasons of life, they keep us in touch with who we were and what we believed before the pressures of middle adulthood distracted us. "It's delightful when you've known somebody long enough that you can see just the way she was as a kid and still is," Bernice Torregrossa, a forty-one-year-old grants analyst for a charitable foundation, observed of a childhood friend. "She always had a strong sense of right and wrong and a sense of indignity at injustice. Now she's very active in Amnesty International."

For women who want to make the world, or at least their community, a better place, allies friendships enjoy a resurgence in midlife, though they've shed their early volatility. Wendy Marsh, a fifty-eight-year-old attorney and rancher in Amarillo, dedicated much of her time to improving the junior college system in Texas. Although she nurtured and treasured friendships dating from boarding school and college, her recent friends had been made through her work on the State Coordinating Board for Higher Education.

"I guess nowadays, friends are people who are intensely interested in the same thing," she said.

But several women ages forty to sixty-four told me of valued friends who weren't interested in the same things they were, who occupied different worlds and held disparate opinions. An opposite friend may be just what a woman needs to spark her midlife psychological development. "It was a yin and yang type of attraction," Albuquerque massage therapist Pam Wilson explained. "Alisa taught me a lot about gentleness. I go rushing into things. Alisa is a slower moving type."

Middle-aged women who manage to find or hang on to true soulmates recognize what a rare treasure they have. "At one point I was leafing through her wedding album, and I turned to the page where there's a picture of her and her bridesmaids," social worker Carol Deanow told me of her friend Carlene. "I shrieked, ran upstairs to my apartment, got my wedding album. We were married within a month of each other, and our bridesmaids wore the same dress. They were empire, this vivid, beautiful emerald green. It was the most extraordinary thing."

Although the impulse may not feel as urgent as it did in early adulthood, women ages forty to sixty-four still welcome lifemates, especially if they choose an unconventional path. When Marsha Hartwell enrolled in Smith College at forty-one, she felt an instant rapport with another student in her forties. "We were speaking the same language, without making an effort to explain ourselves," she said.

With moves less common in middle age than they were earlier, women have a chance to build stable lifemate friendships with neighbors. At forty, attorney Nancy Gertner, now a federal judge, moved into the house where she still lived nine years later. Gradually, she became friends with the pediatrician a few doors away. They developed a friendship their mothers would have recognized from the 1950s.

"Every Saturday morning, she goes to get bread at the bakery down the block," Nancy said. "And she'll drop off the bread at our house and we'll have coffee. We tend to connect like that."

Women who are single and have no family nearby know how precious lifemates can be. *Fort Worth Star-Telegram* government editor Kaye Northcott, fifty-two, told me that as a childless woman who had never married, she counted on friends in similar situations for both companionship and practical help. Political humorist Molly Ivins, her friend of three decades, filled both bills.

"Molly is as entertaining as you can get, and she's also there for you," Kaye explained. "She's the one who brings you dinner or arranges for somebody to mow your lawn or helps you load the bamboo you pulled out of the yard in her truck and take it to the dump."

As their children need them less, middle-aged women may discover the satisfaction of nurturer friendships. Paralegal Pidge Hunt, fifty-five, took her twenty-eight-year-old coworker Rachel under her wing as soon as she joined the firm. Six months later, when Rachel learned that she had multiple sclerosis, her law student husband was so furious at the news that she'd have to quit her job that she decided to divorce him.

"I was her counselor, her shoulder," Pidge said. "Although she has a very caring, concerned, warm, loving mother, sometimes that's a tough relationship. So I was able to be there for her."

By their forties and fifties, many women have the time and money to do things they enjoy, and they turn to playmate friends to help them. Magazine editor Kim Waller looked forward every summer to sailing with two childhood friends in Maine. "Mostly sailing is racing," she said. "We just go sailing. Wind or no wind, we don't care. And we catch up. It's one of the nicest moments of the summer."

Especially for women whose careers are flourishing, workmate friends add zest to midlife. For Laura Kramer, a forty-nine-year-old sociology professor, Nanette, a fellow sociologist, was a workmate and a mentor. When they'd met twenty-two years earlier, they were at the same point in their careers but very different points in their family lives. "I remember her six-year-old pushing my baby in a stroller," Laura said, laughing. "She's a person that I can talk to about my research. I can talk to her about my teaching. I can talk to her about my children. I can talk to her about my parents."

At fifty-three, the Rev. Betsy Alden, a Methodist minister and community college teacher, found herself taking on the mantle of mentor for younger women. Some of these relationships had become both mutually caring and personally satisfying, because they allowed Betsy to pass along what life and her profession had taught her.

Women tend to shed the role of protégée when they hit middle age. As she entered her forties, Sister Elena, a family therapist in Houston's barrios, found herself renegotiating her relationship with her mentor, the nun who'd inspired her to join her order and had encouraged her through a decade of graduate school and internship. After Sister Elena had been working as a full professional for a few years, she expected her friend to treat her as an equal. But, as is often the case, changing the form of the friendship meant risking conflict. Sister Elena finally told her friend directly, "You're not my mother."

Recalling those months of adjustment, Sister Elena observed: "It was harder for her I think, dropping the older sister/other mother role, but we got through that period."

But there is one sort of mentor women ages forty to sixty-four actively seek out: A model for creative aging. "I went to her for menopause," real estate agent Jody Miller said of a friend three decades older. "She gave me great advice."

Such friends help take away the terror of growing old. At fifty-four, Sue Wood was developing a friendship with a painter ten years her senior. "It's such a joy to be around people like that," said Sue. "If I could be like that, then what would be the matter with aging?"

Often, women who came of age in the 1960s and 1970s aren't satisfied with the examples of aging set by their mothers. Graduate student

Faith Lagay found a different model in Ellie Porter, an exuberant and unabashedly unconventional woman of seventy-two. "What can I do to try to retain the kind of passion and interest in people that Ellie has, so I can still have it when I'm her age?" Faith mused.

By forming and nurturing her friendship with Ellie, she had already taken the first step.

✥ Diverging Lives, Converging Hearts ✥

Each year brings events and opportunities that push us toward some people and away from others. By midlife, women recognize the importance of maintaining connection as the personal landscape shifts. One thing that makes this a challenge nowadays is that women the same age can be experiencing very different changes.

Success had created a gap between Beth Madison and Ashley, the constant companion of her twenties. "We worked together every day," Beth recalled. "We went to lunch every day. We were married to hard-working businessmen and could do dinner parties and decorate houses."

Then, following a divorce, Beth launched her own benefits consulting firm; at the time of our interview, it employed nineteen people. "I became a completely different person," she admitted. "I suspect I was more challenging for her to keep up with than she was for me, because I knew who she was. She didn't change."

Another thing that can cause a gap between middle-aged women is the timing of motherhood. Carol Goodenow, a developmental psychologist with the Malden, Massachusetts, schools, explained that social scientists traditionally identified women's life stages with their maternal status—single, married with no children, married with a preschooler, then a combination of the ages of their oldest and youngest child. "Obviously," she said, "there are a lot of people who don't fit into those categories so neatly anymore. There's no place to put a woman who's forty-eight with no children. She's not just prechildren. She's made whole different choices."

And those choices can have a profound impact on her friendships at midlife. As they enter their forties, two friends may be dealing with children anywhere from infancy to adulthood. "Although Blanche and I are only nine years different in age, we're light years apart in the stages of our lives," said Beth, forty-five, who had had her children in her early twenties. "She has a little boy who's just three, and I have an eight-month-old grandson."

Six of the women I interviewed had borne or adopted their only children right around their fortieth birthdays. Since most moms with infants were in their twenties or early thirties, these women had trouble finding lifemates. Many of their contemporaries were worrying about whether their kids were having unprotected sex or how to pay next year's college tuition.

At forty-four, Silicon Valley corporate trainer Nancy Nadler had to struggle to maintain her female friendships, given the demands of her job and her seven-year-old son. Even by telephone, a good heart-to-heart talk was hard to arrange. "When you have a baby, it's one thing," Nancy observed. "Now, I have a seven-year-old who listens. If I say something like, 'Oh, my God!' he runs over to the phone: 'What happened? Tell me!' "

Envy is also an issue for late-life moms. Despite recent medical advances, a successful pregnancy at forty is much less likely than at thirty. After years of following a strict vegetarian regimen designed to promote pregnancy, Houston photographer Janice Rubin, forty, had just had a baby. Relating to friends her age who were having less success in their own attempts to become pregnant required an emotional balancing act. "I want to help them any way I can," she explained. "At the same time, I don't want to wave my happiness in their faces."

Janice could share her joy with friends who had ten-year-olds, but she didn't have what new moms long for—a true lifemate.

ᷜ Loyalty and Laughter ᷜ

With middle age come the resources, and often the personal power, that enable women to pursue friendships. "We see each other more now that she's in Vienna than we did when she was living in Denver and I was living in New York," said publicist Carol Edgar, who got together four or five times a year with her friend-since-fourth-grade, U.S. Ambassador to Austria Swanee Hunt. "The early years of my marriage, I was nesting and making a family, so we saw each other less frequently."

Having kids leave the nest or at least enter high school does give women more time for friends. So does higher status at work, which may entail working more total hours a week but also allows more flexibility, including long lunches.

When her tennis partner announced that she wanted to celebrate her fiftieth birthday with her by going to Wimbledon, Kathleen Ownby said yes. Kathleen's younger child was in college, and her position as the director of a nonprofit agency gave her the freedom to set her own vacation schedule.

"We had a wonderful two weeks in London and Paris," Kathleen recalled. "We came back better friends."

But many women find themselves at least as crunched as they did in their thirties, and when it comes to allocating time between family and friends, feelings of obligation tend to win out.

Karen Hyatt, a regional manager for a title insurance company in downtown Los Angeles, commuted an hour and a quarter each way. That left little time for friends, even the one who lived only two miles away. "I don't even see her once a month," Karen said. "If I leave the office right at five, I'm home at six-thirty. The two nights that I work out, I don't get home until ten. When I do get home, I've been on the phone so much at work that the last thing I want to do is get on the phone again."

When Beth Madison told me she had more time for her friends than she'd had in her twenties and thirties, I suspected that what she really had was more resources, along with the wisdom to control them. The same was true of her friends. When her best friend's marriage dissolved, leaving her with a young son to rear, Beth suggested that she move into an apartment in her building. Mornings, Kelly Somoza would dash down the stairwell for a quick cup of coffee at Beth's before they both headed off to work. "There isn't a day when we fail to talk to each other at least twice," Beth said.

Whether they have more resources or just use them better, middle-aged women report less difficulty maintaining friendships than women in their twenties and thirties, as social psychologist Kathleen Sullivan Ricker reported. Women in midlife also seem able to drop the barriers that have kept them from connecting with each other. "I'm pretty competitive, but probably less so than I used to be," said Maryann, the fifty-four-year-old vice chancellor of a state university system. "I am very aware that I used to look around the room and say, 'I'm more important than that person and that person and that person.' I don't do that anymore."

At fifty-nine, Cybil saw her relationships with her closest friends as less dependent and more enriching than they had been earlier. "My model for friendship has changed," she noted. "I had these four leaning posts. We all had our feet on the ground, but we kind of leaned on each other. Now my model is me as the center of a rose with a lot of petals around me. And some of those petals are tighter clustered and some are more peripheral."

By midlife, women have learned that that connection may be closer at some times than at others. Speaking of her friendships that had endured twenty or thirty years, Kaye Northcott explained: "They'll wax and wane. Somebody will be very strong in your life for a while and then not so strong and then come back over time."

And women in midlife have a clearer idea of what they're looking for in friendship. "Expansiveness and openness, lack of judgmentalism, wide range of mind" were the qualities artist Luanne Stovall, forty-two, sought in friendship, because they made possible "the discussing of things that are very important in the lives of people, especially women."

When I asked middle-aged women what was most important to them in friendship, the answer I got was "honesty." "Honesty is something I value a lot," Wendy Marsh said. "I don't have very many friends who don't tell me what they think."

Constancy also ranked as a friendship value among women forty to sixty-four, along with the humor so prized at all ages. "There's enormous loyalty," Martha Holstein said of one of her most enduring relationships. "And I love the laughter."

Approaching her sixties, artist Lilith realized that she would never be able to go everywhere she wanted to go in the world or do everything she wanted to do, but friends allowed her to have those experiences vicariously. "You get more out of life if you have a friend who shares her life with you," she said. "There's an old Chinese saying about being a vessel that other people pour things into, that when you become that kind of vessel, it gives you strength and knowledge and wisdom."

At fifty, Albuquerque artist Felice Lucero figured she'd found what she called "friendship security." She explained: "You have the knowledge that you have nurtured these friendships and they've passed the test of time."

The message I was hearing from my own agemates was twofold: At midlife, the conditions are perfect for female friendship to flower: Resources and flexibility enrich the soil. Experience and increased self-awareness furnish the sunlight. And tears and laughter provide the water. This is the season to cultivate this garden, for the joy it offers now, for the sustenance it will offer later.

꙰

II

Reaping the Harvest: Ages Sixty-five and Over

When I am an old woman, I shall wear purple
With a red hat which doesn't go, and doesn't suit me, . . .
And make up for the sobriety of my youth.

—Jenny Joseph, "Warning"

Jenny Joseph's ode to late-life liberation has become so popular
among women rounding the long curve from middle age to the
years beyond that when I asked for help finding it, my local reference librarian marched me into a back office and handed me a copy
taped to a gray metal shelf above a colleague's computer. "You can
Xerox this," she said.

As I did, to get the words just right, I remembered the first time
I'd seen them, calligraphed artfully, scattered with pressed pansies and
other dried flowers, and set in a frame in my mother's bathroom. That
was in 1987, and she was dying, at seventy, of a very aggressive lung
cancer. Months before the diagnosis, a friend had given her the poem.
It was a conspiratorial whisper, a declaration of independence from
earlier roles and expectations. And it was from a female friend who
was encouraging her to cut loose and mine life for all the zest that lay
hidden beneath the surface. I'd known that late-life female friends
tended each other in illness and supported each other in handling the

losses of husbands and the disappointments of grown children. But the glimpse of this other, slightly subversive function was a revelation.

Reams of research confirms that one of the main things women sixty-five and over do for their friends is help them extend both life's duration and its quality. Next to the scores of studies on children and adolescents, the greatest body of academic work on female friendships examines those late in life. The results are striking: Women in this age group report that friendships with one another are more important and sustaining than even affectionate and frequent contacts with children and siblings, in which a sense of obligation on both sides may dampen pleasure. When University of Illinois gerontologists Jocelyn Armstrong and Karen Goldsteen studied thirty women, sixty-five to ninety-three, they found that friends, not family members, comprised more than half their informal support networks. Another study, conducted by clinical psychologist Theresa Irene Newsome, revealed that elderly women experienced at least as much genuineness and empathy with their friends as they did with their daughters.

Alone with their female agemates, women in late life are free from the responsibilities of nurturing, advising, and setting a good example. They can be angry, eccentric, bawdy; in short, having spent most of their lives in an era that denied women freedom, they are free with one another to be themselves.

For women in good health, old age doesn't seem quite real. "You will find that when you get there, you will say, 'How did this happen?'" one stylish seventy-five-year-old I interviewed predicted.

The dark side of the years beyond sixty-five—physical and often mental deterioration and the impending deaths of partners, friends, and eventually oneself—lends an immediacy to joy and pleasure. Not only is there less need to postpone gratification and inhibit self-expression; doing so no longer seems prudent. If a seventy-five-year-old woman doesn't join her college roommate on a barge tour of France this year, one of them might be unable to go next. If an eighty-five-year-old woman doesn't tell her best friend she loves her today, one of them might not be around tomorrow.

Sara Williams told me about the joint birthday party her bridge group threw for two members, one turning seventy, the other seventy-five. Inspired by Jenny Joseph's poem, they took purple as their theme. Everyone wore purple. Purple balloons danced across the ceiling. Following the color motif, Sara made a centerpiece of radicchio and flowering kale.

The party went beautifully, but not perfectly. Although everyone had signed the two birthday cards, no one remembered to present them to the guests of honor. One guest forgot her purse. Another left a woman she'd promised a ride. Helping clean up, a third absentmindedly stuck some of the silverware in her handbag instead of the dishwasher. Once she got home and discovered her mistake, she called, mortified.

Rather than spoiling the party in retrospect, these mishaps added to its legend. "I think everybody enjoyed the fact that we were all pretty forgetful of what we were doing," Sara said.

Short of death itself, the prospect of mental decline may be the most frightening specter haunting the last decades of life. Yet, the members of Sara's bridge group could make light of it—together. And by doing so, they not only deflected fear but bonded more closely with one another.

Until recently, sociologists and psychologists took a somber view of the human condition at sixty-five and beyond. In the 1963 edition of his classic book *Childhood and Society,* Erik Erikson depicted the last decades of life as a struggle between ego integrity and despair. The best that people this age could hope for was a notion of "world order and spiritual sense," along with "the acceptance of one's one and only life cycle as something that had to be." Short of that, they would suffer from despair on recognizing "that the time is now short, too short for the attempt to start another life and to try out alternate roads to integrity." Erikson's vision of advanced age left no room for giddy abandon, for the energized pursuit of new interests and adventures, for the delights of mellowed love and companionship, for the spurt of courage and creativity that comes with having fewer years to lose, for the opportunity and authority to make lasting contributions to the community and the world.

Toni Dewey, who moved with her second husband to Boulder, Colorado, where she was busy launching the Museum of Women in the West, radiated energy and involvement. At sixty-eight, she was having the time of her life.

"There is something absolutely glorious about getting older," she said, "because the people that I have been fortunate to have as friends are very sensitive human beings, and their shared experiences are enriching in every way."

This shared zest is a far cry from the view that social scientists, and society as a whole, long held of life's latter decades: a period of "disengagement," as sociologist Pat O'Connor put it. O'Connor noted that the number of friends elderly women had varied widely. Some studies found widows who'd begun developing female friendships for the first time in their lives, while O'Connor's own work with the frail elderly revealed that only one in five had a close friend. The women I interviewed ran the gamut: a few were drawing back from attachments outside the family but more were actively building friendships.

"I like a challenge," eighty-four-year-old Elberta Jette of Eugene, Oregon, told me of the parties she still enjoyed giving. "So I like to cook something that somebody would say I couldn't make. I like to knit things that someone would say I couldn't do."

In her 1987 study of women in their late seventies to their late eighties, Australian psychologist Alice Day discovered that although half her subjects lived alone, most led active social lives. That's also what I found talking to women like Ellie Porter, seventy-two. Single and childless, she considered her friendships absolutely essential. "This is where the isolated organism connects," she explained.

Social science bears her out. Dutch sociologist Pearl Dykstra found that when it came to loneliness, an older person's lack of friends was a greater culprit than her lack of a partner.

Fortunately, women tend to nourish and maintain friendships well into old age. The stereotype of the socially isolated elderly widow doesn't bear out, particularly for women who are relatively healthy, but also for women like my late mother-in-law, whose lively social circle I described in the introduction. Chronic obstructive lung disease had left her housebound, but it hadn't curtailed her female friendships. With help from flexible friends, women who care about remaining connected often can do so. But although the stereotype of women over sixty-five may be wrong, it is perniciously powerful. Our culture's negative image of doddering, ditzy little old ladies, absorbed in their aches and pains, often keep women in late life from developing and valuing friendships with their female agemates.

Since the 1980s, social scientists have begun to take a different view of late life, particularly the role of friendship. Part of what female friends do in the years sixty-five and beyond is no different from what they do earlier: They affirm and support, stimulate and entertain, comfort and accompany one another. Small wonder that older people with confidants, compared to those without, are less likely to be anxious or depressed and more likely to be satisfied with their lives.

Ellie Porter told me: "One of the reasons I don't want to go crazy or get to be a dependent old woman or a poverty-stricken old woman is so my friends won't be burdened by that. Life is something of a fight, and you don't want to let your buddy down."

For Ellie, the support of friends helped her remain physically healthy. But the relationship between physical and social vitality is hard to pin down. Because getting together with friends is easier for women in good health than for those who are frail, health may promote friendship, rather than vice versa. Yet the weight of research showing the importance of friends, even a single close friend, to physical well-being indicates that something must be going on here. When Lenard Kaye and Abraham Monck of Bryn Mawr College looked at the lives of 210 retirement home residents, they discovered that as their personal support networks declined, so did their health. This also happens to elderly women living in the community, rather than in institutions: Those isolated from friends and family do worse, both physically and psychologically, than those surrounded by people who know and care about them.

One way that even casual friends enhance one another's lives at this age is by helping each other continue exploring the world around them. Elderly women will go places together that they never would alone. In rural areas and car-dependent cities, a woman prompted by failing eyesight or sluggish reflexes to give up driving would be isolated if not for friends offering a lift to church or the supermarket. Having one member who had a big car and loved to drive helped Sara Williams's bridge group continue playing. "Doreen's husband wanted her to have a good car, and he knew he was going to die," Sara said. "So he went out and paid cash for this Lincoln. She adores that car. She wants everybody to ride, of course."

Transportation, along with shopping and running errands, is the main form of practical help close female friends give one another in late life. But the equality assumed in friendship is so important that some women in late life find it difficult to request such favors.

Women who've developed and maintained networks of friends their own age can take a matter-of-fact approach to asking for such assistance—and offering it. The accepted social convention seems to be that it's fine to ask for help doing something necessary to maintain general independence, with the understanding that the favor can be returned in a different coin. For example, a woman might reciprocate weekly rides to the supermarket directly by insisting on buying a tank of gas or more subtly by giving her friend a jar of homemade peach preserves.

"Most older women at some time or another need help to go to the doctor or need food to be brought in or whatever," explained sociologist Helen Gouldner. "There's a whole question of reciprocity here. Some can't pay back in money; they can't pay back in kind; there's no way except to express their gratitude, and so there's some stress in the relationship."

Karen A. Roberto discovered something surprising about the distribution of that stress: Older women who thought they were giving more than they were getting actually felt more grateful for the friendship. Those on the receiving end of too much largesse often reported that the friend made them feel bad.

Some of the women I interviewed preferred their friendships free of dependency on either side. Nonie Thompson still entertained regularly, relished deep-sea fishing, and served on several boards, including that of her family's charitable foundation. When she had a practical problem, she hired someone to help her. She looked to friends for companionship only, and she expected them to do the same. She observed: "I think there are a lot of people out there who enjoy having a friend dependent upon them. That is not part of my problem."

As important as the exchange of practical help may be to many women, the heart of female friendship in late life is what it has been all along: talk. Talking to friends, late-life women exchange information that can be crucial to their physical well-being while they offer one another support and stimulation. "You clear up things about doctors," explained Vera, an eighty-year-old retired English teacher in Lawrence, Kansas. "Then we get into something in the ever-so-exciting political field and argue about that for a while."

Families form a perennial topic. "She always wants to know what my kids are doing," Vivian Hall, seventy-three, of Orange County,

California, said of one friend. "I want to know what her kids are doing and what cute things her grandchildren say."

Perhaps because maturity increases discretion, perhaps because the generation born in the first third of the twentieth century has always considered certain topics private, some subjects are seldom broached. Vivian told me: "When it comes to my sex life or my life with my husband or that kind of thing, I don't share things like that, even with my closest friends."

But the older women I interviewed did confide in one another about their important relationships—sharing irritation at a retired husband trying to micromanage their lives, frustration with a daughter dating the same sort of man she just divorced, or worry about a sister with Alzheimer's disease. As they recounted these conversations they'd had with their friends, a refreshing frankness shone through, as if at age sixty-five or seventy the rules had changed and they no longer had to pretend they were coping beautifully with life's stresses. These women sounded like they were letting out a breath they had held for decades.

⤳ Forms That Flourish ⤳

As women move into their sixties and beyond, many broaden their friendship circles. After retirement and with their children grown, they have the free time to rediscover personal interests—to take up landscape painting or tennis, to go back to school or cruise the Greek islands. They also have the experience and contacts to tackle worthwhile public projects—to volunteer in the schools, to rescue a historic landmark. Along the way, they pick up workmates and playmates.

Speaking of the friends she'd made in five years of trying to launch the Museum of Women in the West, Toni Dewey told me: "Some of those friendships are the most rewarding personally and deepest that I've have ever had." Among these was her relationship with Gay, one of the scores of volunteers working to raise the $28 million needed to construct the building and develop the exhibits.

"What I liked about Gay was how truly smart she is, really smart, a very strategic thinker and a doer," Toni told me.

Toni relished her playmates, as well. She loved Chicago Bulls basketball, a passion she shared with Mardie, a friend from her days in the Windy City. "She and I are the greatest Chicago Bulls fans who ever lived," Toni told me. "Last year she invited me to come in to see a game. I flew in for the weekend, and we went. I bought a hat and a tee-shirt."

In late life, doing things with friends takes on an importance that it hasn't had since the early twenties. Fifty-four percent of women ages sixty-five to seventy-four are married, compared to twenty-nine percent of those over seventy-five. As they lose their husbands and partners, women turn to female friends as companions in favorite activities—like going to movies or eating at restaurants—traditionally undertaken in pairs.

Like adolescent girls, elderly widows enjoy hanging out in ensembles. When Sara Williams's bridge group got together every week, conversation trumped card playing. "This is not serious bridge; this is "fun" bridge," Sara explained.

Sara and Doreen had a close friendship apart from the group. In fact, they were soulmates. "We have so many of the same kinds of views," Sara told me. "And we think the same things are funny. We're both survivors. No matter what comes along, we get through it. And I think that makes us closer."

The years past sixty-five see a resurgence of soulmate friendships. Having at least one friend with similar reactions and a similar philosophy becomes increasingly important as women turn their attention to the meaning of their lives and deal with the loss of loved ones.

"When you have the same philosophy about life, people, and inspiration, you love each other very much, and it's an undying love," explained Genevieve Williams, an eighty-seven-year-old retired history teacher in Houston. In sixty-five years of friendship, the only thing she and her soulmate Elaine had disagreed on was whether or not the church door should be painted red.

Lifemates provide older women with the reassurance that they aren't the only one who ever felt/thought/reacted that way. With the specter of senility looming, such affirmation is as crucial to well-being now as it was in their teens.

Although Gertrude Barnstone didn't grow up in a religious family, she felt a special connection to Mitzi, who, like her, was Jewish and an artist. Gertrude explained: "Her children are about the ages of mine, so we can talk to each other about when your children give you pure hell, that sort of thing."

Gertrude had a different type of friendship with Sue, who lived just a few blocks from her. "It's very strange, because she's younger than I, that she's almost maternal with me," Gertrude observed. "She and her husband are a real comfort zone. They frequently ask me to lunch or to supper, and it's lovely."

Even though she was in vigorous health and looked a good decade younger than her seventy years, Gertrude found herself on the receiving end of this nurturer-nurtured friendship, and she discovered she liked it. Other women in late life take on nurturer roles for those who are older and frailer. During her mid-seventies, Mary Ellen Wilson developed a close and caring connection with Lena, an Englishwoman eighteen years her senior whom she met through her church. For years, Mary Ellen drove Lena to the supermarket and listened, fascinated, to stories of her life in the Far East. When Lena fell in her kitchen and couldn't get up, it was Mary Ellen she called, and Mary Ellen who called 911.

In the middle sixties and beyond, the death of loved ones and the development of life-threatening diseases become common enough that women have all-too-frequent opportunities to establish crisis friendships with women experiencing similar traumas. But sometimes women who endured a crisis together earlier in their lives can experience a lifelong bond.

Retired newspaper columnist Dorothy Goff, eighty-eight, and her friend Donelle met as neighbors in Texas City in 1946, a year before the tragic April morning when a French ship loaded with fertilizer exploded in the harbor, injuring 4,000 people and killing 512, still the greatest industrial disaster in American history. As the wounded stumbled dazed down their street, Dorothy helped Donelle strip her bed and tear the sheets into bandages to bind their cuts. Though it had happened long ago, this incident had bonded them forever.

Whatever form old friendships may have taken initially, women sixty-five and over know that shared experience adds immeasurably to their worth. "Over the years I have come to describe real friends as people who have shared history together," said Toni Dewey, the retired Motorola executive. "However long that history is, what matters is having gone through certain phases of your life with someone."

Gerontologist Karen Roberto noted that the average length of the relationships older women had was forty years. And when I asked Chicago anthropologist Madelyn Iris what struck her most about the friendships of the older women artists whose lives she was studying, she told me it was their longevity.

"I don't really know why it surprised me, because my mother, who's in her late seventies now, has one friend from before high school," she reflected. "She has newer friends. Those are couples friends. But the women that she goes shopping with alone or goes to lunch with or whatever, those are her old friends."

Even when they live far apart—or when failing physical faculties turn a fifteen-minute drive into a complicated undertaking—late-life women consider their oldest friends their best friends. In fact, studying older women's friendships, sociologist Rebecca Adams found that the older the friendship, the stronger the bond.

Retired Evanston, Illinois, bank executive and senior center director Pat Taylor considered her childhood friend Sherry in California at least as close as friends who lived nearby. "I don't think she has another person who knows her as well or has felt as close to her from home," Pat told me. "She and I have a connection that's always been there."

For women who've lived most of a century, carrying a friendship from childhood forges a link to experiences so different from today's that they seem almost mythic. Growing up as a school superintendent's daughter in small-town Nebraska, Shirley Johnson, seventy-two, was best friends with Terry, a farm girl. "I spent a lot of time out there," Shirley told me. "I learned to take a bath in a cup of water."

As adults Shirley and Terry had never lived in the same part of the country. Yet they stayed in touch and held each other in their hearts, almost like family.

❧ The Widening Gap ❧

The more interviews I conducted with women age sixty-five and over, the more uncomfortable I became with the notion of lumping them into one age group. Clearly, some were settling back, reflecting on their lives, enjoying unstructured time; and others were withdrawing into a world circumscribed by frailty. But still others were every bit as active in their professions, families, and communities as the forty- and fifty-year-olds I'd talked to.

"I like people, and I like action," Ruth Altshuler declared. "As many interesting things as I've done and continue to do, I'm still not jaded. Everything is fun."

Dressed in an exquisitely tailored suit cut just below the knee to reveal elegant calves, she marched into the restaurant at the Mansion on Turtle Creek, Dallas's toniest hotel, distributing warm smiles but making it clear that she knew how to use the authority conferred by her age and social position. She had been a trustee of Southern Methodist University since 1968, chairman of the local board of the Salvation Army for four years, and the only female campaign chair of the Dallas United Way. Her idea of fun was persuading people to invest their time and money in her favorite charities, and she showed no sign of slowing down.

At first, I tried raising the dividing line between mid and late life from sixty-five to seventy. But that still left me with the dilemma of what to do with individuals like Ruth or Vivian Hall, who remained at seventy-three a formidable political activist and one of the most enthusiastically social people I'd ever met.

The social scientists whose work I was reading seemed to be having the same problem. Several had decided to split late life into two stages—the young-old and the old-old. But they were still arguing about when one let off and the other began. Some put it at seventy-five, others at eighty-five. What they seemed to be getting at was the distinction between vigorous maturity and frailty. Granted, a woman of ninety is more likely to be frail than one of sixty-five, but this passage depends less on birthday than on individual genes, income, good and bad habits, attitude, and accident—such as a hip-shattering fall or a bump on the head.

British sociologists Jay Ginn and Sara Arber proposed a solution. They distinguished among three meanings of age: chronological, social, and physiological. The first is a simple matter of the year one was born, which determines retirement for some and Social Security and Medicare eligibility for all. The second reflects both how old a person feels and how other people react to that individual. The third encompasses the biological changes that proceed more quickly in some than in others.

As a result of all these factors, two friends who met in college, for example, may find themselves at different stages of life at age seventy. One might easily pass, even to her doctor, as middle-aged, and she might still be running her own shop or accounting firm. The other, hit by chronic health problems in her late fifties, might have retired eight years earlier and consider herself an old woman. If these two have built a soulmate friendship, the widening gap will make little difference; but if they were playmates, sharing a passion for tennis or shopping, or even if they were lifemates, their friendship will have to change or die. At the season during which female friends need one another most, they have to work hardest to keep the connection.

A year before our interview, Pat Taylor had retired. Now she had the time and money to travel, something she'd long enjoyed doing with Stephanie, her close friend since 1949. But a recent trip to Italy demonstrated that a difference had arisen between them. One day in Rome, after spending the morning at the Vatican, Pat suggested they explore some ruins on a nearby hill. Stephanie declined, saying she wanted to go back to the hotel for a nap. She was so exhausted that they needed to take a cab.

"Other times when we've been on trips, she's gotten tired, but this time was very dramatic," Pat explained.

As women move through late life, age-related health problems pose an increasing challenge to connection. Explaining how chronic illness affects elderly women's lives, gerontologist Karen Roberto discussed research she'd conducted on the impact of osteoporosis. Roberto told me: "Someone that we had interviewed early on said, 'We used to have all-day shopping excursions. I can't do that anymore because of my osteoporosis, but I still like to shop. So now on Monday we might go here, and on Tuesday we might go there.' Her osteoporosis plays a part in shaping the structure of the friendship, what it looks like on the outside. I don't think it affects the inside of the friendship."

But, Roberto acknowledged, chronic disease does test a close relationship, and the impact on casual friendships can be dramatic. The more physical problems elderly women have, the less socially connected they feel. When women of any age feel the need for new close friends, the first place they look is to casual friends and acquaintances. Older women active in business, church, and community affairs automatically keep that wider social circle replenished. But for a frail woman, maintaining that pool of prospects requires energy and mobility she may simply not have. Once that pool empties, she has nowhere to go to replace friends as they die or become mentally incapacitated.

All too often, what results is a tragic cascade: Declining health prompts a woman to withdraw from her friendships. This retreat leads to worse health, resulting in further isolation, and so on. At the bottom is the loneliness, boredom, and sense of futility that afflict all too many women in late life. Researchers have found that as many as a third of older women say that they have no one to whom they feel very close. This admission rings sadder than any description of physical limitations or of dependence on government agencies ever could.

Physical deterioration isolates some elderly women but not others. Although such health problems as osteoporosis cause many late-life friendships to wither, one study demonstrated that older women in poor health tend to spend more, rather than less, time with their closest friends than they had previously. At the bottom of the discrepancy may lie one unavoidable truth about female friendship from sixty-five on: Women who've built and maintained solid connections during life's prime can count on them during its decline.

Retired teacher Sara Williams wouldn't dream of pulling back from Doreen, her soulmate for thirty-six years. If anything, Doreen's health problems brought out Sara's affection and protectiveness. "She does things she shouldn't do," Sara fussed fondly. "She's had two serious heart attacks, one bypass surgery, seven hernia surgeries. And she still, if somebody says, 'I need so-and-so,' tells them: "Oh, I can do that.' "

Among the late-life women who gave me accounts of reforming treasured friendships challenged by physical decline, one theme rang out repeatedly: Both parties to the friendship spoke to each other openly, matter-of-factly, sometimes even humorously about the intruding condition, without making it the focus of their conversation.

Despite the difference in their ages and their health, retired banker and senior center director Pat Taylor had become increasingly close to her friend Aurora. When Pat had lost her husband in her forties, Aurora, then the only widow among her friends, had given her empathy and affirmation that only someone who'd been there could. Now nearing ninety, Aurora had developed an excruciating back problem, but Pat hadn't allowed that to threaten their friendship. "She and I are able to talk straight to each other," Pat said.

Although arthritis and heart disease are the most common chronic afflictions of old age, mental impairment creates the biggest social obstacle. As the most prevalent of the sixty-some conditions that cause dementia, Alzheimer's disease strikes 18.7 percent of people ages seventy-five to eighty-four and 47.2 percent—close to half—of those age eighty-five and over. Research suggests that women may be more vulnerable than men. Because it often alters its victims' personalities, as well as robbing them of their memories, Alzheimer's makes maintaining friendship especially difficult.

Having Margie, her friend since 1948, develop Alzheimer's disease put Pat Taylor to a tough test. When Pat and I spoke, the illness had so far left Margie's memory of people intact. She still knew who Pat was and recalled the details of their relationship. And rather than withdraw from it, Pat saw her old friend even more frequently than before, traveling from Evanston to Minneapolis at least every three months.

"It's difficult, but it's okay in one sense," she reflected. "It's not okay to see a friend having this. On the other hand, I'm sure that I was supposed to be her friend at this point."

Research demonstrates that day-to-day contact with friends helps those with late-life loss of memory hold on to external and internal reality. Yet maintaining a close relationship with someone whose once even temper has grown short, whose once quick wit has become addled, and whose once clear memory has become all but erased may be impossible, as well as heartbreaking. If she can't remember yesterday's visit, is there any continuity to the friendship? If she confuses you and her sister and the nightshift aide, are you friends in the present tense, or in the past?

After a year of being out of touch, Nan Birmingham got a call from her friend Aileen, whose voice was slurred. "I thought, 'I bet she's drunk,' and then I thought, 'She's had a stroke,'" Nan told me. "I said, 'Where are you, Aileen?' And she said, 'I'm in the convalescent home.' And I said, 'When are you going home?' And she said, 'Never.' And I just fell apart."

Phoning Aileen's husband, Nan learned that her friend who'd once been a sparkling Broadway comedienne had developed a degenerative nerve disorder. Nan, who was divorced and living alone, went to see her, and they both ended up sobbing. That was Nan's last visit.

"I sent her cards, and I sent her little funny things," Nan told me. "I couldn't put myself up against it, because I would come back and be a basket case, and I don't have people around to pull me together."

Nan's was a common response. Dementia is one of the reasons gerontologist Karen Roberto found late-life women giving for no longer calling someone a close friend. "Friends tend to withdraw with the onset of Alzheimer's," she explained. "They don't know how to respond to a person who is not acting the way that they knew them to act. It makes them feel very uncomfortable, and for self-preservation reasons, they stay away."

Just as marriage and motherhood alter the friendships of women in their twenties and early thirties, widowhood alters those after age sixty-five. As long-married women lose their husbands, they draw other widows closer, first as crisis friends and mentors, then as life-mates. Widowhood also changes what longstanding friends do with and for one another. Compared to wives, widows receive more practical help from their friends. They also give more. And, not surprisingly, they spend more time with friends. Married women are busy tending husbands.

Marital status shapes the outlines, if not the heart, of female friendship late in life. Talking with thirty late-life women about their social supports, Madelyn Iris found that many had friends they'd carried with them since childhood, whom they valued more than the couples friends they'd made during their marriages and with whom they longed to spend time one-on-one. But now that their husbands were retired, they couldn't manage it. "A lot of women said, 'This man never leaves me alone,'" Iris recalled.

Contradicting the stereotype of the isolated elderly spinster, women who have always been single often have the strongest social networks in their seventies and eighties. Freed of marriage, motherhood, moves dictated by husbands' jobs, and similar challenges to friendship, the lives of those who've always been single often have a continuity that those of their married sisters lack. But that comparatively smooth progression can create its own friendship challenges.

"There's a barrier between a single woman and married women," said Delia, a never-married sixty-nine-year-old public relations executive. "I feel a slight resentment on their part that I have escaped all of the problems that they have had. With the friends that I grew up with, I definitely feel this little kind of 'Why isn't she depressed? How did she get off free?'"

Delia's old friends may have felt sorry for her in their thirties, when they had husbands and she didn't; but now they envied her; and envy was challenging the bond. Although she kept in touch with these history friends, she felt closer to her single lifemates.

⁊ Necessary Losses ⁊

However cheerfully women undertake the passage into the last decades of life, this remains a season of unavoidable losses. Although most children outlive their parents, the death of an adult daughter or son is not uncommon as women move from their sixties to their seventies, eighties, and beyond. Over the course of late life, death and serious illness become, if not routine, normal. And female friends help each other withstand these repeated blows by affirming emotions (including ambivalence), by drying tears and tolerating mood swings, by mirroring resilience and competence, and by offering companionship and, when appropriate, distraction.

The first significant late-life loss many women experience isn't the death of a loved one; it's retirement. School districts, government agencies, and large corporations may mandate retirement at sixty-five or seventy. When stay-at-home mothers face a similar challenge to their sense of usefulness in their forties and fifties, as children leave the nest, they can use the newly free time to do things with friends and expand their social circles through volunteer or paid work. But women who have spent much of their adult life in jobs outside the home thrive, and even come to depend, on the social stimulation of the workplace.

When they were working at the same college, Mitsuye Yamada and three female colleagues found getting together easy. After retirement, they never seemed able to arrange it. "The four of us kept talking about having lunch, and somehow we kept calling each other and saying, 'I can't go because . . .' " Mitsuye said.

Then something happened that no committee meeting or trip to visit grandchildren could push off their calendars: One of the four died. Mitsuye recalled: "At her funeral we looked at one another and said, 'We should make an effort to get together, because we need each other.' So now we get together for lunch someplace the first Monday of every month. We decided that unless we make this concerted effort to keep in touch, we just won't do it."

Eleanor Tinsley, sixty-nine, had been a Houston political pioneer. I interviewed her seven months after term limits had forced her to retire from city council. During her sixteen-year career as a council member and her preceding stint on the school board, Eleanor had won significant victories—desegregating the city's schools, curbing billboards, banning smoking in municipal auditoriums.

The workmate relationship she and her top aide Madelyn Appel shared brought zest to Eleanor's public life. "The fun and excitement was getting legislation passed," Eleanor told me. "She was there at the moment it occurred, and she was thrilled with me. 'We got those eight votes!' It was a real feeling of accomplishment. We were like ballplayers who win a game."

Because their jobs demanded so much, Eleanor and Madelyn seldom saw each other outside the office. Since Eleanor's retirement, they had gotten together only two or three times, for coffee down at City Hall. Theirs had been a close, caring friendship; but it had been a workmate relationship, and now the work was over. Although Eleanor still referred to Madelyn as one of her dearest friends, much of what connected them was gone.

Something similar happens to every woman who retires from a job that put her in regular contact with people she enjoyed and cared about, especially if she found the work they did together meaningful. The separation from her workplace "home" can be almost as traumatic as the dissolution of a marriage. In fact, cultural anthropologist Mark Luborsky described a successful retirement transition as a kind of death followed by rebirth into a new position in society.

Continued contact with friends from work can cushion the blow. After retirement, women who'd originally bonded in the workplace provide one another with a bridge to that former life. Studying middle-class women, British gerontologist Dorothy Jerrome discovered that they responded to retirement by adopting a variety of friendship strategies. Some worked on strengthening and deepening existing relationships; some made new friends; others developed the role of "good neighbor."

Sara Williams had retired from teaching math more than a decade before our interview. But she got together every three months with her former colleagues, one of whom, Elva, had become a close friend. "She's my middle-of-the-night person," Sara said, referring to their late-hours phone calls. "She stays up late, and she knows I stay up late. When you can't sleep, you have to have somebody to talk to."

Elva also had helped her through an even greater late-life crisis: the death of her husband. "When my husband died, Elva was there for me," Sara said. "She had been there the whole time. She was the one who came almost every day when he was at home to see him, and she made him feel good because she always left some lipstick on his face."

Studying the support networks of rural women whose husbands had died, Karen Roberto and Jean Scott observed that initially, a widow's social life revolves around her family; but between one and four years later, contacts with children, siblings, and grandchildren begin to decrease, and interactions with friends become more important. Friendships that develop in bereavement support groups help buffer the stress of the loss, which is why the American Association of Retired Persons set up a national program pairing the newly widowed with individuals who had made a satisfactory adjustment.

"Not that I don't miss him," sixty-five-year-old Florence Marquez said of her late husband, a mail carrier, who'd been dead three years. "But I find myself doing things that I would have wanted to do before and not have the responsibility of having to come home and make dinner, take care of somebody."

Another inevitable loss challenges friendship in late life: the declining health of friends themselves. Studies show that the amount of contact women in their early eighties have with their friends depends largely on their mood, but that as they move through that decade, deteriorating health places an increasing strain on connection. Once neither friend can drive, getting together becomes difficult. Once emphysema makes one friend short of breath, long telephone conversations become exhausting. Physical limitations as common as arthritis make it difficult to entertain company, go out for dinner, or even dial a phone. By the time women reach their nineties, friendship becomes precarious. "I have one friend who's still alive, but I haven't heard from her in two years," Dorothy Goff said sadly. "She's my longest living friend, but we only kept in touch at Christmas."

The longer an individual lives, the fewer agemates she has and the more likely her surviving friends will have moved to be closer to children or younger siblings. Ruth Altshuler recalled her mother, who'd lived to be eighty-eight, saying toward the end of her life, "We couldn't go a second table at bridge today. Everybody either is dying or has lost her mind." Her mother's complaint "was funny, but sad and true," Ruth noted. "As you get older, friends start fading away."

Past age sixty-five, the experience of having a close friend die becomes common enough that fifteen of the twenty-five women I interviewed in this age group talked about it. Mannie Tuteur, seventy-three, had lost so many friends recently that she and her husband were having trouble keeping her address book current. "My husband goes through the book, and every time somebody dies, he puts an *X*," she complained. "I said, 'Stop doing that! I can't stand it.' I'm going to do a new address book."

Compounding the loss of the friend herself, women have to contend with traditions that treat them as secondary mourners. Although obituaries increasingly acknowledge dear friends and some families even ask a close friend to deliver a eulogy, funerals remain a family affair, coordinated by and designed to comfort spouses, daughters, sons, and siblings and their children. A granddaughter who has seen the deceased no more than a handful of times in the past decade is expected to cry and to be consoled; the close friend who was part of her daily life is expected to bring a pie or casserole to help feed the assembled family and to offer them that consolation.

But these unrelated women have a consolation geographically distant children and grandchildren lack: They were there to enjoy and ease their friends' last days.

First one member of Sara Williams's bridge group died suddenly of a heart attack. Then another succumbed slowly to repeated strokes. But the one that touched her deepest was her dear friend Chloë. Suffering from a crippling condition that gradually hardened her spine, Chloë nevertheless traveled around the world, determined to see and do everything possible while she could still walk. Eventually, cancer and a heart attack sent her to the hospital for her final weeks but left her cordial personality and determined wit intact.

One evening Sara and another friend came to stay with her while her husband attended a Lions Club meeting. "She kept nodding off," Sara recalled. "And she kept saying, 'Oh, my goodness! Here you all came to visit with me, and I'm going to sleep.' I said, 'You don't have to entertain us, Chloë. We just came to sit with you.' That's the last time I saw her. She died the following Sunday."

To help deal with the loss of this important relationship, Sara turned to her surviving friends, mostly in her church. "Because we're a close group, a small church, we really are a good support group for one another," she explained.

Sara understood that, ultimately, women mourning lost friends can expect the greatest support and understanding from other, long-standing, surviving friends and from new friends they may form around the crisis. When gerontologists Karen Roberto and Pat Ianni Stanis polled older women about the deaths of their dear friends, they found that the experience actually brought them closer to other friends. Roberto and Stanis also pointed out the need for society to recognize the importance of the loss and to give surviving friends recognition and support.

For decades, Vera, an eighty-year-old retired high school English teacher, and her friends Ginny and Jill and their husbands had done things as couples. After the men died, the three widows continued the pattern. Then, five years before I interviewed Vera, Jill developed terminal cancer. The disease took their ensemble friendship to a deeper level.

Vera recalled: "One day I went to the hospital and she said, 'The doctor told me I have two weeks.' I said, 'Two more weeks in the hospital?' And she said, 'No. Two more weeks to live.' I started to tear up, and she said, 'It's all right. I think it's kind of exciting.'

"You know, I've never heard a person say that about dying. I thought that was glorious. She just regarded it as another step: 'Boy, I'm going to find out now what it means to die.' "

The grief Vera and Ginny shared for Jill strengthened their friendship. But some elderly women respond to losing a particularly dear friend by shutting down socially. During the sixteen years she'd lived in her Miami Beach high-rise retirement home, Esther, ninety, had made only one close friend. Then Dottie died, and Esther had become isolated.

"I'm left with no one since then," Esther told me. "I tried. I tried. But maybe it's because I'm old. You get old and—I forget what they call it—nothing pleases you. Everything is wrong."

Death is the ultimate crisis that friendships endure, and all friendships that last encounter it. When it comes unexpectedly, friends are left to deal with their loss and their personal vulnerability. Nothing brings home feelings of mortality like the death of someone close who's the same age and sex.

A generation ago, doctors tended to withhold news of impending death from the terminally ill. Nowadays, patients are more likely than not to know the grim prognosis. When there is such warning, a close friend can help validate the dying woman's life and put it into perspective. With the end of life in sight, female friends are uniquely positioned to affirm its significance. They serve one another as mirrors reflecting each other's irreplaceable qualities in a way that encourages and supports this final step in full psychological development.

Often, spouses, siblings, and children are in such a state of denial about a woman's impending demise—or the guilt she feels at abandoning them is so great—that she can't discuss her death with them. But she can with an intimate friend.

Some women explicitly ask their best friends to be at their bedsides when they die—both for the comfort and sense of continuity only friends can give and to see that their wishes are carried out. Pat Taylor, still in excellent health, had told her friend Marjorie what kind of medical care she would and wouldn't want if she were terminally ill. Then she'd given Marjorie her durable power of attorney, second to her daughter, who lived a thousand miles away. "Marjorie knows me well enough and is not too sentimental," Pat explained.

Other women, however, withdraw. That's what my late Aunt Gina did. Living out her last months at home in Florida, she accepted phone calls from her one great, loyal female friend, a woman she'd known for fifty years. But Gina wouldn't let Helen fly out from California to visit her. When I asked why, my aunt told me that she wanted Helen to remember her as she had been, not as she'd become.

Letting a friend in on the end—laying vanity aside, accepting the total vulnerability of death, being utterly ourselves right before we cease to be ourselves at all—is the ultimate act of intimacy. Some women can't bring themselves to ask for it; some can't bring themselves to offer it. But those who can share one of life's greatest gifts, on both sides, and discover that, finally, there is no comfort like friendship.

✢ Friends for Life ✢

Although new friends can never replace the old, they nonetheless bring zest to late life. Researchers have found that women in late life typically take one of two approaches to friendship: Either they have a small circle of close, longstanding friends, who often don't live nearby; or they build larger networks of newer friends, whom they see regularly. When old, dear friends die, the loss is profound for any woman, but those without a network of recent friends are hit hardest. Their social worlds contract with each death. If they outlive the last one, they risk retreating into isolation.

New friends, sociologist Rebecca Adams noted, are more likely than old ones to involve each other in the world around them. But as women get older, making new friends gets harder. After sixteen years of widowhood, retired high school English teacher Vera had remarried a year before our interview and moved from St. Louis to Lawrence, Kansas. "Moving into a strange town at seventy-nine makes it difficult to find friends," she told me. "At my age you're not going to work every day or anything like that."

Vera had become cordial with the wives of her husband's two golfing buddies, and she'd volunteered at the hospital, where she met "a lot of nice ladies" working in the gift shop. "But they haven't developed into anything yet," Vera said.

Despite such difficulties, most women do continue acquiring new friends throughout their lives. About a third of the women sixty-five and over I interviewed described how they'd done so. Travel had introduced some of these women to companions with similar interests; but the secret, several women said, was getting out and doing something—anything—and being open to the people met in the process.

Mary Ellen Wilson, seventy-seven, walked three miles around a track at her Denver neighborhood park each day for exercise. One morning, she struck up a conversation with Beverly, seventy-six, whose doctor had ordered a similar regimen to help prevent a second heart attack. Before long, Mary Ellen, a retired librarian, discovered that Beverly shared her delight in books and plays, and they started going to the theater together.

For many women in late life, the most congenial incubator for new friendships is church or temple. Both Genevieve Williams and Sara Williams (who are not related) told me about their pew groups, which functioned as ensemble friendships. Virtually every Sunday for the past twenty years, Genevieve had arrived at Houston's Trinity Episcopal Church extra early to save the fifth row on the right side. Genevieve and one of the women who sat with her were both eighty-seven, another was eighty-nine, and two others were their age or older. "I call it Elderly Row," Genevieve said.

Retirement homes offer opportunities to form new friendships, especially since residents can enjoy one another's company without worrying about transportation. Edgewater, where seventy-year-old retired Methodist missionary Beverly Walter lived, hosted game nights— bridge one evening, board games another. Sometimes a musical ensemble would come perform, or a church group would organize a beach outing for residents. But the best friend Beverly had made in her six years at Edgewater was Anaïs, a lonely recent widow who just happened to move onto her floor.

Encountering each other in the hall and in the elevator, they discovered that they both hailed from the Northeast, liked classical music, and enjoyed reading. "We share books," Beverly said. "She reads a book and she likes it and she lends it to me, and I read a book I like and I make sure she gets it."

Hearing Beverly describe her friendship with Anaïs echoed my own memories of college dorm life. Here were all these people, mostly women, roughly the same age and income level, living in the same building and interacting every day. At an age when mobility becomes a challenge, living just down the hall or only two floors up from a friend is even more significant than it is at nineteen.

But some of the same issues crop up at both stages of life. After striking up a conversation in the retirement home dining room, Dorothy Goff discovered that she had a lot in common with Alice. They knew some of the same people and enjoyed the same television programs. They became close friends. Along with two other women, Dorothy and Alice established a women's social room they called Petticoat Junction, after one of their favorite television shows. Most evenings, they would hang out there from 6:00 to 9:00, playing cards and watching TV. Then a new unmarried man moved into the building, and Alice dropped Dorothy for him.

"It really hurt me," Dorothy admitted.

At any age, opening up to friendship means risking rejection. Taking the risks involved in forming new friendships requires that individuals maintain their identity and sense of worth. The upscale retirement condominium where Genevieve Williams had moved recently encouraged her individuality from the beginning. When she and her grandson came to look the place over, the staff member who took them around quickly discerned that Genevieve had traveled widely and asked her to show her slides from a different country every week. This clever strategy both secured evening programs for some time to come and introduced Genevieve to her neighbors as a woman worth knowing.

"I'm meeting quite a number of very nice friends, older ladies who've had an interest in life," Genevieve said enthusiastically.

Nursing homes, on the other hand, can be lonely places. Perhaps because dependency strips people of status and self-confidence, these facilities have trouble promoting friendships among residents. The environment seems more congenial in retirement communities that accept elderly people who are still relatively independent but offer them various levels of assistance, all the way up through skilled nursing, as their health deteriorates with age. Because all these options are in one building, women who become friends in health can continue seeing each other even after a stroke or fall relocates one to the nursing floor.

Meeting new people and getting together with friends may take more doing for women who don't live in retirement homes, but being surrounded by neighbors of various ages gives them a broader pool of acquaintances to choose from. The more active and involved the women I interviewed were, the more they were likely to mention cultivating young friends. "As you grow older, people unfortunately die," observed Mannie Tuteur, who still worked for a labor union in Chicago. "I'm in the process of developing relationships with younger women."

Ellie Porter recognized that her close friend Faith Lagay considered her a mentor for creative aging. But the pleasures of their relationship went far beyond that. When they'd met four years earlier in a graduate philosophy of ethics class, where even Faith was twenty years older than most of their fellow students, Ellie had felt an immediate attraction. "I thought, 'Oh, my God, an available, single, intelligent, appealing woman'—there ain't many around that can go play with me," Ellie explained.

Some late-life women find the best "new" friends among old friends. They use class reunions, grandchildren's weddings, or pilgrimages to hometowns as occasions to reconnect.

At first Sara Williams didn't recognize her old roommate Juliana when they saw each other at their sixty-third college reunion; but once she did, she was delighted. "We talked all through lunch that day," Sara recalled. "I found out what all her family were doing. She had four or five sisters and four brothers. I knew them, because I had spent time at their house. We've talked on the phone since then—people, what we know about them, who's still alive of our group."

Continuity is one of the earmarks of late-life female friendship, Karen Roberto told me. In one study that examined social support networks over time, she'd asked a large group of women age sixty-two and older to name one of their closest friends, then posed the same question twelve years later. Many mentioned the same person both times. She was amazed to see how stable these friendships were.

What struck me most as I listened to women ages sixty-five to eighty-nine was how clearly the qualities that characterized the best in female friendship at any age stood out now. Almost all mentioned fun and laughter, and they still ranked honesty among the most important friendship qualities. "I have true friends, people who know me," Florence Marquez said. "A friend is a person who can be honest when they praise you."

Close female friendships, cultivated over the decades, count among a woman's most significant achievements. "It makes me feel so good to have my kids know that these are mother's friends," University of Oregon vice provost Nancie Fadeley, sixty-five, admitted. "Every once in a while, my daughter says, 'Mom, you really have neat friends.' I feel as if I am raised in my children's eyes."

Women who lack these uniquely rewarding late-life intimacies— whether because they never learned to be friends with other women, because they bought the cultural directive to devalue those relation-ships, or because illness or poverty isolates them—miss the support they may need to recognize and understand the validity and fullness of their own existence. Women who cultivate female friendship throughout their lives reap a harvest of insight and affirmation that will provide the nourishment they need at the end of their journey.

Part Three

KEEPING FRIENDS

LET ME CONFESS SOMETHING: For much of my life, I was terrible at making and keeping friends. When it came time to choose basketball teams in junior high phys ed, I was dependably the next-to-last choice, even though I stood taller than average and could sink foul shots. During high school, I hung out with a group of kids who worked on the student paper and the literary magazine, but I didn't really have a best friend. Attending a women's college helped some, but I was so focused on meeting guys on weekends that I ignored the rich potential for connection that surrounded me all week. I was in my mid-thirties before I started reaching out to other women for companionship and affirmation. It took me another decade to become a good friend myself.

Reading reports of research on friendship and interviewing girls and women for this book, I recognized why I'd been so inept. Part of the problem was internal. Like everyone, I brought a lot of baggage to my relationships, including my competitiveness, my conviction that conflict always destroyed connection, and my notion that females were shallow, silly, and generally inferior to males. I'd also been dealing with external challenges to friendship, particularly the moves my family made every few years for my father's job.

Fortunately, most women have less trouble developing female friendships than I did. But each of us brings all of herself to any close relationship, including all our unresolved personal issues, our doubts and insecurities, our fears that baring our hearts will lead to having them broken. Considering that we also face the potholes and road-blocks that our own overbooked schedules and our families' expectations place in our paths, it's surprising that so many friendships do thrive.

But once we learn to recognize these internal and external threats to friendship, we can begin to deal consciously and constructively with them. Cultivating close friends isn't easy; it requires developing and practicing the art of connection. Besides helping us maintain and repair friendships that falter, working at connection enriches friendships that are steady and enables us to initiate and build strong new ones. Luckily, the skills to do this can be learned—at any season of life.

12

ᴥ

Finding It Hard

To be sure, friendship is not available to everyone, as Aristotle explained; it is a state of character, not an activity.

—Judith Shklar, *Ordinary Vices*

I've always had this hunch that women's friendships are not as hunky-dory as they are presented," twenty-eight-year-old University of Oklahoma graduate student Margie Boldt told me. "You go into Hallmark, and you think we must just love each other," she said, referring to the racks of sentimental friendship cards. "I just don't believe that it's all peaches and cream."

Margie spoke from experience. Her relationship with her childhood best friend Suellen had left her gun-shy about getting close to other women. "I had this shadow for the first twenty-one years of my life," Margie explained. "Everything I did, she did. At college, she joined the same sorority. She joined the same cheerleading squad. She dated a guy in the same fraternity as my boyfriend. I felt both competitive and defensive."

As I interviewed women for this book, I kept hearing notes of discord disrupting the harmony of friendship. They echoed themes too common to be coincidental: shame, insecurity, dependency, jealousy, envy, competitiveness, judgmentalism, depression, shyness, self-absorption, fear of abandonment or other betrayal, and a whole range of neurotic needs—all disrupt the harmony of connection.

✤ Maternal Matters ✤

Many psychologists and psychiatrists trace trouble forming and maintaining female friendships to trouble in our relationships with our mothers. The way we interact with our mothers beginning in infancy colors how we relate to other women for the rest of our lives, explained University of Wisconsin–Milwaukee women's studies professor Chava Frankfort-Nachmias. Unresolved issues with our mothers get played out with other women who get close.

The mutual push-pull of mothers and daughters churned through the friendships many women described to me. Take Marissa Heller's. The Columbia senior and her soulmate Nicole had been best friends since they were six months old. "I love her more than anything, but there are times that I can't deal with her," Marissa confessed.

Women say the same thing, often in the same words, about their mothers. As in a mother-daughter relationship, Marissa and Nicole each struggled to maintain her individuality while remaining connected. And like mothers and daughters, they both looked to each other for comforting but resisted taking each other's advice.

For any woman, the maternal relationship is laced with inevitable conflict: A baby comes into the world feeling merged with its mother, as if they were one person. But to become autonomous individuals, children must inevitably separate. For girls, this separation is especially difficult; because, after all, she and her mother are the same sex, a girl *could* become a younger copy of her. In early childhood, this has some appeal. Consider those matching mother-daughter dresses that make a five-year-old feel just like Mommy. Then consider the way adolescent girls insist on making their own generational fashion statements, even if the look is unflattering. Teenage clothing fads are less about style than they are about declaring, for all the world to see, "I'm not my mother."

Eva Margolies noted in *The Best of Friends, The Worst of Enemies:* "Even if a little girl has a mother who pushes her to become independent, . . . the task of breaking away from her mother is monumental." A girl may vacillate between angry adolescent attempts to repudiate her mother and a yearning for her unconditional love. This difficult transition may account for some women's discomfort with conflict, or anything else that threatens connection.

On top of the merger-separation tension that afflicts all mothers and daughters, many women suffer from what psychologists and psychiatrists call attachment problems. In 1951 British psychoanalyst John Bowlby published a study on maternal deprivation. Over the next three decades, after closely watching both humans and monkeys, he and his colleagues Mary and Len Ainsworth identified three different styles of attachment between mothers and their infants. Mothers who felt secure about themselves and their relationships and who responded to their babies warmly and consistently produced *securely attached* children who developed into adults who were comfortable with close relationships. Mothers who couldn't connect with others and rejected their babies emotionally produced *avoidantly attached* children who grew up to be incapable of close, reciprocal relationships. And mothers who were anxious about their relationships and responded sometimes with warmth and other times with anger or frustration produced *ambivalently attached* children who sought close relationships but never quite trusted them.

Avoidantly attached children become adults who either can't ask for what they want or else demand it aggressively—and who have trouble giving to others spontaneously. The ambivalently attached person is likely to be charming and extroverted on one hand and impulsive and self-destructive on the other. By contrast, a securely attached adult can balance work and play and maintain close, mutually rewarding relationships.

Cecile, a forty-five-year-old physician assistant for a medical clinic in Northern California, knew that how she responded to her female friends reflected her ambivalent tie with her mother. Cecile saw her mother as a forceful woman who could be warm and nurturing one minute, brusque and impatient the next. Cecile had never been sure which side would come forward at any given time. "That's why with women, I can't take that kind of pulling the rug out from underneath me," she explained.

Maternal history isn't destiny. Many women whose mothers were unresponsive, anxious, or downright hostile do learn to make and keep close female friends. And being aware that friendship problems with women in general or with a particular kind of woman may have roots in childhood issues helps a woman overcome this challenge.

Sometimes, no matter how secure a girl's attachment to her mother may be, illness or accident deprives her of her mother's love and support, damaging her ability to relate to other women. In her best-seller *Motherless Daughters,* Hope Edelman, who lost her mother to cancer at fourteen, explained:

> In a crowd of other women, as a female, she feels alone. Fierce independence and self-sufficiency are her shield . . . When the person she relied on most has left her, the only companion she can unquestionably count on is herself.

A mother's mental illness can leave the same scars as her death. After our interview, Mary Ruth, a fifty-two-year-old poet and teacher, wrote to me describing the lasting effects of her mother's depression: "I have all of the difficulties most women have in relating to other women, plus a few more. A lot of distrust and anxiety."

Women like Mary Ruth may yearn for close female friendships, but they have trouble relaxing and enjoying them. And when something challenges the relationship, whether that challenge is something internal such as a disagreement or a life event such as marriage or a move, the first impulse of a woman whose mother suffered from serious emotional problems is often to withdraw self-protectively, rather than confront the problem and work it through with her friend.

If we accept the idea that women unconsciously identify their friends with their mothers, every close female friendship offers an opportunity to repair any damage from that first close connection, but only if both parties let it. For example, a woman whose mother nurtured and comforted her when she was sick or hurt but never encouraged her originality or celebrated her victories can develop close friendships with women who both nurture her and affirm her strengths. On the other hand, if they aren't careful, female friends can settle into familiar but unproductive patterns in which they withhold affection or information, offer advice instead of empathy, rebel, and generally replay the worst aspects of their relationships with their mothers.

Of course, a woman's mother isn't the only early influence on her friendships. Everyone else in the household plays a part. In fact, a team of Boston University psychologists discovered that having a warm and demonstrative parent of either sex led people to have better friendships at midlife.

The way a girl relates to her siblings, especially her sisters, also influences how she relates to her women friends when she grows up. Children and adolescents try out ways of interacting with their peers on their siblings first. A girl who gets her way by bossing a little sister or manipulating an older one will tend to use that same strategy with her friends; a girl who learns more positive relational skills, such as listening well or dealing constructively with conflict, will be likely to apply those in her friendships. Social scientists have also found that a person who had a warm childhood relationship with a brother or sister will often be more satisfied with friends of that sibling's sex than the other. Conversely, if two sisters spend their childhoods sniping at each other, they will tend to grow up reluctant to make themselves vulnerable to other women.

Charity Gourley, sixty-one, certainly had that experience as the youngest of five children—a brother and three sisters. "There was a lot of fighting," Charity told me. "I have very, very difficult relationships with my sisters, and to this day there is a lot of tension. There is a lot in terms of my relationships with women in general. It seems to be my nature to always be on the defensive, expecting an attack."

Women come to their friendships with different needs and different expectations. Cybil, a fifty-nine-year-old science professor, gave me an example: "I need 'Good morning' and 'Good evening.' Ella needs half a day every six weeks. So a very lovely—for a while—friendship became very sulky and very crabby."

Cybil wanted daily contact, but a brief phone call satisfied her. Her friend, on the other hand, wanted long conversations but could go for weeks between those, while Cybil's tight schedule made it hard to arrange those four-hour blocks of time. Each woman felt the other wasn't doing her share to maintain the connection.

In *Between Women,* Luise Eichenbaum and Susie Orbach point to unrealistic expectations as the culprit behind many common complaints about woman-to-woman relationships. Women expect their female friends to be endlessly "giving and flexible." Like the ideal mother, they should know intuitively what we want. If they don't, we are often disappointed.

Even the best female friendship, like the best mother-daughter relationship, falls short of what we secretly yearn for it to do: It can heal us, but it can never heal us perfectly.

↬ Inside Out ↬

Certain personality characteristics make it hard to find and keep friends. Insecurity, self-absorption, depression, shame, judgmentalism, shyness, addictions, and eating disorders all undermine a woman's ability to connect.

To be a good friend, a woman first has to be an individual. If her personal boundaries aren't clear, she may find herself in a moral muddle, thinking, as Harvard developmental psychologist Carol Gilligan commented, "that she is responsible for the actions of others while others are responsible for the choices she makes." She'll offer advice, even when a friend clearly doesn't want to be told what she should do; and when the friend resists it, she'll feel frustrated and angry. And because she has trouble setting limits with all the people closest to her, she will have trouble telling her family that she needs time for her friends.

A woman with porous personal boundaries faces another friendship problem: She may repeatedly find herself mired in relationships in which she feels she gives a lot and gets little in return. Gussie, a forty-four-year-old real estate agent, knew that this trait had cost her valued friends. When she felt overloaded, she either erupted or withdrew. Before she could set limits on how far she would go for friends, Gussie had to develop the conviction that she was worthy of friendship by virtue of who she was, not what she was willing to do.

When social psychologist Frances Marie Costa studied 596 people in their twenties, she found high self-esteem to be one of the most important predictors of a person's ability to form satisfying friendships. Self-esteem and female friendship go together: Friendship builds self-esteem, but a woman needs a certain level of self-esteem to be a good friend.

How we feel about ourselves influences whether we're comfortable initiating a friendship or even suggesting a shared activity. Maryann, an outwardly self-confident fifty-four-year-old university administrator, admitted that she'd never felt comfortable picking up the phone and calling a friend to suggest doing something. "It's a fear of rejection," she said. She worried that friends would say no, not because they were genuinely busy or didn't think they'd like the movie, for example, but because they didn't like *her*. As a result, Maryann wound up seeing a lot of movies and plays alone, rather than risking a real or imagined rebuff.

Women who suffer from depression also have trouble making and keeping friends. Depression renders a woman's moods unpredictable, which makes her hard for friends to relate to. The depressed woman often doesn't feel like making social plans, and if she allows herself to be cajoled into lunch or a walk, she can't enjoy it. Believing that her friends can't possibly understand how hopeless she feels makes her feel even worse. This may explain why one team of University of California researchers was able to confirm that misery really does love company: Depressed people prefer being around other depressed people—even though they don't cheer each other up.

For most of her fifty-two years, Karen Hyatt had battled depression. Worse still, she didn't dare let anyone see her distress. "Because of my insecurities about my value to anyone, I always had to be perfect," she told me.

Karen's depression made it hard for her to connect with other women, and her deep sense of shame at being depressed further hindered the connection. Unlike guilt, which springs from feeling we've done something unworthy of us, shame undermines our sense of self; we feel that *we* are unworthy, rather than our behavior. Clinical psychologist Judy Jordan explained:

> [S]hame is . . . a felt sense of unworthiness to be in connection, a deep sense of unlovability, with the ongoing awareness of how very much one wants to connect with others.

Shame isolates us by making us conceal parts of ourselves that we feel are unworthy of love. We may choose not to tell even our closest friends that we had a one-night stand or came close to clobbering our two-year-old, fearing that these actions show us to be promiscuous women or bad, dangerous mothers. But when we share such experiences, along with our feelings of anxiety and guilt, and a friend responds with empathy, rather than judgmentalism, both we and the friendship grow.

On the other hand, a woman may react to a friend's disclosures judgmentally, erecting another common block to close friendship. Judgmentalism can be an outward expression of blurred personal boundaries. If one friend feels responsible for the welfare and reputation of the other, she may drive that friend away by refusing to accept her right to take her own course and make her own mistakes.

Such a response had ruptured one of Nedra's most important friendships. At the time of our interview, she was in her mid-forties, married, with a seven-year-old child and a high-powered job. But a decade and a half earlier, her life had looked bleak. Nedra had just ended a six-month affair with a married man. "I wasn't a very good second woman," she explained. "He wasn't going to leave his wife. I didn't really want him to, but I wanted more attention."

Although she'd initiated it, the breakup left Nedra devastated, alone, and lonely. One evening over dinner, she poured out her pain to her close friend Babette.

"She said the equivalent of, 'Well, that's what you get for dating a married man,' " Nedra recalled, still outraged at receiving such a lack of empathy when she was so vulnerable. "I was just really stunned, and I was pissed off because I felt like, 'It's easy for you to say. You have a marriage. You have a son. You don't know what it's like to be alone.' We didn't speak to each other for almost a year."

Judgmentalism often rises to the surface when a woman feels threatened by another woman's different lifestyle choices. Nothing demonstrates this more clearly than the tension between mothers who have jobs and those who choose to stay home. Physician Sharon Itaya suspended her medical career for about nine years, from the time her daughter was born until her son entered kindergarten. "No one has been so direct as to say, 'I don't agree with what you're doing,' " she told me near the end of that period. "But there certainly are a lot of questions about what I'm doing and a lot of ways in which I've been made to feel self-conscious about having wasted all this time and education and opportunity in order to stay home."

Although making different choices challenges close friendships, it needn't damage them. In fact, if each friend can discuss her own feelings and experiences involving her choice nonjudgmentally, the friendship and both women in it can grow. But when one friend thinks the other's choice invalidates hers, she disrupts the connection. The only way around this dilemma is through it: If a woman tells her friend, for instance, "I feel like if I was right to put my career on hold to stay home with my kids, you must be wrong, and if you were right to keep your job and hire a nanny, then I must be wrong," and the friend responds empathically, rather than defensively, the women and the friendship will emerge stronger.

Self-absorption is another major friendship killer. Two women can't connect if one only wants to talk about her experiences, her problems, and her feelings and quickly brings discussion of anything else back to herself. "But enough about me," Bette Midler's character announced in *Outrageous Fortune*. "What do *you* think about me?" Sociologist Steve Duck noted that such self-absorbed prattle "excludes the listener and, by so doing, implicitly derogates the importance of the other person."

If a friend is going through a crisis, that's one thing: Being there for her during a divorce, for example, means suspending the expectation of reciprocity. For a few months, one friend will do more than her share of talking, the other more than her share of listening. But this license is temporary. The friend who listened will eventually claim her right to talk about *her*self.

Shyness is the quiet cousin of self-absorption. Whether a woman is chronically shy or struck shy in certain situations, such as big parties, her focus is on herself—in this case, on her social discomfort. "I become scattered and lose my sense of self," Jean, an internationally ranked triathlete, admitted. "I become shy, jittery. I become agoraphobic. Sometimes I have to retreat."

Introversion keeps women from putting themselves in situations where they'd meet potential friends. When she does go to a party or a PTA meeting, a shy woman will fade into the background, rather than initiate a conversation or speak up on an issue. As chapter 3 explained, attraction is the first step in developing a friendship. If no one notices a woman, no one can be attracted to her. Shy women go out of their way to avoid being noticed. When shy women do make friends, these friends tend to be fewer and less diverse than those of their more outgoing peers, and introverts interact with their friends less.

Jean led a solitary life in a semirural part of Hawaii, where she raised organic vegetables. "I was getting sort of stuck in patterns, staying by myself a lot," she said. "And I don't want to be that way. I want to experience life and grow and expand, and that means reaching out to get to know people and do things with them. It's something I want, but it doesn't come easy for me."

Loneliness is most common in people who sense that their interests and ideas differ from others', as Jean knew hers did. But in Jean's case, something else also contributed to her loneliness: She seemed unable or unwilling to take part in the casual socializing that often opens the door to friendship.

For three nights, I was a guest in the house where Jean and her boyfriend had been staying for several weeks. Although we all went our separate ways during the day, each evening our hosts prepared dinner, and we all sat down together to eat and chat—all of us except Jean. She was a vegetarian, so it was understandable that she would prepare her own meals. But instead of bringing her beets and carrots to the table, Jean ate them alone, standing up in the kitchen. She seemed either not to know that participating in the social ritual of dinner was an obligation of a houseguest or not to understand what would be expected of her had she joined us. In thirty-six years, she hadn't picked up the skills she needed to function socially.

The lack of such social skills as initiating and carrying on a conversation, expressing appropriate gratitude for presents and favors, and coordinating activities with others underlies what sociologist Pat O'Connor described as "trait," as opposed to "state," loneliness. The latter comes in the wake of a situation that disrupts an individual's social world. Going away to college, losing a spouse or lover, opting to quit work to stay home with young kids—any of these puts a person in a state of loneliness that eventually ebbs. Trait loneliness, on the other hand, is something a person carries with her. It's part of *her,* not the result of her situation. That form of loneliness can last a lifetime.

Once a friendship begins, deficient social skills can imperil its progress and longevity. Steve Duck noted that some socially inept individuals "have a poorly developed idea of what relationships mean to normal adults, and they will do the wrong things simply because their guiding principles are faulty." They may not understand, for example, that when a woman says "I haven't told this to anyone else," she implies an obligation to keep the secret.

Because nothing heals and affirms like spilling a dark secret to a friend and having her accept and understand, nothing threatens female friendship like the inability to keep confidences. Woman after woman told me about developing a promising friendship to a certain point but no further when they discovered their first important secret spilled. Former Fort Worth city councilwoman Shirley Johnson had learned not to confide in one friend because "she never respected information." The way Shirley saw it, "It was always her privilege to be in the know and tell everybody."

Social skills go beyond manners, but manners do matter. Some may be mere convention, but others communicate how one person feels about another. Being late for lunch occasionally is one thing. Being chronically late for dates with a friend is another. Looking distracted while she pours her heart out, interrupting her, and the countless other little ways a woman unconsciously shows that another isn't very important to her can all erode a friendship.

Vera, a retired high school teacher, had to work at her friendship with Willa, a symphony musician with a generous heart but an abrasive mouth. Both lived in the same town house complex. When it snowed, the maintenance crew shoveled everyone's front steps. If they didn't get to Willa's unit before she was ready to go out, she'd call and demand immediate service. In the same situation, Vera would take her old broom and sweep her steps herself. Hearing that, Willa said, "You should wear a tee-shirt with 'Kick Me' on the back."

That stung, Vera told me: "But then I thought, This is just Willa's way of talking. It didn't occur to her that it might have hurt me."

Willa was lucky that Vera was willing to look beyond this flaw. Many women might not have. In fact, social psychologist Martin Johnson concluded that social skills were more important than proximity or appearance in determining who got selected for friendship. People "will tolerate an ugly extravert," sociologist Steve Duck noted, "but not a beautiful social cripple."

Fortunately, social skills can be learned. But the impulses behind them have to come from the heart. Otherwise, the effect will be artificial, and artificiality is one of the most annoying social habits of all.

↜ Body Blocks ↜

Despite the gray chill lingering over New York that early April, Berenice Fischer's apartment, which looked out on Greenwich Village, pulsed with warmth. Berenice, a professor of educational philosophy at New York University, and Roberta Galler, a psychotherapist in private practice, were telling me about their four decades of friendship. The harmony of their shared history echoed themes I'd heard from other women. But another note reverberated beneath it: a childhood bout with polio that had left Roberta first with a brace, then in a wheelchair. From the time she and Berenice met in college, they'd had to take her disability into account.

"When we make plans together, the conditions that impose limitations on me impose limitations on her," Roberta explained. Before making a date to see a play or try out a restaurant, they had to make sure that the theater or room could accommodate Roberta's wheelchair.

From the start, Roberta's disability was the major difference between two friends who were otherwise very similar. As such, it challenged the relationship. Yet for years the two friends mentioned none of these tensions—fearful that giving voice to their difference would threaten their connection. For instance, as roommates in their twenties, they never discussed what Roberta experienced navigating the stairs to their third-floor apartment. After decades of "unspoken accommodation," they finally began talking about how Roberta's disability affected their friendship. In a chapter they coauthored for a book called *Women with Disabilities,* they identified three major challenges to every friendship between a disabled woman and a woman without disabilities—or even with different or less severe ones.

The first challenge is that just meeting and getting to know other women is difficult for the disabled. Take parties. A person with mobility impairments needs to sit in one place and cannot stand and mingle. Likewise, a blind woman may have to stay in one spot, and she won't be able to pick up visual clues about the people she meets or make eye contact with them. A deaf woman has to be skilled at reading lips to make conversation with someone who doesn't sign, and even a woman with a less severe hearing impairment will have to contend with the limitations of her hearing aid in the buzzing crowd.

The second challenge Berenice and Roberta pinpointed involved reciprocity. Because one friend must accommodate the other's physical limitations and often give her practical help, the relationship begins off balance. Many disabled women attempt to achieve equilibrium by being extra supportive or endlessly comforting.

One disabled woman Berenice and Roberta interviewed told them that she compensated by being an emotional Rock of Gibraltar. "You can't feel like a basket case in every department," she explained. Because she was physically needy, she never let herself appear emotionally needy. In her efforts to contribute as much to her relationships as her friends without physical disabilities, this woman played the emotional nurturer for all her friends and missed out on the rich range of friendship variety described in chapter 5.

The third issue a disabled woman and her friend must face together is the responsibility for how they accommodate the impairment. A blind woman's sighted friend learns how to hand her the keys to her front door and to walk on her left, to give her room to swing her cane. But the shared responsibility reaches beyond how the two relate as a pair; it entails a commitment to improving conditions for disabled people in general. They can't escape the impact public policy has on their relationship. Picking up a wheelchair-bound friend for a movie helps her; launching a campaign to have lifts added to buses, so that she can get there on her own in the future, empowers her.

The sad truth is that friendship, no matter how strong, may not be enough to overcome the barriers a severely handicapped woman faces. Poet Mitsuye Yamada and Dahlia, an artist, had been best friends since they met in 1945. Both were Japanese-Americans who had been held in West Coast internment camps during World War II and had been allowed to leave only because they'd been accepted at a college far inland. They were lifemates. Then an automobile accident left Dahlia a quadraplegic.

For a proud, independent commercial artist, being paralyzed from the neck down was devastating. "I think one of the things that really got to her was that she could not do anything for herself," Mitsuye told me. "You have an itch on your head, and you have to ask somebody to scratch it, and then you have to thank that person for scratching your head for you."

Back in the early 1960s, the rights of the disabled had yet to be raised as a public issue. Dahlia needed even more practical assistance from friends than paralyzed people need now, but she figured out a way to reciprocate. She subscribed to art magazines from all over the world and shared what she learned.

By the end of 1963, total dependency had eroded Dahlia's spirit. Three years earlier, Mitsuye's husband had been transferred from New York to California, so Dahlia no longer had her day-to-day companionship and encouragement. But even if she had, she might have made the same decision. After giving her hired caregiver several days off, she stopped eating or drinking anything, including water. When the caregiver returned, she found Dahlia dead.

Perhaps Dahlia would have considered her life worth living if buses, buildings, and sidewalks had been modified to accommodate wheelchairs in 1963, as they have been since the Americans with Disabilities Act was enacted in 1990. Accompanied by a friend or her caregiver, she could have gone to museums and art openings. Nowadays, disabled women, even those with impairments as severe as Dahlia's, are no longer imprisoned in their homes. With the help of friends, they can get out and enjoy the cultural and social assets of their communities.

Although it may not be as obvious as paralysis or deafness, alcoholism can be another serious obstacle to female friendship. It cost Ruth Altshuler a friend she'd had since childhood. When Ruth learned that her husband was killed during World War II, Alma had been the first one to come by and comfort her. They'd traveled together and shared endless laughs. "She was a lot more daring than I and had the best sense of humor of anybody I've ever known in my life," Ruth told me.

But then, when they were both about fifty, the friendship began to fray. Ruth had become a high-powered organizer and fund-raiser. Alma was in and out of Alcoholics Anonymous, but her sober stretches didn't last long. Ruth recalled: "By this time, her husband had died, and all she wanted to do was to go to the country club at eleven in the morning and drink bloody Marys and play cards and then go home and go to bed at five o'clock."

Alma had died three and a half years before our interview. Ruth still thought about her almost daily, although they hadn't seen each other much toward the end. "Those last few years, she just left me alone," Ruth explained. "If I would call, it would be okay, but our friendship was never the same."

Like alcoholism, eating disorders can fracture female friendships by fostering secrecy on the part of one friend and why-can't-I-save-her-from-herself guilt on part of the other. When her soulmate began going on and on about how many grams of fat she'd eaten or how much she'd exercised that day, twenty-one-year-old Saundra felt something else: a disquieting vulnerability. Saundra had ridden the binge-and-diet roller coaster all through high school herself. To protect herself from falling back into that self-destructive pattern, she felt that she had to distance herself from her friend's experience. At the same time, Saundra felt guilty—like she ought to be doing something to help her friend change—but she wasn't yet secure enough in her own recovery to do it.

"I consider having an eating disorder separate from my life now," Saundra explained. "Hearing about it from her, it'll come up in me, and I just don't want to be around her when it's a big issue in her life. I want to be there to help her, but it's hard to help somebody when you're trying to help yourself."

Women's often conflicted relationships with their own bodies can make friendship difficult. Secretly, many women feel flawed if they don't measure up to the prevailing ideal of beauty, as ashamed of their healthy bodies as they might be of a major deformity. In her 1980 book *Among Women,* Louise Bernikow referred to the "tyranny of beauty" as major distrupter of female friendship. What drives women apart isn't beauty itself but how one's looks make the others feel. Granted, a beautiful friend—or even a friend who has an exceptionally lovely feature or two—can make an insecure woman feel envious of her looks or jealous of the attention they attract. ("I wish I had her hair," we think; or "With her looks, no wonder men are crazy about her, and I haven't had a date in three months.") A friend with a great figure can prompt another connection-disrupting emotion—guilt. Our bodies are the one aspect of beauty over which we have some control. We may not be able to add two inches to the length of our legs, but with diet and exercise we can drop fat and improve muscle tone. To a women who is (or feels) overweight or out of shape and isn't doing something about it, a friend's perfect size-six figure can seem like a reproach.

Beauty can make it hard for women to connect. Dotria Rowe, fourteen, had a pert, perfect figure; a pretty, heart-shaped face; unblemished café-au-lait skin; and lustrous, straight black hair hanging down to her waist; but girls she'd hardly met often took a fierce dislike to her. "I have a lot of girls that want to fight me," she said.

Her mother, Pinkey, explained that other African-American girls took one look at Dotria and assumed that she was stuck up—because of her hair. "These young black girls have this thing with hair," Pinkey said. "Most black people, their hair doesn't grow very long. So they love long hair, and if a girl has it, they think that that girl thinks that she is *something.*"

But another woman's beauty also may be a catalyst for connection. The girls and women I interviewed mentioned some aspect of a friend's appearance as the initial attraction more often than common background, considerate nature, or positive attitude—more often, in fact, than anything except sense of humor and shared interests.

"I always have been attracted to pretty women with striking personalities," said Janice Rubin, a forty-year-old photographer. "Even as a fifteen-year-old, my best friend was a woman who was stunningly beautiful, and I just liked to be around her. I enjoyed watching the attention that she got when we were out in public together."

Because Janice was secure in her own value, apart from her looks, she could enjoy having a beautiful friend.

Some beautiful women told me that their appearance helped them make friends. Liz Foreman, a thirty-two-year-old brunette with sculpted features and a perfectly proportioned figure, admitted that she thought her looks helped her in all her interactions with others. "People say it's so hard to be beautiful, but you know what: It makes life a lot easier," she said.

In a study of thirty pairs of college roommates, Wellesley researchers found that women who were similarly attractive were happier about living together. Compared to pairs in which one was beautiful and the other plain, they felt better integrated into each other's social lives. Their looks also gave them a point of connection: Each understood what the other was going through as a plain, beautiful, or moderately attractive woman.

Sometimes the reactions of others can drive two beautiful women together. Lilith, a fifty-seven-year-old artist, had been best friends with Phoebe since their early twenties. "Men found us both very attractive, and a lot of women were competitive with us," Lilith told me.

"Part of the bond between us was that we both knew the downside: It was very important to both of us that people recognized our talents and our intelligence, and they got overlooked completely. Achieving some kind of distinction was important to us. And supporting each other in doing that was part of it."

Being beautiful women the same age made Lilith and Phoebe life-mates. Feeling the same way about people's response to their beauty made them soulmates. Because they had both their looks and their frustration in common, they were able to validate each other's worth apart from their beauty. Their friendship helped them keep in touch with their intelligence and talents and to develop that side of themselves, as well as to acknowledge both the joys and the drawbacks of being beautiful.

❧ The Two Green-Eyed Monsters ❧

Envy and jealousy are twin enemies of friendship. Envy involves the desire for possessions, position, privileges, or attributes. I wish I had a car, a job, a vacation, or looks as nice as Sally's, and (here's the destructive part) I resent that I don't. At its most extreme, envy slides over into covetousness: I wish I had *her* BMW, *her* law practice, *her* week in Paris, *her* hair—and that she didn't.

Jealousy, on the other hand, is about feelings. It always involves a third party and the attention, affection, devotion, admiration, or other positive emotions that we want that person to direct our way. We become jealous of someone when we think that she's receiving more attention or affection from that third party than we are, as when two sisters vie for their parents' favor, or any affection at all if we have or long for an exclusive claim, as when a woman suspects her lover isn't faithful. I may envy a popular friend's social success, but if I feel miserable when my husband spends a half hour talking animatedly with her at a party, then I'm jealous of her.

The things we're prone to envy depend on the attributes we lack but feel are important to have. That lack may not be rational; it's our perception that counts.

"It's very easy to be accepting and loving and happy for someone else when you're in a good place yourself," Marilyn Schultz, a school psychologist, said. "I've seen that through the years with my friends. The envy was there when I was unhappy."

After Pat Taylor was widowed, she found herself seeing less of Jocelyn, her friend of forty years. Not only was Jocelyn's husband still alive; he'd retired from a successful business career. The couple had the time and the means to "bat off around the world," as Pat put it, while Pat had to work. "I suppose maybe it would be envy," she said of the strain in the longstanding connection. "It's just that I knew there were some things I couldn't do but they could."

Occasional envy is only natural, and it can serve as a signpost to self-awareness and personal growth. Instead of feeling guilty for these emotions and trying to repress them or berating ourselves for having them, we should analyze them in order to discover what we truly feel is lacking in our lives and in ourselves.

English professor Claudia Vangerven treasured sharing her love of poetry with a friend in the same field but admitted that envy sometimes arose when one of them published in a prestigious journal. "It's not that I don't want her to do this," Claudia explained. "But it makes me feel that I haven't done enough."

Even when envy doesn't directly disrupt or destroy a friendship, it can rob it of one of its great pleasures: vicariously sharing success and good fortune. "I hesitate to tell Jodie when really good things happen," psychotherapist Jane Burka admitted. "She doesn't react with the same enthusiasm as my other friends."

Often, we envy just one facet of a friend's life. Beth Madison, fifty-one, divorced and childless, admitted that she envied one friend's beautiful children, another's journey of spiritual self-discovery, and several more's stable marriages. She also knew that her friends might envy her success in business. "Envy comes and goes," Beth said.

But many women have trouble accepting their own envy, let alone staying connected to someone who engenders it. Envy violates the ideal of female friendship. If something good happens for a friend, we're *supposed* to feel unalloyed delight. Both our love for her and our identification with her seem to demand that response. Envy is an ungenerous emotion, a holdover from early childhood, when with eyes like calipers we measured the relative size of slices of cake. A centimeter in our favor and we felt smug. A centimeter in our sister's and we were furious at the injustice. When news of a friend's trip to Paris or promotion to partner brings back echoes of that pique, we get a double whammy: first from envy, then from shame at our envy.

Awareness of envy's destructive potential makes many women wary of engendering it. As a Red Cross volunteer working to support the rescue team searching for victims of the Oklahoma City bombing, twenty-nine-year-old park ranger Tina Fellows was interviewed by Barbara Walters. Tina's pleasure at the recognition was mixed with guilt that she was chosen and her roommate wasn't. "I felt really bad," Tina told me. "I could feel it hurt her a little bit because she put in as much time as I had."

Whether we envy a friend's success or worry that she will envy ours, we fear the loss of connection. "The constant tension for women is not just about who is going to look better or who is going to have more, but the notion that somehow this will take them away from the relationship," explained clinical psychologist Judy Jordan.

As bad as envy feels, jealousy feels worse. Jealousy cuts two ways in friendship: We resent her taking someone's affection from us, and we resent her giving her affection to others instead of to us. Either scenario can sever the connection.

Faith Lagay had been close friends with Cath off and on for more than twenty years. When both women lived in Houston, they jogged together several times a week and poured out their problems with men and their frustrations with their families and their jobs. Then Faith moved an hour away to go to graduate school. Living so far apart ruled out near-daily visits, but they could get together on weekends. The trouble, as Faith saw it, was that when they did, Cath expected her undivided attention.

"We had a falling out last fall," Faith told me. "She was coming down here and staying overnight, and I suggested that we have a walk on the beach in the morning with a woman who's interested in a lot of the same things she is. To Cath that meant, 'She's got her friends in Galveston now, and she doesn't need me. Here I went down to see her, and she arranged this walk (which was two hours out of the visit) with another friend.' "

Sometimes jealousy arises because two friends have different perceptions of the closeness of their friendship. One sees it as relatively casual, the other as one of her most significant relationships. Sara Williams reckoned that she and Olive had been friends for twenty-two or twenty-three years, but she suspected that Olive felt closer to her than she did to Olive. Ironically, what made Sara less close to Olive was Olive's habit of putting down Sara's other friends. "She's got a jealous nature, and that's just the truth," Sara said.

Although Olive had always been nice to Sara, periodically she would say mean things about Sara's soulmate Doreen. "She doesn't like the fact that we're such close friends," Sara explained. "I'll just say, 'Well I've known Doreen thirty-six years, and I have never heard anything bad about her.' Then Olive just shuts up and doesn't say anything about her anymore. Maybe she'll wait six months and make some little remark."

Soap operas and sitcoms are full of another kind of jealousy between female friends—the romantic triangle variety: two friends competing for the same man, who must choose one over the other. Contrary to popular belief, however, sexual rivalry is not the main cause of friendship ruptures. For example, when sociologist J. L. Barkas studied the close friendships of twenty-seven women living alone in one block on New York's Upper East Side, she found that of the fifty relationships that had derailed, only two had broken up over men.

While romantic jealousies don't automatically spell the end for female friendships, they do disrupt them. Even the fear that a friend might steal a lover can shatter the connection. For instance, when Vicki Jo Radovsky was in her late twenties, she was involved with Aaron, a backup musician in a Country-and-Western band. He treated her inconsiderately and even admitted that he lusted after her best friend, Tory—a particular blow, given that Tory was trim and Vicki Jo had always felt self-conscious about her own buxom figure.

After months of listening to complaints about Aaron's behavior, Tory decided to try to get him to change his ways. She went over to his house for a heart-to-heart—without telling Vicki Jo first.

"When she told me she went over to his house, I freaked out," Vicki Jo said. "Whether to intercede on my behalf or dance naked in the living room, there was no difference as far as I was concerned, because I knew that he thought she was attractive and of course he would prefer her over me. I couldn't compete on that level. So the mere fact that she presented herself to him in any way was so threatening that I couldn't see beyond that."

Even though she knew that her own insecurity was fueling her fury, Vicki Jo broke off the friendship.

Sexual jealousy threatens lesbians' friendships, too. Political science professor Carol Conoway, forty-eight, shared both intellectual interests and a love of the outdoors with her nonsexual friend Barbara, who also encouraged her to face challenges squarely and be her best self. Nonetheless, this rewarding relationship came perilously close to ending when Barbara started seeing one of Carol's ex-lovers. "This made me really furious," Carol said. "I felt betrayed. But I got over it because being her friend meant the world to me."

If both women really value a friendship and understand how to deal constructively with conflict, they can do more than "get over" jealousy. By addressing their feelings directly, avoiding accusations, listening as openly as they speak, they can grow, and so can their friendship.

↝ Competitiveness ↝

Some women derive their sense of self-worth from the amount of attention they receive from men. They don't really want to grab all the men for themselves. (After all, what would they do with them?) They just need to know that they could have any of them. "She's a very male-oriented woman," Dallas publicist Julia Sweeney observed of her friend Sarita. "It doesn't matter who the man is—she's going to flirt with him and try to get him."

But by competing for male attention, women discard one of the very qualities that makes them feel good about themselves: their empathy. Instead of supporting each other in their shared desire to meet men who might make suitable romantic partners, women who compete in this way ignore other women, even their friends, when men are around.

Roberta, a twenty-eight-year-old lesbian, suspected that one of the reasons she'd been able to stay close to her college best friend, Beryl, was that Beryl didn't consider her a rival for men. "She's a very successful heterosexual," Roberta said. "She was never at a loss for admirers and boyfriends, and that was something that never came between us, I think because I wasn't competing with her. She is generally pretty competitive with women, has a very competitive mother."

If a mother or father is competitive, that parent may pass that competitiveness along to a child or even compete through her. Consider the soccer mom who gets really angry when her daughter's team loses, or the father who asks, when his daughter tells him she made a ninety-eight on a test, "Did anyone make ninety-nine or a hundred?" A girl reared in such a family faces an obstacle in forming close friendships, especially with girls who are as good as she is at sports or schoolwork.

Growing up, university press officer Jay Vanasco was chums with two girls next door. Alessandra was a little older; Maxine, a little younger. Although their friendship continued into their twenties, so did their rivalry. "Our parents were always comparing us," Jay told me. "We're still really good friends, but I would never call them at three in the morning, because I wouldn't want them to know I was in trouble."

Jay liked Alessandra and Maxine, but she didn't feel comfortable showing them her vulnerable side, for fear of giving them an advantage in the competition.

But many of the women I interviewed said they had never felt any sense of rivalry with their friends. "It always seemed amazing to me that there are all these myths about women and how they can't get along," said newspaper editor Kaye Northcott. "You know—the cat-fight thing, women and competition. I've never experienced that in my life. Is it some sort of male-created myth?"

Other women said that they felt competitive with their friends, but that they didn't mind it. "She's like a domestic goddess," Lisa Taylor said of her friend and fellow mom Laurel. "She sews all these toys and dresses. She makes sure that her family eats the purest foods. She's intensely creative with her home environment. She's defined her areas of control, and within those areas, she excels so beautifully."

Lisa explained that having Laurel to compete with made her feel good, because Laurel showed her that reaching a higher level was possible.

A woman secure in her own worth can enjoy high-achieving friends without competing with them. "I know women who are more talented than I am and women who have achieved more, but knowing myself and my talents, I can admire them," explained Ponnie Katz, a sixty-seven-year-old community activist near Boston. Such friends serve as real-life models for success, and—let's face it—they also raise the less obviously accomplished friend in other people's eyes. If someone who's that brilliant, that fine a musician or tennis player, that effective a community leader chooses Mary as a friend, then others conclude that Mary must have traits that make her worth knowing.

But as much as we might wish we could, few of us are content to bask in reflected light. We want the spotlight to be trained on us. For the most part, female competition arises from the need for attention present in all of us—the fear that we may be overlooked. Sometimes it barely disguises that fear at all.

"No matter what you bring up, she has a better story," Polly, sixty-three, said of one competitive acquaintance. "You come back from Syria, and she says, 'I went to Jerusalem,' just to let you know that she's having those experiences, too."

Some women deal with competition by pretending that they only succeed by working harder than their competitors. A track star who trains four hours a day or a solo violinist who practices relentlessly will attract less resentment than one who wins without much effort. "I always at least gave the impression that I was working very hard," explained Yale freshman Joanna Winslade, who'd graduated second in her high school class. "I think if I had looked like I wasn't working at all, people that were working very hard would have been upset."

A common interest normally helps friends bond, but competitiveness may keep them from sharing what's important to them both. Recent college graduate Jennifer Lee told me she couldn't talk to her friend Adrienne about academics, even though doing well in school and getting into a good graduate school were important to both of them—and even though Jennifer had chosen ethnic studies and Adrienne physics. "You can't talk about grades with her, because regardless of the fact that they're not comparable, she will try to compare them," Jennifer said.

In art school, Nora Antil and her friend Carrie had shared a studio. Both had been top students; but while Nora went on to pursue a related career as a residential designer, Carrie decided to become a midwife. She made it clear that she wouldn't welcome Nora's entry into her new field. "I remember she turned to me one day and said, 'Don't you get interested in this; this is mine,' " Nora recalled. "I think she felt that I would overshadow her."

The problem, however, isn't that we compete with our friends. It's that doing so makes us feel awful. Women have been taught that competition is antithetical to the essential female friendship virtues of loyalty, trust, and support. We haven't been brought up to deal with friendly competition. Men have. When social psychologist Stephen Deberry explored the way competition made people feel, he found that although both women and men liked their partners, and themselves, better when they were collaborating rather than competing, men felt more comfortable with competition than women did.

For competitive women, making and keeping friends can be difficult. "I have this one friend who is really competitive," said Kathleen Ownby, the director of a nonprofit agency. "No one is ever going to beat her. She has to know the best people, the best things. She is going to do it the only way, the best way. That doesn't allow you to be close friends."

Jean, a triathlete, had discovered that truth from the other side. "I like competitions, and I think that they can be healthy," she told me. "You can admire other athletes and use them as inspiration. If you happen to be in a race with somebody you know is better than you, you can measure how you are doing by how close you are to them. But outside the race, it gets sticky. Can you go up to that woman who passed you and tell her that her race was outstanding, instead of harboring this brewing kind of a feeling like, 'Damn, she got me'?"

Jean confessed she had trouble making friends with other female athletes, even though they had so much in common—their commitment to their sport, the long hours of training, the fear of injury. But a sense of always being judged, and always judging, separated her from her potential lifemates. "You're either looking at them and wishing you were like them," she explained, "or thinking, 'I should be grateful I've come a long way and I'm not back where that woman is.'"

Jean's struggle between her yearning to connect with other female athletes and her desire to beat them echoes in offices, in classrooms, and on playgrounds where mothers compare how well their children swing along the parallel bars. Women strive to win, but in winning the competition, they fear losing something they value more—the connection. Many women I interviewed told me they would rather retreat from a friend than compete with her. "Whenever I sense competition in a relationship, I'm out," said Cat, a fifty-year-old poet.

Essential, underlying competition is one of the features that distinguish congenial workplace relationships from close friendships. Connie Clark, forty-eight, explained that even she and her fellow kindergarten teachers competed with one another: "You want to know: 'Did the principal think that I am the better teacher? Am I going to get that doctor's kids, or is it one of those other teachers?' Therefore, we are friends and we work together every day, but you are not going to get that closeness."

Many women take competition on the job personally, rather than accepting it as integral to the business or profession they've chosen. Because so many women tend to draw their models for working together from family life, they often expect other women to support them unfailingly, like good mothers or good daughters. When the women they work with don't give them this support, they feel betrayed. Even something as minor as having a female colleague challenge an idea raised in a staff meeting can trigger that sense of betrayal.

As more women spend more of their lives in the workplace, we may become better at competing openly and directly—and better at understanding the special challenges of on-the-job friendships.

~ Fear of Conflict ~

My mother told me that she'd never felt anger. I was convinced then, as I am to this day, that she considered this remarkable assertion an honest reflection of her experience. It took years of therapy for me to learn that her denial of anger wasn't an ideal for which I should strive and decades of living for me to understand why my mother considered it one.

For a woman who grew up in a physically or verbally violent environment, the ability to rouse someone to anger confers a kind of negative power, seizing control by pushing the other person to lose it. But for most of us, anger—whether others' or our own—is deeply disquieting. That's because anger often leads to conflict, and for many women few things produce more anxiety.

"I'm not good about confronting conflict," said Beth Madison, head of her own benefits consulting firm. "People who perpetually put me in that situation, I eventually avoid."

Beth's aversion was typical. "Most of my women clients suffer some pain around trying to deal with conflict in relationships," wrote psychotherapist Judy Jordan. Yet, she noted, when a woman frequently alters her experiences ("You're right. That movie was sentimental and manipulative.") or holds back parts of herself (She's such a happy, devoted mother. I can't tell her I sometimes wish I didn't have kids.)

to avoid conflict with a friend, she robs the friendship of vitality and loses touch with her own feelings. The relationship suffers, as well as the woman's sense of herself.

Jean Baker Miller, the Stone Center psychiatrist who proposed the theory that women grow through their connection with others, told me that while we possess a wide array of relational skills, including empathy, attentive listening, and supportiveness, "The thing that women *aren't* good at is conflict. If you can get through the conflict, female friendship is very growth enhancing."

As I noted earlier, a female friendship has the greatest power for fostering personal growth when the women in it risk conflict—when it enters the testing stage. But because conflict threatens connection, it makes many women so uncomfortable that they conceal their opinions and feelings—often even from themselves—rather than admit their differences. Sometimes, of course, confrontation does end a friendship. Yet, in constantly ducking conflict, we also risk losing friends. Many friendships simply collapse under the weight of unspoken grievances. Rather than deal with anger, disappointment, or other difficult issues, many women withdraw.

That's what Melanie did. From the time Melanie moved into her neighborhood in seventh grade, Sally Good considered her a very close friend. When they found themselves in the same city in their thirties, Sally was a divorced mother trying to support her three children through a video dating service that never quite got off the ground. Melanie, on the other hand, had a husband and a secure job as a C.P.A. for a major oil company.

Melanie's descriptions of her workplace rekindled Sally's entrepreneurial imagination. All those people skipping breakfast in the rush to dress, drop off the kids, and get to the office on time had to be ravenous by ten o'clock. Hoping to profit from their hunger, Sally persuaded Melanie to join her in business, supplying fresh cinnamon rolls and breakfast burritos to local offices.

For four months, the two friends struggled to make the venture work, rising at three A.M., putting in twelve- to fifteen-hour days, and taking out just enough to cover basic living expenses. Then one morning, Sally woke up to find the business's books neatly stacked on her front porch. No note. No explanation.

"I don't know if she wasn't seeing enough profit or if the daily stress was too much," Sally said. "But I think she was so afraid of disappointing me that she couldn't come to me about it."

Melanie's inability to confront Sally cost both women a friendship that had taken decades to build. Theirs wasn't the only account I heard of women sacrificing a friendship to duck a confrontation—just the most extreme. Karla, a social worker in her fifties, never said anything when her soulmate Leonora disappointed her. For more than a decade the two had rented a vacation house together. Then, four or five years before our interview, Leonora had bought a beach cottage. During most of the summer, she rented it out; but for two weeks, she and Karla used the place.

What bothered Karla was that even though she paid half the rate Leonora charged her renters, Leonora kept the house full of her own company, to the point that there was no comfortable place to put Karla's college-age son for a weekend. Still, Karla never told Leonora that she didn't like the present arrangement. "I was choosing not to raise it because she would be very hurt," Karla explained. "I just choose not to deal with those things because that's really not worth the friendship."

But Karla told me that she doubted that she'd share the cottage with Leonora again. Rather than risking offending her friend, she'd give up the pleasure of vacationing with her.

The women I interviewed seemed comfortable describing their disappointment in their friends to me. Women may be "extremely practiced" at venting irritation to third parties and yet be "novices when it comes to talking *directly* with a friend about an upset or a hurt between them," psychotherapists Luise Eichenbaum and Susie Orbach observed in their book *Between Women: Love, Envy, and Competition in Women's Friendships.*

Compounding our fear that conflict will destroy our relationships is the notion that women are natural peacekeepers and that, therefore, any urge to fight is unnatural. Most of us were raised to cooperate, to soothe and smooth over differences, to play well with others—and, especially, not to challenge or talk back to our mothers. This latter childhood edict may be why many women feel more comfortable risking conflict with husbands, brothers, boyfriends, fathers, or male bosses than with women.

"If I argue with a man, I just blow it off," said Cecile, a forty-five-year-old physician assistant at a medical clinic. "The stakes are just really, really high in relationships with women. To have a fight with a female coworker—I would die first."

One reason some women are willing to engage in conflict with men but not with other women may be that men seem more comfortable with conflict, less likely to take disagreement personally. But conflict between friends always has a personal side. Even disagreeing about the merits of a movie can make each friend wonder whether she is as smart or perceptive as the other. Sidestepping such concerns disrupts the connection. On the other hand, talking openly about them while remaining sensitive to each other's feelings can lead to personal growth and a stronger friendship.

~+ Fear of Intimacy ~+

At the same time that women fear disconnection, we may also fear intimacy. We all waver between the desire for closeness—to reveal who we really are to another and be loved despite our flaws—and the fear of rejection if we do so.

"I have a problem with loving people back who say they love me," admitted artist Gail Penrice. "I think that's because of a barrier I may put up for myself. I can't handle rejection."

The more we reveal of ourselves, the more we make ourselves vulnerable. The women sociologist Helen Gouldner and her coauthor Mary Symons Strong interviewed for their book differed in their tolerance for vulnerability. To explain this difference among women, Gouldner used the metaphor of peeling an onion: Some people could only allow others to peel back the top layers of their selves, leaving them incapable of having very close friendships.

That variation among individuals even exists within friendships. Developmental psychologist Sophie Bronstein discovered that, in each of the twenty-six pairs of close friends she studied, "there was one partner who had substantially more positive attitudes toward intimacy than the other."

Intimacy involves revealing ourselves—disclosing what we feel and think. But not all such opening up is intimate. Self-disclosure takes different forms, some of which make us more vulnerable than others. In one form of self-disclosure, we discuss our personal fantasies and anxieties and what's going on in our closest relationships. In another form, we stick closer to the surface, revealing our opinions about public issues, movies, situations at work.

The amount of intimate information a woman feels comfortable disclosing and receiving depends on her personality. Some women are trusting; they expect empathy and nurturing when they reveal their hopes and anxieties. Others are wary; they expect rejection or manipulation. Psychologists have found that sensation seekers tend to be more uninhibited about sharing their most personal thoughts and feelings, even with casual friends. Perhaps they like the sense of relief that comes from unburdening themselves or the excitement of waiting for the response.

Cultural mores also play a role in how much women disclose to one another. Contrasting the attitudes toward intimate disclosure in her native Britain and in the United States, where she'd spent her adult life, novelist Margot Livesey wrote:

> [A]fter initial repudiation, I have come to a renewed appreciation of repression. There are things that cannot or should not be told. There are other ways of being friends besides simply pouring out one's heart.

Sociologist Pat O'Connor has questioned whether self-disclosure is essential to intimacy. Certainly, the two aren't the same. O'Connor noted the rise of talk shows "as a public forum for the kind of talk we see as characteristic of friendship—even intimate friendship." Indeed, in North America they serve as venues for emotional striptease acts. Although the experiences recounted by a mother who seduced her daughter's boyfriend may be intimate, her exchange with thousands of television viewers isn't. But the size of the audience is beside the point. After hearing a two-hour litany of family woes recounted on the flight from Chicago to Denver by a seatmate whose name we don't even know, we may feel annoyance or we may feel compassion, but we don't feel intimacy. Intimacy requires context, a sense of knowing what's on the surface before we delve beneath.

In *Just Friends,* sociologist Lillian Rubin described interviewing a man who had discovered his wife was having an affair. Although he enjoyed a very close relationship with his male best friend, the aggrieved husband never mentioned the betrayal to him.

For a woman to conceal such a crisis from a similarly valued friend would be unthinkable. When a woman withholds something important about her life from a close friend, she undercuts the friendship. If you don't know that a friend has just had a miscarriage, how can you possibly help her, emotionally or otherwise? If she doesn't tell you that she thinks she's up for partner at her accounting firm, how can you share her anticipation? If she doesn't trust you to keep her confidences, how can *you* trust *her*?

After twenty years, Faith Lagay counted Rochelle among her dearest friends. Yet, she vacillated when it came to calling their relationship "close." "I just don't know Rochelle that well," Faith explained. "She's very private. There's a reserve. So I'd say our friendship is still in the early stages, even though it's older than some that are closer."

Not everyone I interviewed was open to intimacy with another woman. Some were wary of intense feelings—on their own parts or on their friends'. They worried that they wouldn't be able to cope with a friend's raw sadness or joy or couldn't reciprocate her deep affection. They felt that if they got too close, they would become emotionally dependent on their friend, or their friend would become emotionally dependent on them. They also were afraid that if they knew how much a friend hurt but didn't have a solution to offer, they would be letting her down. Several women I interviewed told me about having had a close early friendship end badly: They had an awful fight, or the friend moved away and didn't answer letters, or she slipped into alcoholism or allowed a jealous, controlling husband to discourage the relationship. "Since then," I heard repeatedly, "I haven't allowed myself to get that close. I don't want to be hurt like that again."

Other women hold back from close friendship because they confuse emotional and sexual intimacy. They worry that loving another woman, wanting to spend time alone with her, wanting to hold her hand or hug her means they may be latent lesbians—or that their friend might misinterpret physical expressions of affection or nurturing as sexual advances. For fear of disrupting the connection, many women hold back, yet wish they didn't have to. Homophobia—our own and society's—puts us literally out of touch with our friends.

"In all of the friendships that I have had, there is some element that makes this person appealing, so that I wish we could hold hands," said physician assistant Cecile, a married mother of two. "I wish that we could do the things that we would have done when we were little."

Gradually, that attitude is changing. Over recent years, I've noticed that when my close friends come to visit, they often prolong an initial hug, so that we walk to the front door with our arms around each others' waists. At parties, I see women friends touching each other on the shoulder, hand, or knee as they make a conversational point. Just a few weeks ago, on the beach near my house, I observed a trio of college girls on spring break, their arms draped over each others' shoulders, laughing.

❧ Buying the Lies ❧

Until late in this century, women have been asked to believe two lies: Other women aren't worth our time, and neither is friendship. Behind these two lies were the beliefs that men were more interesting and important than women, and romantic and family bonds were the only significant relationships available for women.

Faith Einerson said that her mother distrusted and felt contempt for other women and discouraged her friendships with girls. "It was okay for me to have boys as friends," Faith said. "That was good. Girlfriends were not good. She had almost no women friends. I think she really devalued women.

"I shared, I'm sure, my mother's attitude toward other girls: that they were shallow and stupid. I didn't know until I was in college that women could be interesting and funny and that the same things I got from male friends, I could get from women friends, and better."

But even a generation after the women's movement prompted women, feminist or not, to begin expressing themselves openly and taking one another seriously, even with hit TV series and movies featuring competent heroines, many of the women I interviewed, especially the younger ones, dismissed women as not worth the trouble of getting to know. For instance, describing the dangerous mistakes her lab partner made in chemistry experiments, Amber, a college junior, summed them up as "female stuff, real dingy." With these words, she unconsciously parroted the cultural message so many young women are taught.

In addition to robbing us of the pleasure and power of female friendship, such attitudes make each woman who holds them her own enemy. "[I]n devaluing other women," psychiatrist Jean Baker Miller wrote, "women inevitably devalue themselves."

As a defense against this, some women tell themselves that they're a rare, even unique, exception to the rule. Psychotherapist Irene Stiver told me about treating a successful female professional who suffered from panic attacks. This patient had enormous contempt for women. The breakthrough in her treatment came when one of Stiver's colleagues asked her: "Why are you so contemptuous of women when you're one of them?"

"It blew her away," Stiver said. "She had always said internally, 'I'm not one of them. Women are incompetent.' Women will say that. They don't see how much impact the general culture has on them."

But even women who recognize the value of other women may still give friendship short shrift. As their lives get busier, they give everything else—their families, their jobs, their community and church activities—priority over their friendships. Sociologists have found that busy middle-aged women will choose to spend time with relatives, rather than friends, even though the friends make them feel better. Many women consider maintaining a cohesive extended family a duty and maintaining their own personal friendships a self-indulgence.

Every woman whom Cecile considered a friend was an avowed feminist. Yet Cecile never felt that they placed high priority on her bond with them. "I've often felt that I just didn't really count, you know, wasn't very important," she said.

As long as our culture disregards the worth of female friendship, women will have trouble recognizing its value themselves. Some women never really believed these lies. Although they still have to contend with the ways these cultural messages influence others, at least they don't have to fight them in themselves. And many women, with the help of their friends, learn to tune out the lies and to begin creating their own affirmations of female connection.

13

✳

Challenges to
Friendship

There is an ethos within women's relationships . . . an ethos that
requires staying in the same place together or moving forward
together at the same time.

—Luise Eichenbaum and Susie Orbach, *Between Women*

The girls and women I interviewed told me similar stories of
life events that disrupted female friendship. Chief among these
challenges are moves, marriage, motherhood, misfortune,
money, divorce, and divergent values. But these seven primary challenges have plenty of company. Anything that sets two friends on
different roads tests their bond.

When University of Puget Sound psychologist Lisa Wood examined what caused female friendships to wither, three-quarters of the
time the culprit was what she called "developmental differences." (The
next three contenders—lack of reciprocity, betrayal, and jealousy—
didn't even come close.) Wood told me that the term included any
major divergence in roles or status: If one friend marries or has a child
and the other doesn't, if one takes a demanding job and the other
works part time, if one gets rich and the other can barely make ends
meet, maintaining the connection gets difficult.

That had happened frequently to anthropologist Madelyn Iris. "I have very intense, intimate relationships with women for periods of time," she noted. "Then my life changes, and I move on. I'm not doing what I was ten years ago. I don't have the same goals I had then. Other people are not so changed."

Madelyn's experience was typical. Sociologists have found that the number of a woman's friendships that have withered tends to reflect the number of significant changes that have occurred in her life.

⤳ Moves ⤳

Margaret Valentine was my best friend during most of the 1970s. Then I left Austin for Houston, and she stayed in Austin but changed addresses. My 1980 Christmas card came back undelivered. We reunited when Margaret called two years later to say that her daughter Kathy had made *Rolling Stone* with her all-girl rock group the Go-Gos. For the next few years, we saw each other off and on when assignments took me to Austin. But around 1990, Margaret sold her condo and decamped for England to tend to her aging mother. I haven't heard from her since. Meanwhile, I've moved to Galveston.

Margaret and I shared a lot, including our membership in a peripatetic generation. The trend started with World War II. When World War I had ended, the young men who'd fought it had come back home. After World War II, however, they went wherever the booming American economy needed workers. Small wonder the children they raised knew how to pack but not how to put down deep roots. If a job could prompt relocation, why couldn't a hankering to try a different climate, or a new lifestyle?

"We're the first generation to discover that you could go anywhere you want," said bioethicist Judy Ross, fifty-nine. "My mother still lives where she has for eighty years. She doesn't have to worry about keeping in touch with anybody other than the kids."

The U.S. Census Bureau reported that between 1980 and 1996, 32 percent of people ages twenty to twenty-four and 31 percent of those ages twenty-five to twenty-nine moved at least once. And that didn't include most members of the armed forces.

When I asked her how many close friends she had, Rudi, a forty-year-old army sergeant major, replied: "It's hard to say, because maybe my definition of friends is different from what people who don't move's definition is. I have a lot of people that I write. I have a lot of people that I call. I have a lot of people that I go to dinner with when I'm in town."

But just because moving and having friends move is common doesn't mean it doesn't hurt. When her best friend Mona's husband was transferred three hundred miles away, forty-six-year-old artist Chula Sanchez was heartbroken. Five years later, the pain remained palpable.

"It was like the breakup of a marriage," Chula said. "I've never found anybody to replace her. We see each other once a month, but it's not the same."

Woman after woman told me that what she missed most was the day-to-day contact, that sense of being part of the minutiae of one another's lives. For the first seven years of their friendship, social worker Carol Deanow saw her friend Carlene every day, because they lived in the same apartment building. Then, ten years before our interview, Carlene left Brookline, a city right next to Boston, for Cape Cod.

Although the drive was less than an hour and a half, Carol and Carlene only managed to get together a couple of times a year, usually at a restaurant somewhere between their homes. "But meeting for dinner doesn't do it," Carol explained, "because at that point you are telling each other about your lives rather than sharing your lives."

The only way they might have maintained their former sense of being intertwined would have been to arrange long telephone conversations once or twice a week. And even those wouldn't offer the same connectedness as a face-to-face heart-to-heart.

↤ Marriage and Motherhood ↦

From the first time a girl cancels plans to Rollerblade with a friend because a boy asks her to a movie, primary pairing disrupts female friendship. "Relationships with men get in the way of relationships with your female friends," said Nancy O'Connor, thirty-seven. "Once my husband and I started dating, and the same thing when my best friend met her husband, you pull away from your group."

When I interviewed recent college graduate Jennifer Lee her wedding was two weeks away, and it was straining her fifteen-year best friendship with Adrienne, her maid of honor. As children and adolescents, they'd spent all their free time together. Then a few months before they graduated from high school, Jennifer met the man who would become her fiancé. Until then, neither girl had dated. Suddenly, Jennifer found herself dividing her time.

"It's been a little rough ever since then," Jennifer admitted. "I avoid talking about him unless she asks first."

Having Adrienne serve as maid of honor had piled more pressure on the faltering friendship. "Other than me, she's the primary person who's supposed to be handling things," Jennifer said. "That's just not happening, and I think part of it is the issue that she has with my fiancé. I don't know if that's something that we'll ever be able to resolve."

Romance and marriage present the greatest challenges to friendship during early adulthood, as chapter 9 explained. But they can disrupt the connection between friends of any age. Albuquerque guidance counselor Reyna Luna, forty-nine, had been single for as long as thirteen years between marriages. Around the time of her last wedding, she noticed one of her best friends pulling away. When Reyna asked her what was wrong, the woman replied: "You're the friend I have fun with. Now we don't do things together."

If the friend had invited her to do something, Reyna would have made the time, she insisted. But the woman hadn't. Instead, she'd behaved as if they'd had a falling out. "I really think she was angry with me for getting married," Reyna said.

Some friendships strain to the point of breaking well before the wedding is planned, as soon as one woman or the other gets wrapped up in a serious romance. Medical ethicist Martha Holstein recounted what happened when her friend Kristine got involved with Mel. Kristine kept canceling plans with Martha because Mel wanted to do something else. The last straw came just before Martha's departure from San Francisco for graduate school. Kristine left a message on Martha's answering machine saying that she'd come to Martha's goodbye party—unless the ski conditions were good at Tahoe. Martha was outraged.

As it turned out, the forecast for the Sierras was bad, so Kristine and Mel came to the party. But because Mel got restless, Kristine left early. Two months after Martha moved, she had her first contact from Kristine—a letter saying that Mel was moving to France, alone. Kristine was devastated. "And I didn't do anything," Martha admitted.

One of our culture's unwritten rules is that the needs of the couple relationship trump the needs of the friendship. Misunderstandings often arise because it's hard to decide when a friend becomes part of a couple. A woman in an intense romance may consider herself half of a pair after three dates; her friend may assume that she can make independent social plans right up to the wedding. Compounding this potential confusion is the question of how much weight to give the needs of a friend and those of a husband or romantic partner.

When University of Wisconsin–Milwaukee sociologist Stacey Oliker interviewed twenty-one married women on their best friendships, just over half told her that they occasionally had to choose between their friends and their husbands. But an unspoken agreement that obligations to family came first kept the issue from causing conflict: The husband always won, except when the friend's basic welfare or that of her children was at stake. A woman might inconvenience her family by taking in a friend's kids so that she could tend her dying mother, but she wouldn't insist her husband fix dinner so that she and her friend could go out.

Even if one woman is married when the friendship begins, having the other friend wed can strain the bond. True, the two now have one more thing in common, but they also have to juggle a fourth person's schedule and expectations. And they have to consider how well all four personalities mesh.

"Integrating men into women's friendships is one of the hardest things to navigate," observed psychotherapist Jane Burka who was divorced. "You come together as couples, and it almost never works that all four really like each other."

Sometimes the men get along fine, but neither friend takes to the other's guy. Maddy, a fifty-two-year-old Los Angeles philosophy professor, found herself in that situation with Jane. Maddy considered Jane's husband Tony "weird." As for Jane's reaction to Maddy's boyfriend Ned, "It was one of those early childhood unresolved things," Maddy explained. "They each reminded the other of the wrong person."

She continued: "Even though Tony and Ned are good friends, when we're together as couples, it just doesn't work, so we quit making an effort to do that."

Whatever her objections to the lover or spouse, a friend is well advised to keep them to herself. Criticize him and you attack your friend's wisdom and judgment in a crucial life choice. And you risk her telling him what you think of him. Of course, if a woman starts sporting unexplained bruises, always has to borrow lunch money, or becomes uncharacteristically self-critical, her best friend should voice her suspicions. But in trying to save her friend, she may lose the friendship.

Even if there's no violence, economic exploitation, or emotional abuse, a stormy affair or marriage puts a woman's friends in an awkward position. When trouble erupts, she's bound to pour out her side of the crisis to her best friend. That vivid description of her heartache will linger long after the romantic partners themselves have made up. Even a friend who has nothing personal against the husband or lover will have a hard time being pleasant in the future. And if they've always disliked each other, being civil will be a special trial.

That had happened to Roberta, twenty-eight. From the time her college soulmate Beryl started dating the man who became her husband, Roberta hadn't liked him, and Beryl's recent marital troubles had worn thin what Roberta called the "veneer of politeness" she'd managed to maintain whenever she was around him.

"She told me a lot about the problems in their relationship," said Roberta. "I was the repository of all this negative stuff that she didn't always want to deal with. It really put a strain on our friendship. I haven't talked to her in probably six months now."

An additional challenge to that relationship was Beryl's eighteen-month-old son. Pushed further aside by "the vortex of attention the baby absorbs," Roberta found her friendship foundering. As much as she longed to rescue it, she had no idea how.

In *The Secret Between Us,* Laura Tracy asserted that most women "believe that female friendships are purchased with borrowed money on borrowed time." That's never truer than when a woman has preschool children.

"I want to go out and party when I go to L.A., but she's grounded," Pamela Rabin, a thirty-seven-year-old single saleswoman at Neiman Marcus in Dallas, said of a friend with two- and four-year-old daughters. "I go to her house. She says, 'Good morning. Would you like some coffee?' And that's about all we get to say, because the girls take over."

A mother and her childless friend struggle to stay connected even if the friend has decided to postpone motherhood or is certain that she doesn't want kids. When one friend has a baby and the other doesn't, the strain can be painful. When one has a baby and the other can't have one, it can be excruciating. "I have a patient who went through five years of infertility treatment," psychotherapist Jane Burka said. "This woman had a friend who was going through infertility treatment at the same time and had a successful pregnancy. The envy was so strong that they could not sustain each other through any of this."

Some childless women adjust to a friend's maternity by assuming the role of godmother or indulgent aunt. But for many childless women, helping a friend herd a three-year-old through a shopping mall or an art gallery ranks below helping her strip old wallpaper. Some women are childless by choice.

"People say children are fabulous," said Gussie, a forty-four-year-old real estate agent. "I don't happen to feel that way. I don't find children interesting and pleasant to be with. I find them exhausting. So every time friends have children, we have to relate on a different basis, because now they're involved with their children, and I don't want to be."

Even among mothers, children challenge friendships. When Stacey Oliker asked married women what bonded them to their close friends, shared child-rearing values ranked high on the list. Conversely, disagreement in this sensitive area threatens the connection. Vida, thirty-six, recalled what happened during her annual weekend at a bed-and-breakfast with five friends from college, now all moms. "This was a very trusted circle where you could say, 'I had an affair,' you could say anything, and you would get nothing but support," she said. But when one woman mentioned casually that she didn't believe in day care, the group erupted. "Without realizing it, she was attacking their choices," Vida explained.

Nothing freezes female friendship like a woman feeling her children are threatened. Much as Nancy O'Connor and Imogene liked each other, their boys hadn't gotten along since they met as preschoolers. Nancy told me that not only was Imogene's son mean to Danny himself; he'd rallied other boys to pick on him. After five years, Nancy insisted Imogene do something.

Imogene decided to handle the problem by convening her son's fourth-grade friends to discuss what they didn't like about Danny.

When Nancy heard about the "Danny-bashing session," she marched up to Imogene's and chewed her out. "Her judgment had just completely blown me away," she explained. "I couldn't talk to her for a long time after that."

By our interview, Nancy and Imogene had resumed a cordial relationship, but it was no longer close.

⚬ Other People ⚬

Reared in an upper-middle-class black family, Carol Conoway had been relatively protected from racism. Certainly, the last place she expected to experience it was at Bryn Mawr. After having a wonderful time over Christmas break visiting her dorm mate Evelyn and her family, she had returned a few days early to study. Shortly before classes resumed, Carol was hard at work in the library when she heard Evelyn's familiar footsteps approaching. She was delighted that her friend was back on campus, but something in those steps sounded strange.

"When she reached my carrel, she hugged me and said 'Hello,' " Carol recalled. "Then she said that she had very bad news, that her parents had really been upset that she brought home a black friend. She was ordered to cut off our friendship.

"It was like something had forced a cinderblock into my stomach. Nothing like this had happened before in my life."

Of all the external pressures that threaten female friendship, the toughest can be other people: parents, siblings, husbands and lovers, and even other friends. Maybe they feel jealous of the relationship. Maybe, like Evelyn's parents, they are expressing their own prejudices. But often their motivation for meddling is a desire, however wrongheaded, to protect the best interests of the person they care about.

Parents are the people most likely to interfere in a friendship. Not infrequently, mothers and fathers exert pressure on their daughters either to drop lower status friends and socialize "up" or to "stop putting on airs" and abandon higher status friends. Parental interference cost computer specialist Faith Einerson one of her closest high school friendships. On the surface, she and Jaycie stopped being best friends because Jaycie got serious about tennis, which Faith couldn't play. But underneath, Faith suspected, lay snobbery. Faith's mother was a secretary, and the wealthy people she worked for were friends and social peers of Jaycie's parents.

As an adult, a woman may be forced to cut back on friendship because of an aging parent's demands on her time. Taylor, a forty-eight-year-old accountant, was her mother's sole companion. "I do everything with my mom," she told me. "We get along tremendously, but at the same time there's no room for anybody else in my life."

Other friends, on either side, can get in the way as well. During Chrystal Hunter's senior year in high school, another girl befriended her close friend since ninth grade. "She started spending more time with the other girl, and I just backed out of it," Chrystal explained.

Romance always challenges a friendship, but a possessive lover poses particular challenges. "My first serious boyfriend wanted all of my time," said eighteen-year-old college freshman Joanna Winslade. "Semi-intentionally, he alienated me from my friends—by getting upset when I would say I'm going out with the girls, and by creating a sort of bubble around me of intimate space, couple space."

Even sensitive and supportive husbands often resent the time and attention their wives give their friends, and they may fear, often unjustly, that the women friends spend their time together complaining or laughing about their men. Usually, such worries are misplaced. In fact, sociologist Stacey Oliker even found that during marital disputes women friends often generate empathy for each other's husbands, first by experiencing it themselves and then by engendering it in the complaining wives.

When her marriage is in trouble, a woman may withdraw emotionally and physically from her friends rather than confide in them and ask for help. As long as a woman thinks her marital problems might be solved, she may be reluctant to confide in her friends for fear of being disloyal to her husband or becoming a subject of gossip. She may also recognize that if the marriage heals, she may have difficulty maintaining a friendship with a woman who knows all the gory details of the dispute.

Distressed by the separation of a couple they'd been friends with for years, retired banker Pat Taylor and her husband became particularly attentive to each of them during the crisis. When the couple got back together, they pulled away from Pat and her husband. "They built a whole new circle of friends," Pat said, adding philosophically: "You have to have a clean plate, you know. People know too much after you've said things you wouldn't say if you knew you were going to be living together again."

That friendship never recovered, but some do—once the couple deals with the marital problems or splits. Contact dwindled to four or five phone calls a year after Verna, Kathy Thomas Barr's friend of fifteen years, married an alcoholic rancher in Central Texas. "He became more isolated and withdrawn, and he expected her to do the same," Kathy said. "She was afraid to leave him alone, because she knew that he would drink heavily. Then last year her sister got married, and he refused to go to the wedding, and she said, 'That's it.' "

Later, Verna remarried. This time she chose an outgoing man who encouraged her friendships. After that, she and Kathy visited each other every few months.

Physical and emotional abuse threaten a woman's female friendships, as well as her survival. Caught in an abusive relationship, she needs her friends desperately, to provide both a reality check and practical help extricating herself. Yet instead of reaching out, many women let their net of female support unravel. The first thing an abusive husband often does is to try to isolate his wife from other women. This isolation makes it easier for him to beat or berate her, and it also makes it easier for him to control her.

Meg's alcoholic husband Joe didn't hit her, but he did feel threatened by her women friends. Once a friend who lived in another city called to say she'd be in town, and Meg invited her over that Saturday, when Joe would be out playing golf. "I bought cold cuts for lunch, and I bought extra so Joe and I could have them for dinner," Meg explained. "It was a summer afternoon, and I didn't feel like cooking. Angie and I had a delightful time, sitting in the backyard just giggling and acting silly and renewing the friendship. When Joe got home that evening, Angie had left, and I said, 'We're just going to have cold cuts for dinner.' He said, 'Did you buy those for Angie?' I said, 'Well, yeah, and I bought extra for us tonight.' And he got incensed and said, 'I will not have leftovers from Angie.' It was truly bizarre."

To preserve her marriage, Meg cut her ties to her female friends—without telling them why. "It was like a slow strangulation of the friendships," she said. "I didn't realize it at the time, but that isolation kept me in that marriage for five years when I should have gotten out after the first year."

Whatever demands family members and romantic partners make, women must acknowledge the importance of female friends and take the time to nurture their friendships. Their personal growth, and sometimes even their survival, depends on it.

↜ Widowhood and Divorce ↜

In my interviews, I heard many stories of women providing comfort and support to friends whose marriages had disintegrated. Many formed new friendships with others in similar circumstances: crisis friends to endure together the trauma of breakups, mentors to teach them the ropes of single motherhood and midlife dating, and lifemates and playmates to share the stress and freedom of being on their own.

A newly divorced or a newly widowed woman has had her life upended. She was once half a couple, but she is now on her own. Whichever way it happens, the end of a marriage produces bereavement; however, the quality of that sense of loss is different. Widows may feel anger at being abandoned; but except in cases of suicide or extreme recklessness, pleasant memories of the marriage don't get buried under the rubble of deceit and betrayal.

The age at which the two events typically occur also makes a difference in how a woman responds to them. The average age for a woman at divorce is about thirty-three; for a woman at a husband's death, sixty-nine. Divorce tends to leave women without partners when their children are young and their earning power has yet to peak; widowhood, when their children are grown and they've had time to prepare for retirement.

For many widows, losing a husband to death entails losing friends, too. If the husband suffered a long terminal illness, the wife may have curtailed time with her friends in order to care for him. Once he dies, she may feel too exhausted or griefstricken to rekindle those friendships. Or friends she and her husband saw as couples, even if the primary bond was between the two women, may have trouble integrating a widow into their social lives. Or the widow may envy her friends who still have husbands, and that resentment may poison those friendships.

Divorced women face the same friendship challenges as widows, plus many of their own. Studying people sixty to sixty-five, sociologists Laurie Hatch and Kris Bulcroft concluded that widowed women were better at keeping close friends than their divorced or separated agemates. One reason may be that centuries of custom help a new widow's friends know what to do to help her cope with her loss. They can put up out-of-town family during the funeral, bring a cake or covered dish to the wake, help the widow sort through and dispose of her husband's belongings. Each of those rituals offers opportunities for talk, for comforting, for reconnection.

Society has yet to develop norms for dealing with divorce. Maybe someday, best friends will throw showers to replace whatever housewares exes take with them. Maybe someday, newly single women will lick their wounds with a traditional girlfriend vacation after the decree is final. But for now, we have no template for this transition.

During a divorce, many women turn to their families for emotional and economic support; in the breakup's aftermath, sociologist Robert Milardo noted, a sense of duty and obligation to relatives discourages bonds with friends. Yet to adjust successfully to their new lives, divorcing women need longstanding friends—especially females and especially those who've gone through similar experiences. Friends tend to interfere less and be less judgmental than family.

Even among women who accept it as a regrettable commonplace, divorce is one of the most demanding tests of friendship. By maintaining connection during a friend's divorce, a woman makes a clear commitment to their relationship. "It was like an acid test; anybody who stuck with me was pretty impressive," explained forty-nine-year-old Laura Kramer, whose divorce more than a decade earlier had dissolved some friendships and fortified others.

The impact a divorce has on a friendship often depends on whether a woman's friends are married or single. Simple logistics play a role. When both women are married, their availability for friendship is the same; but when one of them divorces, it isn't. A recent divorcée is apt to feel at loose ends socially during evenings and weekends, which her married friends consider couple time. Although she may receive an occasional invitation to join them for dinner or a movie, issuing one herself is awkward.

"My friends have been wonderful about including me, but it's more in bigger events," said Linda Girard, fifty-one and divorced two years. "I'm not real comfortable calling and saying, 'Do you and Jeff want to go to the movies tonight?' "

Whether a married woman is conscious of it or not, fear can cause her to back off from a friend who's separating or divorcing. Two of attorney Sarah Scott's closest friends remained loyal during her divorce and four-year child custody battle, but many other friends vanished. "What I was going through was so frightening," Sarah said. "It was like having cancer. I had been in this mothers' group for five or six years, and those women all fell away. The whole relationship had been based on mother and child, and here was the possibility that I might have my child taken away. I lost every friend I had made through being a mother during that process."

Grieving over the death of her marriage, a newly divorced woman may withdraw from the world like a widow in mourning. Two years after her husband left, community organizer Sylvia Castillo, fifty-one, still didn't feel up to socializing. Now she was facing a birthday party and a baby shower. "If somebody can go with me, I will go for a while," she told me with a shrug.

What hurts the most is when a valued girlfriend takes the hus- band's side. As a young mother, Lilith had ranked Marlys, the wife of one of her husband's colleagues, among her two closest friends. But when Lilith said she and her husband were separating, Marlys told her, "I can't be there for you, and furthermore, we have to be there for your husband, because he's in the law firm."

Lilith was devastated. "I remember crying and actually beating my hands against the wall," she said, "because I had thought I could count on her, and I knew that getting out of this marriage was going to be a nightmare."

Even a split that's relatively free of rancor takes its toll on friendship. "I came out of the divorce with more of our friends remaining my friends than my husband's," social worker Carol Deanow said. "I think we both knew that it's very difficult for friends to really and truly remain friends with both. We did not have a contentious divorce and have coparented extremely well, but it still didn't work out."

Being forced to choose between couple friends can be agony. Throughout their late thirties and early forties, Julie Penrod-Glenn and her friends Ingrid and Nadine were a tight trio. By rare good fortune, Ingrid and Nadine's husbands and Julie's boyfriend got along—so well, in fact, that the men formed their own independent bond.

Then Ingrid and Stuart split up.

Julie and Nadine did their best to remain loyal to Ingrid, even though they still liked the man she portrayed as a villain. But the friendship shattered over Julie's wedding. Julie asked her two best friends to serve as attendants. Ingrid agreed—until she learned that her ex would be a wedding guest.

"She became hysterical," Julie recalled. "Not only wouldn't she be in the wedding; she wouldn't *come* to the wedding if we were going to invite him. She stood on the couch and yelled and screamed and threatened to hit me. I was terrified."

The three-way female friendship skidded downhill from there. Had Ingrid been able to reach beyond her own pain and anger to empathize with her friends, she might have recognized that by forcing them to exclude either her ex-husband or her, she would be the ultimate loser. As it was, she lost two close, supportive friends, just when she needed them most.

⤳ Misfortune ⤳

Compared to other relationships, friendship is relatively free of rules. One of the few rules there are goes like this: True friends stick by one another in adversity.

Adhering to that unwritten edict in an acute emergency is one thing. But sticking by a friend in the face of a lasting misfortune is another matter. As with divorce, a disquieting sense of vulnerability may pull friends out of connection.

Physical and mental disabilities present challenges to friendship. When two women—one able-bodied, the other disabled—become friends, they face this difference from the beginning. But a serious illness or accident that occurs *after* the relationship is established presents additional problems: It upsets the balance of reciprocity. It alters how and when two women can see each other. It may rule out activities they once shared. Suddenly, the friendship must change or die.

Studying the impact of ill health on female friendship, British sociologist Dorothy Jerrome found that friends faced with serious sickness or injury tended to do one of three things: One of them might with-draw, the ill friend might deny the seriousness of her affliction to protect the friendship, or the two might bond more closely.

When Carol Safran received her third diagnosis of breast cancer, her close friends rallied around her, even those who lived half a conti-nent away, like Fanny. Carol confided to Fanny that she dreaded the radiation treatments. So, early on the mornings of the treatments, Fanny phoned Carol, ready with a pep talk. Carol would admit: "I'm freaking out about the radiation. Tell me what I can think about to get through it."

And Fanny would say: "Just say as you're lying there at eight-thirty, 'I'm going to get out of here by nine o'clock.' " The calls worked, and they bonded Carol and Fanny even more firmly than they'd been before.

Of all the misfortunes a woman can suffer, those involving loss of children rank among the biggest challenges to her friendships. Two of the women I interviewed recalled being delighted to find themselves pregnant simultaneously with a friend, only to have their shared joy wrenched away by the other woman's stillbirth. "It was hard for me to show up with my new little son in the middle of her grieving," said Claudia Vangerven, a professor of literature.

Losing a grown child can also shatter friendships. Science teacher Cybil's son was in college when he shot himself. "A lot of people couldn't deal with it," Cybil recalled. "They're pleasant, but they don't look you in the eye, and some topics just don't happen anymore. I still see Myrna occasionally at the store, and she tells me how her children are. And I want to say, 'Jesus Christ, Myrna, ask me how I am. Ask me how my one remaining kid is.' "

Raising a chronically ill or disabled child also challenges a woman's friendships. On top of the emotional issues come the practical de-mands of providing care for a person who may never outgrow com-plete dependency.

Some friends demonstrate their commitment by relieving the bur-den. When Bernice Torregrossa mentioned that she wanted to attend a three-day conference but couldn't because no one would take her younger daughter, Cecilia volunteered. In addition to cerebral palsy, the little girl suffered from moderate mental retardation, plus some of the symptoms of autism. "She had terrible separation anxiety because she was so dependent," Bernice explained. "The minute I walked out of the room, she was going to start screaming."

Yet here was Cecilia, who had several kids of her own, volunteering without being asked.

Other once-close friends shrink from even casual contact. "Every woman in my position has had a friend who's walked away," said Dolores, whose second son, Jason, was born with multiple disabilities. Her friend Bernadine had two children about the same age and was considering having a third. Over coffee a couple of years after Jason's birth, Bernadine declared that she had decided against another child. "I couldn't stand it if I had a child like Jason who was mentally retarded," she explained.

That sank the friendship.

Bernadine could have shared the same information in a way that affirmed Dolores as a woman and a mother if she had said, for instance, "I've decided not to have another child. At my age, I'm worried that something might go wrong. When I see you with Jason, I'm amazed at all you're doing to help him reach his potential, and at the love and good grace with which you do it. But I'm just not that patient and not that strong."

Instead, Bernadine's comment had been the opposite of empathic. In making it, she had disregarded Dolores's feelings, including the love and protectiveness she felt toward her son. And that had broken the connection.

⚮ Changes in Money and Status ⚮

As a cultural ideal, friendship has nothing to do with money or social status. But connecting across difference is always hard, no less so when the difference is something we'd prefer to ignore.

"Differences in your financial situation are an awkward reality," observed sociology professor Laura Kramer, a divorced mother. "For example, I have a friend who has a lot more money than I do, and I don't want to make her self-conscious about it by asking her advice."

It wasn't just a matter of differing means; it was a matter of differing attitudes. At present, Laura was considering whether to paint her house herself or to have it painted. She knew that one friend would say, "Just hire someone." But there were others who'd tell her what she could expect to pay either way and leave the decision up to her. "They would never say, 'Oh, it's only three hundred dollars,' " she explained. "They would realize that maybe they think that's low, but I don't."

Once a friendship is established, an abrupt shift in financial fortune can jolt the two women out of connection. "Your personal fortunes can change dramatically, and so can the fortunes of your friends," observed Cecile, who had grown up in an upper-middle-class family but had spent much of her adult life on the financial edge, working in public health clinics.

One day, she met a successful builder in the Berkeley-Oakland area. Within ten months, they were married. After fire destroyed their house, the insurance settlement allowed them to replace it and to buy and build on other property. "Meanwhile, I have close women friends who are still renting apartments," Cecile said from her living room overlooking San Francisco Bay. "I have actually hesitated to pursue a friendship when I wasn't sure what the person was going to think if I brought her home."

A sudden rise in one's friend's fortunes triggers issues that may not have been addressed before in the friendship. Suppose, psychologist Lisa Wood hypothesized, you suddenly have more money: "You are really excited about buying all new furniture for your house, and you've got all these people coming in, and they're doing the wallpaper and sanding the floors. You're on Cloud Nine. And here's your close friend, who isn't poor but is not getting to do any of that stuff. She's trying really hard to be generous and saying, 'I'm so happy for you. I can't wait to come over and see it.' But it gets wearing after a while."

The financially fortunate friend may notice the friendship slipping but have no idea that she's being insensitive. If the other woman admits that she's on a tight budget and doesn't want to hear about all the fun her friend is having spending money, she may—or may not— save the friendship. And even if she does, the newly flush friend may begin seeking out new playmates, to share shopping sprees, and new mentors, to help her gain acceptance from the established rich.

As women become socially mobile, new friends can become increasingly important. "People can't lug their families with them up the social ladder," University of Delaware sociologist Helen Gouldner explained.

Lugging old friends is almost as hard. In eighth grade, Debbie Grotfeldt and her best friend Ramona shared similar circumstances: Both had single mothers who earned low wages. Then, during their junior year, Ramona got pregnant and married an abusive man. Debbie went to college and married a man who treated her as an equal. Three decades later, Ramona still lived in the same little Illinois town, where she was on her second marriage. Debbie was in Houston running a nonprofit organization and accompanying her artist husband to exhibits of his work in New York, Europe, and Latin America.

Despite the disparity that tugged at them, Debbie and Ramona struggled to stay connected, like swimmers caught in a current. Often, under similar circumstances, one friend or the other lets go, and the relationship sinks.

Even among people who place little value on money, possessions, or lineage, academic and professional credentials count socially. And because they do, success or failure at acquiring them may divide friends. For instance, when one friend's career advances, the other may feel abandoned.

One day while she was in graduate school, psychologist Lisa Wood had what she described as "one of those crystallizing conversations" with her friend Clara, who was also working on her Ph.D. Clara said she'd recognized that her doctorate was so important to her because it would allow her to live an intellectual life. "I was really admiring of her, very proud of her, and confident for her," Wood told me.

Then Clara dropped out.

When Wood finished her degree, Clara was extremely envious and upset. At first Wood didn't notice. Pursuing the life of the mind had come down to hunting for work in a tight academic job market. No sooner had Lisa landed her post at the University of Puget Sound than she and Clara had a big blowup. "It was over a lot of things," Wood recalled. "But one of the things she said was: 'You think you're so great because you're a professor.' And that's not what I was thinking at all. I was thinking, 'I'm really glad that I have a job.' "

Some people live most of their lives in the public eye, and for them, a real friend is both refuge and tonic. Talk-show hostess Oprah Winfrey met Gayle King when they both worked at a Baltimore television station in 1976. They'd been best friends ever since. In 1990 Winfrey told *Ebony* that she knew she could call King at any hour, about anything, and that King would give her something she couldn't get from an army of sycophants—the truth. Four years later, Winfrey explained to *New Woman*: "Gayle helps keep me grounded and centered."

Provided both women commit themselves to maintaining their connection and each understands and acknowledges her own issues about power, money, and recognition, a real friendship can survive the strain of fame. From 1970 to 1976, Kaye Northcott and Molly Ivins shared an office and a job, editing a feisty liberal political journal called the *Texas Observer.* They became close friends. Then Molly took a job at the *New York Times,* and her career accelerated. Returning to Texas, she became a popular newspaper columnist. A book of her columns sat on the best-seller list for weeks on end. Molly began appearing places like *Nightline* and served a short stint on *60 Minutes.*

The friendship weathered Molly's public glory, perhaps in part because Kaye didn't seek that for herself. "I've never been envious of Molly's fame," Kaye said, "but I've always been envious of Molly's talent."

Even more important than that lack of envy was the commitment the two women had to their friendship. They both worked at staying in connection.

⤳ Divergent Values ⤳

When a good friend reveals herself to be a bad person, can she still be a good friend?

Foundation grants analyst Bernice Torregrossa lost a friend over that issue. "She was very vibrant," Bernice said, "but she tended to cut corners morally—like thinking that it didn't matter if you walked the check. Not armed robbery, but ways of doing things that weren't right."

As with money and class, differences in values can keep two women from becoming friends, or at least close friends, in the first place. "I certainly have many acquaintances that I have a lot of differences of opinion with," writer and editor Gabrielle Cosgriff, fifty-eight, said. "But I wouldn't be really close friends with people who had vastly different opinions on the things I take seriously: friendship, the way you treat people, and being honest and open and not bigoted."

Female friendships have a better chance of weathering abstract differences on values than disagreements about how each conducts her life. Because of the values they imply, career choices sometimes separate friends. When Beth Madison decided to go into business, she found some of the friends she'd made during the late sixties and early seventies pulling back. Most of her friends had become doctors, academics, high school teachers, or clerics, and here she was opening an insurance firm. The reaction of one once-close friend stung especially. Beth explained: "I had the feeling that she was judging my lifestyle choices and felt that I wasn't going to be worth knowing because I was going to work for money."

Even when a woman considers her own sexual behavior moral, it can cost her friendships with women who adhere to a different code. Reared Catholic, Karen Roberto was best friends from fifth grade through high school with a girl who later became a nun. But when Karen fell in love at nineteen with the man she later married, diverging sexual values pulled the women apart. At first, Karen simply didn't tell her friend that she was having sex, let alone enjoying it. But when Karen and her boyfriend moved in together, the fraying thread that held the friendship together snapped. The nun simply wasn't able to maintain a close connection with a woman living in what the church viewed as a state of mortal sin.

Women who have a firm sense of themselves and their own boundaries may be able to maintain a close friendship despite their friend's making a choice they consider morally wrong. One Catholic woman, for instance, described trying to argue a friend out of having an abortion, but then accompanying her to the doctor and staying with her to make sure she'd be all right. But remaining connected to a friend who persists in living her life in a way that violates our values—that places a strain on connection from both sides, a strain few friendships can endure.

☙ Fights and Misunderstandings ☙

As half of the original writing team for *I Love Lucy*, Madelyn Pugh Davis was always inventing fights between Lucy Ricardo and Ethel Mertz. Madelyn explained the formula to me: Lucy and Ethel would fall out over something minor, like wearing the same dress to a party.

Then, after an exaggerated exchange of pique, they'd make up before the credits rolled.

In real life, fights between women friends are too traumatic—betrayals, slights, disappointments, and words spoken in haste too hurtful to forget—for the relationship to heal in half an hour. But young girls do fight easily and make up quickly. Eleven-year-old Olivia Cory gave me an example: When a big, red rubber ball hit her friend Dee during phys ed, Dee, thinking Olivia had thrown it, angrily stormed off. The next weekend, the two spent an hour happily Rollerblading. By the time they unbuckled their skates, they knew they were best friends again.

That incident had occurred twelve months before our interview. "This year, we're like closer friends—maybe not closer, but we're less steamy," Olivia told me. "We don't blow up at each other."

As Olivia and Dee approached adolescence, they were learning to express disappointment, anger, and irritation appropriately. Too often, girls and women learn instead to dodge disagreement, only to have it boil over in a bigger fight later.

When they were both divorced and in their mid-thirties, Carolyn started dating a man her friend Margot had just broken up with. The first few times he'd invited her out, Carolyn had declined; but he persisted. "I finally asked her if she would mind if I went out with him," Carolyn recalled. "And she said no, not at all, that she was finished with him."

But as soon as Carolyn started seeing him regularly, Margot angrily accused her of being insensitive—even though Margot had explicitly given her the go-ahead. "She looked at it as I went out with lots of guys, so I could have skipped that one," Carolyn told me. "And she was right. I could have."

Sometimes expressing a complaint directly does destroy a friendship. Because she'd always been allergic to cigarette smoke, Charity Gourley, sixty-one, didn't keep ashtrays in her house. Noticing their absence, her friend Paula, a smoker, brought her own and left it so she could use it when she visited. "It took me several years before I was able to ask her not to smoke in my house," Charity said. "She was really insulted when I did that, and that fractured our relationship."

Sociologist Pat O'Connor noted that the cause of a split often comes down to "a breach of the friendship contract." But unlike marriage, friendship lacks formal rules and sanctions. We may generally agree that friends don't slander each other, betray each other's confidences, or have sex with each other's spouses or lovers. But what about issues like hospitality, encouragement, reciprocity, practical support—being there for each other?

Frequently, perceived lack of reciprocity sparks a quarrel. Whenever Ina, her friend since junior high, felt down, family court judge Susan Baker Olsen could spot it, and she'd invite Ina to go somewhere for a heart-to-heart. But either Susan hid her troubles better or Ina was less sensitive. At the end of a hard day at work, Susan asked Ina if she wanted to go have a drink, adding: "I have something that I really want to talk about." Ina replied that she didn't really drink. Susan responded: "I don't really drink, either. We could get a Coke or something." Ina said: "No, I guess I'll just go home." Frustrated, Susan shot back: "Forget it!" And Ina asked: "Is there some reason you wanted to have a Coke?"

Susan thought she had made her desire for her friend's time clear from the start. "I thought that she should pick up if I wanted to talk about something, but she didn't," Susan told me.

Having a close friend let us down in a crisis or react in a way we never expected can be shattering. The friendship has weathered the comfort and strengthening stages described in chapter 3, but it doesn't pass the testing stage. And the failure can be over something relatively trivial. Take an unexpected response to a joke; it can suddenly make a woman feel like she doesn't really know her friend at all. That happened to Cecile during a phone call with a friend. "I was angry with my husband, she seemed unhappy with her boyfriend, and I jokingly suggested that we switch partners for the night," Cecile recalled. "She hung up. I felt like she had slapped me across the face. And suddenly a twenty-year relationship evaporated."

The cooling of this once-close friendship may have been inevitable. But in many cases, it isn't. Learning how to manage conflict, how to fight well and make up well, is essential to healthy, life-enhancing female friendships. Fortunately, approaches to making up, like most of the other skills involved in maintaining female friendships, can be learned.

14

⚬

Seventeen Steps
to Having Friends for Life

Make new friends, but keep the old;
One is silver, and the other's gold.

— Round sung by Girl Scouts

The day after I drove up to Houston for lunch with my busy lawyer friend Maida, a handwritten note arrived, dated and postmarked the previous day. It was a short note that said only: "I am often grateful that Betsy Hunter [the woman who introduced us] sent you into my life, and I was grateful again today!"

I tucked the note away where I could find it whenever my spirits needed buoying.

Despite competing demands from families, jobs, and other commitments, busy women have figured out ways to nurture close friendships and to repair damaged ones. I asked each person I interviewed what advice she'd give others. The examples that illustrated their points were as diverse as the women themselves; but the underlying wisdom came down to just seventeen ingredients.

✢ 1. Make Friendship a Priority ✢

"Friendships are hard work," ceramicist Chula Sanchez observed. "You have to weed them and water them. They don't grow on their own."

That doesn't mean the work can't be fun. Benefits consultant Beth Madison suggested that, if you're single, you should get two season subscriptions to your favorite performing arts group or sports team, so you can invite a friend to go with you. But like any close relationship, a female friendship also needs time when the two women can be alone or at least speak privately by phone.

Arranging a regular date for a meal or an activity helps structure space for friendship in busy lives. On the first Monday of every month, medical practice administrator Sharon Healy got together with two friends for dinner. "It seems so mechanical," she admitted, but it maintained the connection.

Vida, a thirty-six-year-old medical educator and the mother of a two-year-old, got together once a year for a weekend with her far-flung college friends. They took turns planning the reunion. For the most recent one, the designated planner had rented an entire bed-and-breakfast. "They had a sitting room, and I think nobody really ever sits there," Vida said. "We just took it over and talked forever."

✢ 2. Value Friendships for What They Are ✢

Friendship comes in different varieties, and one secret of sustaining them is appreciating each for what it brings to your life, rather than fretting over its limitations.

"Some of my best friends have the best senses of humor," Wendy Marsh observed. "I don't know that I would call on them for the deepest problems, but with humor you can get through a lot."

Another woman told me of her close friendship that puzzled everyone who knew her, even her husband. This friend turned every conversation topic back to herself, she regaled casual acquaintances with the details of her personal life, and she blatantly inflated her accomplishments. Yet the woman I interviewed was able to look beyond these flaws to her friend's unflagging loyalty and her knack for knowing exactly what kind of support to give in a crisis. To those who didn't know her well, her friend may have seemed self-absorbed, but she had been able to reach beyond herself and form an empathic connection.

❧ 3. Learn How to Listen ❧
and When to Remain Silent

Being able to listen well is essential for tending female friendships. Jay Vanasco told me that if she wanted to discuss a personal problem, she'd call her friend Mae. "She has this incredible skill of listening not only to what you're saying, but what you mean and will tell you what you mean," Jay said.

Psychologists call that "active listening." When a friend is talking about something important, push everything else out of your mind. Don't split your concentration by trying to figure out what to say next. That's easy: Paraphrase what she says—and what she implies.

For example, a friend may say to you: "My mother is driving me crazy. She keeps dropping hints that she wants to move in with us."

Instead of immediately jumping in with a solution, you might say: "It sounds like you really don't want her living with you, but you don't know how to tell her."

She acknowledges what you said or clarifies it. You paraphrase her statement. She digs a layer deeper. In this way, you can help her acknowledge her ambivalence about her mother. At best, your friend may leave your tête-à-tête ready to deal with her mother assertively. But even if she doesn't, she'll feel stronger, better about herself—loved, understood, supported.

One thing that active listening *doesn't* involve is offering advice. By giving, instead, emotional and practical support that helps her solve her own problems, a woman strengthens both her friend and her friendship. Whatever the problem, let your friend control the pace of her revelations. After all, she may feel that's one of the few things in her life she can control.

For women, the virtue of loyalty is tightly bundled with that of discretion. Loyalty begins with two rules: Never talk about her behind her back. Never betray a confidence.

The tricky part is identifying a confidence. When a friend says, "I'm in line for promotion to vice president for customer relations when Joe leaves in June," does she want you to keep the news to yourself or spread it? The best strategy is to ask.

❧ 4. Express Your Feelings Directly ❧

The one topic that close women friends almost never talk about is the relationship itself. Yet simply saying "Our friendship means a lot to me, even though we may not see each other for weeks" can help keep the rapport alive despite time pressure.

As with any human relationship, being close female friends requires that we don't expect one another to be perfect, that we value the friendship for what it is and each other for who we are and accept the shortcomings in both. On the other hand, expressing disagreement and anger appropriately and being able to receive them constructively are crucial to maintaining close, long-lasting friendships.

Yale freshman Joanna Winslade had one complaint about her college best friend Holly. "She is always, always late," Joanna said. Rather than allow irritation to erode their friendship, Joanna broached the issue early on. Joanna recounted the discussion: "She said she doesn't mean to and things just happen. And I said I understand when things happen sometimes; but if they happen all the time, then there is something going on that you need to pay attention to."

By telling Holly how her chronic lateness made her feel, Joanna maintained the connection—even though she didn't succeed at getting Holly to break the habit. Recognizing that Holly wasn't going to change, Joanna adapted. "Whatever time I wanted things to happen, I'd set them up for earlier," she said.

Linda Girard told me her friend of seventeen years, Louanne, had taught her to be open about the negative feelings she'd been taught to conceal. "She's so honest about herself," Linda said. "She has said things to me like, 'I feel like you never want to do anything with me,' and that makes me feel really bad. If anyone else were to say that to me, I think I would backpedal and try to make excuses. With Louanne, I can say, 'I'm really sorry you feel that way, and that's certainly not what I intended, and I appreciate your candor.' Her honesty and her openness create a place for me to be different from the way I am in other relationships."

~ 5. Handle Conflict and ~ Competition Constructively

Six months after communications and management consultant Nan Kilkeary and her friend and workmate Dana left the corporate world to start their own firm, they recognized that in risk tolerance, they stood at opposite ends of the scale. Dana wanted to expand only after they had money in the bank to cover the cost. Nan wanted to charge ahead with limited funding.

Nan told Dana that they needed to confront their differences. As they sat in Nan's living room discussing candidly what made them comfortable and uncomfortable, both friends recognized that they were incompatible as business partners. "It was scary," Nan recalled of the conversation. "But we decided to terminate the business relationship and keep the friendship."

Some of the sagest advice I heard on handling conflict came from ten-year-old Eva Kuhn. When a friend became hurt or angry at a remark, Eva took a two-step approach: First, she repeated what she'd just said, in case the other girl had misunderstood. Then, Eva explained why she'd said it.

Eva also had a strategy she used when she was the one stung. "If you have an argument and somebody says something bad to you, you don't immediately burst into tears or snap back at them," she advised. "You should calmly say, 'Why did you do that? Was it something that I did? Are you having family problems?' "

Only recently, Susan Baker Olsen had learned how to engage in constructive conflict with her friend Ina. "We pretty much can say anything that we want to each other," Susan told me. "It wasn't too many years ago that I didn't feel like I could, because I was afraid that she was going to be so hurt that she just couldn't deal with it.

"I just decided that I had to tell her something and be assertive about it, or else it was going to be the end of our friendship. So I just started telling her in 'I' words."

A woman who complains "When you don't return my phone calls for three days, I feel hurt" is asking for help and soothing; one who says, "You obviously don't value our friendship—you don't return my phone calls for three days" is making an accusation.

One secret to constructive conflict is letting go—of the need to win, of resentment at losing. In the wake of her divorce, Carol Edgar felt predictably vulnerable, especially when it came to selling her apartment. That was one reason she wanted her close friend Wilda, an attorney, to handle the sale. Unfortunately, the arrangement strained their friendship. Fortunately, Carol knew how to limit the damage.

"She really, really got angry with me on the telephone, and I suddenly felt as if I were her child instead of her client," Carol recalled. "Finally, I said, 'Look, this is going nowhere. Let's just hang up. Let's just let it go.' And then two days later, she called to apologize. I credit her for having the courage and initiative to take that action. When she called, I didn't say, 'Well, how could you do such a thing?' I said, 'Well, that was really hard for me.' Then we decided not to re-argue and try to find out who was right and who was wrong. And I think that's the key."

~ 6. Take the Initiative in Making Up ~

After a fight, make the first move at reconciliation, especially if you were the injured party. Called before a board of ministry to defend her decision to divorce her then-husband, Methodist minister Betsy Alden asked Abigail, a fellow clergywoman she'd known since seminary, to accompany her as her advocate. Abigail declined, saying that she didn't want to be put in a position of having to discuss things Betsy had told her in confidence. "She had reasons that I did understand, but it felt like a betrayal at that point to me," Betsy said. "That sort of estranged us for a while."

Then, one day, Betsy realized that it was Abigail's fiftieth birthday and called her. Betsy opened with: "I know it's your birthday, and I was thinking of you. We haven't been in touch a lot recently, but we need to be."

Betsy didn't even refer to the rift.

Four months later, the two shared a room at a conference. "She made a big point of saying that she was so grateful that I had taken that initiative," Betsy recalled.

Because Abigail herself felt that she'd caused the rupture, she hadn't been able to reach out to repair the friendship. If Betsy hadn't, both women would have lost an important relationship.

❧ 7. Stay in Touch ❧

The secret to keeping friends is maintaining connection, and essential to maintaining connection is staying in touch. My mother was a fine and faithful correspondent. Even when my brother and I were preschoolers, she wrote someone a letter every evening. A card file of addresses sat on top of her desk; as we moved from city to city for my father's corporate career, it grew fat.

Although holiday letters and Christmas card notes seem like one more task shoehorned into an already stressful season, they are an effective way to maintain at least a tenuous connection with the people who've left our daily lives but not our hearts. Of course, staying in touch throughout the year is better. And it isn't that difficult. All it takes is a postcard or a quick phone call.

Charity Gourley considered Hester her model for nurturing friendships. They'd met when they were living in Tanzania with their medical-missionary husbands. Although Charity had been back in the States for twenty years, the friendship continued because Hester was such a good correspondent. "She keeps postcards beside her telephone," Charity told me. "She is always calling people, and she is always sending a quick postcard to someone."

When Mali List's college friend Georgina graduated, Mali gave her a stack of preaddressed postcards. "I believe in letter writing, even if the person doesn't write me back," Mali said. "When I was studying in Italy, I wrote all of my friends religiously. If they didn't write me back, that was fine; they were getting a letter that said, 'Here's what I'm up to.'"

Television pioneer Madelyn Pugh Davis advised: "Don't let the friendships fade away. Call them or drop a card or have lunch. If you lose touch, then you feel embarrassed because you don't know anything that they are doing. Then you say, 'I can't call, because I haven't called in so long.'"

❧ 8. Adapt to Change ❧

Maintaining a long-term friendship means learning to tolerate change in the relationship. A close friend moves, marries, gets promoted to a demanding new job, or has a baby. Or she suddenly declares a topic—say, her relationship with her lover—off limits.

Developmental psychologist Sophie Jacobs Bronstein found that in most friendships, intimacy matters more to one partner than the other, and that changes like these tend to upset that partner more. The way to move the relationship through this test is for the two to talk about it openly; often, the friend who's more troubled by the change has to bring up the subject.

Although both friends must be committed to preserving their relationship through life's sea changes, one may be more ingenious than the other at devising ways to stay connected. Beth Madison shared a strategy for helping a friendship survive a friend's move to another town: Give her a few weeks to get settled; then come visit. She advised: "Say, 'You've got to be lonely up there, so I'll come up and we'll go discover Chicago.' "

Patty Kilday and her friend Joy met on the staff of their college paper. After graduation, both married and became journalists, but then their lives diverged. Patty's marriage lasted. She balanced raising three sons with a job on a daily newspaper. Joy's marriage didn't. She became a foreign correspondent specializing in international trouble spots: the Middle East one year, Bosnia another. But instead of letting the friendship unravel as their lives diverged, they knit an even tighter connection. Joy made a point of establishing a relationship with each of Patty's boys, sending them letters, postcards, and interesting presents from everywhere assignments took her. "They're the only kids we know who have real Iraqui money," Patty told me.

Understanding that Patty's children were the focus of Patty's life, Joy made them part of hers.

↜ 9. Be There for Your Friends ↜

The old adage holds true: To have a friend, you have to be a friend. Often, that comes down literally to being there.

Being there for a friend can be as simple and straightforward as pitching in to help at a party. Or it can be as sensitive as comforting a friend after the death of a loved one. "You always feel unequal to the task of sympathy," noted retired city councilwoman Eleanor Tinsley. "Some people are better at it than others, but I think we always need to do *something*. The wrong thing is to do nothing."

When a friend is experiencing tough times, being there means making allowances for lapses brought on by the circumstances. Going through a rough divorce, one of Beth Madison's best friends stood her up for a dinner date. The next morning the woman called, miserable and apologetic. "I feel like dog meat," Beth's friend said. "Life's a mess now. I screwed up. Sorry."

When university administrator Maryann, fifty-four, and her husband separated, her friend Rosalie hit on a way to help her through the traumatic transition. Maryann's husband had arranged to come collect his things on a Saturday morning. Later that same day, Rosalie would help Maryann throw a brunch for her closest friends at what was now *her* house. After eating, they'd all go over to the best nursery in town and buy plants for their gardens.

"It was brilliant," Maryann told me. "She invited five or six women over to my house for brunch with the idea that my vanity and pride would kick in and that I could not meet them at the door in my ruffled bathrobe with my tear-streaked face, that I would of course have to put on a nice feed and have the good linen and stuff out. We all had a wonderful time. We went out and bought flowers, which, of course, is a symbol of life and rejuvenation. By the time they left me, I felt so much better than I could have under any other circumstance."

Eased by presence of friends, the death of a loved one doesn't have to become the death of love. In her early fifties, Bobye List was the only widow in her social group. When her husband was terminally ill, their friends had rallied around. "I don't think it's because we're so special," she told me. "If you have good friends, they form a community around you."

No one is better equipped to help a woman through life-altering illness than a friend. Shirley Defoe, fifty-two, valued her mentor Josephine for her wisdom, humor, and spirituality. A recent stroke had left Josephine's larynx paralyzed, but Shirley still visited and talked to her. "That's what friendship's about," Shirley explained. "You're not just their friend when they're healthy. You're friends no matter what."

Staying connected, day to day, as a friend's life ebbs is both the most daunting challenge and the most significant service of female friendship. Cybil had been a bedside companion to several friends as they died. For each woman, she first let her friend know that she didn't mind talking about dying. Women who couldn't bring themselves to discuss the impending end with their husbands or children unburdened themselves to Cybil about everything from speculations about an afterlife to the hymns they wanted at their funerals. Next, she went through boxes of family photos with them. As Cybil wrote on the back, capturing identities of individuals and details of events that otherwise would be lost to future generations, she helped her dying friends do deeper work. She explained: "It's a good technique for having a person review her life and pull it into a perspective that contents her enough that she can let it go."

That important presence both soothes the dying friend and eases her guilt at abandoning the people she loves. As she lets go, she knows her friends will comfort one another and her family.

↝ 10. Know Your Limits ↝

In friendship, dependability ranks as a cardinal virtue. One of the few unspoken rules of friendship is that a friend will do what she says, show up on time, and remember important occasions. Yet as much as some women might love their friends and value their friendships, they can't seem to manage this. That's because the root of reliability is knowing your limits.

Marguerite Salmon's friend Emerald had that down. "She's very grounded," Marguerite said. "She has a good sense of what she wants and what she doesn't want, so if I ask her to do something or help me with something and she can't, she'll say, 'I can't.' Or she'll say, 'I can't right now, but I can at this other time.' She is somebody that I know I can count on."

Knowing your limits extends to knowing just how much of yourself you're comfortable disclosing, and how fast. Taylor, a forty-eight-year-old accountant, grew up in a very private family. No one discussed personal problems. But in her forties, she faced two crises that she couldn't keep to herself: First, she developed breast cancer. Then, a few years later, her husband moved out. She needed her friends' support, but she didn't want to answer probing questions.

"With the cancer diagnosis, if I didn't want to talk to somebody about it, I just said that," she explained. "I wanted to talk to people when I felt like talking to people. I did it on my own time. And I really learned something through that. It was the same with my separation."

By learning to be assertive about intimacy, Taylor became more comfortable with it.

✧ II. Master the Art of Reciprocity ✧

In two of my friendships, I'm usually the one who initiates contact. In two others, my friend is. When I'm on the receiving end, I'm always glad to get the call. To be sure my friend knows that, I try to set up a date to do something together, or at least to talk again, before I get off the line. Where I'm the one who gets in touch, I sense a similar welcome. In fact, one of those two women often sounds relieved, as if she'd been waiting for me to phone. I suggest lunch. We set a date. We have a great talk over quesadillas. Then I don't hear from her until I call again. I've had to learn that that's okay.

Although reciprocity is an ideal in friendship, seldom is the balance exact. Some women are better organized than others. Some are busier. Some can take two-hour lunches; others have to be back at their desks at one o'clock sharp. Some battle bouts of depression during which they can't bring themselves to reach out. Doing 60 percent of the work may be what it takes to maintain a life-enhancing friendship.

Trust and loyalty are essential in establishing a close friendship; reciprocity and communication are essential for maintaining it.

Occasionally, Jan Williams told me, she would receive an expensive gift from a friend with a lot more money, or a powerful friend would do her a favor. Rather than fretting because she couldn't return the gesture in kind, Jan sent a book as a thank-you. As a writer and community college English teacher, she kept up with the latest literary releases, and she had an unerring sense of which book was right for which friend.

When one woman has both the means and the inclination to be extravagantly generous, little acts of thoughtfulness help keep a friendship in balance. That's how New York publicist Carol Edgar had been able to maintain reciprocity with her lifelong friend Swanee Hunt, the heir to a legendary Texas oil fortune. "I like to do things that make her feel taken care of," Carol explained. "I arranged for a case of bubble bath to be delivered to her. She says, 'Every time I slip into my Calgon bath, I think of you.' You know, baths are very soothing. I guess that's maybe what our friendship is—soothing and healing."

Travel challenges any friendship, but especially one between two women of different means. To preserve balance, they can choose a mode of transport and accommodation that the less affluent friend can afford. Even if the better-heeled woman could pay for both to go first class, they fly coach and stay in $80-a-night hotels or drive and camp out. Or they compromise: At expensive restaurants she picks up the tab but lets her friend do the same the next night at someplace modestly priced.

"Ivy has a tremendous amount of money, and I have nothing," sculptor Gertrude Barnstone said of one dear friend. "And sometimes she will do wonderful things. Like to go to her nephew's wedding in Santa Fe, she sent me a big fat check to get the ticket to go out there, which I hadn't solicited." So Gertrude fabricated a work of art, a little table, for Ivy as a thank-you.

⇜ 12. Give Gifts from the Heart ⇜

This past Christmas, the presents I received were exceptionally thoughtful, as if each friend and relative had carefully considered my whims, my tastes, and the way I live and entertain. My husband's brother and sister-in-law sent a necklace of semiprecious stones in colors that match half of what's hanging in my closet. My nephew and ex-sister-in-law mailed two packets of hard-to-find wild mushrooms— one porcinis, the other morels (for which I have a special weakness). My running partner gave me an exquisite hand-glazed Mexican plate, not unlike ceramic pieces I had already but half a century older and far finer. A Houston couple, frequent weekend guests, must have noticed that not a blade in my kitchen had a decent edge; they sent a beautifully balanced four-inch version of a chef's knife.

I appreciated the things themselves, but more than that I appreciated the care and understanding that had gone into their selection. These weren't just fulfillments of seasonal expectations; they were gifts from the heart.

Such symbols of friendship needn't wait for special occasions. "When you see something that you think she'd like, buy it and send it to her," advised Betsy Alden. "It doesn't have to be a birthday or Christmas."

During her officers' training, Army physical therapist Charlene Guardia received regular C.A.R.E. packages from her high school friend Leanne. "She sent me homemade cookies lots of times," Charlene recalled. "She sent me socks with bats on them at Halloween, little cute things like that. She's a very thoughtful person that way. She's a good friend to have."

Real estate agent Jody Miller, forty-seven, had two friends who understood the art of giving gifts from the heart. Heather had a gorgeous hand-knit ski sweater. When Jody was going out to someplace casually elegant, Heather would urge her to borrow it. "I'd keep it in a plastic bag the whole time and only wear it to a place where I wouldn't get something on it," Jody explained. "Then one day, she gave it to me."

The other friend, Loraine, a ceramicist, gave Jody and her husband graceful pots with exquisite glazes. "Living with art that you love that somebody you love made—that makes a friendship so rich," Jody observed.

✤ 13. Learn to End Friendships ✤ Without Making Enemies

From the time we're toddlers, we're taught that friendship is forever. Sometimes that's the way female friendship functions. But sometimes there comes a point when even a once-close friendship just doesn't work for us any longer. It isn't pleasurable. It isn't supportive. Maybe it's even mutated into something destructive—one of the enabling, foul-weather, draining, or treacherous relationships described earlier.

We shed friends naturally as we move from place to place or job to job. Preserving a friendship under such circumstances takes work. If a woman doesn't want it to continue, extricating herself is simply a matter of doing nothing.

"I just don't call her," one seventy-five-year-old woman said of a former friend who lived in another town and finally made one too many nasty comments when she was drinking.

But to actively end a friendship—that's different. Merely acknowledging that we might want to stop being someone's friend brings a nagging sense of failure and guilt. As women we're brought up to avoid hurting others, especially those who've made themselves vulnerable to us, as friends have.

Martha Holstein did manage to end a friendship with grace, kindness, and sensitivity. Her friend, who was single, wanted the relationship to satisfy all her emotional needs. Martha was married, had two young children, and was in graduate school. She just couldn't commit to being there whenever her friend needed her. She tried disentangling herself by pleading her genuinely jammed schedule, but her friend responded by becoming even more demanding. Finally, Martha said simply, "I can't be the friend you want me to be."

That statement was honest in the most literal sense. And it worked. Martha freed herself from the relationship. But she did it with minimum damage to her friend's ego. In those few, well-considered words, she assumed the burden of inadequacy herself, instead of placing it on her dependent and hence vulnerable friend. It's like a boyfriend saying "I can't love you the way you deserve," instead of saying "I don't love you."

⁓ 14. Reconnect with Old Friends ⁓

After emerging from her failed marriage, the first thing Meg wanted to do, even before she went apartment-hunting, was rebuild the female friendships she'd let disintegrate. "I had a lot of friends in California," she said. "I flew to San Francisco and started there with those friends and worked my way down the coast to San Diego. I felt: I've got to get my friends back."

Weddings, graduations, class reunions, and similar occasions make excellent opportunities for reestablishing contact. During the event itself, the primary participants may be too busy to do much beyond say hello, but you can always follow up later.

In the fourteen years since Lucinda had moved from Southern California to San Francisco, Karen Hyatt had lost touch with her until one day an announcement arrived: Lucinda's son was graduating from college. Karen wrote a note explaining that she worked near the campus and could come to the graduation. A couple of days later, she came home to find a message on her answering machine saying that

Lucinda and her family were so excited to hear from her. Although they couldn't get her a ticket to the graduation, they wanted her to join them for dinner afterward.

"It was wonderful," Karen told me. "Lucinda and I were sitting in the restaurant with tears streaming down our faces. And I just looked at her and said, 'You know, nothing changes, does it?' And she said, 'No.' "

❧ 15. Be Open to New Friends ❧

Even if friendships and friends were immortal, we would need fresh friends to stimulate new personal growth. Current friends are one of the best sources of new friends. When a good friend says she thinks you'd like someone, take the trouble to meet her. For one thing, a mutual friend is in a position to judge how well your personalities will mesh. For another, in the course of suggesting the introduction, she has probably presented your best traits, as well as your common interests, to each other, making it even easier to connect.

Luanne Stovall heard that Martha, a fellow artist, was going to be at a particular party. Because both the hostess and another close friend had said they thought they'd enjoy each other, Luanne made a point of engaging Martha in conversation. "She came with very high recommendations," Luanne explained. Predisposed to hit it off, the two women experienced immediate rapport and quickly became friends.

My friend Carol Safran, forty-nine, told me she thought establishing a friendship took "a certain cadence." She explained: "Some people you see seven nights a week after you meet them and other people every other week. That's how it develops. If you have a revealing or intimate conversation, you don't necessarily want to have another one of those the next day."

❧ 16. Help Your Daughters and Mothers ❧ Have Strong Friendships

Because children learn by example, the best way a woman can assure that her daughter enjoys the rich rewards of female friendships is to nurture and value her own. But girls need direct friendship guidance and practical support, as well. Every time an adult woman asks a girl about her friends, every time she listens to a girl's accounts of friendship's joys and troubles and treats them as seriously as she would the pleasures and pains of romance, every time she includes the girl's friends in plans or ferries the girl to and from her friend's house, she helps build a priceless legacy.

"My parents have always stressed my friendships," said Sherri Jayson. "When I was younger and my friends didn't live in the same neighborhood, they would have to drive me half an hour and pick me up at the end of the day or the next night. My friends' parents would never be willing to do that."

Older women need support for their friendships, too. Daughters who help their elderly mothers fix dinner for their friends, neighbors who offer a lift to bridge club, nieces who give housebound aunts prepaid phone cards to stay in touch with distant friends honor not just the recipients but the lifelong importance of female friendship.

~ 17. Celebrate Friends and Friendships ~

Tradition is fine, but celebrating female friendship doesn't begin or end with the time-honored wedding and baby showers. Two years after Ellie Porter and Faith Lagay met, Faith invited Ellie to join her for a sisterhood Christmas. Ellie was single, Faith was divorced, and Faith's daughter, who had a little girl of her own, was recently separated. In addition to providing a festive way to mark the holiday, the new ritual deepened the friendship.

"Women are making ceremonies to celebrate the cycles of their lives," observed Rabbi Lynn Gottlieb, who wrote about the subject in her book *She Who Dwells Within: A Feminist Vision of Renewed Judaism.* The age for Jewish bat mitzvahs, thirteen, corresponds roughly to the start of menstruation, the biological landmark for a girl's transition to womanhood. Further milestones follow: High school and college graduation, a wedding, and the birth of a first child all offer opportunities for celebration. So do crossing into menopause, becoming a grandmother, and retiring from paid work.

To create an appropriate ritual to celebrate a friend's transition from one season of life to another, Lynn recommended asking her to suggest objects that symbolize the season she is leaving and the one she is entering and arranging them on an altar. The symbols needn't be serious to be significant. For example, a girl turning thirteen might include a Barbie doll for her childhood and a bra for her adolescence. The girls and women invited to the party contribute stories about entering that next stage, drawn either from their own lives or from family or cultural history.

But even the simplest shared rituals strengthen female friendship's bond. "Being with my friends is always a celebration," said Claudia Vangerven, an English professor at the University of Colorado. "We go see a movie, and it really knocks us out. We can go get coffee afterward and talk and laugh and giggle. So when I am with my friends, it is a celebration of one another, of openness."

Epilogue

❧

E-mail Is Female, and Other Thoughts on the Future of Female Friendship

"Do you know about the guinea pig chat room?" Bernice Torregrossa asked me at book club.

"It's on-line, for people who have guinea pigs," continued Bernice, whose twelve-year-old daughter had one as a pet. "You trade information about the different breeds, about what you feed them, about what to do if they get sick. And in the course of that, you may get to be friends."

Visiting this chat room once in a while, Bernice had noticed that two women had shifted from chatting solely about guinea pigs to asking about each other's lives. Like talks over coffee or on the phone, these cyber conversations danced in and out of personal and general topics. It all sounded so relaxed, easy-flowing, and virtually cost free.

E-mail is female, I thought. Like the telephone, it's a medium that fits the way girls and women relate. And it seems to be facilitating friendship, easing connection, eroding the barrier of geographical distance. It's a good thing, too, considering how global our lives are becoming.

As I conducted the interviews for this book, girls and women kept bringing up the impact this technology was having on their friendships. Suddenly, we can preserve contact over thousands of miles and a dozen time zones, without worrying about running up astronomical phone bills or synchronizing those few hours when we and our friend in Hong Kong are both awake and at home. Jokes and recipes and baby pictures have gone global. So have the mundane details of daily life. Women who wouldn't have called across town to say, "It's raining so hard here I can't see the street" or "I just finished Amy Tan's new book and can't wait for you to read it" will tap that line and send it off. Several women told me they E-mailed their close friends three or four times a day.

Other forces are at work on the bonds between us, as well. Social attitudes are changing. Women are finally beginning to value themselves and each other fully. Women are making clear to their husbands and lovers from the start that their female friendships are essential, and we are insisting on time for them.

As we begin to accept friendship as a primary relationship, we've started to invent ways to acknowledge it. Our culture marks wedding anniversaries and births of children, but not starts of friendships. "I sometimes will note on a letter to a friend that we are now celebrating the twentieth anniversary of our friendship," said Carol Edgar. "I'm sure in other cultures this may exist, but in our culture, there's just no honoring friendship. It's a huge gap."

Months after our interview, Pam Canty E-mailed me: "I'm now quite interested in pursuing the idea of how women are considering 'the long run.' What will boomer women be doing twenty or twenty-five years from now? I hear a significant amount of fear, but no succinct ideas as to how to dispel it. Most of us don't know what to do. Where will we be, and what's going to happen?"

Many of the young and middle-aged women I interviewed told me that they weren't sure what they would be doing in their later years, but whatever it was, they planned to be doing it together. Speaking of her closest friend, psychoanalyst Jane Burka said, "We're two peas in a pod. We make jokes about we're going to retire together, and she'll have a dog and I'll have a cat."

Sharon Healy spoke of eventually living with a group of friends, as she had as a student. She told me: "My friends have said that we would have to make sure that one of us could see, one of us could walk, one of us could hear—that everybody had one of the senses, so we could take care of one another."

Two women told me they'd gone with friends to look for land to buy together. They planned to build a cluster of small houses, to use for weekend getaways now but full time once they retired. One of them was having a lawyer draw up papers for a joint purchase. Another woman went to far as to sketch out a floor plan of shared housing for me. For other women, the idea was still abstract: They weren't sure just which friends they'd want to live with. They knew they wanted a big, open central kitchen where everyone could cook together. Whatever they built or bought with friends had to have room for visiting children and grandchildren.

As I listened to these descriptions, I thought at first that the women giving them were expressing nostalgia for the 1960s group living arrangements that many of them had experienced as students. But as I kept hearing variations on this residential theme, I detected an underlying message: These women had recognized the sustaining value of female friendship. They knew that their friends had brought them joy and comfort, laughter and insight, that their friends had helped them cope with adversity and develop into their best selves. Whether or not these women and their friends would actually spend their later years living together in the same house, they fully intended to be integral parts of each others' lives through the decades, right to the end. Discussing their fantasies about shared housing was a way to express this commitment. What they were describing was a metaphor for the shared future of female friendship.

Whatever external trappings our connections with one another take in the coming years, whatever ways emerging technologies help us maintain and deepen connection, whatever practical arrangements we adopt in order to make room for friends in our lives, more and more women are taking the first steps toward enjoying the full pleasure and power of female friendship: They are acknowledging it as a primary bond. They are nurturing their friends and being nurtured by them in return. They are empathizing with one another. As a consequence, they are becoming stronger, more giving, more fulfilled; becoming better partners in all their relationships; becoming more effective at work, at home, and in the world around them. Above all, they are experiencing the comfort and joy of connection.

Appendix A

꘏

The Friendship Interviews: Method and Questions

This book began as I observed my mother-in-law and her friends and contemplated my own female friendships. As I started to formulate the concepts I eventually addressed, I began talking to a handful of my friends about their friendships. As I did this, I began reading everything I could find about the subject. I began with books and went on to dissertation abstracts and articles in peer-review journals in the social sciences. Scattered across the country were psychologists, psychiatrists, sociologists, and anthropologists who offered particular insights into specific aspects of female friendship. Because I wanted my book to be both well-grounded and geographically representative, I decided to arrange to speak in person with these two dozen experts and to set up interviews with girls and women in the same communities.

I interviewed 204 girls and women across the United States. The youngest girl I interviewed for this book was eight, the oldest woman ninety. Three-quarters of these girls and women were of European heritage, 11 percent African, 9 percent Hispanic, 3 percent Asian, and 2 percent Native American. Because the immigrant experience forms a significant part of contemporary American life, I included 6 women who were born in other countries; all had become naturalized citizens or permanent legal residents. Eighty of the women were married and living with their husbands; 3 were separated, 48 divorced, and 12 widowed. Thirteen, including 2 who were divorced, volunteered that they were lesbian. Nine lesbians and 5 unmarried heterosexuals described themselves as living with someone in a committed, long-term relationship.

Most of the adults I interviewed had college educations and fell into that broad bulge of the socioeconomic spectrum that ranges from stable working class to upper middle class, but I included a few women struggling to stay above the poverty line and at least two with annual incomes (as opposed to assets) in the millions.

The interviews ranged from forty-five minutes to five hours, but most were one-and-a-half to two hours long. I taped the interviews and had them transcribed verbatim. I asked the questions orally, rather than presenting the women with a written questionnaire. The questions follow.

Women's Friendship Interview Questions

1. For the book I'm writing, I'd like to talk to you about your friendships, primarily close ones with other women. I'd like to begin with those you have now, then

move back through your life by decade. But first, I need to know some things about you. How do you spell your name?

2. May I use your real name, or would you prefer that I use a pseudonym, which would be a first name only? If you'd prefer a pseudonym, is there one you'd especially like me to use? Tell me also if you'd like me to conceal other identifying details about you. If you'd like me to conceal your identity when I write about any specific friendship or incident, just tell me so when it comes up in the course of this interview.

3. How old are you?

4. What's your occupation?

5. What's the highest level of education you've achieved?

6. What do you consider your ethnic background? How much education did your parents have, and how did they earn their living? Are you married or in a long-term primary relationship? Have you ever been? Do you have children? If so, how old are they? Do you have sisters or brothers? If so, how close to you are they in age? [For women with sisters, I asked later for them to compare their relationships with their sisters to their relationships with their close friends.]

7. Not including family members or past or current spouses or romantic partners, how many close friends do you have now? How many of each gender? Is one closer than the others, or is there one you'd particularly like to tell me about? Let's start with her. [If one, even the closest, was a man, I talked about that relationship last, and in contrast.]

8. [For each close friend we had time to discuss] How long have you known her? How did you meet? What attracted you to her? When and how did you know that you'd become close friends?

9. Do you live in the same city/town/area? Have you ever?

10. How often do you get together, talk on the phone, write each other? What do you do together?

11. Can you identify any stages or milestones in the development of this friendship? Do you recall anything happening that has deepened or solidified your relationship, made you feel really committed to each other?

12. What do you value most about her or about your friendship? Is there a crisis she helped you get through, a time she was there for you in an important way? Have you ever had a serious disagreement or a fight? How did you repair the friendship, or did it weaken or dissolve? How do you handle conflict, competition?

13. [After we'd discussed at least one current close friend.] Which friend could you call at three A.M. if you were having romantic, family, or work problems? If you had a practical emergency, such as your car breaking down somewhere remote or your house/apartment becoming uninhabitable? To go to a movie, take a vacation with, share some other enjoyable activity?

14. Have you ever lost a close friend through disagreement? What happened? Through a move? Because your or her romantic partner, parents, or others didn't like her/you? For a reason you haven't figured out? [Where time allowed, I used these same questions to discuss additional current friendships and friendships earlier in life.]

15. What qualities do you most value in a friend/friendship? [If the woman being interviewed isn't a middle-class, heterosexual Euro-American] Are there any friendship traditions or types that are unique or especially significant to your background?
16. Is there anything about your mother's/daughter's friendship patterns that might help me?
17. Is there anything I haven't asked about that you think I should include?
18. What questions about female friendship would you like to see this book answer?

Although each interview addressed every question, in most cases, women used these as jumping-off points, adding experiences and insights that I hadn't prompted directly. As I spoke with sociologists and psychologists, I learned that this open-ended method of interviewing is common in social science research.

Finally, I tallied the responses. When a girl or woman responded that she didn't know the answer to a question, I went on to the next. For this reason, the responses for qualities valued in friendship in general and the people chosen for help and fun don't add up to 204. The results follow.

Tally of Friendship Data

1. WHAT ATTRACTS (*for each friendship, not for each person interviewed*)

shared interests	48
humor/made me laugh	47
physical appearance/presence/style	43
shared outsider status	30
shared situation	25
intelligence	20
extroversion/outgoingness	20
daring/spirit	16
naturalness/genuineness	13
sweetness/niceness/considerateness	12
optimism/positive attitude	7
strength/energy	7
creativity	5
admirable qualities	4
similar personality	2
charisma/magnetism	2
taste	2
lack of judgmentalism	1

2. FREQUENCY OF CONTACT

	PERSON	PHONE	MAIL	E-MAIL
daily/ every other day	25	10		8
two or three times a week	16	18	5	1
weekly/three times a month	31	18	4	1

	PERSON	PHONE	MAIL	E-MAIL
two times a month	17	16		1
monthly	12	15	1	3
every six weeks/two months	14	5	5	
two to six times a year	26	12	2	
once a year or less frequently	18	2	5	

3. QUALITIES VALUED MOST ABOUT PARTICULAR FRIEND

dependability/being there for me	27
continuity/history/really knowing me	19
admirable qualities	17
humor/making me laugh	16
lack of judgmentalism	12
sharing a spiritual/philosophical interest	12
intellectual stimulation	11
loyalty	10
sharing a favorite work/leisure activity	9
acceptance of me as I am	9
understanding of me	8
good nature/kindness	8
trust/safety	6
good listener/empathic	6
her love/feeling/friendship for me	6
encouragement of my growth	5
sharing resources	5
skill at communication	5
comfort	4
fun	3
good judgment	3
honesty/emotional openness	2
accepting help/making me feel needed	2
not too demanding of time/support	2
not competitive	1
equality/reciprocity	1
difference	1
high self-esteem	1
always taking my side	1

4. QUALITIES VALUED MOST IN FEMALE FRIENDSHIP GENERALLY

honesty/emotional openness	19
dependability/being there for me	15
humor	13
trust	13
loyalty	12

acceptance of me as I am	8
intellectual stimulation	7
willingness to listen	3
equality/reciprocity	2
her love/feeling/friendship for me	2
caring about others/altruism	2
respect	2
sharing a spiritual/philosophical interest	2
virtue/character	2
accepting help/making me feel needed	2
lack of judgmentalism	1
empathy	1
ease of communication	1
warmth	1
encouragement of my growth	1
knowing me thoroughly	1
integrity	1
decency	1
diversity	1
sharing resources	1
being polite/friendly	1
optimism/positive outlook	1

5. WHOM WOULD YOU PICK FOR THE FOLLOWING:

	FEMALE	MALE	RELATIVE	ACQUAINTANCE	HIRED	SELF
personal problem	125	5	27	1	2	9
practical help	40	31	27	5	13	
vacation/movie/other fun	102	8	9	6		2

Appendix B

✝✧✝

The Friendship Interviews: Participants

Most of the 204 girls and women I interviewed about their friendships gave me permission to identify them when quoting them. They appear by their real names in the body of the book. A few asked to remain completely anonymous and to be referred to only by pseudonyms. Others preferred that I use pseudonyms in the text but agreed to let me acknowledge them by name elsewhere. They are as follows: Alice Abbott, Charlotte Abbott, Nora Antil, Debbie Bernsten, Shelly Branch, Bonnie Bryant, Kathryn Casey, Ann Garry, Martha Gehman, Lorna Hall, Marilyn Hazelton, Betty Hoskins, Teresa Kindle, Shan Leonard, Shannon emal-Lundgren, Kathryn Mazaika, Jennie McDonald, Mildred McKenzie, Rochelle Miller, Lynn Randolph, Antoinette Ross, Jyoti Thottam, Saralee Tiede, and Sue Vandergrift.

In addition to the social scientists and clinicians I thanked in the Acknowledgments, the following generously shared their time and their insights with me: Joyce Anter, Frederique Apffel-Marglin, Lynda Behrendt, Nancy Busch, Beth Doll, Barbara Ellman, Chava Frankfort-Nachmias, Phyllis Gillman, Carol Goodenow, Christine Hejinian, Madelyn Iris, Stanley Shapiro, Beverly Tatum, Jeanne Tschann, Susan Turell, Linda Walsh, Nancy Whittier, and Lisa Wood. All of them made this book stronger by deepening my understanding of women's development and of female friendship.

Notes

Introduction

XIII Family therapist Barbara Ellman . . . : Barbara Ellman, telephone interview by author, 12 November 1992.

XIV "So blind have we been . . .": Lillian B. Rubin, *Just Friends: The Role of Friendship in Our Lives* (New York: Harper & Row, 1985), p. 9.

XIV . . . six out of ten of whom spend their last years . . . : U.S. Bureau of the Census, *Statistical Abstract of the United States: 1998* 118th ed. (Washington, D.C., 1998), Table 62.

Part One
THE MEANING OF FEMALE FRIENDSHIP

1 What Our Great-Grandmothers Knew

4 Writing in the mid-1600, . . . : Lillian Faderman, *Surpassing the Love of Men: Romantic Friendship and Love between Women from the Renaissance to the Present* (New York: William Morrow, 1981), pp. 70–71.

5 To Phillips's contemporaries . . . : Rashelle F. Trefousse, "The Reputation of Katherine Phillips" (abstract of Ph.D. diss., City University of New York, 1990).

5 Far from finding close bonds between women threatening . . . : Faderman, *Surpassing the Love of Men*, p. 72.

5 . . . by the mid-eighteenth century . . . : Ibid., p. 109.

5 This may be why one true-life romance . . . : Ibid., pp. 120–21.

5 . . . the popular wisdom of the seventeenth . . . : Ibid., p. 80.

6 "How I love you & . . .": letter from Jeannie Field Musgrove to Sarah Butler Wister quoted in Carroll Smith-Rosenberg, "The Female World of Love and Ritual: Relations between Women in Nineteenth-Century America," *Signs* 1, no. 1 (Autumn 1975): 4.

6 Some scholars of eighteenth- . . . : among them, Lisa Moore, " 'Something More Tender Still than Friendship': Romantic Friendship in Early-Nineteenth-Century England," *Feminist Studies* 18, no. 3 (Fall 1992): 500.

6 ". . . assumed an emotional centrality . . .": Smith-Rosenberg, "Female World": 8.

6 At this time, it was not uncommon for a woman . . . : Faderman, *Surpassing the Love of Men*, p. 174.

6   A few months after they met at college . . . : Carol Lasser, " 'Let Us Be Sisters Forever': The Sororal Model of Nineteenth-Century Female Friendship," *Signs*, 14, no. 1 (Autumn 1988): 158

7   The practice pervaded all classes.: Ibid., p. 180.

7   As early as the mid-1700s . . . : Sheryl Anne Kujawa, " 'A Precious Season at the Throne of Grace': Sarah Haggar Wheaten Osborn, 1714–1796" (abstract of Ph.D. diss., Boston College, 1993).

7   . . . Thomas Paine, William Blake, and . . . : Candace Ward, introductory note to Mary Wollstonecraft, *A Vindication of the Rights of Woman* (Mineola, N.Y.: Dover Publications, 1996).

7   . . . but her primary source of emotional support . . . : Jennifer Lorch, "The Absent Centre: Thoughts on the Friendship between Mary Wollstonecraft and Fanny Blood," *Studies in Sexual Politics* no. 26–27 (October 1988): 23–41.

7   The letters and journals penned in the 1800s . . . : Elizabeth Jameson, "Women as Workers, Women as Civilizers," in *The Women's West,* ed. Susan Armitage and Elizabeth Jameson (Norman, Okla.: University of Oklahoma Press, 1987), p. 149.

7   "For women who went West . . .": Elizabeth Jameson, telephone interview by author 22 July 1996.

7   The American West was a notable exception . . . : Katherine Harris, "Homesteading in Northeastern Colorado, 1873–1920: Sex Roles and Women's Experience," in *Women's West,* p. 169.

7   "All through those early years . . . ": Elizabeth Hamsten, *Read This Only to Yourself: The Private Writings of Midwestern Women, 1880–1910* (Bloomington, Ind.: Indiana University Press, 1982), p. 61.

8   In 1886 Bee Randolph . . . : Harris, "Homesteading," p. 174.

8   Back East, women who decided to pursue . . . : Lillian Faderman, "Nineteenth-Century Boston Marriage as a Possible Lesson for Today," in *Boston Marriages: Romantic but Asexual Relationships among Contemporary Lesbians,* ed. Esther D. Rothblum and Kathleen A. Brehony (Amherst, Mass.: University of Massachusetts Press, 1993), pp. 29–30.

8   Late nineteenth-century author Sarah Orne Jewett . . . : Faderman, *Surpassing the Love of Men,* pp. 197–201.

8   Supported by this stable and caring . . . : Gail C. Keating, "Sarah Orne Jewett's Experiences with Mentoring and Communities of Women" (abstract of Ed.D. diss., Temple University, 1987).

8   But after Sarah's death in 1907 . . . : Faderman, *Surpassing the Love of Men,* p. 197.

8   In 1892 *Psychopathia Sexualis* . . . : William H. Harris and Judith S. Levey, ed., *The New Columbia Encyclopedia* (New York: Columbia University Press, 1975), p. 1500.

8   . . . describing "inversion," or the adoption . . . : Faderman, *Surpassing the Love of Men,* p. 314.

8   Five years later, British psychologist Havelock Ellis . . . : *Columbia Encyclopedia,* p. 858.

8   . . . likening one of his wife's . . . : Liz Stanley, "Romantic Friendship? Some

Issues in Researching Lesbian History and Biography," *Women's History Review* 1, no. 2 (June 1992): 193–216.

9   Sigmund Freud's 1905 *Three Essays* . . . : *Columbia Encyclopedia,* p. 1016.

9   Since 1869, German sexologists . . . : Faderman, *Surpassing the Love of Men,* p. 239.

9   Mary Grew of Providence, Rhode Island, . . . : Ibid., p. 27.

9   During the 1910s and 1920s, women began to . . . : Christina Simmons, "Companionate Marriage and the Lesbian Threat," *Frontiers* 4, no. 3 (Fall 1979): 54–59.

10   "In this framework, traditional . . .": Ibid, p. 54.

10   Harkening back to the alliances forged . . . : Doris Kearns Goodwin, *No Ordinary Time: Franklin and Eleanor Roosevelt: The Home Front in World War II* (New York: Touchstone/Simon & Schuster, 1994), pp. 207–208.

10   English writer Vera Brittain's friend . . . : Rita Miriam Kissen, *Vera Brittain: Writing a Life* (abstract of Ph.D. diss., University of Massachusetts, 1986).

10   Poets Marianne Moore and Elizabeth Bishop . . . : Robin Riley Fast, "Moore, Bishop, and Oliver: Thinking Back, Re-Seeing the Sea," *Twentieth Century Literature* 39, no. 3 (Fall 1993): 364.

10   But the aspirations promoted for women . . . : Brett Harvey, *The Fifties: A Women's Oral History* (New York: HarperCollins, 1993), p. 116.

10   By the 1950s, women were told that . . . : Ibid., p. 17.

11   As Susan Faludi observed . . . : Susan Faludi, *Backlash: The Undeclared War Against American Women* (New York: Crown Publishers, 1991), pp. 52–53.

11   Of the six million women who joined . . . : Susan J. Douglas, *Where the Girls Are: Growing Up Female with the Mass Media* (New York: Times Books, 1994), pp. 46–47.

11   Very few of the female rituals . . . : Smith-Rosenberg, "Female World," p. 22.

12   . . . the sense of anxious emptiness Betty Friedan . . . : Betty Friedan, *The Feminine Mystique* (New York: Laurel/Dell, 1983), p. 20.

13   In the wake of those first heady . . . : Anita Shreve, *Women Together, Women Alone* (New York: Viking, 1989), p. 5.

13   As the movement's motto . . . : Ibid., p. 44.

13   "One of the greatest contributions . . .": Barbara Ellman, telephone interview by author, 12 November 1992.

13   Studies have revealed a marked . . . : One of the most extensive of these, a study conducted at Ohio State University, involved 1,427 women. V. Richardson, "Clinical-Historical Aspects of Friendship Deprivation Among Women," *Social Work Research and Abstracts* 20, no. 1 (1984): 19–24.

15   Barbara Tuttle, the only daughter . . . : Harvey, *The Fifties,* pp. 25–27.

16   When sociologist Helen Gouldner discussed . . . : Helen Gouldner and Mary Symons Strong, *Speaking of Friendship: Middle-Class Women and Their Friends* (New York: Greenwood Press, 1987), pp. 107–108.

17   One reason women born after 1950 feel free . . . : Caryl S. Avery, "What Kind of Friend Are You?" *New Woman,* July 1990, P. 43.

19 I'd been told, for example, that working-class . . . : Helen Gouldner, interview by author, Wilmington, Del., 26 March 1996.

19 . . . working-class female friendships emphasize . . . : Karen Walker, "Between Friends: Class, Gender, and Friendship" (abstract of Ph.D. diss., University of Pennsylvania, 1993).

22 "There's a shared experience that women of color . . .": Beverly Tatum, interview by author Northampton, Mass., 5 April 1996.

23 When sociologist Helen Gouldner interviewed . . . : Gouldner and Strong, *Speaking of Friendship,* p. 33.

26 For the 800,000 individuals who move to . . . : from the 804,416 figure for 1994, *1996 World Almanac and Book of Facts* (Mahwah, N.J.: Funk & Wagnalls, 1995), p. 393.

26 . . . interpreting different nonverbal cues . . . : Anna Marie Dew and Colleen Eard, "The Effects of Ethnicity and Culturally Congruent and Incongruent Nonverbal Behaviors on Interpersonal Attraction," *Journal of Applied Social Psychology* 23, no. 17 (September 1993): 1376–89; and Adeyemi I. Idowu and Issa A. Alao, "Touching Behavior among Nigerian Undergraduate Students: An Exploratory Study," *Nigerian Journal of Guidance and Counseling* 2, no. 2 (August 1986): 34–47.

26 . . . developing traits considered socially . . . : Examining what British and Hong Kong Chinese students at a university in England looked for in friends, Robin Goodwin and Daniel Tang reported that sensitivity and humor counted most for the British and creativity and money-mindedness for the Chinese. R. Goodwin and D. Tang, "Preferences for Friends and Close Relationships Partners: A Cross-Cultural Comparison," *Journal of Social Psychology* 131, no. 4 (August 1991): 579–81.

26 To compound the problem, immigrants to the United States . . . : Shalini Dev Bhutani, "A Study of Asian Indian Women in the United States: The Reconceptualization of Self" (abstract of Ph.D. diss., University of Pennsylvania, 1994); and Aloma Mary Mendoza, "An Exploratory Study on the Socioeconomic, Cultural and Sociopsychological Experiences of Caribbean-Born Women in Ontario, Canada" (abstract of Ph.D. diss., York University, 1990).

2 What Friendship Is—and Isn't

29 "It's only just recently in our culture . . .": Helen Gouldner, interview by author in Wilmington, Del., 26 March 1996. *New York Times* health columnist Jane E. Brody touched on some of the research linking friendship and other social support to physical health in the 5 February 1992 edition, p. B8.

29 . . . helps us maintain a sense of social reality . . . : Dorothy Jerrome, "Good Company: The Sociological Implications of Friendship," *Sociological Review* 32, no. 4 (November 1984): 696–718.

29 Addressing the annual meeting of the Institute for Contemporary Psychotherapy . . . : James S. Grotstein, "On Human Bonding and of Human Bondage: The Role of Friendship in Intimacy," *Contemporary Psychotherapy Review* 5 (Fall 1989): 5–32.

29 . . . the women she studied placed . . . : Beverly Minker Schydlowsky, "Friendships Among Women in Mid-Life" (abstract of Ph.D. diss., The Fielding Institute, 1983).

30 Most of the girls and women I talked to . . . : Sociologists have found a similar
range in numbers of close friends. J. L. Barkas, "Friendship Patterns Among
Young Urban Single Women" (abstract of Ph.D. diss., City University of New
York, 1983).

33 "One thing I react very negatively to . . .": Barbara Ellman, telephone interview
by author, 2 November 1992.

34 "Women naturally create . . .": Joan Berzoff, interview by author, in North-
hampton, Mass., 5 April 1996.

35 Married women, in particular . . . : Stacey J. Oliker, *Best Friends and Marriage:
Exchange Among Women* (Berkeley, Calif.: University of California Press, 1989),
p. 113.

35 Another practical function friendships . . . : Kathleen Sullivan Ricker, "The
Friendship Patterns of Two Cohort Groups of Women in Three Career Lifestyles" (abstract of Ph.D. diss., University of Denver, 1987).

36 "We have always done what . . .": Berzoff, 5 April 1996.

36 Some research has even suggested that . . . : J. Philippe Rushton, "Genetic
Similarity, Human Altruism, and Group Selection," *Behavior and Brain Sciences*
12, no. 3 (September 1989): 503–59.

36 Research suggests that friends . . . : Pri P. Shah and Karen A. Jehn, "Do Friends
Perform Better Than Acquaintances? The Interaction of Friendship, Conflict,
and Task. Special Issue: Relationships in Group Decision and Negotiation,"
Group Decision and Negotiation 2, no. 2, (June 1993): 149–65.

36 "It is the kind of spontaneity . . .": Steve Duck and Paul H. Wright, "Reexamining Gender Differences in Same-Gender Friendships: A Close Look at Two
Kinds of Data," *Sex Roles* 28, no. 11/12 (1993): 726.

37 "Expressing anger to an intimate . . .": Oliker, *Best Friends and Marriage,* p. 127.

38 In her studies of both women in therapy . . . : Berzoff, 5 April 1996.

38 When Lionel Tiger's *Men in Groups* . . . : Lionel Tiger, *Men in Groups* (New
York: Random House, 1969), pp. 41–54.

39 As recently as the late 1970s . . . : Paul H. Wright, "Men's Friendships, Wom-
en's Friendships and the Alleged Inferiority of the Latter," *Sex Roles* 8, no. 1
(January 1982): 1–3.

39 When, inspired by the women's movement . . . : Richard Aukett, Jane Ritchie,
and Kathryn Mill, "Gender Differences in Friendship Patterns," *Sex Roles* 19,
no. 1/2 (July 1988): 57; and Sandra Parker, "Conceptions of Friendship: How
Women and Men Perceive Themselves and Others in the Context of Their
Friendships" (abstract of M.A. thesis, University of British Columbia, 1990).

39 Paul H. Wright, one of the early . . . : Wright, "Men's Friendships," 8.

39 Many researchers have observed that men tend . . . : Karen Walker, "Men,
Women, and Friendship: What They Say, What They Do," *Gender and Society*
8, no. 2 (June 1994): 246–65.

39 Others contend that the most frequent reason . . . : Duck and Wright, "Reexamining Gender," *Sex Roles*: 715.

39 But even when the primary purpose is conversation . . . : Lynne R. Davidson and Lucile Duberman, "Friendship: Communication and Interactional Patterns in Same-Sex Dyads," *Sex Roles* 8 no. 8 (August 1982): 809–22.

39 Women, on the other hand, interweave . . . : Ibid.

39 Women's friendships are generally more personal . . . : Robert R. Bell, "Friendships of Women and of Men," *Psychology of Women Quarterly* 5, no. 3 (Spring 1981): 402–17.

39 Women care more about giving one another . . . : Jeanne Marie Tschann, "Adult Friendship: Effects of Gender and Life-Stage on Closeness, Meaning of Friendship and Patterns of Socializing" (abstract of Ph.D. diss., University of California–Santa Cruz, 1983).

39 "I think intimacy is greatly overrated . . .": John Douard, interview by author, 16 October 1995 in Galveston, Tex.

40 Just because males in our culture . . . : Fiona Hart, "The Construction of Masculinity in Men's Friendships: Misogyny, Heterosexism and Homophobia," *Resources for Feminist Research* 19, no. 3/4 (September–December 1990): 60–67.

40 . . . that doesn't mean that men . . . : Gary Phillip Cotter, "Men's Same-Sex Friendships: An Expansion of the Current Intimacy Paradigm" (abstract of Ph.D. diss., The Fielding Institute, 1993).

40 . . . but between heterosexual men . . . : Barbara Kraker, "The Relationship of Gender, Homophobia and Beliefs about Homosexuality to Self-Disclosing Behavior in Same-Sex Dyads" (abstract of Ph.D. diss., New York University, 1986).

40 On the other hand, when women open up . . . : Kim G. Dolgin, Leslie Meyer, and Janet Schwartz, "Effects of Gender, Target's Gender, Topic, and Self-Esteem on Disclosure to Best and Midling Friends," *Sex Roles* 25, no. 5/6 (September 1991): 312.

41 Differences in the patterns . . . : Joyce F. Benenson, "Gender Differences in Social Networks," *Journal of Early Adolescence* 10, no. 4 (November 1990): 472–95.

41 For men, the number of close male friends . . . : Beverly Minker Schydlowsky, "Friendships Among Women in Mid-Life" (abstract of Ph.D. diss., The Fielding Institute, 1983).

41 . . . while other studies indicate . . . : Claude S. Fischer and Stacey J. Oliker, "A Research Note on Friendship, Gender, and the Life Cycle," *Social Forces* 62, no. 1 (September 1983): 124–33.

41 From middle to late life . . . : Marion Crawford, "What Is a Friend?" *New Society* 42, no. 785 (October 20, 1977): 116–17.

41 For 80 percent of its existence . . . : William H. Harris and Judith S. Levey, ed., *The New Columbia Encyclopedia* (New York: Columbia University Press, 1975), p. 1677.

41 Men went off together to track . . . : Janet Mancini Billson, *Keepers of the Culture:*

The Power of Tradition in Women's Lives (New York: Lexington Books/The Free Press, 1995), pp. 59–60.

41 A study of Polish university students . . . : Valerian J. Derlega and Ewa Gurnik Stepien, "Norms Regulating Self-Disclosure Among Polish University Students," *Journal of Cross-Cultural Psychology* 8, no. 3 (September 1977): 369–76.

42 ". . . that intimate relationships among men . . .": Walter L. Williams, "The Relationship Between Male-Male Friendship and Male-Female Marriage: American Indian and Asian Comparisons," in *Men's Friendships: Research on Men and Masculinities,* vol. 2, ed. Peter M. Hardi (Newbury Park, Calif.: Sage Publications, 1992), p. 186.

42 "When I bring something up, a male friend . . .": Linda Walsh, telephone interview by author, 21 August 1995.

43 Although men and women can provide . . . : Linda Sapadin, "Friendship Patterns: A Comparison of Professional Men's and Women's Cross-Sex and Same-Sex Friendships" (abstract of Ph.D. diss., City University of New York, 1986). Related to this phenomenon, clinical psychologist Gary Degroot studying male college students found that the higher the quality of their nonsexual friendships with women, the lower their anxiety about dating. Gary John Degroot, "The Relationship between Cross-Sex Friendships, Sex-Role Orientation and Dating Anxiety Among College-Age Males" (abstract of Ph.D. diss., California School of Professional Psychology, 1992).

43 In study after study, men have described . . . : Sapadin, ibid.; Richard Aukett, Jane Ritchie, and Kathryn Mill, "Gender Differences in Friendship Patterns," *Sex Roles* 19, no. 1/2 (January 1988): 57.

43 . . . while women have reported . . . : Paul H. Wright and Mary Beth Scanlon, "Gender Role Orientation and Friendship: Some Attenuation, but Gender Differences Abound," *Sex Roles* 24, no. 9/10 (May 1991): 551–66.

43 ". . . friendships that involved at least . . .": Leigh E. Elkins and Christopher Peterson, "Gender Differences in Best Friendships," *Sex Roles* 29, no. 7/8 (October 1993): 497–508.

43 In forming and maintaining a friendship with a man . . . : J. Donald O'Meara, "Cross-Sex Friendship: Four Basic Challenges of an Ignored Relationship," *Sex Roles* 21, no. 7/8 (October 1989): 525–43.

43 Her helpful suggestion doesn't diminish . . . : Susan McWilliams and Judith A. Howard, "Solidarity and Hierarchy in Cross-Sex Friendships," *Journal of Social Issues* 49, no. 3 (Fall 1993): 199.

44 If a woman is married or seriously involved . . . : Bonnie Shapiro Auerbach, "The Therapeutic Value of Friendship" (abstract of Ph.D. diss., California School of Professional Psychology, 1987).

44 A more delicate situation arises when . . . : Michael Monsour, Brigid Harris, Nancy Kurzwell, and Chris Beard, "Challenges Confronting Cross-Sex Friendships: 'Much Ado about Nothing?' " *Sex Roles* 31, no. 1/2 (July 1994): 62.

45 . . . life partnerships growing out of friendships . . . : Of the three lesbian courtship scripts Suzanna Rose, Debra Zand, and Marie A. Cini identify, the

friendship script is the most common; the other two center on romance and sexual attraction. S. Rose, D. Zand, and M. A. Cini, "Lesbian Courtship Scripts," in *Boston Marriages: Romantic but Asexual Relationships Among Contemporary Lesbians,* ed. Esther D. Rothblum and Kathleen A. Brehony (Amherst, Mass.: University of Massachusetts Press, 1993), pp. 71–74.

46 A woman may become suspicious . . . : Jeanne L. Stanley, "The Partnered Lesbian and Her Friends: The Impact of Friendship on Self-Esteem and Relationship Satisfaction" (abstract of Ph.D. diss., University of Pennsylvania, 1993).

47 "Women's friendships are extraordinarily valuable . . .": Jean Baker Miller, telephone interview by author, 5 April 1996.

47 "Friends love you, but they don't have a stake in the outcome.": Linda Walsh, telephone interview by author, 21 August 1995.

48 The less support our traditional families . . . : Auerbach, "Therapeutic Value."

48 . . . so prevalent during adolescence, . . . : Jacques D. Lempers and Dania S. Clark-Lempers, "Young, Middle, and Late Adolescents' Comparisons of the Functional Importance of Five Significant Relationships," *Journal of Youth and Adolescence* 21, no. 1 (February 1992): 53–96.

50 The majority of the three hundred men and women . . . : Lillian B. Rubin, *Just Friends: The Role of Friendship in Our Lives* (New York: Harper & Row, 1985), p. 18.

50 However, they felt freer to show family members . . . : Ibid., p. 19.

50 "For whatever our anger or disillusion . . . ": Ibid., p. 22.

51 But for a woman in her twenties, the better . . . : Frances Marie Costa, "Friendship Patterns in Young Adulthood: A Social Psychological Approach" (abstract of Ph.D. diss., University of Colorado at Boulder, 1983).

51 Because a friend's visit is a matter . . . : Gary R. Lee and Constance L. Shehan, "Social Relations and the Self-Esteem of Older Persons," *Research on Aging* 11, no. 4 (December 1989): 427–42.

52 . . . these relationships supported marriage by giving . . . : Oliker, *Best Friends,* p. 59.

52 More than half the women . . . : Ibid., p. 54.

52 Women *listen* to their friends . . . : Ibid., p. 125.

52 Surprisingly, women often express empathy . . . : Ibid., p. 125.

53 Perhaps because women are better than men . . . : Jeanne Marie Tschann, "Adult Friendship: Effects of Gender and Life-Stage on Closeness, Meaning of Friendship and Patterns of Socializing" (abstract of Ph.D. diss., University of California–Santa Cruz, 1983).

53 A husband may object to his wife's . . . : Oliker, *Best Friends,* p. 45.

54 In *Women Make the Best Friends: A Celebration* . . . : Lois Wyse, *Women Make the Best Friends: A Celebration* (New York: Simon & Schuster, 1995), pp. 148–51.

55 These heart-to-hearts help women define . . . : Sandra L. Titus, "A Function of Friendship: Social Comparisons as a Frame of Reference for Marriage," *Human Relations* 33, no. 6 (June 1980): 409–31.

55 O'Connor challenged the contention . . . : Pat O'Connor, "Women's Confidants

Outside Marriage: Shared or Competing Sources of Intimacy?" *Sociology* 25, no. 2 (May 1991): 241.

55 Oliker asserted that for the majority of women . . . : Oliker, *Best Friends,* p. xii.

55 . . . and that close friendships both support . . . : Ibid., p. 107.

56 But when women friends connect . . . : Jean Baker Miller, telephone interview by author, 5 April 1996.

56 ". . . women friends engender and reinforce . . .": Oliker, *Best Friends,* abstract.

3 The Seven Stages of Friendship

57 Examining my own friendships and those that other . . . : Clinical psychologist Joel Block and his coauthor Diane Greenberg described six developmental stages for women's friendship as "come-ons versus put-offs," "common ground: uncommon chemistry versus superficial sociability," "mutual respect versus disparaging comparisons," "trust versus mistrust," "self-disclosure versus self-enclosure," and "intimacy versus alienation." J. Block and D. Greenberg, *Women and Friendship* (New York: Franklin Watts, 1985), pp. 62–77. Sociologist Steve Duck identified four stages, after that of mutual attraction, in the development of any kind of relationship: "reducing uncertainty about the partner, exploring one another's feelings, growing together into the relationship and stabilizing the relationship." S. Duck, *Understanding Relationships* (New York: Guilford Press, 1991), p. 63.

58 For his 1961 Ph.D. dissertation . . . : Michael Gurevitch, telephone interview by author, 31 October 1996. (His dissertation, awarded by the Massachusetts Institute of Technology's Department of Political Science, was "The Social Structure of Acquaintanceship Networks.")

58 Take complaining—not the kind . . . : Diana Boxer, telephone interview by author, 20 November 1996, and her article "Social Distance and Speech Behavior: The Case of Indirect Complaints," *Journal of Pragmatics* 19, no. 2 (February 1993): 103–25.

58 While interviewing seventy-five women . . . : Helen Gouldner and Mary Symons Strong, *Speaking of Friendship: Middle-Class Women and Their Friends* (New York: Greenwood Press, 1987), p. 27.

58 First, women exclude those . . . : Ibid., p. 28.

59 . . . attitude dissimilarities like . . . : Michael Sunnafrank, "On Debunking the Attitude Similarity Myth," *Communication Monographs* 59, no. 2 (June 1992): 164–79. University of Minnesota communications specialist Sunnafrank reported that while contrary to popular belief similarity in attitudes doesn't create attraction, dissimilarity in attitudes may put people off if they discover it early enough.

59 Yet, surprisingly, acquaintances made . . . : Gouldner and Strong, *Speaking of Friendship,* p. 32.

60 "Women did not make close friends . . .": Helen Gouldner, interview by author in Wilmington, Del., 26 March 1996.

61 "Even closest couple friends . . .": Lyn Beth Bendtschneider, " 'We All Like to

Dance and Play Dominoes': The Nature and Maintenance of Couple Friends" (abstract of Ph.D. diss., University of Iowa, 1994).

62 Professional ethics dictate that . . . : Kerry Gayle Aikman, "Ethics in Psychotherapy: The Practice of Nonsexual Dual Roles" (abstract of Ph.D. diss., Loyola University of Chicago, 1994); and Sharon Kay Anderson, "A Critical Incident Study of Nonromantic/Nonsexual Relationships Between Psychologists and Former Clients" (abstract of Ph.D. diss., University of Denver, 1993).

63 Half of the more than four thousand women . . . : Victoria Secunda, "The New Woman Friendship Report," *New Woman,* August 1992, p. 73.

63 . . . some social scientists have dubbed it . . . : Arthur Aron, Donald G. Dutton, Elaine M. Aron, and Adrienne Iverson, "Experiences of Falling in Love," *Journal of Social and Personal Relationships* 6, no. 3 (August 1989): 243–57.

63 "There's sometimes this instantaneous attraction. . . .": Helen Gouldner, interview by author in Wilmington, Del., 26 March 1996.

63 Each of us has what Gouldner and Strong call . . . : Gouldner and Strong, *Speaking of Friendship,* p. 42.

63 As they talk, they look at each other . . . : Steve Duck, *Understanding Relationships* (New York: Guilford Press, 1991), p. 54.

64 "To initiate is to make a *choice* . . . ": Daniel J. Levinson in collaboration with Judy D. Levinson, *The Seasons of a Woman's Life* (New York: Alfred A. Knopf, 1996), p. 34.

64 . . . what sparks friendship is mutual behavior . . . : Duck, *Relationships,* p. 29.

65 "Usually, after an initial attraction . . .": Gouldner, 26 March 1996.

65 . . . they are more likely to arrange to get together . . . : Duck, *Relationships,* p. 35.

65 Friendships germinate best under conditions . . . : Stacey J. Oliker, *Best Friends and Marriage: Exchange Among Women* (Berkeley, Calif.: University of California Press, 1989), pp. 83–84.

65 In an article for *Cosmopolitan* . . . : Susan Jacoby, "The Delicate Art of Making Friends," *Cosmopolitan* May 1995, p. 220.

66 . . . which are off-limits . . . : When British psychologists Robin Goodwin and Iona Lee compared topic taboos between close friends in Britain and in mainland China, they found that more subjects were off-limits for Chinese than Britons and for men than for women. R. Goodwin and I. Lee, "Taboo Topics among Chinese and English Friends: A Cross-Cultural Comparison," *Journal of Cross-Cultural Psychology* 25, no. 3 (September 1994): 325–38.

67 . . . learning to read each other's facial expressions . . . : H. L. Wagner and Jayne Smith, "Facial Expression in the Presence of Friends and Strangers" *Journal of Nonverbal Behavior* 15, no. 4 (Winter 1991): 201. University of Manchester psychologists Wagner and Smith reported that women could tell a friend's emotions from her facial expression more accurately than she could a stranger's.

67 . . . anticipate reactions . . . : Ellen S. Sullins, "Interpersonal Perception Between Same-Sex Friends," *Journal of Social Behavior and Personality* 7, no. 3 (1992): 395–414.

67 . . . and gauge the appropriate amount of physical contact. . . . : Valerian J.

Derlega, Robin J. Lewis, Scott Harrison, Barbara A. Winstead, et al., "Gender Differences in the Initiation and Attribution of Tactile Intimacy," *Journal of Nonverbal Behavior* 13, no. 2 (Summer 1989): 83–96.

Note: None of the above three studies connect these abilities with any given stage of friendship development. The first two point out that people are able to read friends better than strangers or acquaintances, the third that women feel more comfortable touching their friends than men do. My own extension is that developing the ability to relate to each other in these three ways is a joint developmental task of any female friendship.

68 . . . gossip "can serve a crucial function . . .": Deborah Tannen, *You Just Don't Understand: Women and Men in Conversation* (New York: Ballantine Books, 1991), p. 96.

68 "It's like animals that have rituals . . .": Linda Walsh, telephone interview by author, 21 August 1995.

68 When a group of Temple University psychologists . . . : Marianne Jaeger, Anne Skleder, Bruce Rind, and Ralph Rosnow, "Gossip, Gossipers, Gossipees," in *Good Gossip,* ed. Robert F. Goodman and Aaron Ben-Ze'ev (Lawrence, Kan.: University Press of Kansas, 1994), pp. 154–68.

70 ". . . the amount of fun and relaxation experienced . . .": Robert B. Hays, "The Day-to-Day Functioning of Close Versus Casual Friendships," *Journal of Social and Personal Relationships* 6, no. 1 (February 1989): 21–37.

70 "Friends are often appreciated . . .": Duck, *Relationships*, p. 13.

70 . . . each incorporates the other into her inner life.: "A Study of Women's Relationships: Involvement and the Psychological Sense of Community," Karen Asher Holtzblatt (abstract of Ph.D. diss., University of Toronto, 1982).

71 Gifts also strengthen friendship . . . : Gouldner and Strong, *Speaking of Friendship,* p. 108.

71 But one form of reciprocity . . . : Ibid., p. 71.

71 "Over the long run, each . . . ,": Ibid.

72 . . . many of the women they talked to admitted . . . : Ibid., p. 30.

72 Strengthened friendships become . . . : Ibid., p. 98.

74 "That's my spot," she said . . . : Elizabeth Berg, "Losing Kate," *New Woman,* July 1993, p. 127.

76 "There were people who had deeper . . .": Lynda Marie Behrendt, telephone interview by author, 1 September 1995.

77 ". . . merged self-other boundaries.": Joan Berzoff, interview by author in Northampton, Mass., 5 April 1996.

77 ". . . almost like entering into an altered state.": Ibid., "Valued Female Friendships: Their Function in Adult Female Development" (Ed.D. diss., Boston University, 1985), p. 203.

77 "It really makes sense when . . .": Berzoff, 5 April 1996.

4 Becoming Our Best Selves: How Female Friendship Encourages Our Development

78 In 1921, when she was thirty-seven, . . . : Doris Kearns Goodwin, *No Ordinary*

Time: Franklin & Eleanor Roosevelt: The Home Front in World War II (New York: Touchstone/Simon & Schuster, 1995), p. 207.

78 "In the space of two years . . .": Ibid., p. 208.

79 . . . the importance women place on relationships . . . : The evolution of contemporary thought on women's psychological development is a fascinating intellectual adventure story, a gripping tale of bias and breakthroughs. For the interested reader, enlightening (and often entertaining) sources include: Carol Gilligan, *In a Different Voice: Psychological Theory and Women's Development* (Cambridge, Mass.: Harvard University Press, 1993; original edition, 1982); Joan A. Lang, "Self Psychology and the Understanding and Treatment of Women," *Review of Psychiatry* 9 (1989); ibid., "Notes Toward a Psychology of the Feminine Self," in *Kohut's Legacy: Contributions to Self Psychology,* ed. Paul E. Stepansky and Arnold Goldberg (Hillsdale, N.J.: The Analytic Press, 1984).

80 "in a relational voice . . .": Gilligan, *Different Voice,* p. xiii.

80 . . . she explained that females' development . . . : Jean Baker Miller, *Toward a New Psychology of Women* (Boston: Beacon Press, 1986), p. 83.

80 "Women really do take the responsibility . . .": Ibid., telephone interview by author, 5 April 1996.

80 In the common everyday activities women perform . . . : Miller, *New Psychology,* pp. xix–xx.

81 "The female protagonist becomes . . .": Jack Zipes, *Don't Bet on the Prince: Contemporary Feminist Fairy Tales in North America and England* (New York: Methuen, 1986), p. 32.

81 . . . girls want to grow up . . . : Nancy Chodorow, *The Reproduction of Mothering: Psychoanalysis and the Sociology of Gender* (Berkeley, Calif.: University of California Press, 1978), pp. 123–24.

81 . . . for both men and women, the earliest . . . : Ibid., p. 77.

81 "Feminine identification processes . . .": Ibid., p. 176.

81 "The selves of women and men tend . . .": Nancy Chodorow, *Feminism and Psychoanalytic Theory* (New Haven: Yale University Press, 1989), p. 2.

81 . . . even women with young children felt . . . : Phyllis Gillman, "Adult Women's Closest Female Friendships and Their Relationship to Maternal and Marital Status" (Ph.D. diss., Wright Institute, 1986), p. 94.

81 "Women's friendships are crucial to . . .": Ibid., interview by author in Los Angeles, 10 May 1996.

82 "Because you don't have the familial obligations . . .": Miller, 5 April 1996.

82 In 1978 a group of female therapists . . . : Christina Robb, "A Theory of Empathy: The Quiet Revolution in Psychiatry," *The Boston Globe Magazine,* 16 October 1988.

82 Instead of equating psychological growth . . . : Judith Jordan, "Relational Development: Therapeutic Implications of Empathy and Shame," Works in Progress, n. 39 (Wellesley, Mass.: The Stone Center, Wellesley College, 1989), p. 4.

82 That ethic doesn't even work for men . . . : Irene Stiver, interview by author in Newton, Mass., 1 April 1996.

82 The first is a pleasant spark . . . : Miller, 5 April 1996.

83 . . . Second, two people in connection become . . . : Stiver, 1 April 1996.

83 Three years after the theory group . . . : Robb, "Theory of Empathy."

83 "Mutuality doesn't mean . . .": Judy Jordan, interview by author in Lexington, Mass., 2 April 1996.

83 "There isn't typically the power differential," . . .: Ibid.

84 "The more you can bring yourself . . .": Ibid.

84 "The experience of intimate bonding in friendship . . .": Kerry Ann Moustakas, "Encounters of Intimate Bonding: An Heuristic Investigation of Friendship" (abstract of Ph.D. diss., Union Institute, 1993).

85 "Most women are always thinking . . .": Stiver, 1 April 1996.

85 . . . a friendship that requires that one . . . : Jordan, "Relational Development," p. 3.

85 Instead of fostering growth in both women . . . : Karin Schultz, "Women's Adult Development: The Importance of Friendship," *Journal of Independent Social Work* 5, no. 2 (1991): 19–30.

85 "In order to stay in the illusion . . .": Jordan, 2 April 1996.

85 . . . by revealing her true self to a friend . . . : Christine Luhe Hejinian, "An Exploration of the Role of Same-Sex Close Friendship in Women's Adult Development" (abstract of Ph.D. diss., Wright Institute, 1981.)

86 "When women are willing to risk . . .": interview with Christine Hejinian in San Francisco, 16 May 1996.

86 . . . not the macho denial of fear . . . : Judith Jordan, "Courage in Connection: Conflict, Compassion, Creativity," Works in Progress, no. 45 (Wellesley, Mass.: The Stone Center, Wellesley College, 1990), p. 2.

88 For women without sisters . . . : Joan Berzoff, "Valued Female Friendships: Their Function in Female Adult Development" (Ed.D. diss., Boston University, 1985), p. 91.

88 "Women are always working on their relationships . . .": Ibid., interview by author in Northampton, Mass., 5 April 1996.

88 "I really do feel that friendship . . .": Gillman, 10 May 1996.

88 If a little girl's mother . . . : Berzoff, "Valued Female Friendships," pp. 121–22.

88 "Even women who have had very difficult . . .": Christine Hejinian, interview by author in San Francisco, 16 May 1996.

88 The theme of maternal reparation winds . . . : Janice M. Bowman Swanson, "Speaking in a Mother Tongue: Female Friendship in the British Novel" (abstract of Ph.D. diss. University of California–Santa Barbara, 1981).

89 By providing insight and empathy . . . : Berzoff, 5 April 1996.

90 Studies by psychologists and sociologists . . . : This seems to be true for women of all backgrounds. For example, among these studies are one that Irish sociologist Pat O'Connor conducted among working-class women. P. O'Connor, *Friendships Between Women: A Critical Review* (New York: Guilford Press, 1992), p. 65.

90 "Women friends reflect parts of the self . . .": Berzoff, 5 April 1996.

90 . . . friendship both reinforces the importance . . . : Hejinian, 16 May 1996.

90 Friends do each other good . . . : Pat O'Connor, *Friendships Between Women,* p. 84.

91 Married women in particular rely on female friends . . . : Stacey J. Oliker, *Best Friends and Marriage: Exchange Among Women* (Berkeley, Calif.: University of California Press, 1989), p. 107.

91 If it weren't for Emily Dickinson's . . . : Marilyn Elaine Matis, "We Demand the Flame": The Assembly of Emily Dickinson's Female Audience (abstract of Ph.D. diss., State University of New York at Buffalo, 1983).

5 The Ten Forms of Female Friendship

92 ". . . friends of the road . . .": Lillian B. Rubin, *Just Friends: The Role of Friendship in Our Lives* (New York: Harper & Row, 1985), p. 106.

92 . . . identified three types of female friendships . . . : Helen Gouldner and Mary Symons Strong, *Speaking of Friendship: Middle-Class Women and Their Friends* (New York: Greenwood Press, 1987), p. 60.

92 . . . divided close female friendships into . . . : Pat O'Connor, *Friendships Between Women: A Critical Review* (New York: Guilford Press, 1992), p. 66.

93 . . . described five kinds of women's friendships . . . : Joel Block and Diane Greenberg, *Women and Friendship* (New York: Franklin Watts, 1985), pp. 38–43.

94 . . . both men and women are capable . . . : Recent research seems to bear this out. Clinical psychologist Cynthia Mitchell found that gender was only one factor determining the four basic same-sex friendship patterns she identified: "expressive-confirming," "active-affirming," "possessive-ambivalent," and "competitive-accepting." C. Mitchell, "Adult Friendship Patterns: The Implications of Autonomy, Connection and Gender" (abstract of Ph.D. diss., Boston University, 1986).

94 A month earlier, the Rev. Jim Jones . . . : Ida Harper Simpson, "Communal Living," *Microsoft Encarta* (Microsoft and Funk & Wagnalls, 1993), entries B224 and B1061.

95 All women are outsiders . . . : Barbara Ellman, telephone interview by author, 12 November 1992.

95 "Sometimes you become so connected . . .": Carmen Renee Berry and Tamara Traeder, *Girlfriends: Invisible Bonds, Enduring Ties* (Berkeley, Calif.: Wildcat Canyon Press, 1995), p. 101.

97 Nursing a baby prompted . . . : Cathy Arden Kaats, "Friends and Mothers," *New Woman,* September 1990, p. 77.

97 "We actually looked at each other . . .": Ibid, p. 77.

98 In her work with young adults . . . : Susan Bodnar, "Friendship and the Construction of the Person in Adult Development" (abstract of Ph.D. diss., City University of New York, 1992).

99 "The value of relationships with . . .": Beverly Tatum, interview by author in Northampton, Mass., 5 April 1996.

99 "When four or five motherless women . . .": Hope Edelman, *Motherless Daugh-*

ters: The Legacy of Loss (New York: Delta/Bantam Doubleday Dell, 1994), p. 182.

100 At 9:02 on the morning of . . . : Federal Emergency Management Agency (FEMA) reports, 24 May 1995 through 29 October 1996, compiled and transmitted via the Internet.

101 After studying the people . . . : Janice A. Vermiglio-Smith, "The Human Consequences of Exposure to a Natural Disaster Threat" (abstract of D.P.A. [Doctor of Public Administration] diss., Arizona State University, 1993).

102 We may be eager to put . . . : Joel D. Block and Diane Greenberg, *Women & Friendship* (New York: Franklin Watts, 1985), pp. 42–43.

105 In her book *The Best of Friends* . . . : Eva Margolies, *The Best of Friends, the Worst of Enemies: Women's Hidden Power over Women* (Garden City, N.Y.: Dial/Doubleday, 1985), pp. 182–83.

105 "The more time that passed . . .": Ibid., p. 183.

106 Writing anonymously, one woman . . . : "I Was Making Myself a Doormat," *Good Housekeeping,* January 1989, pp. 20–23.

106 "[T]hey were all in the same spot . . .": Ibid, p. 23.

106 This "tyranny of feelings" includes . . . : Janice G. Raymond, *A Passion for Friends: Toward a Philosophy of Female Affection* (Boston: Beacon Press, 1986), p. 155.

108 "I came to love her obsessively. . . .": Joan Berzoff, "Valued Female Friendships: Their Functions in Female Adult Development" (Ed.D. diss., Boston University, 1985), p. 95.

109 Working for Sears in Queens . . . : James Servin, "Cookin' with Salt-N-Pepa," *Bazaar,* November 1994, p. 111.

109 "[T]he thing that drives the S-N-P machine . . .": Ibid., p. 116.

110 "To know that there are other women . . .": Irene Stiver, interview by author in Watertown, Mass., 1 April 1996.

112 Studying young adults who used . . . : Denise Kandel and Mark Davies, "Friendship Networks, Intimacy, and Illicit Drug Use in Young Adulthood: A Comparison of Two Competing Theories," *Criminology* 29, no. 3 (1991): 460–61.

113 In *Friendships Between Women* . . . : O'Connor, *Friendships,* pp. 19–21.

114 "In my own experience . . .": Tatum, 5 April 1996.

117 "As roommates, we shared not just living space . . .": Audrey Edwards, "Sisters Under the Skin," *New York Times Magazine,* 19 September 1993, p. 34.

118 When social psychologist Priscilla Roberts . . . : Those four famous pairs were anthropologists Ruth Benedict and Margaret Mead, political activists Christabel Pankhurst and Annie Kenney, writers Virginia Woolf and Vita Sackville-West, and photographers Lisette Model and Diane Arbus. Priscilla Roberts, *Female Mentor Relationships* (Ph.D. diss., Wright Institute, 1987).

118 "[N]ot only have women's relationships . . .": Lee H. Campbell, "Women and Mentoring: The Tradition, the Process, the Vision" (abstract of Ph.D. diss., Union Institute, 1992).

118 "Women do what mothers have . . .": Joan Berzoff, interview by author in Northampton, Mass., 5 April 1996.

119 . . . woman-to-woman mentorships (unlike those . . . : Lee Campbell observed this after studying female college students and professional women. Lee H. Campbell, "Women and Mentoring."

119 "People just don't move away from this area . . .": Nancy Busch, interview by author in Bronx, N.Y., 7 February 1996.

121 "Most people who see old friends . . .": Rubin, *Just Friends,* p. 35.

122 "Today I can scarcely bear . . .": Mary Cantwell, "Lawless Friendship," *New York Times Magazine,* 17 March 1996, p. 68.

124 "(1) Women's friendship groups tend . . .": Jennifer Lee Grimes, "Women's Friendship Groups: An Exploration of Bonding among Women in Three Groups" (abstract of Ph.D. diss., Wright Institute, 1987).

125 When forty-two-year-old Susan . . . : E. Bingo Wyer, "Support Group: That's What Friends Are For," *Good Housekeeping,* December 1995, p. 30.

Part Two

THE SIX SEASONS OF FEMALE FRIENDSHIP

133 When she queried women in midlife . . . : Beverly Minker Schydlowsky, "Friendships Among Women in Mid-Life" (abstract of Ph.D. diss., Fielding Institute, 1983).

134 . . . the Midlife Passage that . . . : Gail Sheehy, *Passages* (New York: E. P. Dutton, 1976; 1977 Bantam ed.), pp. 350–64.

134 . . . Levinson had divided male . . . : Daniel J. Levinson with Charlotte N. Darrow, Edward B. Klein, Maria H. Levinson, and Braxton McKee, *The Seasons of a Man's Life* (New York: Ballantine Books, 1978), pp. 18–21.

134 But that range . . . : Ibid., p. 53.

134 "To my surprise, the findings . . .": Daniel J. Levinson in collaboration with Judy D. Levinson, *The Seasons of a Woman's Life* (New York: Alfred A. Knopf, 1996), p. 5.

134 These transitions could be smooth or . . . : Ibid., p. 35.

135 . . . his eras and transitions were defined . . . : Levinson, et al., *Man's Life*, p. 54.

6   First Bonds Beyond the Family: Ages Eight to Twelve

138 "[B]est friendships in preadolescent . . .": Alyse J. Danis, "In Girls' Own Voices: The Interpersonal and Developmental Implications of Best Friendships Among Preadolescent Females" (abstract of Ed.D. diss., University of San Francisco, 1994).

138 "(1)The ability to share . . . " Ibid.

139 In order to remain emotionally connected . . . : Carol S. Fullerton and Robert J. Ursano, "Preadolescent Peer Friendships: A Critical Contribution to Adult Social Relatedness?" *Journal of Youth and Adolescence* 23, no. 1 (1994): 45.

139 In a study that demonstrated . . . : Marie-Josephe Chauvet and Peter Blatchford, "Group Composition and National Curriculum Assessment at Seven Years," *Educational Research* 35, no. 2 (Summer 1993): 189–96.

139 Close, reciprocated friendship . . . : For her master's thesis in social psychology,

Cyma Gauze studied 138 fourth-, fifth-, and sixth-graders and found that this effect was particularly crucial for children growing up in troubled households. Cyma M. Gauze, "Peer Relations as Moderators of Family Influences on Pre-Adolescent Self-Esteem" (abstract of M.A. thesis, Concordia University, 1991).

139 . . . and serves as a buffer against anxiety . . . : Ian M. Goodyer, Caroline Wright, and Patricia Altham, "Recent Achievements and Adversities in Anxious and Depressed School-Age Children," *Journal of Child Psychology and Psychiatry and Allied Disciplines* 31, no. 7: 1063–77.

139 "A reciprocal friendship is when you . . .": Sharon Vaughn, interview by author in Coral Gables, Fl., 23 January 1996.

139 One study of fourth- through sixth-graders showed . . . : Nancy Brandon Tuma and Maureen T. Hallinan, "The Effects of Sex, Race, and Achievement on School Children's Friendships," *Social Forces* 57 (1979): 1274.

139 When both friends feel similarly . . . : William M. Bukowski, Betsy Hoza, and Michel Bolvin, "Measuring Friendship Quality during Pre- and Early Adolescence: The Development and Psychometric Properties of the Friendship Qualities Scale," *Journal of Social and Personal Relationships* 11, no. 3 (August 1994): 471–84.

140 Studies have found that some children who are rejected . . . : Among those studies are one conducted among 326 third-graders by Deborah Lowe Vandell and Sheri E. Hembree of the University of Wisconsin Department of Educational Psychology (D. L. Vandell and S. E. Hembree, "Peer Social Status and Friendship: Independent Contributors to Children's Social and Academic Adjustment," *Merrill Palmer Quarterly* 40, no. 4 [October 1994]: 461–77); and one conducted by University of Michigan developmental psychologists Jeffrey Parker and Steven Asher among 881 third- through fifth-graders (J. Parker and S. Asher, "Friendship and Friendship Quality in Middle Childhood: Links with Peer Group Acceptance and Feelings of Loneliness and Social Dissatisfaction," *Developmental Psychology* 29, no. 4, [July 1993]: 611–21).

140 "When girls are disliked . . .": Vaughn, 23 January 1996.

140 . . . children younger than that . . . : Vaughn, 23 January 1996.

141 . . . provided neither was aggressive.: Tiffany M. Field, Paul Greenwald, Connie J. Morrow, Brian T. Healy, et al., "Behavior State Matching During Interactions of Preadolescent Friends Versus Acquaintances," *Developmental Psychology* 28, no. 2 (March 1992): 243.

141 . . . social life begins as early as thirteen months . . . : Carollee Howes and Leslie Phillipsen, "Gender and Friendship: Relationships Within Peer Groups of Young Children," *Social Development* 1, no. 3 (September 1992): 230–42.

141 . . . children are capable of forming . . . : Barry H. Schneider, Judith Wiener, and Kevin Murphy, "Children's Friendships: The Giant Step Beyond Peer Acceptance," *Journal of Social and Personal Relationships* 11, no. 3 (August 1994): 323–40.

141 By the time they're a year and a half, . . . : "Les relations affinitaires à la crèche [Friendships in the Day Care Center]" *Enfance* 47, no. 4 (1993): 377–91.

141 By two, children start developing . . . : Cornelius F. Van Lieshout, Marcel A. Van Aken, and Emiel T. Van Seyen, "Perspectives on Peer Relations from Moth-

ers, Teachers, Friends and Self," *Human Development* 33, no. 3–4 (July–October 1990): 225–37.

141 Studies have shown that very young children . . . : Among these studies have been those conducted by Carollee Howes and her colleagues at the University of California at Los Angeles. Howes and Phillipsen, "Gender and Friendship." C. Howes, Kristin Droege, and Catherine C. Matheson, "Play and Communicative Processes Within Long- and Short-Term Friendship Dyads," *Journal of Social and Personal Relationships* 11, no. 3 (August 1994): 401–10. Shira M. Rosenblatt and C. Howes, "Alternative Influences on Children's Development of Friendships: A Social-Developmental Perspective," *American Journal of Community Psychology* 23, no. 3 (1995): 432.

141 Frequent playmates start helping . . . : Roberta Orthel Shreve, "Friends in the Process of Meaning-Making: A Study of Vygotsky's Concept of Internalization" (abstract of Ed.D. diss., University of North Dakota, 1993).

141 Friends this age often collaborate . . . : Robert Keith Sawyer, "The Performance of Pretend Play: Enacting Peer Culture in Conversation" (abstract of Ph.D. diss., University of Chicago, 1994).

141 The closer the friendship . . . : JoEllen Vespo, "Features of Preschoolers' Relationships," *Early Childhood Development and Care* 68 (March 1991): 19–26.

141 As school age approaches . . . : Ibid.; and Cheryl L. Slomkowski and Melanie Killen, "Young Children's Conceptions of Transgressions with Friends and Nonfriends," *International Journal of Behavioral Development* 15, no. 2 (June 1992): 247–58.

141 . . . asked five-year-olds to make a picture . . . : Robyn M. Holmes, "Children's Artwork and Nonverbal Communication," *Child Study Journal* 22, no. 3 (1992): 157–66.

142 This practice of secret sharing . . . : Ken J. Rotenberg, "Development of Children's Restrictive Disclosure to Friends," *Journal of Genetic Psychology* 156, no. 3 (1995): 289.

142 They help young children cope with . . . : Laurie Kramer and John M. Gottman, "Becoming a Sibling: 'With a Little Help from My Friends' . . . *Developmental Psychology* 28, no. 4: 685–99.

142 . . . to the dangers of growing up . . . : Thomas A. Rizzo and William A. Corsaro, "Social Support Processes in Early Childhood Friendship: A Comparative Study of Ecological Congruences in Enacted Support," *American Journal of Community Psychology* 23, no. 3 (1995): 403.

142 When a close friend moves away . . . : Kathryn A. Park, "Preschoolers' Reactions to Loss of a Best Friend: Developmental Trends and Individual Differences," *Child Study Journal* 22, no. 4 (1992): 233–52.

142 These imaginery companions serve as buffers . . . : Mineko Inuzuka, Yoshiko Satoh, and Kayo Wada, "The Imaginary Companion: A Questionnaire Study," *Japanese Journal of Child and Adolescent Psychiatry* 32, no. 1 (1991): 32–48.

142 During the first few years of elementary . . . : Anna Craft, "Five- and Six-Year-Olds' Views of Friendship," *Educational Studies* 20, no. 2 (1994): 181–94.

142 . . . and to share with others.: Sherri Painter Pataki, Cheryl Shapiro, and Margaret S. Clark, "Children's Acquisition of Appropriate Norms for Friendships and
Acquaintances," *Journal of Social and Personal Relationships* 11, no. 3 (August
1994): 427–42.

142 By age nine or ten, kids say they're willing . . . : Fullerton and Ursano, "Preadolescent Peer Friendships," 48.

142 . . . by age ten or twelve, they expect friends . . . : Lynne Zarbatany, Kristen
Ghesquiere, and Karen Mohr, "A Context Perspective on Early Adolescents'
Friendship Expectations," *Journal of Early Adolescence* 12, no. 1 (February 1992):
111–26.

142 . . . by age twelve or thirteen, they can . . . : Fullerton and Ursano, "Preadolescent Peer Friendships."

142 . . . being careful about taking turns . . . : Field, Greenwald, Morrow, Healy,
et al., "Behavior State Matching," 248.

142 . . . reciprocating small favors . . . : Peggy A. de Cooke, "Children's Understanding of Indebtedness as a Feature of Reciprocal Help Exchanges between Peers,"
Developmental Psychology 28, no. 5 (September 1992): 948–54.

143 . . . deep friendships begin to emerge around . . . : Fullerton and Ursano,
"Preadolescent Peer Friendships," 50.

143 . . . used "chums" to denote a particular . . . : Harry Stack Sullivan, *The Interpersonal Theory of Psychiatry* (New York: W. W. Norton, 1953), pp. 245–46.

143 Sullivan described these intense . . . : Ibid., p. 245.

143 As early as preschool, girls tend . . . : Candice Feiring and Michael Lewis,
"The Development of Social Networks from Early to Middle Childhood: Gender
Differences and the Relation to School Competence," *Sex Roles* 25, no. 3/4 (Au-
gust 1991): 237–53.

143 "Girls . . . expected and received more . . .": M. L. Clark and Monnie L. Bittle,
"Friendship Expectations and the Evaluation of Present Friendships in Middle
Childhood and Early Adolescence," *Child Study Journal* 22, no. 2 (1992): 115–35.

143 . . . compared how two pairs of sixth-graders . . . : Deborah Tannen, *You Just
Don't Understand: Women and Men in Conversation* (New York: Ballantine Books,
1990), pp. 264–65.

144 "All the girls' talk is about . . .": Ibid., p. 265.

144 When boys disagree, they tend to be direct . . . : Robert Cohen, telephone
interview by author, 3 February 1997. Marie A. Sell, Robert Cohen, Arthur C.
Graesser, Melissa K. Duncan, Glen E. Ray, Christine D. MacDonald, and Michelle Crain, "The Form and Function of Speech Act Exchanges in Children's
Dyadic Interactions," *Discourse Processes* 18 (1994): 119.

145 But even in mixed-age classrooms . . . : Anne B. Smith and Patricia M. Inder,
"The Relationship of Classroom Organization to Cross-Age and Cross-Sex
Friendships," *Educational Psychology* 10, no. 2 (1990): 127–40.

145 In cases in which these nontraditional . . . : Joseph P. Allen, "Social Impact of
Age Mixing and Age Segregation in School: A Context-Sensitive Investigation,"
Journal of Educational Psychology 81, no. 3 (September 1989): 408–16.

146 "After a few near tumbles . . .": Maya Angelou, *I Know Why the Caged Bird Sings* (New York: Bantam Books, 1993), p. 119.

147 "We often choose friends based on . . .": Vaughn, 23 January 1996.

147 "Cindy was less my kindred . . .": Nancy Kelton, "Lifelong Friends," *Parents,* March 1993, p. 201.

147 In addition to their one-on-one friendships . . . : Linda Walsh, telephone interview by author, 12 August 1992.

148 But although some preadolescent girls . . . : When University of Washington developmental psychologist Mary Gillmore and her colleagues studied the patterns of friendship among 919 fifth-graders, they found that even children who got in trouble themselves were more attached to friends who didn't. Mary R. Gillmore, J. David Hawkins, L. Edward Day, and Richard F. Catalano, "Friendship and Deviance: New Evidence on an Old Controversy," *Journal of Early Adolescence* 12, no. 1 (February 1992): 80–95.

149 Studies show that companionship motivates . . . : One of these is the study Susan Duncan conducted on 422 seventh- and eighth-graders. Susan Catherine Duncan, "The Role of Cognitive Appraisal and Friendship Provisions in Children's Experience of Affect in Physical Activity" (abstract of Ph.D. diss., University of Oregon, 1992).

150 "Friendships are really challenging . . .": Beth Doll, University of Colorado at Denver psychologist, telephone interview by author, 20 February 1997.

151 Some forms of psychological trauma . . . : Lorraine Ashton Everett, "The Female Relational Self in the Context of Preadolescent Chum Friendship" (abstract of Ph.D. diss., Fielding Institute, 1991).

152 But a recent study of seventh-graders . . . : Patricia A. Aloise-Young, John W. Graham, and William B. Hansen, "Peer Influence on Smoking Initiation During Early Adolescence: A Comparison of Group Members and Group Outsiders," *Journal of Applied Psychology* 79, no. 2 (April 1994): 281–87.

152 . . . the younger children thought such restrictions . . . : Marie S. Tisak and John Tisak, "Children's Conceptions of Parental Authority, Friendship, and Sibling Relations," *Merrill-Palmer Quarterly* 36, no. 3 (July 1990): 362.

152 "By sixth grade, they think they have the . . .": Marie Tisak, telephone interview by author, 31 January 1997.

153 One study has shown that when it came . . . : Ian Goodyer, Caroline Wright, and Patricia Altham, "The Friendships and Recent Life Events of Anxious and Depressed School-Age Children," *British Journal of Psychiatry* 156 (May 1990): 693.

154 "Conflict is what gives kids . . .": Beth Doll, 20 February 1997. For more on how children deal with conflict, see Willard W. Hartup, Doran C. French, Brett Laursen, Mary Kathleen Johnston, and John R. Ogawa, "Conflict and Friendship Relations in Middle Childhood: Behavior in a Closed-Field Situation," *Child Development* 64 (1993): 452–53; and Frances E. Aboud, "Disagreement Between Friends," *International Journal of Behavioral Development* 12, no. 4 (December 1989): 495–508.

156 But "that's the way girls bond,": Vaughn, 23 January 1996. For more on the phenomenon of cliques, see Carol Gilligan, Preface to *Making Connections: The Relational Worlds of Adolescent Girls at Emma Willard School,* ed. Carol Gilligan, Nona P. Lyons, and Trudy J. Hanmer (Cambridge, Mass.: Harvard University Press, 1989), pp. 11–12.

156 When a girl is actively disliked . . . : Vaughn, ibid. With Gary X. Lancelotta as first author, Vaughn reported one study on which she based her description in "Relation Between Types of Aggression and Sociometric Status: Peer and Teacher Perceptions," *Journal of Educational Psychology* 81, no. 1 (1989): 86–90.

7 Challenges and Changes: Ages Thirteen to Seventeen

158 In this short time, she must decide . . . : Susan Harter and Ann Monsour, "Developmental Analysis of Conflict Caused by Opposing Attributes in the Adolescent Self-Portrait," *Developmental Psychology* 28, no. 2 (March 1992): 251–60.

158 ". . . recognize the interrelationship . . .": Beth Doll, "Children Without Friends: Implications for Practice and Policy," *School Psychology Review* 25, no. 2 (1996): 178.

159 . . . concerns about being too outspoken . . . : Jill MacLean Taylor, Carol Gilligan, and Amy M. Sullivan, *Between Voice and Silence: Women and Girls, Race and Relationship* (Cambridge, Mass.: Harvard University Press, 1995), p. 39.

159 In a landmark study of female development . . . : Lori Stern, "Conceptions of Separation and Connection in Female Adolescents," in *Making Connections: The Relational Worlds of Adolescent Girls at Emma Willard School,* ed. Carol Gilligan, Nona P. Lyons, and Trudy J. Hanmer (Cambridge, Mass.: Harvard University Press, 1989), p. 75.

160 . . . interviewed inner-city students at risk . . . : Richard Alan Spurling, "Factors Affecting the Transition to Grade Nine as Perceived by Students in an Urban Setting" (abstract of Ph.D. diss., University of Connecticut, 1992).

160 Other studies demonstrate that prodding . . . : Among these are one recounted by Taylor, Gilligan, and Sullivan, *Between Voice and Silence,* p. 55.

160 Although close friends can be a crucial . . . : Thomas J. Berndt, "Friendship and Friends' Influence in Adolescence," *Current Directions in Psychological Science* 1, no. 5 (October 1992): 156–59; and Karen A. Frankel, "Girls' Perceptions of Peer Relationship Support and Stress," *Journal of Early Adolescence* 10, no. 1 (February 1990): 69–88.

160 One program, developed in the United States . . . : Kimberley Shaw, review of Mosh Smilansky, *Friendship in Adolescence and Young Adulthood* (Gaithersburg, Md.: Psychosocial and Educational Publication, 1991), in *Journal of Clinical Child Psychology* 22, no. 1 (March 1993): 123.

160 Another program, devised in Australia . . . : Alan Ralph, Annette Spano, Heather Whitely, Linda Straong, et al., "Social Training for Adolescents: Making Positive Steps," Special Issue: Social Competence of Children and Adolescents, *Behavior Change* 8, no. 4 (1991): 183–93.

160 It occurs in social context; . . . : For studies demonstratiing this, see Barbara Ann Miller, "Adolescents' Relationships with Their Friends" (abstract of Ed.D. diss., Harvard University, 1991); Nona P. Lyons, "Listening to Voices We Have Not Heard," in *Making Connections,* p. 62; and Susan Marie Overhauser, "The Significance of Friendship Intimacy and Family Warmth for Adolescent Identity Development and Individuation: A Developmental Study" (abstract of Ph.D. diss., University of Minnesota, 1993).

161 . . . both girls and boys involved in romantic . . . : Tiffany Field, Claudia Lang, Regina Yando, and Debra Bendell, "Adolescents' Intimacy with Parents and Friends," *Adolesence* 30, no. 117 (Spring 1995): 136.

162 . . . and are more likely to confide . . . : Elizabeth Monck, "Patterns of Confiding Relationships Among Adolescent Girls," *Journal of Child Psychology and Psychiatry and Allied Disciplines* 32, no. 2 (January 1991): 333–45.

162 For girls who've had . . . : Judith P. Salzman, "Save the World, Save Myself," in *Making Connections,* p. 121.

162 For a girl growing up . . . : Taylor, Gilligan, and Sullivan, *Between Voice and Silence,* p. 95.

163 . . . the number of friends a mother doesn't know . . . : Candice Feiring and Michael Lewis, "Do Mothers Know Their Teenagers' Friends? Implications for Individuation in Early Adolescence," *Journal of Youth and Adolescence* 22, no. 4 (August 1993): 337–54.

163 . . . parents often view adolescent friendships . . . : Lillian B. Rubin, *Just Friends: The Role of Friendship in Our Lives* (New York: Harper & Row, 1985), p. 110.

164 . . . one of the most popular topics . . . : Penelope Eckert, "Cooperative Competition in Adolescent 'Girl Talk,' " *Discourse Processes* 13, no. 1 (January–March 1990): 91–122.

165 Several studies of female high school athletes . . . : Among those studies are Richard M. Ryckman and Jane Hamel, "Female Adolescents' Motives Related to Involvement in Organized Team Sports," *International Journal of Sports Psychology* 23, no. 2 (April–June 1992): 147–60; Roberta Vasko Kraus, "Toward a Theory of Team Effectiveness in Women's High School Volleyball" (abstract of Ph.D. diss., University of Denver, 1990); Bruce Keeler, "The Quality of Adolescent Peer Relationships in the Sport Domain and Their Contribution to Global Self-Worth" (abstract of Ph.D. diss., University of California–Los Angeles, 1992;) and Janet Lynne Enke, "Cultural Production, Reproduction, and Change Within an Athletic Context" (Ph.D. diss., Indiana University, 1992).

165 In a study of eleven- to nineteen-year-olds advertising . . . : Shmuel Shulman, Inge Seiffge-Krenke, and Lily Dimitrovsky, "The Functions of Pen Pals for Adolescents," *The Journal of Psychology* 128, no. 1 (January 1994): 96.

165 . . . more than three-quarters of the adolescents . . . : Ibid., p. 91.

165 Girls tend to choose friends . . . : M. L. Clark and Marla Ayers, "Friendship Similarity During Early Adolescence," *The Journal of Psychology* 126, no. 4 (July 1992): 402.

165 . . . both boys and girls tend to pick . . . : Ibid., p. 401.

167 "Young people can . . . be remarkably . . .": Erik H. Erikson, *Childhood and Society* (New York: W. W. Norton, 1963), p. 262.

167 . . . the tug-of-war between individuality . . . : Rubin, *Just Friends,* p. 111.

168 . . . as girls move from the five- through fourteen-year-old . . . : U.S. Bureau of the Census, *Statistical Abstract of the United States: 1998,* 118th ed. (Washington, D.C., 1998), Table 132.

168 . . . and become almost eight-and-a-half times as likely . . . : Ibid., Table 141.

168 Scores of studies on the use . . . : Susan T. Ennett and Karl E. Bauman, "The Contribution of Influence and Selection to Adolescent Peer Group Homogeneity: The Case of Adolescent Cigarette Smoking," *Journal of Personality and Social Psychology* 67, no. 4 (October 1994): 653–63. A study of 4,059 British eleven-through sixteen-year-olds showed that researchers who focus only on a specific behavior, such as smoking, miss the point: Kids tend to seek out other kids who are similar to them in attitudes, beliefs, academic performance, socioeconomic status, and a host of other characteristics, as well. Richard J. Eiser, Michelle Morgan, Philip Gammage, Neil Brooks, et al., "Adolescent Health Behavior and Similarity-Attraction: Friends Share Smoking Habits (Really), but Much Else Besides," *British Journal of Social Psychology* 30, no. 4 (December 1991): 339–48.

168 Smokers pick other smokers . . . : Susan T. Ennett, Karl E. Bauman, and Gary G. Koch, "Variability in Cigarette Smoking Within and Between Adolescent Friendship Cliques," *Addictive Behaviors* 19, no. 3 (May–June 1994): 295–305; Patricia A. Aloise-Young, John W. Graham, and William B. Hansen, "Peer Influence on Smoking Initiation During Early Adolescence: A Comparison of Group Members and Group Outsiders," *Journal of Applied Psychology* 79, no. 2 (1994): 281; and Erica Van Roosmalen and Susan A. McDaniel, "Adolescent Smoking Intentions: Gender Differences in Peer Context," *Adolescence* 27, no. 105 (Spring 1992): 87–105.

168 Even though the influence of peers . . . : James Youniss and Denise L. Haynie, "Friendship in Adolescence," *Journal of Developmental and Behavioral Pediatrics* 13, no. 1 (February 1992): 59–66.

168 . . . adolescents who have strong relationships . . . : Gertie Witte, "Adolescent Deviance and Alcohol Consumption: The Influence of Parents and Friends" (abstract of Ph.D. diss., McGill University, 1993).

168 Adolescents who have a lot of drug-using friends . . . : Among the many studies coming to this conclusion are one of small-town adolescents conducted by a team from Texas A&M (B. E. Pruitt, Paul M. Kingery, Elaheh Mirazee, Greg Heuberger, et al., "Peer Influence and Drug Use among Adolescents in Rural Areas," *Journal of Drug Education* 21, no. 1 [1991]: 1–11) and another of young Native Americans (Fred Beauvais, "Drug Use of Friends: A Comparison of Reservation and Non-Reservation Indian Youth," *American Indian and Alaska Native Mental Health Research* 5, no. 1 [1992]: 43–50).

168 After interviewing thirty-seven high school . . . : Randy R. Kafka and Perry

London, "Communication in Relationships and Adolescent Substance Use: The Influence of Parents and Friends," *Adolescence* 26, no. 103 (Fall 1991): 587–98.

169 But the tendency among girls . . . : Michael Windle, "A Study of Friendship Characteristics and Problem Behaviors Among Middle Adolescents," *Child Development* 65 (1994): 1766.

169 A senior participating in the study . . . : Lyn Mikel Brown, "When Is a Moral Problem Not a Moral Problem? Morality, Identity, and Female Adolescence," in *Making Connections,* pp. 88–89.

169 In 1995, the most recent year . . . : Bureau of the Census, *Statistical Abstract,* Table 150.

169 . . . the official cause of death for . . . : Ibid., Table 141.

169 A study of 409 Virginia high school students . . . : Debra E. Cole, Howard O. Protinsky, and Lawrence H. Cross, "An Empirical Investigation of Adolescent Suicidal Ideation," *Adolescence* 27, no. 108 (Winter 1992): 816.

169 Describing hopelessness as . . . : Ibid., p. 814.

170 In fact, almost a third of the friends . . . : David A. Brent, Joshua A. Perper, Grace Moritz, Chris Allman, et al., "Psychiatric Effects of Exposure to Suicide Among the Friends and Acquaintances of Adolescent Suicide Victims," *Journal of the American Academy of Child and Adolescent Psychiatry* 31, no. 4 (July 1992): 629–39. Two other papers by the same authors discuss different aspects of the same study: "Psychiatric Sequelae to the Loss of an Adolescent Peer to Suicide," *Journal of the American Academy of Child and Adolescent Psychiatry* 32, no. 3 (May 1993): 509–17; and "Bereavement or Depression? The Impact of the Loss of a Friend to Suicide," *Journal of the American Academy of Child and Adolescent Psychiatry* 32, no. 6 (November 1993): 1187–97. For another study of friends of suicidal adolescents, see Philip Hazell and Terry Lewin, "Friends of Adolescent Suicide Attempters and Completers," *Journal of the American Academy of Child and Adolescent Psychiatry* 32, no. 1 (January 1993): 76–81.

170 By puberty, girls grasp that friendship has . . . : Steve Duck, *Understanding Relationships* (New York: Guilford Press, 1991), p. 154.

170 Because they're not quite sure of who they are . . . : Beth Doll, "Children Without Friends," 168.

170 After finding that adolescents with the strongest . . . : Susan Moore and Jennifer Boldero, "Psychosocial Development and Friendship Functions in Adolescence," *Sex Roles* 25, no. 9/10 (1991): 534.

170 "[F]riendship may lead to developmental . . .": Ibid., p. 534

171 As a girl learns to listen . . . : Beth Doll, "Children Without Friends," 175.

171 To experience empathy, a girl first must . . . : Ibid., p. 174.

172 Chronic turmoil at home exaggerates the normal . . . : Robert H. Aseltine, Susan Gore, and Mary Ellen Colten, "Depression and the Social Developmental Context of Adolescence," *Journal of Personality and Social Psychology* 67, no. 2 (August 1994): 252–63.

172 Even though these new friendships may be . . . : Katina K. Kostoulas, Irving

H. Berkovitz, and Hatsuko Arima, "School Counseling Groups and Children of Divorce: Loosening Attachment to Mother in Adolescent Girls," *Journal of Child and Adolescent Group Therapy* 1, no. 3 (September 1991): 177–92; and Joseph Guttman, "Adolescents from Divorced Families and Their Best-Friend Relationship: A Qualitative Analysis," *Journal of Divorce and Remarriage* 20, no. 3/4 (1993): 95–110.

8   Flourishing amid Firsts: Ages Eighteen to Twenty-two

176 Between 1973 and 1995, membership . . . : Statistics compiled biennially by the National Panhellenic Conference show a 45.09 percent increase in enrollment in college social fraternities and sororities from 1973 to 1995.

178 . . . the more responsive one friend was . . . : Michael Steven Losoff, "Responsiveness in Adolescent Friendships" (abstract of Ph.D. diss., University of Texas at Austin, 1989).

181 . . . what she called "sustaining" friendships . . . : Kirsten Jan Tyson-Rawson, "College Women and Bereavement: Late Adolescence and Father Death" (abstract of Ph.D. diss., Kansas State University, 1993).

183 . . . roommates even tend to synchronize . . . : Aron Weller and Leonard Weller, "Menstrual Synchrony Between Mothers and Daughters and Between Roommates," *Physiology and Behavior* 53, no. 5 (May 1993): 943–49.

184 . . . sexual bonding takes place in the context . . . : David Lee Mitchell, "The Interaction Between Friendship-Based Primary Networks and Sexually Interdependent Primary Relationships: The Development and Test of a Model Linking Social Networks and Microrelationships" (abstract of Ph.D. diss., University of Florida, 1992).

185 Female undergraduates report feeling even more . . . : Janet Frances Maurer, "Reported Stress of College Seniors as a Function of Gender and Sex Role Orientation" (abstract of Ph.D. diss., University of Pennsylvania, 1981).

9   Real-World Drift: Ages Twenty-three to Thirty-nine

187 In Daniel J. Levinson's model . . . : Daniel J. Levinson, in collaboration with Judy D. Levinson, *The Seasons of a Woman's Life* (New York: Alfred A. Knopf, 1996), p. 20.

189 Comparing women ages twenty to thirty-nine with those . . . : Kathleen Sullivan Ricker, "The Friendship Patterns of Two Cohort Groups of Women in Three Career Lifestyles" (abstract of Ph.D. diss., University of Denver, 1987).

191 Sharing change is what makes . . . : Susan Bodnar, "Friendship and the Construction of the Person in Adult Development" (abstract of Ph.D. diss., City University of New York, 1992).

191 The twenties are the most mobile . . . : U.S. Bureau of the Census, *Statistical Abstract of the United States: 1998* (118th ed.) (Washington, D.C., 1998), Table 32.

191 In any given year, about a third . . . : Ibid.

193 . . . Although full-time employment reduced . . . : Carol Shaver Goodenow, "Friendship Patterns of Adult Women: Relationship to Life Span Development

and to Psychological Well-Being" (abstract of Ph.D. diss., State University of New York at Buffalo, 1985).

193 "[E]ven seasonal cannery work, under . . .": Patricia Juanita Zavella, "Women, Work and Family in the Chicano Community: Cannery Workers of the Santa Clara Valley" (abstract of Ph.D. diss., University of California–Berkeley, 1982).

193 In 1997, more than three-quarters . . . : Bureau of the Census, *Statistical Abstract,* Table 645.

194 And even two women with equal . . . : For some of the sociological research demonstrating this, see Pat O'Connor, *Friendship Between Women: A Critical Review* (New York: Guilford Press, 1992), p. 27; and Helen Gouldner and Mary Symons Strong, *Speaking of Friendship: Middle-Class Women and Their Friends* (New York: Greenwood Press, 1987), p. 85.

195 . . . for first weddings, the early . . . : Bureau of the Census, *Statistical Abstract,* Table 158.

195 . . . by the year 2010, a third of all Americans . . . : Ibid., Table 63.

195 . . . those who do so by choice tend to . . . : Frances Elizabeth Bonds-White, "An Exploratory Study of the Adult Development of a Group of Never-Married Women from 22–82" (abstract of Ed.D. diss., Temple University, 1987).

195 . . . in 1995 only 19 percent of American women . . . : Bureau of the Census, *Statistical Abstract*, Table 62.

195 The 1990 census revealed that . . . : Bureau of the Census, *Statistical Abstract,* Table 62.

196 . . . single women like to get together with friends . . . : Stacey J. Oliker, *Best Friends and Marriage: Exchange Among Women* (Berkeley, Calif.: University of California Press, 1989), p. 86.

196 . . . many married women have to content themselves . . . : Irish sociologist Pat O'Connor found this so prevelant that she made these "mental constructs" a separate form of female friendship. (O'Connor, *Friendship Between Women*, p. 57.)

197 . . . although most American babies still are born . . . : Bureau of the Census, *Statistical Abstract,* Table 94.

197 . . . although on average the number of friends they had . . . : Julie Dryden Carbery "The Changing Significance of Friendship Across Three Young Adult Phases" (abstract of Ph.D. diss., University of Texas at Dallas, 1993).

197 While experts agree . . . : Pat O'Connor, *Friendship Between Women,* pp. 76–77.

198 . . . "[m]others of young children have fewer . . .": Oliker, *Best Friends,* p. 93.

198 . . . far from being isolated, mothers of young . . . : Linda Bell and Jane Ribbens, "Isolated Housewives and Complex Maternal Worlds—The Significance of Social Contacts between Women with Young Children in Industrialized Societies," *Sociological Review* 42, no. 2 (May 1994): 227–62.

198 . . . female friendships dwindle once women have . . . : Nancy Chodorow, *The Reproduction of Mothering: Psychoanalysis and the Sociology of Gender* (Berkeley, Calif.: University of California Press, 1978), pp. 200–201.

198 . . . The friendships among mothers with . . . : Phyllis B. Gillman, "Adult Women's Closest Female Friendships and Their Relationship to Maternal and Marital Status" (Ph.D. diss., The Wright Institute, 1986), p. 94.

198 These women communicated with their friends . . . : Ibid., p. 109.

199 "They would be desperate to find . . .": Carol Goodenow, interview by author in Malden, Mass., 1 April 1996.

200 . . . having a son or daughter start school . . . : Steve Duck, *Understanding Relationships* (New York: Guilford Press, 1991), p. 121.

206 . . . these bonds either had formed around their . . . : Pat O'Connor, "Women's Confidants Outside Marriage: Shared or Competing Sources of Intimacy?" *Sociology* 25, no. 2 (May 1991): 251.

207 . . . marriage changed the functions . . . : Leslie L. Smith, "Women's Friendships with Other Women: A Reflection of Object Relations" (abstract of Ph.D. diss., Boston University, 1982).

207 . . . the younger women included more friends . . . : Mary J. Levitt, Ruth A. Weber, and Nathalie Guacci, "Convoys of Social Support: An Intergenerational Analysis," *Psychology and Aging* 8, no. 3 (September 1993): 323–26.

10 Friendship's Second Flowering: Ages Forty to Sixty-four

214 . . . women in midlife rated their current close . . . : Martin S. Fiebert and Kimberly S. Wright, "Midlife Friendships in an American Faculty Sample," *Psychological Reports* 64, no. 3, pt. 2 (June 1989): 1127–30; and Kimberly Sue Wright, "Friendship in Midlife: Gender Differences and Similarities in a Faculty Sample" (abstract of M.A. thesis, California State University at Long Beach, 1988).

214 . . . the importance they attached to these . . . : Beverly Minker Schydlowsky, "Friendships Among Women in Mid-Life" (abstract of Ph.D. diss., Fielding Institute, 1983).

215 . . . introduced this particular season with a five-year . . . : Daniel J. Levinson in collaboration with Judy D. Levinson, *The Seasons of a Woman's Life* (New York: Alfred A. Knopf, 1996), p. 20.

215 ". . . after about forty . . . biological senescing . . .": Ibid., p. 21.

215 . . . posited the concept of "unfinished identity" . . . : Zoya Sandomirsky Slive, "Mid-Life Transition: A Study of the Psychosocial Development of Married Women in Middle Adulthood" (abstract of Ed.D. diss., Boston University, 1986).

217 While studying women fifty-five and older who had . . . : Madelyn Iris, interview by author in Chicago, 24 March 1996.

219 ". . . who had maintained contacts with other . . .": Cleo S. Berkun, "Perception of Changing Appearance, Aging and Mood in Middle Aged Women" (abstract of D.S.W. diss., University of California–Berkeley, 1981).

221 A woman's social adjustment to widowhood . . . : Pat O'Connor, *Friendships Between Women: A Critical Review* (New York: Guilford Press, 1992), p. 129.

222 In a study of middle-aged women whose mothers . . . : Julia Gamble Kahrl, "Maternal Death as Experienced by Middle Aged Daughters: Implications for Psychoeducational Interventions" (abstract of Ph.D. diss., Ohio State University, 1988).

227 . . . social scientists traditionally identified . . . : Carol Goodenow, interview by author in Malden, Mass., 1 April 1996.

228 Despite recent medical advances . . . : Although no figures are available on the number of women who try to have babies after forty and their relative rate of success, a search of the gynecological literature turned up study after study documenting the difficulty. For example, K. E. Smith and R. P. Buyalos found a spontaneous abortion (miscarriage) rate of 20.0 percent in pregnant women forty and older, compared to 3.8 percent for women thirty-one to thirty-five. K. E. Smith and R. P. Buyalos, "The Profound Impact of Patient Age on Pregnancy Outcome After Early Detection of Fetal Cardiac Activity," *Fertility & Sterility* 65, no. 1 (January 1996): 35–40.

229 . . . when it comes to allocating time between family . . . : Linda J. Waite and Scott C. Harrison, "Keeping in Touch: How Women in Mid-Life Allocate Social Contacts among Kith and Kin," *Social Forces* 70, no. 3 (March 1992): 637–54.

229 . . . middle-aged women report less difficulty maintaining . . . : Kathleen Sullivan Ricker, "The Friendship Patterns of Two Cohort Groups of Women in Three Career Lifestyles" (abstract of Ph.D. diss., University of Denver, 1987).

231 . . . for the sustenance it will offer later.: For a study demonstrating that women who cultivate friendships in midlife have more support from friends in old age, see Jean K. Quam, "The Utility of Friendship for Older Women: An Application of the Task Specific Model" (abstract of Ph.D. diss., University of Wisconsin–Madison, 1981).

11 Reaping the Harvest: Ages Sixty-five and Over

233 . . . Women in this age group report that friendships . . . : Among the studies demonstrating this value in friendships are those described in the following: James E. Lubben, "Gender Differences in the Relationship of Widowhood and Psychological Well-Being among Low Income Elderly," *Women and Health* 14, no. 3/4 (1988): 161–89; Gary R. Lee and Constance L. Shehan, "Social Relations and the Self-Esteem of Older Persons," *Research on Aging* 11, no. 4 (December 1989): 427–42; Jeffrey Shinri Nagafuji, "Activity Preferences and Well-Being of Elderly Japanese" (abstract of M.S.W. thesis, California State University–Long Beach, 1994); and Larry C. Mullins and Elizabeth Dugan, "The Influence of Depression, and Family and Friendship Relations, on Residents' Loneliness in Congregate Housing," *Gerontologist* 30, no. 3 (June 1990): 377–84.

233 . . . friends, not family members, comprised more . . . : Jocelyn M. Armstrong and Karen S. Goldsteen, "Friendship Support Patterns of Older American Women," *Journal of Aging Studies* 4, no. 4 (Winter 1990): 391–404.

233 . . . elderly women experienced at least as much . . . : Teresa Irene Newsome, "The Therapeutic Functions of Friendship for Elderly Women: An Examination of Quality, Quantity, and Continuity" (abstract of Ph.D. diss., University of Kentucky, 1985).

234 The best that people this age could . . . : Erik H. Erikson, *Childhood and Society* (New York: W. W. Norton, 1963), p. 168.

234 Short of that, they would suffer from despair . . . : Ibid., p. 169.

235 . . . a period of "disengagement," . . . : Pat O'Connor, *Friendships Between Women: A Critical Review* (New York: Guilford Press, 1992), p. 125.

235 . . . the number of friends elderly women had . . . : Ibid., p. 120.

235 In her 1987 study of women . . . : Alice Taylor Day, *Remarkable Survivors: Insights into Successful Aging Among Women* (Washington, D.C.: Urban Institute Press, 1991), abstract.

235 . . . when it came to loneliness, an older person's . . . : Pearl A. Dykstra, "Loneliness Among the Never and Formerly Married: The Importance of Supportive Friendships and a Desire for Independence," *Journal of Gerontology* 50B, no. 5 (1995): S327.

235 The stereotype of the socially isolated elderly widow . . . : In fact, sociologist Helen Gouldner called it "absurd," particularly for relatively healthy women. Helen Gouldner, interview by author in Wilmington, Del., 26 March 1996.

235 Our culture's negative image of doddering . . . : Ruth Harriet Jacobs, "Friendships Among Old Women," *Journal of Women & Aging* 2, no. 2 (1990): 19–32; and O'Connor, *Friendships Between Women,* pp. 131–32.

236 . . . older people with confidants . . . : For four of the many studies supporting this, see Charles A. Guarnaccia and Alex J. Zautra, "Use of Confidant Reports to Assess the Affective State of Older Adults," *Clinical Gerontologist* 9, no. 2 (1989): 68–71; Mary Frances Demellier, "Intimate Friendships and Adaptation to Life Stress in Older Adult Females" (abstract of Ph.D. diss., Ohio State University, 1981); Rebecca Gay Adams, "Friendship and Its Role in the Lives of Elderly Women" (abstract of Ph.D. diss., University of Chicago, 1983); and Larry C. Mullins and Mary Mushel, "The Existence and Emotional Closeness of Relationships with Children, Friends, and Spouses: The Effect of Loneliness Among Older Persons," *Research on Aging* 14, no. 4 (December 1992): 448–70.

236 . . . as their personal support networks . . . : Lenard W. Kaye and Abraham Monck, "Social Relations in Enriched Housing for the Aged: A Case Study," *Journal of Housing for the Elderly* 9, no. 1/2 (1991): 111–26.

236 This also happens to elderly women . . . : Mark G. Thompson and Kenneth Heller, "Facets of Support Related to Well-being: Quantitative Social Isolation and Perceived Family Support in a Sample of Elderly Women," *Psychology and Aging* 5, no. 4 (December 1990): 535–44.

236 Transportation, along with shopping . . . : Karen A. Roberto, "Friendships Between Older Women: Interactions and Reactions," *Journal of Women and Aging* 8, no. 3/4 (Fall 1996): 55–73; and Jane Pearson Scott and Karen A. Roberto, "Informal Supports of Older Adults: A Rural-Urban Comparison," *Family Relations* 36 (October 1987): 446–47.

237 "Most older women at some time or another . . .": Gouldner, 26 March 1996.

237 . . . Older women who thought they were giving . . . : Roberto, "Friendships Between Older Women," 55–73; and Karen A. Roberto and Jean Pearson Scott, "Friendship Patterns Among Older Women," *International Journal of Aging and Human Development* 19, no. 1 (1984–1985): 1–10.

237 . . . the heart of female friendship in late life . . . : For studies supporting this idea, see Jean K. Quam, "Older Women and Informal Supports: Impact on Prevention," *Prevention in Human Services* 3, no. 1 (Fall 1983): 119–33; and Beth B. Hess, "Aging, Gender Role, and Friendship," *Educational Horizons* 60, no. 4 (Summer 1982): 155–60.

239 Fifty-four percent of women sixty-five to seventy-four . . . : U.S. Bureau of the Census, *Statistical Abstract of the United States:* 1998, 118th ed. (Washington, D.C., 1998), Table 67.

240 . . . a year before the tragic April morning . . . : *1988–1989 Texas Almanac* (Dallas: A. H. Belo Corporation, 1987), p. 397.

240 . . . the average length of the relationships . . . : Karen A. Roberto, "Qualities of Older Women's Friendships: Stable or Volatile?" *International Journal of Aging and Human Development* 44, no. 1 (1997), p. 13.

241 "I don't really know why it surprised me . . .": Madelyn Iris, interview by author in Chicago, 24 March 1996.

241 . . . the older the friendship, the stronger . . . : Rebecca G. Adams, "Emotional Closeness and Physical Distance Between Friends: Implications for Elderly Women Living in Age-Segregated and Age-Integrated Settings," *International Journal of Aging and Human Development* 22, no. 1 (1985–1986): 55–76.

242 They distinguished among three meanings . . . : Jay Ginn and Sara Arber, " 'Only Connect': Gender Relations and Ageing," in *Connecting Gender and Ageing: A Sociological Approach,* ed. Sara Arber and Jay Ginn (Philadelphia: Open University Press, 1995), p. 5.

242 The first is a simple matter . . . : Ibid., pp. 5–6.

242 The second reflects both how old . . . : Ibid., p. 7.

242 The third encompasses the . . . : Ibid., p. 10.

243 Explaining how chronic illness affects . . . : Karen A. Roberto, interview by author in Greeley, Col., 25 June 1996.

243 "The more physical problems elderly women . . .": Ibid., "Osteoporosis and Older Women: Productive Lifestyle Strategies," *Journal of Women and Aging* 5, no. 3/4 (1993): 55.

244 Researchers have found that as many as a third . . . : Pat O'Connor, "Same-Gender and Cross-Gender Friendships Among the Frail Elderly," *The Gerontologist* 33, no. 1 (February 1993): 25.

244 . . . that older women in poor health tend . . . : Karen A. Roberto and Priscilla J. Kimboko, "Friendships in Later Life: Definitions and Maintenance Patterns," *International Journal of Aging and Human Development* 28, no. 1 (1989): 15.

244 Although arthritis and heart disease are the most . . . : Anne Scott and G. Clare Wenger, "Gender and Social Support in Later Life," in *Connecting Gender and Ageing,* ed. Arber and Ginn, pp. 158–59.

244 As the most prevalent of the sixty-some conditions . . . : Denis Evans, et al., "Prevalence of Alzheimer's Disease in a Community Population of Older Persons Higher than Previously Reported," *Journal of the American Medical Association* 262, no. 18 (10 November 1989): 2551–56.

245 Research suggests that women may be . . . : Lindsay A. Farrer, et al., "Effects of Age, Gender and Ethnicity on the Association Between Apolipoprotein E Genotype and Alzeimer's Disease," *Journal of the American Medical Association* (22 and 29 October 1997): 1353.

245 . . . day-to-day contact with friends helps those . . . : For studies supporting this position, see Barbara Joanne Williams, "Friends in Passing: A Description of Social Interaction and Friendship at an Adult Day Care Center" (abstract of M.A. thesis, California State University–Long Beach, 1992); and Rebecca G. Adams, "Which Comes First: Poor Psychological Well-being or Decreased Friendship Activity?" *Activities, Adaptation and Aging* 12, no. 1/2 (1988): 27–41.

246 "Friends tend to withdraw with the onset . . .": Roberto, 25 June 1996.

246 As long-married women lose their husbands . . . : Trudy Bohrer Anderson, "Primary Resources of Elderly Women" (abstract of Ph.D. diss., University of Nebraska–Lincoln, 1981).

246 Compared to wives, widows receive more . . . : Roberto and Scott, "Friendship Patterns," 1–10.

246 They also give more.: Sally K. Gallagher and Naomi Gerstel, "Kinkeeping and Friend Keeping Among Older Women: The Effect of Marriage," *The Gerontologist* 33, no. 5 (October 1995): 680–81.

246 . . . many had friends they'd carried with them . . . : Iris, 24 March 1996.

246 . . . women who have always been single . . . : Gail Wilson, "Changes in Gender Roles in Advanced Old Age," in *Connecting Gender and Ageing,* ed. Arber and Ginn, p. 109.

247 The first significant late-life loss . . . : For some of the many studies on the impact of retirement on women's relationships, see Henrik Ossian Ostberg, "Retirement, Health and Socio-Psychological Conditions: A Longitudinal Study of 116 Municipally Employed Women in Malmoe, Sweden" (abstract of Fil.Dr. (Ph.D.) diss., Lunds Universitet, 1992); Mary Frances Madigan, "Preparation for Prime Time: Three Business Women at Work and in Retirement" (abstract of Ed.D. diss., Columbia University Teachers College, 1985); Doris Ingrisch, "Conformity and Resistance as Women Age," in *Connecting Gender and Ageing,* ed. Arber and Ginn, p. 55; and Michal E. Mor-Barak, Andrew E. Scahrlach, Lourdes Virba, and Jacque Sokolov, "Employment, Social Networks, and Health in the Retirement Years," *International Journal of Aging and Human Development* 35, no. 2 (1992): 145–59.

248 . . . described a successful retirement transition . . . : Mark Robert Luborsky, "Social and Cultural Foundations of the Retirement Transition" (abstract of Ph.D. diss., University of Rochester, 1985).

248 After retirement, women who'd originally bonded . . . : For studies demonstrating this and discussing ways in which employers and unions can help women maintain some of the friendship benefits of the workplace after they retire, see Doris Francis, "The Significance of Work Friends in Late Life," *Journal of Aging Studies* 4, no. 4 (Winter 1990): 405–24; Doris Francis, "Women Workers,

Workplace Friends, and Retirement: A Union Model," in *Pre-Retirement Planning for Women: Program Design and Research,* ed. Christopher L. Hayes and Jane M. Deren (New York: Springer Publishing, 1990), pp. 89–113; and O'Connor, *Friendships Between Women,* p. 124.

248 . . . they responded to retirement by adopting . . . : Dorothy Jerrome, "The Significance of Friendship for Women in Later Life," *Ageing and Society* 1, no. 2 (July 1981): 175–97.

249 . . . initially, a widow's social life . . . : Karen A. Roberto and Jean Pearson Scott, "Confronting Widowhood: The Influence of Informal Supports," *American Behavioral Scientist* 29, no. 4 (March/April 1986): 499. See also O'Connor, *Friendships Between Women,* p. 129.

249 Friendships that develop in bereavement . . . : Kenneth I. Maton, "Community Settings as Buffers of Life Stress? Highly Supportive Churches, Mutual Help Groups, and Senior Centers," *American Journal of Community Psychology* 17, no. 2 (April 1989): 203–32.

249 . . . which is why the American Association . . . : Molly H. Folken, "The Importance of Group Support for Widowed Persons," *Journal for Specialists in Group Work* 16, no. 3 (September 1991): 172–77.

249 . . . the amount of contact women in their early eighties . . . : Colleen L. Johnson and Lillian E. Troll, "Constraints and Facilitators to Friendship in Late Late Life," *The Gerontologist* 34, no. 1 (February 1994): 82–85.

249 By the time women reach their nineties . . . : Ingrid Arnet Connidis and Lorraine Davies, "Confidants and Companions: Choices in Later Life," *Journal of Gerontology* 47, no. 3 (May 1992): S115.

250 Compounding the loss of the friend herself . . . : Fred Sklar, "Grief as a Family Affair: Property Rights, Grief Rights, and the Exclusion of Close Friends as Survivors," *Omega Journal of Death and Dying* 24, no. 2 (1991–1992): 109–21.

251 . . . the experience actually brought them closer . . . : Karen A. Roberto and Pat Ianni Stanis, "Reactions of Older Women to the Death of Their Close Friends," *Omega Journal of Death and Dying* 29, no. 1 (1994): 1.

252 A generation ago, doctors tended to withhold . . . : Clive Seale, "Communication and Awareness About Death: A Study of a Random Sample of Dying People," *Social Science and Medicine* 32, no. 8 (1991): 943–52.

252 . . . this final step in full psychological development.: Daniel J. Levinson in collaboration with Judy D. Levinson, *The Seasons of a Woman's Life* (New York: Alfred A. Knopf, 1996), p. 21.

252 Although new friends can never replace . . . : For studies comparing the roles of new friends and old friends in late life, see Rebecca G. Adams, "Secondary Friendship Networks and Psychological Well-being Among Elderly Women," *Activities, Adaptation and Aging* 8, no. 2 (March 1986): 59–72; and Karen A. Roberto and Priscilla J. Kimboko, "Friendships in Later Life: Definitions and Maintenance Patterns," *International Journal of Aging and Human Development* 28, no. 1 (1989): 10.

253 New friends, sociologist Rebecca Adams noted, are . . . : Adams, "Secondary Friendship Networks."

253 Despite such difficulties, most women . . . : Anne Scott and G. Clare Wenger, "Gender and Social Support in Later Life," in *Connecting Gender and Ageing,* ed. Arber and Ginn, p. 162.

255 Nursing homes, on the other hand, . . . : For studies comparing social interaction in various kinds of assisted-living settings, see Janet E. Bitzan and Jean M. Kruzich, "Interpersonal Relationships of Nursing Home Residents," *The Gerontologist* 30, no. 3 (June 1990): 385–90; Gary F. Meunier, "Encouragement Groups with Nursing Home Elderly," *Individual Psychology Journal of Adlerian Theory, Research and Practice* 45, no. 4 (December 1989): 459–64; Candace Stacey-Konnert and Jon Pynoos, "Friendship and Social Networks in a Continuing Care Retirement Community," *Journal of Applied Gerontology* 11, no. 3 (September 1992): 298–313; and Jane Woolley, "Voluntary Confinement: An Ethnographic Study of a Lifetime Care Retirement Community" (abstract of Ed.D. diss., Columbia University Teachers College, 1994).

256 Continuity is one of the earmarks . . . : Roberto, 25 June 1996.

Part Three
KEEPING FRIENDS

12   Finding It Hard

262 The way we interact with our mothers beginning . . . : Chava Frankfort-Nachmias, interview by author in Evanston, Ill., 26 April 1996.

262 . . . "Even if a little girl has a mother . . .": Eva Margolies, *The Best of Friends, the Worst of Enemies: Women's Hidden Power over Women* (Garden City, N.Y.: The Dial Press/Doubleday, 1985), p. 18.

263 This difficult transition may account . . . : Luise Eichenbaum and Susie Orbach, *Between Women: Love, Envy, and Competition in Women's Friendships* (New York: Penguin Books, 1987), pp. 56–58.

263 In 1951, British psychoanalyst John Bowlby . . . : Robert Karen, *Becoming Attached: Unfolding the Mystery of the Infant-Mother Bond and Its Impact on Later Life* (New York: Warner Books, 1994), pp. 126–76, 382–83, 391–92. The summary of attachment styles and their consequences also relies on Steve Duck, *Understanding Relationships* (New York: Guilford Press, 1991), pp. 119–20. For other studies on the impact of maternal attachment styles on friendships, see Shmuel Shulman, James Elicker, and Alan Stroufe, "Stages of Friendship Growth in Preadolescence as Related to Attachment History," *Journal of Social and Personal Relationships* 11, no. 3 (August 1994): 341–61.

264 "In a crowd of other women, as a female, . . .": Hope Edelman, *Motherless Daughters: The Legacy of Loss* (New York: Delta/Dell, 1994), pp. 181–82.

264 . . . every close female friendship offers . . . : Christine Hejinian, interview by author in San Francisco, 16 May 1996.

265 . . . having a warm and demonstrative . . . : Carol E. Franz, David C. McClelland, and Joel Weinberger, "Childhood Antecedents of Conventional Social Accomplishments in Midlife Adults: A 36–Year Prospective Study," *Journal of Personality and Social Psychology* 60, no. 4 (April 1991): 586–95. For more on how

family warmth and strong friendships work together, see Susan Marie Over-hauser, "The Significance of Friendship Intimacy and Family Warmth for Ado-lescent Identity Development and Individuation: A Developmental Study" (abstract of Ph.D. diss., University of Minnesota, 1993).

265 Children and adolescents try out ways . . . : J. Kelly McCoy, Gene H. Brody, and Zolinda Stoneman, "A Longitudinal Analysis of Sibling Relationships as Mediators of the Link between Family Processes and Youths' Best Friendships," *Family Relations* 43 (1994): 406.

265 . . . a person who had a warm childhood relationship . . . : Gerald Wayne Greenfield, "Effects of Relationships with Siblings on Friendships" (abstract of Ph.D. diss., University of Colorado at Boulder, 1988).

265 Women expect their female friends . . . : Eichenbaum and Orbach, *Between Women,* p. 18.

266 . . . "that she is responsible for the actions . . .": Carol Gilligan, *In a Different Voice: Psychological Theory and Women's Development* (Cambridge, Mass.: Harvard University Press, 1993; original edition: 1982), p. 82.

266 . . . she found high self-esteem to be one . . . : Frances Marie Costa, "Friendship Patterns in Young Adulthood: A Social Psychological Approach" (abstract of Ph.D. diss., University of Colorado at Boulder, 1983).

267 Depression renders a woman's moods unpredictable . . . : Susan M. Poslusny, "Women's Friendship in Depression: The Lived Experience of Depressed and Non-Depressed Friends" (abstract of Ph.D. diss., University of Illinois at Chi-cago Health Sciences Center, 1990).

267 Depressed people prefer being around other . . . : Karen S. Rook, Paula R. Pietromonaco, and Megan A. Lewis, "When Are Dysphoric Individuals Dis-tressing to Others and Vice Versa? Effects of Friendship, Similarity, and Interac-tion Task," *Journal of Personality and Social Psychology* 67, no. 3 (September 1994): 548–59; and Abram Rosenblatt and Jeff Greenberg, "Examining the World of the Depressed: Do Depressed People Prefer Others Who Are De-pressed?" *Journal of Personality and Social Psychology* 60, no. 4 (April 1991): 620–29.

267 Unlike guilt, which springs from. . . . : Judith V. Jordan, "Relational Develop-ment: Therapeutic Implications of Empathy and Shame," Works in Progress, no. 39 (Wellesley, Mass.: The Stone Center, Wellesley College, 1989), p. 6.

267 "[S]hame is . . . a felt sense . . .": Ibid.

267 Shame isolates us by making us conceal . . . : Ibid., interview by author in Lexington, Mass., 2 April 1996.

268 Nothing demonstrates this more clearly . . . : Jan Jarboe, "The Mommy Wars," *Texas Monthly* 17, no. 7 (July 1981): 78–81.

269 . . . "excludes the listener . . .": Steve Duck, *Understanding Relationships* (New York: Guilford Press, 1991), p. 73.

269 Introversion keeps women from putting themselves . . . : Helen Gouldner and Mary Symons Strong, *Speaking of Friendship: Middle-Class Women and Their Friends* (New York: Greenwood Press, 1987), p. 73.

269 When shy women do make friends . . . : Elizabeth Goering and Patricia

Breidenstein-Cutspec, "The Web of Shyness: A Network Analysis of Communicative Correlates," *Communication Research Report* 6, no. 2 (December 1989): 111–18.

270 Loneliness is most common in people who sense . . . : Brad Bell, "Emotional Loneliness and the Perceived Similarity of One's Ideas and Interests," *Journal of Social Behavior and Personality* 8, no. 2 (June 1993): 273–80.

270 The lack of such social skills as . . . : Pat O'Connor, *Friendships Between Women: A Critical Review* (New York: Guilford Press, 1992), pp. 109–10.

270 . . . some socially inept individuals . . . : Duck, *Relationships,* p. 166.

271 . . . social skills were more important . . . : Martin A. Johnson, "Variables Associated with Friendship in an Adult Population," *Journal of Social Psychology* 129, no. 3 (June 1989): 379–90.

271 People "will tolerate an ugly extravert". . . : Duck, *Relationships,* p. 165.

272 For instance, as roommates in their twenties, . . . : Berenice Fisher and Roberta Galler, "Friendship and Fairness: How Disability Affects Friendship Between Women," in *Women with Disabilities: Essays in Psychology, Culture, and Politics,* ed. Michelle Fine and Adrienne Asch (Philadelphia: Temple University Press, 1988), p. 175.

273 Because one friend must accommodate the other's . . . : Ibid., p. 180.

273 . . . she compensated by being an emotional . . . : Ibid., p. 184.

273 The third issue a disabled woman and her friend . . . : Ibid., pp. 186–88.

275 . . . "tyranny of beauty" . . . : Louise Bernikow, *Among Women* (New York: Harmony Books, 1980), p. 98.

276 . . . women who were similarly attractive were happier . . . : Linda L. Carli, Roseanne Ganley, and Amy Pierce Otay, "Similarity and Satisfaction in Roommate Relationships," *Personality and Social Psychology Bulletin* 17, no. 4 (August 1991): 419–26.

278 . . . it can serve as a signpost to . . . : Luise Eichenbaum and Susie Orbach, *Between Women: Love, Envy, and Competition in Women's Friendships* (New York: Penguin Books, 1987), p. 111.

278 Instead of feeling guilty for these emotions and trying to repress . . . : Ibid., p. 99.

279 "The constant tension for women . . .": Jordan, 2 April 1996.

280 . . . of the fifty relationships . . . : J. L. Barkas, "Friendship Patterns Among Young Urban Single Women" (abstract of Ph.D. diss., City University of New York, 1983).

281 Instead of supporting each other . . . : In Laura Tracy, *The Secret Between Us: Competition among Women* (Boston: Little Brown, 1991), p. 115, the author wrote: "[W]hen we compete for me, we stop trying to empathize with each other. Instead, we try to cancel each other out."

283 For the most part, female competition arises . . . : Eichenbaum and Orbach, *Between Women,* p. 117.

284 . . . although both women and men liked their partners . . . : Stephen T. Deberry, "The Effect of Competitive Tasks on Liking of Self and Other," *Social Behavior and Personality* 17, no. 1 (1989): 67–80.

285 Many women take competition on the job . . . : Laura Tracy, pp. 134–35.

285 For a woman who grew up in a physically or verbally . . . : Eichenbaum and Orbach, *Between Women*, p. 142.

285 "Most of my women clients suffer some pain . . .": Judith V. Jordan, "Courage in Connection: Conflict, Compassion, Creativity," Works in Progress, no. 45 (Wellesley, Mass.: The Stone Center, Wellesley College, 1990), p. 6.

285 . . . when a woman frequently alters her experiences . . . : Jordan, "Relational Development," p. 3.

286 "The thing that women *aren't* good at . . .": Jean Baker Miller, telephone interview by author, 2 April 1996.

287 Women may be "extremely practiced" . . . : Eichenbaum and Orbach, *Between Women*, p. 147.

288 . . . differed in their tolerance for vulnerability.: Helen Gouldner and Mary Symons Strong, *Speaking of Friendship: Middle-Class Women and their Friends* (New York: Greenwood Press, 1987), p. 113.

288 To explain this difference among women . . . : Helen Gouldner, interview by author in Wilmington, Del., 26 March 1996.

288 . . . in each of the twenty-six pairs of close friends . . . : Sophie Jacobs Bronstein, "The Experience of Dyadic Friendship Between Women" (abstract of Ed.D. diss., Temple University, 1988).

288 Self-disclosure takes different forms . . . : Jeanne Tschann, interview by author in San Francisco, 16 May 1996.

289 . . . sensation seekers tend to be more . . . : Robert E. Franken, Kevin J. Gibson, and Philip Mohan, "Sensation Seeking and Disclosure to Close and Casual Friends," *Personality and Individual Differences* 11, no. 8 (1990): 829–32.

289 "[A]fter initial repudiation, I have come to a renewed . . .": Margot Livesey, "The Valley of Lost Things," in *Between Friends: Writing Women Celebrate Friendship,* ed. Mickey Pearlman (Boston: Houghton Mifflin, 1994), p. 12.

289 . . . whether self-disclosure is essential . . . : O'Connor, *Friendships Between Women,* p. 30.

289 . . . "as a public forum . . .": Ibid., p. 178.

289 Although he enjoyed a very close relationship . . . : Lillian B. Rubin, *Just Friends: The Role of Friendship in Our Lives* (New York: Harper & Row, 1985), pp. 67–68.

292 "[I]n devaluing other women . . .": Jean Baker Miller, *Toward a New Psychology of Women,* 2nd ed. (Boston: Beacon Press, 1986), p. xv.

292 This patient had enormous comtempt . . . : Irene Stiver, interview by author in Watertown, Mass., 1 April 1996.

292 . . . busy middle-aged women will choose to spend . . . : Linda J. Waite and Scott C. Harrison, "Keeping in Touch: How Women in Mid-Life Allocate Social Contacts Among Kith and Kin," *Social Forces* 70, no. 3 (March 1992): 651.

13   Challenges to Friendship

293 . . . three-quarters of the time the culprit . . . : [no by-line] "Psychology Study Shows Why Close Friendships End," *Arches* (newsletter of the alumni association of the University of Puget Sound, Tacoma), December 1995.

293 . . . the term included any major . . . : Ibid., interview by author in Tacoma, Wash., 22 May 1996.

294 . . . the number of a woman's friendships . . . : Helen Gouldner and Mary Symons Strong, *Speaking of Friendship: Middle-Class Women and Their Friends* (New York: Greenwood Press, 1987), pp. 129–30.

294 . . . between 1980 and 1996, 32 percent . . . : U.S. Bureau of the Census, *Statistical Abstract of the United States: 1998*, 118th ed., (Washington, D.C., 1998), Table 32.

297 . . . just over half told her that they occasionally . . . : Stacey J. Oliker, *Best Friends and Marriage: Exchange Among Women* (Berkeley, Calif.: University of California Press, 1989), p. 113.

297 The husband always won, except when . . . : Ibid., p. 75.

297 Criticize him and you attack your friend's . . . : Barbara Hustedt Crook, "Love Her, Hate Him: When a Good Friend Goes for a Man You Can't Stand," *Cosmopolitan*, March 1989, p. 120.

298 . . . "believe that female friendships . . .": Laura Tracy, *The Secret Between Us: Competition Among Women* (Boston: Little Brown, 1991), p. 197.

299 When one friend has a baby and the other . . . : Jane Burka, telephone interview by author, 23 April 1997.

299 . . . shared child-rearing values ranked high . . . : Oliker, *Best Friends,* p. 94.

301 . . . during marital disputes women friends often . . . : Ibid., p. 125.

301 As long as a woman thinks her marital problems . . . : Pat O'Connor, *Friendships Between Women: A Critical Review* (New York: Guilford Press, 1992), p. 103.

303 The average age for a woman at divorce . . . : Bureau of the Census, *Statistical Abstract,* 1998, Table 160.

303 . . . for a woman at a husband's death . . . : Bob Schoen and Robin Weinick, *Demography* 30, no. 4 (November 1993): 737.

304 . . . widowed women were better at keeping . . . : Laurie Russell Hatch and Kris Bulcroft, "Contact with Friends in Later Life: Disentangling the Effects of Gender and Marital Status," *Journal of Marriage and the Family* 54, no. 1 (February 1992): 230.

304 Society has yet to develop norms for dealing . . . : Patrick C. McKenry and Sharon J. Price, "Alternatives for Support: Life After Divorce: A Literature Review," *Journal of Divorce and Remarriage* 15, no. 3/4 (1991): 1–19.

304 . . . a sense of duty and obligation to relatives . . . : Robert M. Milardo, "Changes in Social Networks of Women and Men Following Divorce," *Journal of Family Issues* 8, no. 1 (March 1987): 78–96.

304 Yet to adjust successfully to their new lives . . . : Maureen Baker, "Women Helping Women: The Transition from Separation to Divorce," *Conciliation Courts Review* 22, no. 1 (June 1984): 53–63.

304 Friends tend to interfere less . . . : Milardo, "Changes in Social," 78–96.

304 When both women are married . . . : Luise Eichenbaum and Susie Orbach, *Between Women: Love, Envy, and Competition in Women's Friendships* (New York: Penguin Books, 1987), pp. 189–90.

307 . . . One of them might withdraw . . . : Dorothy Jerrome, "Frailty and Friendship," *Journal of Cross-Cultural Gerontology* 5, no. 1 (January 1990): 51–64.

309 A sudden rise in one's friend's fortunes . . . : Wood, 15 June 1996.

309 "People can't lug their families with them . . .": Helen Gouldner, interview by
author in Wilmington, Del., 26 March 1996.

310 . . . when one friend's career advances, the other . . . : Eichenbaum and Orbach,
Between Women, p. 79.

310 Talk-show hostess Oprah Winfrey met . . . : Patricia Keogh, "Friends Who Get
Along Famously," *New Woman*, February 1994, pp. 85–86.

310 . . . she knew she could call King . . . : Laura B. Randolph, "Sisters of the Spirit:
Networks Help Celebrities Deal with Fame and Pain," *Ebony*, July 1990, p. 36.

311 "Gayle helps keep me grounded . . .": Keogh, "Friends," 85.

313 . . . the cause of a split often comes down . . . : O'Connor, *Friendships Between
Women*, pp. 149–50.

14 Seventeen Steps to Having Friends for Life

322 . . . in most friendships, intimacy matters more . . . : Sophie Jacobs Bronstein,
"The Experience of Dyadic Friendship Between Women" (abstract of Ed.D.
diss., Temple University, 1988).

Index